*Less managing. More teaching. Greater learning.*

# INSTRUCTORS...

Would you like your **students** to show up for class **more prepared**?
*(Let's face it, class is much more fun if everyone is engaged and prepared…)*

Want an **easy way to assign** homework online and track student **progress**?
*(Less time grading means more time teaching…)*

Want an **instant view** of student or class performance?
*(No more wondering if students understand…)*

Need to **collect data and generate reports** required for administration or accreditation?
*(Say goodbye to manually tracking student learning outcomes…)*

Want to **record and post your lectures** for students to view online?
*(The more students can see, hear, and experience class resources, the better they learn…)*

A: With **McGraw-Hill's *Connect*,™**

## INSTRUCTORS GET:

- Simple **assignment management**, allowing you to spend more time teaching.
- **Auto-graded** assignments, quizzes, and tests.
- **Detailed visual reporting** where student and section results can be viewed and analyzed.
- Sophisticated **online testing** capability.
- A **filtering and reporting** function that allows you to easily assign and report on materials that are correlated to learning objectives and Bloom's taxonomy.
- An easy-to-use **lecture capture** tool.
- The option to **upload course documents** for student access.

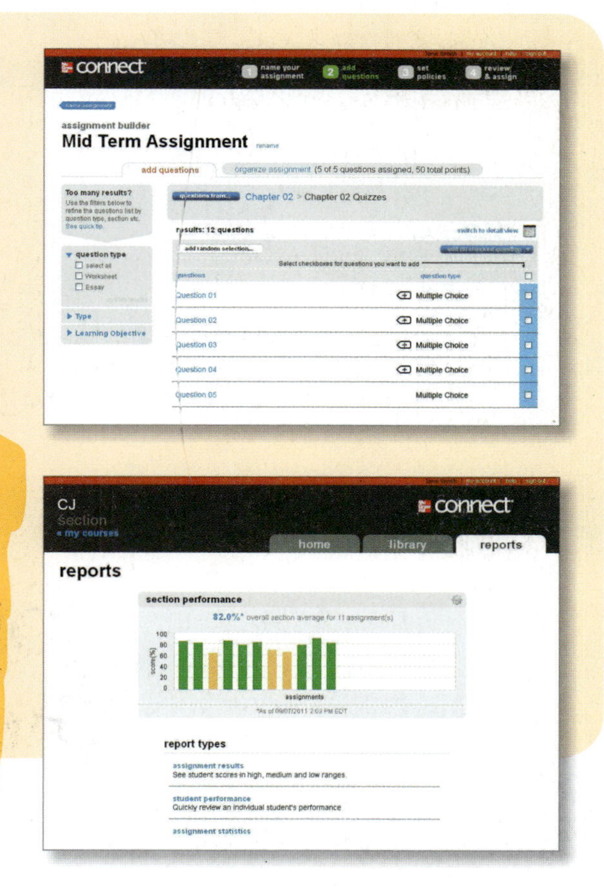

GINA ANTONACCI
Humber College

**CJ**
**First Edition**



ISBN-13: 978-0-07-069695-2

ISBN-10: 0-07-069695-0

1 2 3 4 5 6 7 8 9 10 DOW/DOW 1 9 8 7 6 5 4 3

Printed and bound in the United States of America.



Editorial Director: Rhondda McNabb
Publisher: Kim Brewster
Sponsoring Editors: Karen Krahn & Marcia Siekowski
Marketing Managers: Stacey Metz & Tracy Yan
Developmental Editor: Lindsay MacDonald
Senior Editorial Associate: Marina Seguin
Supervising Editor: Jessica Barnoski
Photo/Permissions Research: Allison McDonald, McDonald Editorial Services
*i*Learning Sales Specialist: Lisa Gillman
Copy Editor: Ann Firth
Production Coordinator: Scott Morrison
Cover Design: Sarah Orr, Artplus Limited
Cover Image: Pics_Nathan Lau_77887700_GettyRF
Interior Design: Sarah Orr, Artplus Limited
Page Layout: Liz Harasymczuk
Printer: R.R. Donnelley/Willard

**Library and Archives Canada Cataloguing in Publication**

Antonacci, Gina
CJ / Gina Antonacci. -- 1st ed.

Includes index.
ISBN 978-0-07-069695-2

1. Criminal justice, Administration of--Canada--
Textbooks. I. Title.

HV9960.C2A58 2013 364.971 C2012-905973-0

# About the Author

Gina Antonacci began her career as a Probation and Parole Officer in Toronto before becoming a Senior Staff Development Officer, providing training and development to Probation Officers and Correctional Officers.

As a full-time faculty member in the School of Community and Social Services at Humber College, Gina taught in the Law and Security Administration and Police Foundations Programs. She is currently the Dean of the School of Social and Community Services at Humber College. Gina has a Bachelor's degree from the University of Toronto and a Master of Science in Criminal Justice Administration from Niagara University.

*Like everything else, this is for Melissa, Alanna, and Jenna.*

# Brief Contents

# Contents

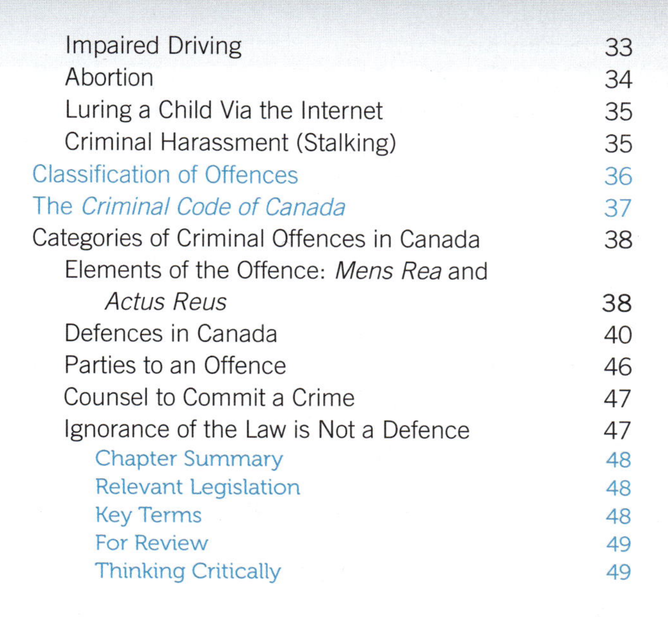

## CHAPTER 7 Community Corrections 156

## CHAPTER 8 Youth Justice 182

## CHAPTER 9 Restorative Justice 210

## CHAPTER 10 The Victim in the Criminal Justice System 226

The Future
NEXT EXIT

# Preface

The Criminal Justice System is dynamic—it is always changing. It is a reflection of who we are as a society as it mirrors our values, our beliefs, and our attitudes about acceptable behaviour. The criminal justice system provides us with many opportunities to examine our societal beliefs and to understand the relationship between the law and ourselves, collectively and individually.

Each of us is affected by the workings of the criminal justice system—directly or indirectly. We read about difficult cases, we empathize with victims, and we search for ways to improve the system. We are also given the opportunity to challenge ideas, engage in debate, and examine evidence-based research, all with the goal of arriving at our own personal view of the critical issues. We are invited to contemplate difficult concepts such as fairness, justice, and punishment. We learn to recognize the systemic impact of racism and sexism, and we can analyze the relationship between social problems and the criminal justice system.

The goal of this text is to provide students with a user-friendly overview of the main players, major processes, and contemporary issues within the criminal justice system so that they may engage with the criminal justice system both in their course of study and in their lives, in general. The text includes information about each of the major components of the criminal justice system—courts, police, and corrections. There is also an emphasis on the role of the victim and the role of the media. There are many current and classic examples of cases that highlight laws and procedures.

The cover image of this text was chosen because it represents the belief that people and experiences can change and that freedom, both physical and emotional, is within reach. There is a great deal of sadness and pain within the criminal justice system, but there is also an opportunity for growth and transformation. Our criminal justice system, through its policies and practices, supports the belief that people can change. There is an onus on us all to embrace the dynamic nature of criminal justice and continue to strive for a criminal justice system that is more effective, more efficient, and more sensitive to the needs of everyone who comes into contact with it.

It is my hope that each student who uses this text will become engaged in the issues and the cases by talking about them, analyzing and understanding them so that they may become passionate about the criminal justice system, not only for the duration of their course of study, but for their entire lives.

# Inside *CJ*

Each chapter opens with a current **case study** introducing the reader to the chapter's main topics. Many of the cases highlight recent news stories and are directly relatable to the chapter content.

**Learning Objectives** are listed on the opening spread and are tagged throughout the chapter. The objectives encompass the concepts that are most important to each particular chapter. They act as a study tool for students, testing their knowledge on each chapter's main topics.

### The Ex-Colonel's Conviction and "Old Fashioned" Police Work

A once-decorated career soldier who rose to the rank of Colonel pleaded guilty to a total of 88 charges—two charges of murder, two for sexual assault, and the remaining charges for theft—on October 7, 2010, in Superior Court in Belleville, Ontario. Russell Williams, a married, career soldier, was a high profile Colonel who had been stationed at various posts around the world. At the time of his arrest he was the Commander of the Canadian Forces Base in Trenton, Ontario. This "Jekyll and Hyde" case shocked both the military world and Canadians across the country.

Williams was convicted of the murders of Jessica Lloyd, 27, and Corporal Marie-France Comeau, 38, a Trenton-based air attendant under the command of Colonel Williams. Both victims were asphyxiated. Comeau was found dead in her home, and Lloyd was discovered in a wooded area outside of Tweed, Ontario. The sexual assaults, for which Williams was convicted, involved home invasions near his cottage.

The police engaged in old fashioned police work in order to zero in on Williams as a suspect in this case. Tire tracks left at the scene of Jessica Lloyd's home were compared to the tires of vehicles stopped at a police roadblock. Williams was identified as a suspect when his tires proved to be a match. His boot print was also matched to the boot prints found in the yard of Lloyd's home. Jim Smyth conducted the police interview that led to Williams' confession. Smyth, a detective sergeant with the OPP's behavioural sciences unit, was praised for his superior interviewing skills.

By pleading guilty to the offences, neither a preliminary hearing nor a trial were required. Several days of evidence and victim impact statements followed Williams' guilty plea.

**LEARNING OBJECTIVES**

By the end of this chapter, you should be able to:

- **LO1** Describe the history of policing in Canada.
- **LO2** Identify the organization of policing in Canada.
- **LO3** Identify the legislation that governs police in Canada.
- **LO4** Describe the role and function of policing.
- **LO5** Explain the recruitment, selection, and training process.
- **LO6** Recognize the stresses related to police work.
- **LO7** Outline types of police accountability and oversight.
- **LO8** Identify ways in which policing is evaluated.
- **LO9** Describe the role of private police in Canada.

Russell Williams was interviewed by Detective Sergeant Jim Smyth.

The footprints and tire tracks of the accused were critical pieces of evidence obtained by police.

On October 18, 2010, Williams was sentenced to life imprisonment, with no possibility of parole for 25 years. Williams, who was 47 at the time of the sentencing, will be eligible for parole when he is 72 years of age.

Soon after the conviction, Williams was stripped of his rank and formally evicted from the military. In what was a profoundly symbolic act, uniforms and military apparel belonging to Williams were burned in a furnace at Canadian Forces Base Trenton where Williams once served as the Unit Commander.

Police gathered evidence at the home of Jessica Lloyd.

## MYTH VS FACT — Bounty Hunters Beware!

Bounty hunters appear regularly on American television; however, they do not exist in Canadian law. In fact, bounty hunters are illegal in Canada. Canadians (in Canada) are protected from being apprehended by bounty hunters. In 1993, American bounty hunter Daniel Kear came to Canada to apprehend Sidney Jaffe at his Canadian residence and return him to Florida where he was to face trial. Kear was subsequently extradited to Canada where he was convicted of kidnapping Jaffe.

**Myth vs. Fact** boxes clarify preconceptions students may have about the Canadian criminal justice system.

# JUST or BUST?

**Just or Bust?** boxes are designed to encourage debate in class and to consider all sides of an argument.

Should people be sentenced to custody for unpaid fines? What are the implications of doing so?

## IN THE NEWS

### Honour-Based Violence

**Honour-based violence** is violence that occurs when family members kill or commit a violent act against another family member because they believe that the victim has dishonoured the family name and reputation. There is not a specific offence related to honour-based violence. Offenders are charged with the relevant criminal code offence, while honour is the motivation for committing the crime. A recent Ontario case highlighted honour-based crime when the Shafia family—father Mohammad, second wife Tooba, and son Hamed—were convicted of first degree murder in the deaths of four family members. Mohammad Shafia's first wife, Rona Amir, and Tooba and Mohammad Shafia's three daughters were found dead in a vehicle at the bottom of a Kingston canal in 2009. According to the accused, the daughters rebelled by engaging in what others in Canadian society might describe as typical behaviour of young girls—wearing makeup, dating boys, refusing to wear traditional clothing. During the trial, evidence was presented showing that the girls and Rona Amir [illegible] to threats of violenc[illegible]

Mohammad Shafia, 58, his second wife Tooba Mohammad Yahya, 42, and their son Hamed, 21, were found guilty of first-degree murder after a jury found them guilty of murdering four other family members. They were each sentenced to life imprisonment.
Photograph by: Stringer, Reuters

Though they represent a small number of homicide cases overall, honour killings are high profile cases because of the message that they send. In honour killings, the life of the family member is far less important than the shame the family perceives. This is a strong and disturbing message for most people, making honour-based crime difficult to understand. It is estimated that there have been at least 15 honour killings in Canada since 2002 (Keeping, 2009). After the Shafia verdict, a number of Muslim leaders made it clear that honour killing is not faith-based. Several Islamic religious leaders denounced honour killings publicly, and recognized the need to educate Muslims about gender equality. Imam Syed Soharwardy, the founder of the Islamic Supreme Council of Canada, explained that such violence is clearly condemned in the Qur'an but can be present in remote regions of Muslim countries as a result of the misinterpretation of religious doctrine (CBC, 2012).

**In the News** features news stories relevant to each chapter's content.

**Flashback** takes the reader back in time to explain developments in legislation, cases that have made an impact on the criminal justice system, and other equally important developments that have an impact on the current system.

## FLASHBACK:

### THE KARLA HOMOLKA PLEA BARGAIN: "A DEAL WITH THE DEVIL"?

Perhaps the most famous plea bargain in Canadian history is the deal that Karla Homolka made with the Crown arising from her role in the deaths of Ontario teenagers Kristen French, Leslie Mahaffy, and Homolka's own 15-year-old sister, Tammy Homolka. Homolka made the deal in exchange for her testimony against her then-husband Paul Bernardo. At the time that the deal was struck, the police did not have the videotaped evidence that surfaced later. The tapes revealed that Homolka might have been more involved in the crimes than she had originally claimed. The Crown honoured the agreement and did not rescind the deal with Homolka when the tapes were found. This very public case left many Canadians with a view of plea bargaining gone bad.

## Wrongful Conviction

PROFILE

The names of the wrongly convicted have become well known to Canadians. Their stories are a constant reminder of the fallible nature of the criminal justice system.

### Steven Truscott

Steven Truscott was sentenced to hang for the 1959 death of Lynn Harper, a classmate. At the age of 14, Truscott was a death row inmate until his sentence was commuted to life imprisonment. He was paroled in 1969 to live an anonymous life in Ontario. Truscott always maintained his innocence and after numerous investigations into the facts of the case, the Ontario Court of Appeal overturned the conviction in August of 2007. In July, 2008, Truscott received $6.5 million in compensation.

### Donald Marshall Jr.

In 1971, at 17 years of age, Donald Marshall Jr. was convicted of murdering his friend, Sandy Seale in Sydney, Nova Scotia. He was sentenced to life imprisonment. He was released in 1982 following an RCMP review where the Nova Scotia Court of Appeal declared him not guilty. A royal commission in 1990 determined that systemic racism had contributed to the wrongful conviction. Roy Ebsary was eventually convicted of manslaughter in Seale's death. Donald Marshall Jr. spent 11 years in jail and was eventually given a lifetime pension of $1.5 million in compensation for his ordeal. Marshall died in 2009 at age 55.

**Profile** boxes feature prominent figures that have made a difference in the Canadian criminal justice system.

**Focus On...** boxes take a closer look at a topic within the chapter and relate it to a real-world example.

## FOCUS ON Hate Crime in Canada

**Hate crimes** refer to criminal offences that are motivated by hate towards an identifiable group. A group may be targeted based on national or ethnic origin, language, race, religion, sex, age, mental or physical disability, or sexual orientation. Police services across Canada reported a 35 percent increase in hate crimes between 2007 and 2008. Of those, most (55 percent) were motivated by race or ethnicity, followed by religion (26 percent) and sexual orientation (16 percent) (Statistics Canada, 2010). The crimes that were motivated by hate included violent crimes such as assaults and uttering threats (42 percent) and vandalism to property (47 percent). The most violent crimes were those motivated by sexual orientation. Of those crimes, the victim was male in 85 percent of the cases. The most commonly targeted racial/ethnic group was Blacks, followed by South Asians. The most commonly targeted religion was the Jewish faith, with a rise of 42 percent in 2008 over the previous year. Hate crimes against the Catholic faith and the Muslim faith followed. The highest rates of hate crime were in Vancouver, British Columbia and Hamilton, Ontario. Hate crime differs from crime in general, in that most hate crimes are perpetrated by strangers. The victim seldom knows the perpetrator, implying that the victims are random subjects chosen strictly because they are a member of the targeted group.

**hate crimes**
criminal offences that are motivated by hate towards an identifiable group

A hate crime: Jewish graves are vandalized.

**TABLE 2.3 Hate Crime in Canada's Cities**

**Hate crimes reported by police, by type of motivation, by 10 largest census metropolitan areas**

| | 2008 | | | | | |
|---|---|---|---|---|---|---|
| | Race/ ethnicity | Religion | Sexual orientation | Other or unknown | Total | |
| | | | | | number | rate[1] |
| Vancouver | 61 | 40 | 34 | 8 | 143 | 6.3 |
| Hamilton | 29 | 2 | 2 | 0 | 33 | 6.3 |
| Kitchener | 16 | 15 | 0 | 0 | 31 | 6.1 |
| Ottawa[2] | 26 | 19 | 3 | 3 | 51 | 5.6 |
| Toronto | 127 | 93 | 43 | 8 | 271 | 5.4 |
| Calgary | 43 | 8 | 6 | 0 | 57 | 5.3 |
| Edmonton | 20 | 3 | 4 | 0 | 27 | 3.4 |
| Winnipeg | 7 | 5 | 1 | 1 | 14 | 2.1 |
| Québec | 6 | 2 | 4 | 3 | 15 | 2.0 |
| Montréal | 18 | 5 | 7 | 8 | 38 | 1.0 |

[1]. Populations have been adjusted to follow policing boundaries and to reflect missing coverage from the Royal Canadian Mounted Police outside of British Columbia. Rates are calculated per 100,000 population.
[2]. Ottawa refers to the Ontario portion of the Ottawa–Gatineau census metropolitan area.
SOURCE: Statistics Canada, Hate crimes reported by police, by type of motivation, http://www.statcan.gc.ca/daily-quotidien/100614//t100614b1-eng.htm, 20 February 2012. Reproduced and distributed on an "as is" basis with the permission of Statistics Canada.

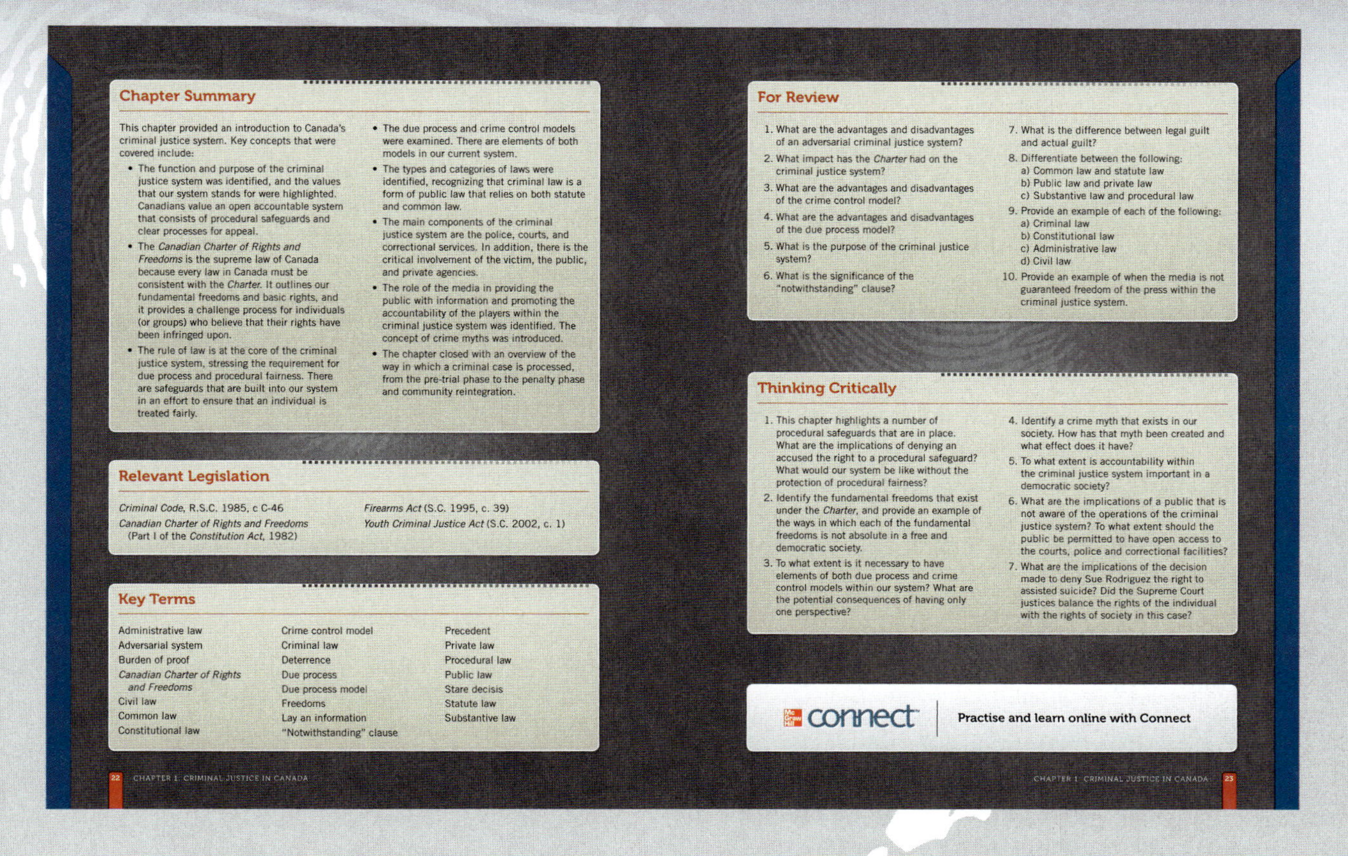

## Chapter Summary

This chapter provided an introduction to Canada's criminal justice system. Key concepts that were covered include:

- The function and purpose of the criminal justice system was identified, and the values that our system stands for were highlighted. Canadians value an open accountable system that consists of procedural safeguards and clear processes for appeal.
- The *Canadian Charter of Rights and Freedoms* is the supreme law of Canada because every law in Canada must be consistent with the *Charter*. It outlines our fundamental freedoms and basic rights, and it provides a challenge process for individuals (or groups) who believe that their rights have been infringed upon.
- The rule of law is at the core of the criminal justice system, stressing the requirement for due process and procedural fairness. There are safeguards that are built into our system in an effort to ensure that an individual is treated fairly.
- The due process and crime control models were examined. There are elements of both models in our current system.
- The types and categories of laws were identified, recognizing that criminal law is a form of public law that relies on both statute and common law.
- The main components of the criminal justice system are the police, courts, and correctional services. In addition, there is the critical involvement of the victim, the public, and private agencies.
- The role of the media in providing the public with information and promoting the accountability of the players within the criminal justice system was identified. The concept of crime myths was introduced.
- The chapter closed with an overview of the way in which a criminal case is processed, from the pre-trial phase to the penalty phase and community reintegration.

## Relevant Legislation

*Criminal Code*, R.S.C. 1985, c C-46
*Canadian Charter of Rights and Freedoms* (Part I of the *Constitution Act*, 1982)
*Firearms Act* (S.C. 1995, c. 39)
*Youth Criminal Justice Act* (S.C. 2002, c. 1)

## Key Terms

Administrative law
Adversarial system
Burden of proof
*Canadian Charter of Rights and Freedoms*
Civil law
Common law
Constitutional law
Crime control model
Criminal law
Deterrence
Due process
Due process model
Freedoms
Lay an information
"Notwithstanding" clause
Precedent
Private law
Procedural law
Public law
Stare decisis
Statute law
Substantive law

22 CHAPTER 1 CRIMINAL JUSTICE IN CANADA

## For Review

1. What are the advantages and disadvantages of an adversarial criminal justice system?
2. What impact has the *Charter* had on the criminal justice system?
3. What are the advantages and disadvantages of the crime control model?
4. What are the advantages and disadvantages of the due process model?
5. What is the purpose of the criminal justice system?
6. What is the significance of the "notwithstanding" clause?
7. What is the difference between legal guilt and actual guilt?
8. Differentiate between the following:
   a) Common law and statute law
   b) Public law and private law
   c) Substantive law and procedural law
9. Provide an example of each of the following:
   a) Criminal law
   b) Constitutional law
   c) Administrative law
   d) Civil law
10. Provide an example of when the media is not guaranteed freedom of the press within the criminal justice system.

## Thinking Critically

1. This chapter highlights a number of procedural safeguards that are in place. What are the implications of denying an accused the right to a procedural safeguard? What would our system be like without the protection of procedural fairness?
2. Identify the fundamental freedoms that exist under the *Charter*, and provide an example of the ways in which each of the fundamental freedoms is not absolute in a free and democratic society.
3. To what extent is it necessary to have elements of both due process and crime control models within our system? What are the potential consequences of having only one perspective?
4. Identify a crime myth that exists in our society. How has that myth been created and what effect does it have?
5. To what extent is accountability within the criminal justice system important in a democratic society?
6. What are the implications of a public that is not aware of the operations of the criminal justice system? To what extent should the public be permitted to have open access to the courts, police and correctional facilities?
7. What are the implications of the decision made to deny Sue Rodriguez the right to assisted suicide? Did the Supreme Court justices balance the rights of the individual with the rights of society in this case?

McGraw Hill connect | Practise and learn online with Connect

CHAPTER 1 CRIMINAL JUSTICE IN CANADA 23

**End-of-chapter content** includes:

- **Chapter Summary** of the key concepts covered in the chapter.
- A list of **Relevant Legislation** found in each chapter.
- List of the **Key Terms**.
- **For Review** questions test the students' knowledge of the topics covered.
- **Thinking Critically** questions encourage the reader to consider some of the issues mentioned in the chapter in a more critical manner.

## Additional Resources

### Instructor Resources

McGraw-Hill Connect™ is a web-based assignment and assessment platform that gives students the means to better connect with their coursework, with their instructors, and with the important concepts that they will need to know for success now and in the future.

With Connect, instructors can deliver assignments, quizzes, and tests online. Instructors can: edit existing questions and author entirely new problems—track individual student performance by question, assignment or in relation to the class overall—with detailed grade reports; integrate grade reports easily with Learning Management Systems (LMS) such as WebCT and Blackboard. And much more.

By choosing Connect, instructors are providing their students with a powerful tool for improving academic performance and truly mastering course material. Connect allows students to practice important skills at their own pace and on their own schedule. Importantly, students' assessment results and instructors' feedback are all saved online—so students can continually review their progress and plot their course to success.

Connect also provides 24/7 online access to an eBook—an online edition of the text—to aid students in successfully completing their work, wherever and whenever they choose.

The Connect Instructor Library and Assignment Bank provide all the critical resources instructors will need to build their courses, including a Test Bank, Instructor's Manual, ready-made PowerPoint® presentations, Homework Activities, Videos, and a Debate Guide.

**The Test Bank** contains multiple-choice, true-false, and short answer questions, each categorized according to learning objective, and text page reference.

**The Instructor's Manual** includes teaching strategies, tips, and creative classroom activities.

**PowerPoint® Presentations** include key lecture points and images from the text to offer instruction support and provide a visual complement to lectures. The slides are comprehensive and can be adapted to meet the needs of any course. As an aid for instructors who wish to create their own presentations, an **Image Library** containing all visual elements from the text is also available.

**Pre-Built Homework Activities Bank** includes Video Exercises, Internet Exercises, and Case Study Quizzes. These activities can be assigned separately or in combination with the Test Bank or your own material for interactive assignments and quizzes.

**Virtual Field Trips** encourage students to explore criminal justice settings in an interactive online environment.

**A Debate Guide** for each chapter poses engaging debate topics and questions in criminal justice to encourage classroom discussion and debate.

### Student Resources

Connect provides students with a powerful tool for improving academic performance and truly mastering course material, plus 24/7 online access to an interactive and searchable eBook. Connect allows students to practise important skills at their own pace and on their own schedule. Importantly, students' assessment results and instructors' feedback are all saved online—so students can continually review their progress and plot their course to success. Additional resources available within Connect include Sentencing Games, Profile Games, Practice Quizzes, Flashcards, and more!

#### SUPERIOR SERVICE

Service takes on a whole new meaning with McGraw-Hill Ryerson and *CJ*. More than just bringing you the textbook, we have consistently raised the bar in terms of innovation and educational research—both in criminal justice and in education in general. These investments in learning and the education community have helped us to understand the needs of students and educators across the country, and allowed us to foster the growth of truly innovative, integrated learning.

### COURSE MANAGEMENT

McGraw-Hill Ryerson offers a range of flexible integration solutions for Blackboard, WebCT, Desire2Learn, Moodle, and other leading learning management platforms. Please contact your local McGraw-Hill Ryerson *i*Learning Sales Specialist for details.

### TEGRITY

Tegrity is a service that makes class time available all the time by automatically capturing every lecture in a searchable format for students to review when they study and complete assignments. With a simple one-click start-and-stop process, you capture all computer screens and corresponding audio. Students replay any part of any class with easy-to-use browser-based viewing on a PC or Mac. Educators know that the more students can see, hear, and experience class resources, the better they learn. With Tegrity, students quickly recall key moments by using Tegrity's unique search feature. This search helps students efficiently find what they need, when they need it across an entire semester of class recordings. Help turn all your students' study time into learning moments immediately supported by your lecture. To learn more about Tegrity, watch a two-minute Flash demo at http://tegritycampus.mhhe.com.

### SUPERIOR LEARNING SOLUTIONS AND SUPPORT

The McGraw-Hill Ryerson team is ready to help you assess and integrate any of our products, technology, and services into your course for optimal teaching and learning performance. Whether it's helping your students improve their grades, or putting your entire course online, the McGraw-Hill Ryerson team is here to help you do it. Contact your iLearning Sales Specialist today to learn how to maximize all of McGraw-Hill Ryerson's resources!

For more information on the latest technology and Learning Solutions offered by McGraw-Hill Ryerson and its partners, please visit us online: **www.mcgrawhill.ca/he/solutions**.

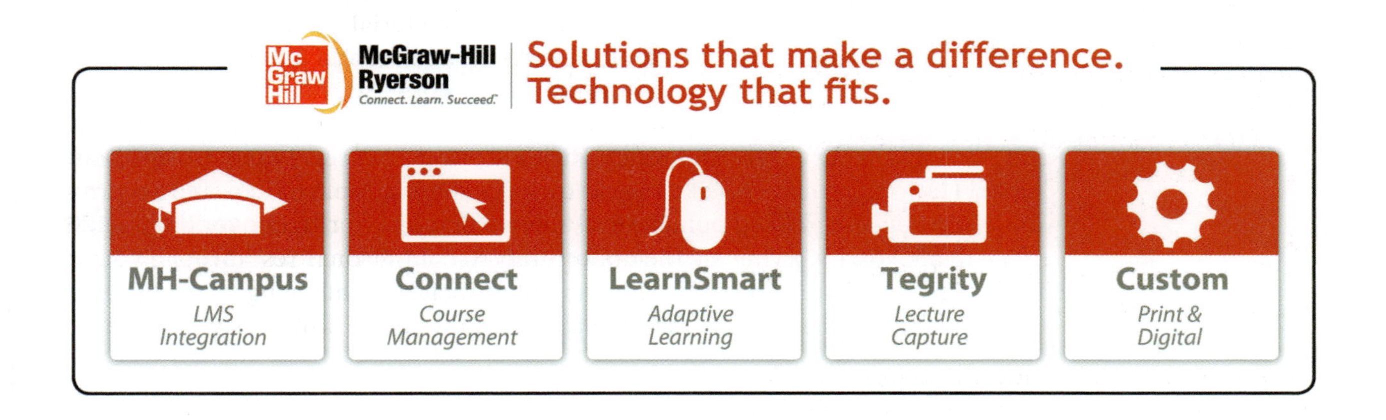

# Acknowledgements

I would like to thank the McGraw-Hill Ryerson team for their ongoing support and encouragement during this process. I am grateful to Sponsoring Editors, Karen Krahn and Marcia Siekowski, and to Supervising Editor, Jessica Barnoski. Thank you to Ann Firth for the careful editing. I would like to extend a special thank you to Lindsay MacDonald, my Developmental Editor, for her patience, support, belief, and kindness. I would like to thank the reviewers who took the time to read and comment on early versions of the text—your feedback was very helpful.

Galib Bhayani, *Kwantlen Polytechnic University*
Lorree Bogden, *Douglas College*
Beth de Beer, *Douglas College*
Loretta Gerlach, *University of Regina*
Walter Greczko, *Niagara College*
Ron Hinch, *University of Ontario Institute of Technology*
Hannele Jantti, *Douglas College*
Richard Jochelson, *University of Winnipeg*
John Jones, *Sault College*
Karin Kaercher, *Camosun College*
Darrell Kean, *Langara College*
Roland J. LaHaye, *Mount Royal University*
Lynne LeRoy, *Durham College*
David Mikelberg, *Humber College*
Darryl Plecas, *University of the Fraser Valley*
Russell Smandych, *University of Manitoba*
Sussan Thomson, *Douglas College*
Brian D. Young, *Camosun College*

I would like to thank my Humber College colleagues, past and present, for the help and assistance they provided to me at various stages of the development process—a special thank you to John Steckley, Henri Berube, Arthur Lockhart, Ron Stansfield, Scott Nicholls, Sandra Nesbitt, Shirley Richards, Rod Spencer, Frank Trovato, and Michael Hatton. I would also like to acknowledge the hundreds of Law and Security Administration and Police Foundations students that I have taught over the past 20 years—thank you for giving me the opportunity to continue to learn through you. It has been especially rewarding to see many of my former students grow to become successful professionals within the criminal justice system.

Finally, to my husband, Russ Fairey and to our daughters, Melissa, Alanna, and Jenna... thank you for many years of love and support, and for teaching me far more than I could ever teach you.

CJ
FIRST EDITION
Mc
Graw
Hill
McGraw-Hill
Ryerson

CHAPTER 1

# Criminal Justice in Canada

## Cannabis in Canada

There are a number of laws that cause us to engage in ongoing examination and debate. Canada has been struggling for many years with the creation of laws that govern the use of marijuana. The most recent challenge to Canadian law was heard in Ontario in April, 2011, when Matthew Mernagh, 37, of St. Catharines, Ontario, was charged with producing marijuana. Mernagh, who suffers from fibromyalgia, scoliosis, seizures, and depression said that he was unable to find a doctor who would support his application for a medical marijuana licence, so he began to grow his own. Justice Donald Taliano, who heard the case, said that doctors across the country choose to ignore Health Canada's medical marijuana program and refuse to sign forms that allow ill people to legally obtain cannabis. Essentially, doctors are the gatekeepers to the medical marijuana program, which began in 2000, because it is only with their approval that a patient can access medical marijuana. Justice Taliano ruled that the medical marijuana program was unconstitutional because sick people cannot get access to medical marijuana through appropriate means and must resort to growing their own, a crime in Canada. Ill people end up being labelled as criminals when they are in a no-win situation requiring them to choose between their health and the law. The federal government responded to the case by launching a consultation phase to examine ways in which to improve the current regulation of medical marijuana. It is expected that the case will result in a revised law that provides for a fair, accessible process. This case illustrates the dynamic nature of our laws and the fact that our laws change as our society evolves. This case also highlights the need to ensure the protection of individuals who are denied procedural fairness in the application of our law.

SOURCE: R. *v.* Mernagh, 2011 ONSC 2121.

### LEARNING OBJECTIVES

By the end of this chapter, you should be able to:

- **LO1** Explain the function and purpose of the criminal justice system.
- **LO2** Explain the rule of law and its significance in Canadian law.
- **LO3** Describe the rights and freedoms guaranteed by the *Canadian Charter of Rights and Freedoms*.
- **LO4** Identify the procedural safeguards that exist in the criminal justice system.
- **LO5** Describe the due process and crime control philosophies of criminal justice.
- **LO6** Identify the types and categories of laws that exist in Canada.
- **LO7** Identify the components of the criminal justice system.
- **LO8** Describe the relationship between the media and the criminal justice system.
- **LO9** Describe the way in which a criminal case is processed through the criminal justice system.

## LO1 The Criminal Justice System

The criminal justice system plays a crucial role in our society. It is a system that consists of processes and procedures intended to manage and respond to crime in our society. The criminal justice system has a number of important functions, which include:

- preventing crimes,
- enforcing laws,
- investigating crimes,
- prosecuting criminal cases through an impartial judicial system—one for adults and one for youths,
- implementing sentences that are imposed by the criminal courts—for adults and youths,
- providing correctional institutions and community supervision for sentenced individuals (adults and youths) at both the provincial and federal levels, and
- meeting the needs of victims.

In performing the functions required to make the criminal justice system work, there are a number of other goals that are attained.

- Protecting society by maintaining the peace, and by preventing and controlling crime.
- Adjudicating cases in a manner that is fair, and results in a just conclusion.
- Providing treatment and rehabilitation intended to ensure that individuals are able to live crime-free lives.

The criminal justice system is responsible for ensuring that the necessary processes and procedures are in place, and that those processes are legal and effective and that they are consistent with the values of our society. Through our laws we demonstrate our commitment to individual rights and freedoms, as well as the needs of society overall. We strive to balance both.

As Canadians, we value the following:

- An open criminal justice system that is transparent. A system that allows the public and the press access to information regarding the daily operations of the system.
- An accountable criminal justice system—with processes for appeal and procedural safeguards.
- A system that respects all of the rights and freedoms within the *Canadian Charter of Rights and Freedoms*, including the fundamental freedoms and the legal rights.
- A system that respects the rights of victims.
- Efficiency. There is a recognition that the criminal justice system operates with public funding, and that it must be both efficient and effective.
- Rehabilitation and the belief that offenders can change. There are numerous sentences available to judges, and programs dedicated to assist offenders to become crime-free members of our society.

### THE RULE OF LAW

LO2

"The hallmarks of a regime which flouts the rule of law are, alas, all too familiar: the midnight knock on the door, the sudden disappearance, the show trial, the subjection of prisoners to genetic experiment, the confession extracted by torture, the gulag and the concentration camp, the gas chamber, the practice of genocide or ethnic cleansing, the waging of aggressive war. The list is endless."

TOM BINGHAM

The rule of law is often referred to in our courts and in written judgements. The rule of law has evolved through history to describe the fundamental rights and beliefs that form the foundation of a fair and just society. The rule of law enforces a minimum standard of fairness to be adhered to within the justice system (Bingham, 2010). There are several principles inherent within the rule of law. The rule of law means that every dispute will be settled in a peaceful manner by engaging in **due process** in our courts before a judge where one's rights will be both respected and protected. Each person is protected by the law and it applies to everyone equally, regardless of

**due process**
the right to be treated within the principles of fundamental justice

**TABLE 1.1 The Principles of the Rule of Law**

| Bingham's Principle of the Rule of Law | Application of the Principle Within the Criminal Justice System |
|---|---|
| The law must be accessible and so far as possible, intelligible, clear and predictable. | Individuals are entitled to information about our laws sufficient to guarantee an understanding of their impact. The laws must be clear and predictable to facilitate accessibility. |
| Questions of legal right and liability should ordinarily be resolved by application of the law and not the exercise of discretion. | It is critical that legal resolution be based upon an objective application of the law as opposed to the subjective discretion of an individual. |
| The laws of the land should apply equally to all, save to the extent that objective differences justify differentiation. | All individuals should be treated equally before the law. Objective differences that justify differentiation can include differentiation for young offenders or Aboriginal offenders. |
| Ministers and public officers at all levels must exercise the powers conferred on them in good faith, fairly and for the purpose for which the powers were conferred, without exceeding the limits of such powers and not unreasonably. | All Ministers and public officers (including police) are entrusted with powers, and they must use those powers within reason. They must not abuse their powers in the exercise of their duties and they must be accountable if they do. |
| The law must afford adequate protection of fundamental human rights. | Fundamental human rights must be protected in law. These fundamental rights and freedoms must be respected and adhered to throughout the criminal justice system. |
| Means must be provided for resolving, without prohibitive cost or inordinate delay, bona fide civil disputes which the parties themselves are unable to resolve. | The ability to resolve disputes must not be so costly that the process is prohibitive to the average person. The process for resolution should not involve unreasonable delays. |
| Adjudicative procedures provided by the state should be fair. | Trials and other procedures should be administered in a fair and impartial manner, at every stage of the trial process. |
| The rule of law requires compliance by the state with its obligations in international law as in national law. | There is a recognition that Canada has an obligation to adhere to relevant international law, such as the Universal Declaration of Human Rights. |

SOURCE: Approximately 154 words from *The Rule of Law* by Tom Bingham (Penguin Books, 2010). Copyright © Tom Bingham, 2010. Reproduced by permission of Penguin Books Ltd.

connect ONLINE ACTIVITY

one's status. The rule of law offers equal protection and a formal process of procedural justice to adjudicate disputes. It guarantees that fundamental freedoms are upheld and that no one is subjected to arbitrary power. In his examination of the rule of law, Tom Bingham identifies eight universal principles that directly apply to the various elements and players within the Criminal Justice System.

## LO3 THE *CANADIAN CHARTER OF RIGHTS AND FREEDOMS*

The ***Canadian Charter of Rights and Freedoms*** (the *Charter*) is a piece of legislation that has a major impact on all aspects of administering justice in Canada. It is Part 1 of *The Constitution Act,* 1982, and it outlines Canadians' basic rights and freedoms. The *Charter* is the supreme law of Canada, meaning that every other law in Canada must be consistent with it. In a relatively short period of time, the *Charter* has had a significant impact on Canadian society. Though the *Charter* addresses our rights as individuals, it has an impact on society as well. It has changed the way in which criminal law is practised, and it has created an awareness of the requirement for due process in our society. It has also led to a society with a clearer understanding of its rights and freedoms.

***Canadian Charter of Rights and Freedoms***
the supreme law of Canada, which outlines our fundamental freedoms and basic rights

The *Charter* guarantees the following freedoms and rights:

- **Fundamental Freedoms**—Section 2
  - freedom of conscience and religion;
  - freedom of thought, belief, opinion and expression, including freedom of the press and other media of communication;
  - freedom of peaceful assembly; and
  - freedom of association.
- **Democratic Rights**—Sections 3, 4, and 5 guarantee us the right to vote, the sitting

The G-20 Summit, hosted in Toronto in 2010, caused us to ask many questions about the limits to peaceful assembly.

of parliament, and the maximum length of time between general elections.

- **Mobility Rights**—Section 6 guarantees Canadian citizens the right to live and work anywhere they choose in Canada.
- **Legal Rights**—Sections 7 to 14 contain the following rights:
  - To life, liberty, and security of the person.
  - To be free from unreasonable search or seizure.
  - To not be arbitrarily detained or imprisoned.
  - To be informed promptly of the reasons for any arrest or detention, and be released if the reasons are not valid.
  - To be able to retain and instruct legal counsel without delay and to be informed of that right.
  - To receive a fair and public trial within a reasonable time, by an impartial tribunal, if charged with a crime.
  - To not be compelled to give evidence against yourself.
  - To be presumed innocent until proven guilty according to law in a fair and public hearing.
  - To be free from cruel and unusual punishment.
  - To be granted reasonable bail if appropriate.

## FLASHBACK:

### QUEBEC LEGISLATURE APPLIED THE NOTWITHSTANDING CLAUSE IN 1988

The province of Quebec applied the notwithstanding clause in 1988 when it sought to protect its sign laws. The provincial government had passed laws that required all commercial signs in the province (inside and outside of establishments) to be in French only. The intent of the law was to ensure that the French language was protected in commercial activities. There were a number of challenges by individuals and groups who believed that the law violated their rights under section 2(b)—the right to freedom of expression. The government of Quebec responded by making some minor amendments that allowed other languages on the inside of commercial establishments. However, language other than French was prohibited on external signs. Five years later when the notwithstanding clause expired it was not renewed. Instead, the Quebec government passed a new law that stated that signs could use more than one language, as long as French was the predominant one displayed (Sharpe and Roach, 2005).

- To receive a court-appointed interpreter, if required.

- **Equality Rights**—Section 15 ensures equal benefit and protection of the law without discrimination based on personal traits such as race, national or ethnic origin, colour, religion, sex, age, or mental or physical disability.
- **Language Rights**—Section 16 makes English and French the official languages of Canada. Section 23 gives minority language education rights in certain circumstances.

**burden of proof**
a duty to produce evidence to prove facts necessary to establish a cause of action or a defence

### SECTION 1: NOT ALL RIGHTS ARE ABSOLUTE

Section 1 of the *Charter* is a critical section because it recognizes that not all rights and freedoms are absolute. This means that there are situations where our *Charter* rights are subject to reasonable limits, which are justified, in a free and democratic society. For example, we do have the fundamental freedom of thought, belief, option, and expression. However, we also have laws that limit certain kinds of expression, such as those prohibited by our hate laws.

### THE "NOTWITHSTANDING" CLAUSE

The **"notwithstanding" clause** (section 33) provides federal and provincial governments with the ability to override specific *Charter* rights in certain situations. They can make a decision that a law operates "notwithstanding" a provision included in section 2 or sections 7 to 15 of the *Charter* (Sharpe and Roach, 2005). The provinces and territories have used this

**"notwithstanding" clause**
the clause allowing federal and provincial governments the ability to override specific *Charter* rights in certain situtations

**TABLE 1.2 *Charter* Procedural Safeguards**

| Stage in the Criminal Justice Process | Procedural Safeguard | *Charter* Section |
|---|---|---|
| At the time of an arrest | • The right to be notified of the reason for the arrest.<br>• The right to remain silent.<br>• The right to consult with a lawyer. | 10. (a) Everyone has the right on arrest or detention to be informed promptly of the reasons therefor.<br>10. (b) Everyone has the right on arrest or detention to retain and instruct counsel without delay and to be informed of that right. |
| Pre-trial | • The right to a hearing regarding pre-trial detention. | 9. Everyone has the right not to be arbitrarily detained or imprisoned.<br>11. (e) Any person charged with an offence has the right not to be denied reasonable bail without just cause. |
| Search or seizure | • The right to be free from unreasonable search and seizure. A search that is reasonable is authorized by law and carried out in a manner that is reasonable. | 8. Everyone has the right to be secure against unreasonable search and seizure. |
| At trial | • The **burden of proof** rests with the Crown.<br>• The accused is presumed innocent and the crown must prove guilt beyond a reasonable doubt.<br>• An accused is under no obligation to present a defence to a charge.<br>• The accused has the right to be tried within a reasonable amount of time.<br>• The accused has the right to an interpreter. | 11. (d) Any person charged with an offence has the right to be presumed innocent until proven guilty according to law in a fair and public hearing by an independent and impartial tribunal.<br>11. (b) Any person charged with an offence has the right to be tried within a reasonable time.<br>14. A party or witness in any proceedings who does not understand or speak the language in which the proceedings are conducted or who is deaf has the right to the assistance of an interpreter. |
| At sentencing | • The accused should receive a penalty that reflects the nature of the offence. | 12. Everyone has the right not to be subjected to any cruel and unusual treatment or punishment. |

power only rarely. When it is used, it can only be invoked for a maximum of five years at which time it no longer has any force and the law can be struck down by the courts.

## ENFORCING THE *CHARTER*

Canadian courts are entrusted with interpreting and enforcing the *Charter*. The courts are the guardians of the *Charter*—it is their job to ensure that the decisions made are consistent with the *Charter*'s philosophy and principles. Judges have the power to strike down and invalidate laws or other government actions, and do so if it is necessary to defend a protected right or freedom. Canadians who believe that a provincial or federal law or action violates their *Charter* rights can initiate a process to challenge the law or action.

If an individual believes that a law violates the *Charter*, a court will hear the case and determine if there is a way to justify the violation under section 1 (the section that indicates that not all rights are absolute). If a law cannot be justified under section 1, a court may declare that the law is unconstitutional. When that happens, part VII, section 52(1) of the *Constitution Act, 1982,* makes it clear that:

> Any law that is inconsistent with the provisions of the Constitution is... of no force or effect.

In some situations the court may suspend the actual declaration to give the government time to respond to the decision, usually with an appeal or an amended law. The Canadian parliament or a provincial legislature has the right to invoke the notwithstanding clause to continue to operate a challenged law.

If someone believes that a government official, such as a police officer, violated the *Charter*, the court will usually make a decision during the hearing of the case. For example, if it is determined that the police engaged in an unreasonable search, the court may determine that any evidence that was introduced as a result of the search is not admissible because it was obtained illegally. The court has the right to make a decision that is believed to be fair based on the type of violation.

## PROCEDURAL SAFEGUARDS

LO4

The *Charter* provides a number of procedural safeguards that are intended to ensure that accused persons are treated fairly throughout the criminal justice process. Procedural fairness is a critical element of a fair and democratic system of law. Some safeguards that are specific to the criminal justice process are listed in Table 1.2.

## CHALLENGES TO THE *CHARTER*

As the supreme law of Canada, every other law in Canada must be consistent with the *Charter*. Since its' inception, we have seen a number of *Charter* challenges. Cases that challenge the *Charter* allege that a Canadian law is not consistent with the *Charter,* and is therefore unconstitutional. *Charter* challenges are important because they have the potential to change the lives of Canadians. Though not limited to criminal law, there have been many *Charter* challenge cases related to criminal law. The following are two well-known cases.

### THE SUE RODRIGUEZ CASE: CHALLENGING ASSISTED SUICIDE

Charter challenges usually begin with average Canadians who believe that one of the freedoms, guaranteed in the Charter, is being denied. In 1992, Sue Rodriguez, a woman from Victoria, British Columbia, made history when she fought for the right to end her own life with the assistance of a physician. Sue Rodriguez had ALS (amyotrophic lateral sclerosis), commonly referred to as Lou Gehrig's disease. Section 241 of the *Criminal Code of Canada* (the *Criminal Code*) prevents anyone from assisting another to commit suicide. It states:

> 241. Every one who
> (a) counsels a person to commit suicide, or
> (b) aids or abets a person to commit suicide,
> whether suicide ensues or not, is guilty of an indictable offence and liable to imprisonment for a term not exceeding fourteen years.

An assisted suicide is when one person, potentially a physician, helps another to commit suicide by providing the first person with a means to die, such as a fatal drug overdose, a lethal injection, or the removal of life support. Often the people

Sue Rodriguez fought for the right to die by being assisted by a physician.

who want assisted suicide are unable to end their own lives, due to their illness. Rodriguez believed that section 241 interfered with her right to "life, liberty and security of the person"—personal liberties—guaranteed in section 7 of the *Charter*. It was her belief that an individual should be able to choose to end one's own life, along with the method, timing, and circumstances of death which, in her case, was influenced by her knowledge that her eventual death would be difficult for herself and her family. In 1993, the Supreme Court of Canada heard her case and in a 5 – 4 decision, they rejected her case (Smith, 1993). In their ruling, the Supreme Court justices recognized that our laws had an obligation to preserve life in order to protect vulnerable people. This obligation was deemed to be more significant than the individual rights of Sue Rodriguez.

In 1994, Sue Rodriguez did eventually end her life, with the help of an anonymous doctor. There were no criminal charges laid in the case.

On June 14, 2012, a landmark decision was delivered by the British Columbia Supreme Court, when it declared section 241 unconstitutional—it discriminates against terminally-ill persons. The court was hearing the case of Gloria Taylor who, like Sue Rodriguez, has ALS and wants the right to choose the time of her death. The federal government was given one year to amend the current *Criminal Code* legislation.

### CHARTER CHALLENGE: POLYGAMY IN CANADA

The laws related to polygamy have long been the subject of debate and judicial review in Canada. Polygamy has been against the law in Canada since 1892. In response to a formal request by the Attorney General of British Columbia, the Supreme Court of British Columbia was asked to decide whether section 293 of the *Criminal Code* (polygamy) is constitutional. Chief Justice Robert Bauman reviewed the laws to determine if they contravene the *Charter*'s guarantee of freedom of religion. In his decision, dated November 23, 2011, "Bauman concluded that Canada's criminal prohibition on polygamy is a violation of the guarantee of freedom of religion in the *Charter*, but accepted that this is constitutionally justified as a reasonable limitation intended to prevent harm to women, children and society" (Bala, 2011).

Polygamy is defined in the *Criminal Code* as:

293. (1) Every one who
- (a) practises or enters into or in any manner agrees or consents to practise or enter into
  - (i) any form of polygamy, or
  - (ii) any kind of conjugal union with more than one person at the same time,

  whether or not it is by law recognized as a binding form of marriage, or
- (b) celebrates, assists or is a party to a rite, ceremony, contract or consent that purports to sanction a relationship mentioned in subparagraph (a)(i) or (ii),

is guilty of an indictable offence and liable to imprisonment for a term not exceeding five years.

Bauman's review of the law was related to the existence of the polygamous community of Bountiful, British Columbia. Plural marriage is a way of life in Bountiful, where men have several wives and teenage girls are usually married very young. It is their religious belief that the more

Winston Blackmore, the religious leader of the polygamous community of Bountiful, British Columbia, with several members of his family.

children a man brings into the world, the greater the likelihood that he will enter the kingdom of God, find salvation, and possibly become a God himself. Winston Blackmore, the religious leader of the polygamous community, was born and raised in Bountiful and it is reported that he has 22 wives and 67 children. The polygamist community is a part of a fundamentalist form of Mormonism and its history can be traced back to the Mormon community in Utah.

The RCMP investigated allegations of polygamy, forcible marriage, child abuse, and sexual exploitation in Bountiful. They eventually laid charges of polygamy against two men in Bountiful—Winston Blackmore and James Oler. It was alleged that Blackmore had 19 marriages and that Oler had marriages to three women. In 2009, a British Columbia judge dismissed the charges against both Blackmore and Oler (CBC, 2009).

At this point, Chief Justice Bauman's decision has not been appealed to the Supreme Court of Canada. As such, our current polygamy law (section 293) remains intact and a part of Canada's criminal code.

## PHILOSOPHIES OF CRIMINAL JUSTICE: DUE PROCESS AND CRIME CONTROL

LO5

The criminal justice system operates while striving to balance two opposite philosophies. These two philosophies (or models) represent two different and extreme, but equally important value systems that co-exist within the criminal justice system. These two models were first articulated by Herbert L. Packer in 1968. The two models are the due process model and the crime control model, and both are apparent in our criminal justice system.

The goal of the **due process model** is to ensure that the criminal justice system is just. There is a focus on ensuring that accused people are treated fairly and that there are procedural safeguards in place to protect the rights of individuals. The model stresses the importance of the presumption of innocence and all of the safeguards that support that assumption. The model reminds us that power is subject to abuse and recognizes a responsibility on the part of the judiciary to identify and respond to any abuse of power.

The due process model stresses the importance of ensuring that procedures are followed and respected. If the procedures are not followed, factual guilt is not relevant in the model. The model expects the criminal justice system to "earn" a conviction by ensuring that the police and the

"A person is not to be held guilty of a crime merely on a showing that in all probability, based upon reliable evidence, he did factually what he is said to have done. Instead he is to be held guilty only if these factual determinations are made in procedurally regular fashion and by authorities acting within competencies duly allocated to them."

HERBERT L. PACKER, *TWO MODELS OF THE CRIMINAL PROCESS*

Procedural fairness was debated in the aftermath of the G-20 summit in Toronto in June, 2010.

courts have proceeded in a fair manner (Packer, 1968).

The due process model also differentiates between legal guilt and factual guilt. Legal guilt refers to an accused who has been found guilty when all the procedural safeguards have been respected. Factual guilt occurs when an accused may be guilty of committing a crime, but is not found legally guilty because a legal procedure has been abused or a right has been withheld. For example, a case may be dismissed because the accused was not tried within a reasonable amount of time. The accused may be factually guilty because he did commit the crime; however, he is not legally guilty because his right to be tried within a reasonable period of time was not respected. As such, the factual guilt is irrelevant because the fact that the accused was denied the constitutional guarantee of procedural fairness is more important than the finding of guilt.

There is an expectation that the criminal justice system will be accurate, fair, and reliable, and that power is limited and is not abused. There is a recognition that the accused is entitled to rights and freedoms and that those rights and freedoms must be respected in order to find an accused person legally guilty of a crime. Procedural safeguards are a critical element of the criminal justice system, regardless of the crime or the criminal.

**crime control model**

protects the public through the capture, prosecution, and conviction of offenders

The **crime control model** focuses on protecting the public through the capture, prosecution, and conviction of offenders. The emphasis is on securing a conviction and

"The presumption of guilt is what makes it possible for the system to deal effectively with large numbers, as the crime control model demands. The supposition is that the screening processes operated by police and prosecutors are reliable indicators of probable guilt. Once a man has been arrested and investigated without being found to be probably innocent, or, to put it differently, once a determination has been made that there is enough evidence of guilt to permit holding him for further action, then all subsequent activity directed toward him is based on the view that he is probably guilty."

HERBERT L. PACKER, *TWO MODELS OF CRIMINAL PROCESS*

incapacitating as many criminals as possible. This model asserts that the criminal justice system needs to process cases in an efficient, quick manner. There is also an environment of attitudes that result in a presumption of guilt. The belief is that if a person is arrested for a crime, he or she is likely guilty of the crime. This model stresses the competence of the professionals within the criminal justice system and trusts that they made decisions and used their discretion in the best interest of our society overall. This model also relies on the principle of **deterrence**, as there is an expectation that if a society sees people being successfully prosecuted and convicted, they will be deterred from committing the same or similar crimes. Proponents of the crime control model support swift justice and harsher penalties (Packer, 1968).

**deterrence**
discouraging the criminal behaviour of persons (or a society) by exposing them to successful conviction

The crime control model and the due process models are abstract views of differing approaches to criminal justice. Today there is an expectation that the criminal justice system ensures that the due process model and the crime control model co-exist. There is a need to ensure that due process is respected. There is also a need to ensure that our society is protected from criminals who threaten public safety. The reality is that our system balances elements of both models, integrating them in order to ensure that we have a criminal justice system that is both fair and effective.

## LO6 TYPES OF LAW IN CANADA

An overall understanding of the types and categories of law in Canada enables one to recognize the role and context of criminal law, the foundation of the criminal justice system. There are two main categories of law: **common law** and **statute law**.

### COMMON LAW

Common law is a body of law that continually develops as it is created by court decisions that become judicial **precedent**. It is law that is not created by parliament and is therefore not codified. When there is no statute law to govern a specific matter, the court looks to common law for a resolution. Common law is adaptable and changes based on the circumstances before the court. Precedent stems from British common law; it is also referred to **stare decisis**, a Latin phrase that means "to stand by what has been decided." This rule requires that other like cases be decided in the same way. A judge can refer to a precedent when adjudicating a similar case. A precedent that is set by the Supreme Court of Canada can only be changed by the Supreme Court by reversing its own decision later, or by the passage of a new law that overrules the court's decision.

**precedent**
is a judicial decision used as a standard in similar, subsequent cases

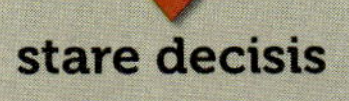

**stare decisis**
refers to precedent; a Latin phrase that means "to stand by what has been decided"

### STATUTE LAW

Statute law is created through the parliamentary process and is a part of a written piece of legislation. It is specific in its intent and its interpretation. A provincial or federal legislature or parliament has the power to create new laws and to amend current laws. The federal parliament in Ottawa creates legislation that is federal, and each province and territory creates its own legislation. At the federal level, laws begin with a process of examination, where senior public servants examine an issue and make recommendations for the law. They then draft the law, which requires approval from Cabinet (a group of Members of Parliament and/or Senators identified by the Prime Minister). This draft is then presented as a bill to Parliament to be examined and debated by members. In order for a bill to become a law it must be approved by the majority in both the House of Commons and the Senate. It then must receive Royal Assent by the Governor General in the name of the Queen (Parliament of Canada, 2005). The provinces and territories follow a similar process to create statute law.

The second categorization is **private law** and **public law**.

### PRIVATE LAW

Private law resolves disputes between individuals and private entities, such as corporations. Examples of private law include contract law, family law, or estate law. In matters of private law, there is no representation on behalf of the state. Private law involves two private parties.

## FOCUS ON The Gun Registry in Canada

The long gun registry in Canada has been controversial since its introduction as part of the *Firearms Act* in 1995. The long gun registry was created by the Liberal government of the day in response to the 1989 massacre of 14 female students at École Polytechnique in Montréal. The *Firearms Act* requires all long-gun owners to be licensed and to register their guns. It also includes harsher penalties for crimes involving the use of guns. At the time, the Liberal government estimated that the registry would cost about $119 million; however, with the revenue that would be generated from the registry it was projected to cost tax payers $2 million. The deadline for all long-gun owners to register their guns was January 1, 2003. By that date, 75 percent of all long-gun owners registered 5.8 million guns Canada wide. In 2002, the federal Auditor General Sheila Fraser revealed that the cost of implementing the long-gun registry was exorbitant. The costs were estimated at $527 million due to a faulty computer system and a number of costs that were unforeseen. Fraser's report indicated that the registry cost taxpayers $1 billion by 2005 and generated about $140 million in income (Auditor General Report, 2006).

This bumper sticker is in response to the gun registry controversy.

Along with the outrage over the cost, there was criticism from various groups and individuals across the country. In addition, Canada's political parties have philosophical differences on gun control policy, which resulted in heated debate on the topic in the House of Commons. The registry was criticized by long-gun owners across the country who believed that it was penalizing peaceful gun owners rather than criminals who acquire illegal firearms. The registry was supported by the Liberal party, the New Democratic Party, and the Bloc Quebecois. Canadian police chiefs have also declared their support for the long-gun registry indicating that they use it on a regular basis to determine if suspects have firearms in their homes. The Conservative government made several attempts to abolish the long-gun registry and in October 2011, the majority Conservative government introduced legislation to scrap the registry. The bill, C-19, received Royal Assent in April 2012.

### PUBLIC LAW

Public law involves the state and the general population, and is administered on behalf of the state. It includes criminal law, administrative law, and constitutional law. In matters of public law, a prosecutor represents the state.

The laws in Canada are classified in several areas, based on type. There are four main classifications: criminal, constitutional, administrative, and civil.

**criminal law**
a form of public law referring to laws that prohibit certain acts

**Criminal law** is a form of public law and refers to those laws that prohibit certain acts. There is a definition of the type of act that is prohibited as well as the penalty that may be received if someone is found guilty of the act. In addition, our criminal law describes the law related to the procedures required to administer the law. For example, the procedures related to a criminal search are identified in our criminal laws.

**Constitutional law** is a form of public law and refers to those laws that identify the powers and limitations of the government and the way in which those powers are exercised. For example, the *Constitution Act* of 1867 identifies the different powers of the federal and the provincial governments.

**constitutional law**
a form of public law referring to laws that identify the powers and limitations of the government and how the powers are exercised

## FLASHBACK:
### THE MONTREAL MASSACRE

The Montreal massacre occurred on December 6, 1989, when Marc Lepine, 25, who had earlier been rejected from the Canadian Armed Forces, roamed the halls of École Polytechnique, the School of Engineering at the University of Montreal, shooting and killing 14 female engineering students. Before and during the 20 minute rampage of terror, Lepine spouted anti-feminist rhetoric (Rathjen and Montpetit, 1999). When he entered one classroom he shouted, "I want the women. I hate feminists!" He separated the women from the men and he executed them. His final act was to take his own life. Lepine left a suicide note, ensuring that his motive was clear. He wrote:

*"Please note that if I am committing suicide today… it is not for economic reasons… but for political reasons. For I have decided to send Ad Patres [Latin: "to the fathers"] the feminists who have ruined my life. …The feminists always have a talent for enraging me. They want to retain the advantages of being women… while trying to grab those men. …They are so opportunistic that they neglect to profit from the knowledge accumulated by men throughout the ages. They always try to misrepresent them every time they can."*

Lepine attached the names of 19 prominent women from the province of Quebec who were in non-traditional occupations. The list included the first female firefighter and a female police captain. Under the list he wrote:

*"[These women] nearly died today. The lack of time (because I started too late) has allowed these radical feminists to survive."*

It appears that it was his intention initially to kill these prominent women, but chose instead to go to the School of Engineering to target the female students. The events of December 6, 1989, changed Canada. It has been designated a day of national commemoration. The long-gun registry was initiated in response to the massacre, as was the White Ribbon Movement, founded by Jack Layton in 1991. Violence against women continues to be a critical issue and requires ongoing awareness and education.

**SOURCES: http://www.gendercide.org/case_montreal.html; http://www.cbc.ca/news/canada/montreal/story/2009/12/06/montreal-massacre-national-day-action-remembrance-violence-against-women.html; Rathjen, H., and Montpetit, C. (1999). *December 6th: From the Montreal Massacre to Gun Control*. Toronto: McClelland and Stewart.**

**Administrative law** is another form of public law and refers to the body of law that addresses the actions of governments and government agencies. The focus of administrative law is the manner in which boards, tribunals, commissions, agencies, or ministers make decisions. The goal is to ensure that there are effective remedies in place for issues related to public administration. One example is law related to unemployment benefits or human rights violations.

**administrative law**
a form of public law that addresses the actions of government and government agencies

**Civil law** is the overarching term for all areas of private law that generally regulate private individuals and groups in our society. Civil law includes family law, contract law, tort law, and estate law.

**civil law**
overarching term for all areas of private law that regulate private individuals and groups in our society

The final category is **substantive law** and **procedural law**.

### SUBSTANTIVE LAW

Substantive law identifies the rights and obligations of citizens in any given jurisdiction. It identifies the substance of law in that it defines an offence by clearly stating the actions that are against the law. A crime that is defined in the criminal code is an example of substantive law.

### PROCEDURAL LAW

Procedural law is a category of law that defines procedures within the justice system. Procedural law provides clear processes to ensure that the system is fair. The procedures related to the gathering of evidence are examples of procedural law.

## LO7 The Adversarial System

The Canadian criminal justice system is an **adversarial system** where two opposing sides present their case before an impartial arbiter. The Crown attorney, representing the government of Canada, and the accused, usually represented by defence counsel, are adversaries during this process. Each party is called upon to gather and present evidence and a legal argument—all within the parameters of the law. The impartial adjudicator is the judge and/or the jury. The judge's role is not only to make the final decision of guilt or innocence, but to also ensure that there is procedural fairness throughout the process. The judge must also consider balancing the rights of the individual with the rights and interests of society as a whole. The goal of the system is to arrive at a just decision that comes from presenting a case in a protected environment, under the scrutiny of a judge, jury, and the public.

**adversarial system**
two opposing parties present their case before an impartial arbiter

The traditional adversarial system has been complemented by the introduction of restorative justice measures that offer less formal and less punitive approaches to dealing with some forms of crime. Restorative justice moves away from the adversarial win/lose approach that is more common in the traditional system. Restorative justice will be examined in more detail later in this text.

### THE COMPONENTS OF THE CRIMINAL JUSTICE SYSTEM

The criminal justice system consists of several components that together share the overall goal of protecting our society. Each of the components will be examined in more detail in dedicated chapters. Each element of the criminal justice system is governed by its own legislation, rules, and regulations. The various components are interrelated and influence one another. Each of the component areas has several layers of jurisdiction. The components are: police, courts, and corrections.

These three main areas have a great deal of influence on each other and they rely on each other's cooperation. They represent a network of agencies and services that provide law enforcement, prosecution, trial, punishment, and the supervision of offenders. It represents a vast network of individuals and agencies. Each component will be discussed in more detail in later chapters.

#### THE POLICE

The police are responsible for enforcing the laws across Canada. Policing is both proactive and reactive in nature. It is proactive when it engages the public in crime prevention and other related initiatives. It is reactive when it responds to crime. The police are the most visible component of the criminal justice system. In 2011, there were 69,438 police officers employed across Canada (Statistics Canada, CANSIM table 254-0002). They begin the criminal prosecution of a case by laying charges in response to criminal activity, and they follow that case through the court system to completion.

The organization of policing in Canada is multi-jurisdictional. There are three levels of

The Royal Canadian Mounted Police is the largest and most recognizable police service in Canada.

policing in Canada and each level has its own jurisdiction and responsibilities. In addition, there are First Nations policing agreements in place for Aboriginal communities across Canada. The Royal Canadian Mounted Police (RCMP) is Canada's federal police agency. The RCMP polices the three territories, all of the provinces except Ontario and Quebec, and has municipal policing agreements with approximately 180 municipalities. Under the *Constitution Act*, each province and territory in Canada is responsible for administering justice, which includes policing responsibilities. All provinces except Ontario and Quebec have entered into agreements with the federal government whereby the RCMP polices their provinces.

## THE COURT SYSTEM

There are several levels and types of courts in Canada. Assigned with resolving disputes fairly, each court is responsible for hearing specific types of cases. The courts are entrusted to interpret the laws and make judgements to guide society on important issues. The levels are as follows:

**Provincial/Territorial Courts** The majority of disputes are dealt with at this level throughout Canada. These courts hear matters related to criminal law, family law, young offenders, traffic offences, and all other disputes that flow from provincial or territorial legislation. Small Claims Court disputes are also heard at this level.

**Provincial/Territorial Superior Courts** Superior Courts hear both civil and criminal cases, of a more serious nature than the provincial courts. Each jurisdiction identifies requirements or limitations related to the types of cases heard in the courts.

**Courts of Appeal** A Court of Appeal in each jurisdiction hears the appeals from decisions that were made in lower courts. The appeals can result from decisions made in any lower court, based on criminal or civil law.

**Federal Courts** Federal courts are responsible for adjudication matters that stem from federal laws. They include cases related to taxation, immigration, citizenship, copyright, and any cases that involved any Crown corporation or federal government department.

**The Supreme Court of Canada** The Supreme Court of Canada is the highest court in Canada. It is an appeal court that has jurisdiction over all areas of law. A decision made by the Supreme Court is a final decision.

Source: Department of Justice Canada (2005)

**FIGURE 1.1** Outline of Canada's Court System

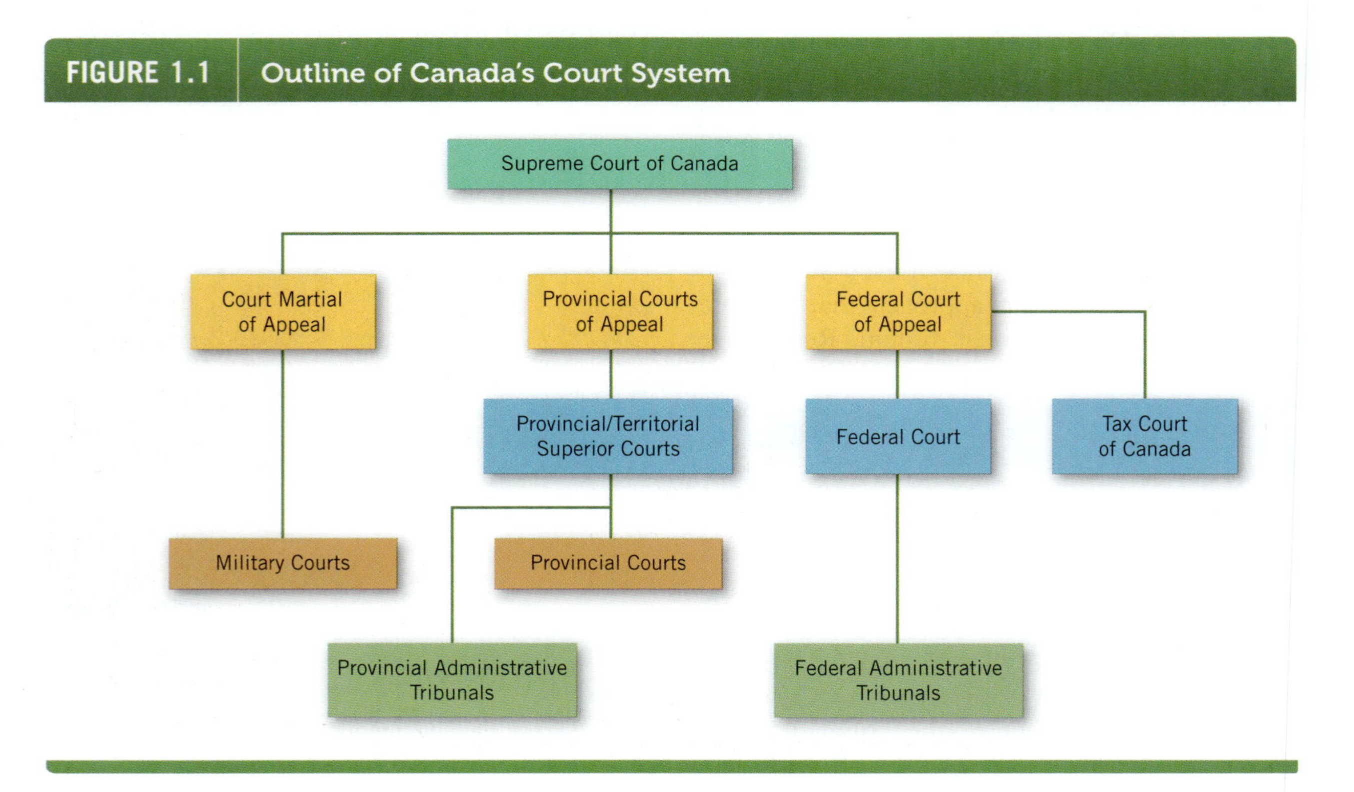

## THE CORRECTIONAL SYSTEM

The correctional system is responsible for administering the sentence that has been imposed by the court. The sentence may be an institutional sentence, which involves incarceration, or it may be a community sentence such as probation. Our correctional system is administered by both the federal and provincial governments. The federal government is responsible for the custody and supervision of offenders who receive a custodial sentence of two years or longer. This includes the provision of parole for federal offenders. The provincial governments are responsible for all offenders who receive a community sentence as well as those who are sentenced to imprisonment for less than two years. This split jurisdiction requires that the two systems cooperate and communicate with each other.

Collins Bay Institution.
This medium-security institution for men opened in 1930.

In addition to the three main elements of the criminal justice system, there is the involvement of the victim, the offender, private agencies, and the public.

The victim and the offender are the principal players in the criminal justice system. The role of the victim varies based on the type of case. The victim could have an active role as a witness during the trial, or by providing a victim impact statement during the sentencing phase of the trial. The offender is expected to be in the courtroom

**FIGURE 1.2** The Criminal Justice Process from Crime to Conviction to Corrections

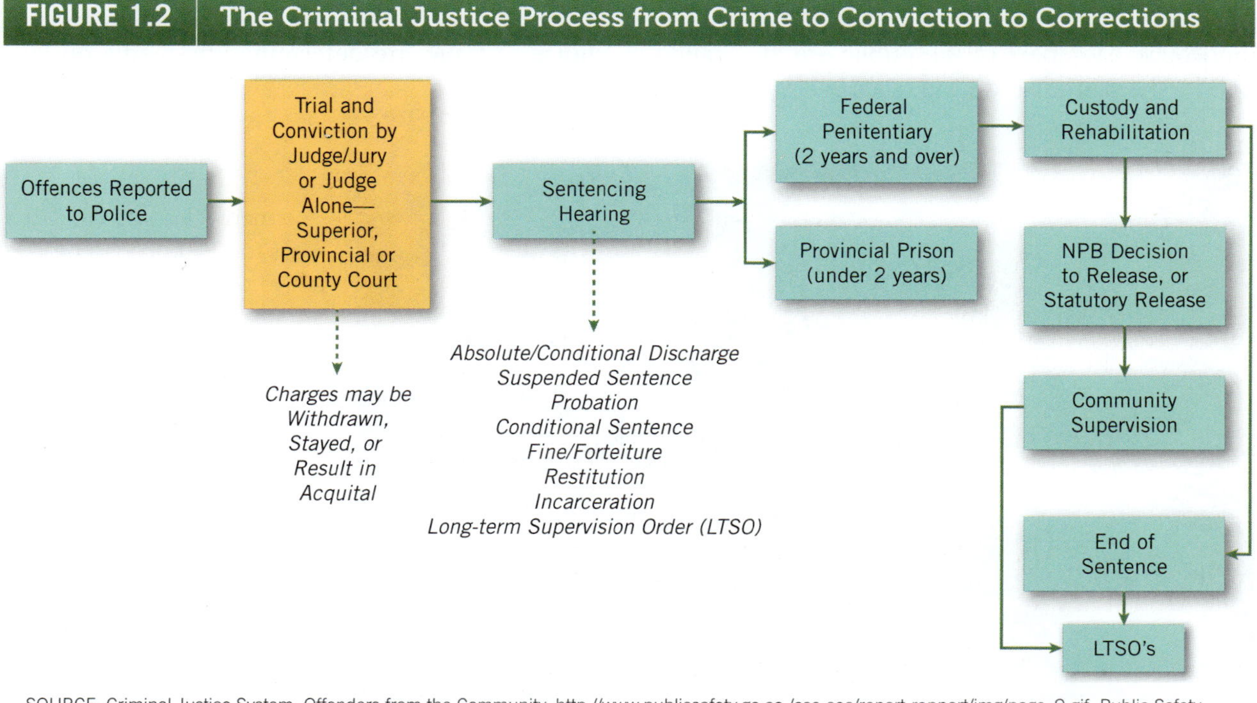


SOURCE: Criminal Justice System: Offenders from the Community, http://www.publicsafety.gc.ca./csc-scc/report-rapport/img/page_9.gif, Public Safety Canada. Reproduced with the permission of the Minister of Public Works and Government Services, Canada.

during the entire trial to be informed and available to his or her counsel.

### PRIVATE AGENCIES

There are many private agencies that contribute to the flow of the criminal justice system. There are agencies that provide services to offenders upon their release. The services include assistance with reintegration into society, teaching specific employment or academic skills, as well as counselling. Some agencies are contracted by the federal or provincial governments to provide services to offenders on their behalf. There are also organizations that provide support and advocacy to victims of crime.

### THE PUBLIC

There are many ways that the public is involved with the criminal justice system. Because we have an open system, the public is welcome to attend open court. Courts are open to the public and there is an area in each court for spectators. The only time a court may not be open to the public is when a judge decides that it is in the best interest of the accused or the victim that spectators not be permitted.

The public is called upon to provide a service to the criminal justice system by serving on juries. Jury members are asked to listen to the facts of a case and make a determination of guilt or innocence. Members of the public are also called upon to be witnesses during trials.

Perhaps the most important way in which the public is involved in the criminal justice system is in the requirement to know the law. Members of the public are expected to be aware of the laws that exist, and they are expected to respect and obey them.

## The Media and the Criminal Justice System

LO8

Though not a component of the criminal justice system, there is a critical relationship between the media and the criminal justice system. The *Charter* protects our right to freedom of the press, and it is through the application of this freedom that Canadians access and learn about the criminal justice system. The media play a pivotal role in educating Canadians about the operation of the criminal justice system and in doing so, play a role in holding the criminal justice system accountable for its actions. Though few Canadians ever take advantage of their right to sit in a courtroom to watch the justice system at work, we are all exposed to media reports and headlines that are designed to be our eyes and ears. In addition to supplying us with information about the cases in the criminal justice system, the media influence the general public's view of crime and the criminal justice system overall. Media coverage, the extent and the choice of topic, are determined by media outlets.

The media has also created ways for the public to be active participants in the criminal justice system while sitting on their couches. Television shows that highlight "most wanted" suspects give members of the public an opportunity to name suspects. Criminal cases are often recreated through Crime Stoppers videos in an effort to prompt the public to provide tips leading to an arrest or conviction.

We are exposed to the coverage, information, and ideas that they choose to cover.

> "Where there is no publicity there is no justice. Publicity is the very soul of justice."
>
> JEREMY BENTHAM

Ray Surette (2011) describes the experience that an individual has when viewing the media coverage of events as a 'mediated experience.' It is through this mediated experience that the public is able to engage in a criminal justice event, from their own home. We are able to view images, hear sounds, and witness raw emotion, often live. It is this mediated experience that shapes the way in which most individuals view the criminal justice system and assess its practises and policies. The challenge is that the media does not always portray a balanced view of crime or the criminal justice system overall. As such, we base our opinions and ideas on a biased view, which is often determined by decision makers who are seeking headlines that sell newspapers and visuals that will entice viewers. Because we often only hear part of a story, usually out of context, we are led to interpret the event based on our limited life experience (Surette, 2011). This uninformed interpretation can lead to beliefs that are problematic because they are not based on evidence. For example, when we hear that a parolee commits a crime while under parole supervision, we are left with the general impression that parole is dangerous because this parolee, profiled in a news story, committed a crime. This leads to a lack of support for parole. Our decision to support parole (or not) is then based on a single incident. We are not given information during the report about the fact that 70 percent of parolees complete their parole successfully (Corrections and Conditional Release Statistical Overview, 2007). This limited access to information is precarious because it leads to interpretations that are based on opinion, not fact. These same opinions can then influence public policy.

The mass media is often involved in creating crime myths, where the public is presented with a distorted view of the world (Kappeler & Potter, 2005). Often media representations of criminal incidents are exaggerated, which can affect the public's perceptions. There are a number of ways in which crime myths are exacerbated, including misusing statistics, presenting opinion as fact, and using undocumented sources of authority. Crime myths may condemn a certain group in our society based on its race, religion, age, or any other demographic attribute. Crime myths tend to exaggerate the amount of crime in our society, resulting in an overall belief in the need for more prisons, police, or more severe punishments for offenders. Essentially, fear is at the root of a crime myth. It is only through an evidence-based analysis of crime-related issues that one can assess the true state and extent of crime in our society.

connect ONLINE ACTIVITY

> "Exaggerating the magnitude of the problem sustains public attention long enough for fear to take hold, leading to calls for institutional control and formal sanctions."
>
> KAPPELER, V.E., AND POTTER, G.W., *THE MYTHOLOGY OF CRIME AND JUSTICE.*

The media's access to the courts is often debated. The media do not have an absolute right to broadcast news related to criminal cases; there are limits to that right. For example, there are times when identifying information is not made public in order to protect the privacy of an accused. Under the *Youth Criminal Justice Act*, protecting the identity of young persons is a statutory requirement. Victims of crime, sexual assault complainants, and witnesses can also be protected under section 486.4 of the *Criminal Code*, which gives judges the authority to order publication bans on any information that could disclose their identity. This type of ban never expires; a victim or witness can never be disclosed even if there is an acquittal. Any information that a judge feels would jeopardize a fair trial can be withheld from publication through a publication ban. A judge has the power to create and impose a publication ban. Most publication bans expire when the case has concluded. Judges also have the power to protect jurors, by ensuring that they are only referred to in the courtroom by an identifying number and not by name.

## MYTH VS FACT

Crimes that are most often depicted on television are those crimes that are least likely to occur in real life. In addition, news reports consistently over-represent violent crime and under-represent property crime (Reiner, 2002). In reality, the rate of violent crime is far lower than the rate of property crime in Canada. In 2010, the property crime rate in Canada was 3,846 incidents per 100,000 population, compared to a much lower violent crime rate of 1,282 incidents per 100,000 population (Brennan and Dauvergne, 2011).

The role of the media as it relates to the various components of the criminal justice system will be examined throughout this text.

## LO9 Processing a Case through the Criminal Justice System: An Overview

Cases weave through the criminal justice system on their way to a final conclusion. There are procedures that are required in order to move the case along to the next stage. The following overview identifies the basic steps and stages that will be discussed in detail in later chapters.

### PRE-TRIAL PHASE

A criminal charge is initiated in the pre-trial phase. Accused persons are notified that they have been charged with a criminal offence in one of the following ways, depending on the severity of the offence:

1. After a crime is committed, the police investigate the crime, identify a suspect, and then they go to a justice of the peace. The police **lay an information** against the suspect, which indicates why they believe the person should be arrested. The justice of the peace will agree or not. If the justice of the peace agrees, he or she will sign the arrest warrant. The police now have the authority to arrest the individual.
2. Police can arrest a suspect when he or she is in the progress of committing a crime.
3. Police can issue a summons requiring the accused person to appear in court on specific day.
4. Police may issue an appearance notice to a suspect, on the spot, requiring him or her to attend court on a specific date.

**lay an information**
documentation against a suspect, indicating why the police believe the person should be arrested

If a person was arrested for committing an indictable offence, he or she will be photographed.

Once an individual has been arrested, the police will determine whether or not they wish to make an application to hold the accused person in custody, prior to trial. In order to detain the accused in custody, there must be a hearing before a justice of the peace within 24 hours of the time of arrest. The judicial interim release hearing (*Criminal Code,* s. 515) is referred to as a bail hearing or a show cause hearing. At the hearing, the onus is on the prosecutor to identify reasons that the accused should not be released before the trial. If the judge decides to release the accused, the prosecutor may identify conditions for release.

### TRIAL PHASE

The trial phase generally consists of several appearances before a court. Depending on the offence and the will of the accused, there are several things that may happen at the first appearance in court:

1. The accused may plead guilty and may be sentenced on the spot.
2. The accused may plead guilty and a date is set for sentencing. The accused may be held in custody until the sentencing date or may be released with a requirement to return on the sentencing date.
3. The accused may plead not guilty and a trial date is set.
4. The accused may plead not guilty and a date for the preliminary hearing is set.

The preliminary hearing determines whether or not there is enough evidence to take a case to trial. Only accused persons charged with certain indictable offences are entitled to a preliminary hearing. If a judge determines that there is not enough evidence to proceed to trial, the accused is released and is free to go. Accused persons can choose to waive their right to a preliminary hearing and proceed directly to the trial (*Criminal Code*, s. 535).

The criminal trial is an adversarial process where the burden of proof rests upon the Crown. The trial begins with a reading of the details of the offence and then there is an opportunity for the accused to plead guilty or not guilty. A trial may last for months or mere moments, depending on the nature of the case before the court. At the conclusion of the trial there is a decision made by the judge or the jury. If the case has been proven beyond a reasonable doubt, then the accused is declared guilty. If the case has not been proven beyond a reasonable doubt, then the accused is declared not guilty and is aquitted.

### SENTENCING

A guilty party may be sentenced immediately, at the conclusion of the trial, or a sentencing date may be determined. The accused may be released into the community pending sentencing or may be held in custody. A judge may wish to order a pre-sentence report (*Criminal Code*, s. 721.1) at this time to provide the court with additional information during the sentencing phase. The victim impact statement (*Criminal Code*, s. 722) is read at this stage, if applicable. Both the Crown and the defence attorneys are entitled to make comments regarding their recommendations for sentencing, based on the facts of the case and the circumstances of the offender.

Once the accused is sentenced, the penalty phase begins.

### PENALTY PHASE

During the penalty phase the offender must fulfill the conditions identified during the sentencing phase. The correctional service is involved in supervising custodial and community sentences. At this point the penalty may involve:

1. Incarceration in a federal facility (if sentenced to two years in jail or longer).
2. Incarceration in a provincial facility (if sentenced to less than two years).
3. Community supervision (includes probation, conditional sentence, community service order, restitution).
4. Fine.

### REINTEGRATION INTO THE COMMUNITY

If an offender is incarcerated, the final phase is reintegration into the community. For many offenders this involves being subject to a form of community supervision, such as parole or mandatory supervision.

## Chapter Summary

This chapter provided an introduction to Canada's criminal justice system. Key concepts that were covered include:

- The function and purpose of the criminal justice system was identified, and the values that our system stands for were highlighted. Canadians value an open accountable system that consists of procedural safeguards and clear processes for appeal.
- The *Canadian Charter of Rights and Freedoms* is the supreme law of Canada because every law in Canada must be consistent with the *Charter.* It outlines our fundamental freedoms and basic rights, and it provides a challenge process for individuals (or groups) who believe that their rights have been infringed upon.
- The rule of law is at the core of the criminal justice system, stressing the requirement for due process and procedural fairness. There are safeguards that are built into our system in an effort to ensure that an individual is treated fairly.
- The due process and crime control models were examined. There are elements of both models in our current system.
- The types and categories of laws were identified, recognizing that criminal law is a form of public law that relies on both statute and common law.
- The main components of the criminal justice system are the police, courts, and correctional services. In addition, there is the critical involvement of the victim, the public, and private agencies.
- The role of the media in providing the public with information and promoting the accountability of the players within the criminal justice system was identified. The concept of crime myths was introduced.
- The chapter closed with an overview of the way in which a criminal case is processed, from the pre-trial phase to the penalty phase and community reintegration.

## Relevant Legislation

*Criminal Code*, R.S.C. 1985, c C-46

*Canadian Charter of Rights and Freedoms* (Part I of the *Constitution Act*, 1982)

*Firearms Act* (S.C. 1995, c. 39)

*Youth Criminal Justice Act* (S.C. 2002, c. 1)

## Key Terms

Administrative law
Adversarial system
Burden of proof
*Canadian Charter of Rights and Freedoms*
Civil law
Common law
Constitutional law
Crime control model
Criminal law
Deterrence
Due process
Due process model
Fundamental freedoms
Lay an information
"Notwithstanding" clause
Precedent
Private law
Procedural law
Public law
Stare decisis
Statute law
Substantive law

## For Review

1. What are the advantages and disadvantages of an adversarial criminal justice system?
2. What impact has the *Charter* had on the criminal justice system?
3. What are the advantages and disadvantages of the crime control model?
4. What are the advantages and disadvantages of the due process model?
5. What is the purpose of the criminal justice system?
6. What is the significance of the "notwithstanding" clause?
7. What is the difference between legal guilt and actual guilt?
8. Differentiate between the following:
   a) Common law and statute law
   b) Public law and private law
   c) Substantive law and procedural law
9. Provide an example of each of the following:
   a) Criminal law
   b) Constitutional law
   c) Administrative law
   d) Civil law
10. Provide an example of when the media is not guaranteed freedom of the press within the criminal justice system.

## Thinking Critically

1. This chapter highlights a number of procedural safeguards that are in place. What are the implications of denying an accused the right to a procedural safeguard? What would our system be like without the protection of procedural fairness?
2. Identify the fundamental freedoms that exist under the *Charter*, and provide an example of the ways in which each of the fundamental freedoms is not absolute in a free and democratic society.
3. To what extent is it necessary to have elements of both due process and crime control models within our system? What are the potential consequences of having only one perspective?
4. Identify a crime myth that exists in our society. How has that myth been created and what effect does it have?
5. To what extent is accountability within the criminal justice system important in a democratic society?
6. What are the implications of a public that is not aware of the operations of the criminal justice system? To what extent should the public be permitted to have open access to the courts, police and correctional facilities?
7. What are the implications of the decision made to deny Sue Rodriguez the right to assisted suicide? Did the Supreme Court justices balance the rights of the individual with the rights of society in this case?

CHAPTER 2

# Crime and Criminal Law

## A Journey of Terror

On July 30, 2008, Tim McLean, 22, was murdered while onboard a Greyhound bus bound for Winnipeg. McLean's seatmate Vincent Li, age 40, engaged in an unprovoked attack on McLean, repeatedly stabbing, dismembering, and eventually beheading him in front of his fellow passengers. On March 29, 2009 the Manitoba Court of Queen's Bench Judge John Scurfield said that Li could not be found guilty of murder because he was mentally ill at the time of the offence. Evidence presented at the trial indicated that Li suffers from schizophrenia and he experienced a major psychotic episode on the day of the offence. He said that he heard voices from God advising him that Tim McLean was evil and that he needed to be eliminated. Li is housed in a provincial psychiatric facility; he will not serve his time in prison. The Manitoba provincial review board continues to assess Li to determine if he will remain in the hospital indefinitely or if he will be discharged, if he is ever considered to be well enough to return to mainstream society. Tim McLean's family is lobbying the Canadian government to amend the *Criminal Code of Canada* to prevent mentally ill persons who commit murder from ever returning to the community. They are pursuing "Tim's Law" to support victims of violent crime. This case illustrates the way in which the defence of 'Not criminally responsible due to a mental disorder' is applied. This defence and others will be examined in this chapter.

SOURCE: CBC.ca.

### LEARNING OBJECTIVES

By the end of this chapter, you should be able to:

- **LO1** Describe the ways in which crime is measured in Canada.
- **LO2** Identify Canada's crime rate and factors that may influence the crime rate.
- **LO3** Understand the criminal justice funnel and its impact on society.
- **LO4** Explain the dynamic nature of our laws and provide specific examples of laws that have been created, repealed, or amended in recent history.
- **LO5** Describe how offences are classified in the *Criminal Code of Canada* and the impact of the classification.
- **LO6** Identify and describe *mens rea* and *actus reus:* the elements of an offence.
- **LO7** Identify the defences that are available to defendants in Canadian courts.
- **LO8** Define the ways one may be a party to an offence in Canada.

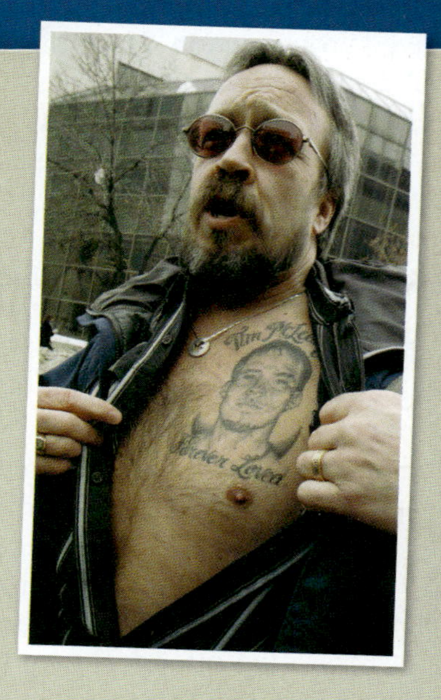

The bus on which the attack occurred (left) and victim Tim McLean's father (top).

Criminal law in Canada falls under the jurisdiction of the federal government. The authority for the federal government to enact criminal law is derived from section 91 of the *Constitution Act, 1867*. Federal law applies across Canada, with the intention of having a consistent application of the law. Criminal laws are codified in the *Criminal Code of Canada* (the *Criminal Code*). There are several other pieces of federal legislation that are related to criminal law, including the *Drug and Substances Act* and the *Youth Criminal Justice Act*.

Though the laws are created under the jurisdiction of the federal government, the provinces and territories have the power to administer the laws, which means that they have the power to enforce and prosecute the laws (the *Constitution Act, 1867*). Each province and territory is responsible for enforcing the laws and prosecuting offenders. They are also responsible for incarcerating offenders who receive custodial sentences less than two years in length.

Our laws are both procedural and substantive. Procedural law refers to laws that provide us with direction on how to proceed within the justice system. For example, our arrest laws are examples of **procedural law** because they guide police on how, when, and under what circumstances an arrest is legal in Canada. They describe a procedure. **Substantive law** refers to laws that define that which is against the law. When the criminal code defines murder, it is substantive. When the code defines assault, it is substantive. In order to have an effective justice system, we require procedural laws to guide our process and substantive laws to define crime.

**procedural law**
law that provides direction on how to proceed within the criminal justice system

**substantive law**
law that defines actions that are prohibited

This chapter will examine crime in Canada and the criminal laws that were created to respond to crime, in our ever-evolving society.

## LO1 Measurement of Crime in Canada

Acquiring an accurate measurement of crime in any jurisdiction is a challenge. We know that all crime is not reported and we also know that there are challenges in ensuring consistent data collection across the country. We rely heavily on the following three data collection instruments to provide us with information on the volume of crime, the severity of crime, and the experience of victims of crime:

- The Uniform Crime Reporting Survey
- The Crime Severity Index
- The General Social Survey: Victimization

It is important to recognize that each of the data sources presents a different view of the nature and extent of crime in Canada.

### THE UNIFORM CRIME REPORTING SURVEY

The police-reported crime rate measures the overall volume of crime in Canada. Data to determine the crime rate is collected from the **Uniform Crime Reporting (UCR) Survey**, which is a census of crime collected by police services across Canada. Each police service across the country is provided with the same crime categories and definitions, and they systematically report the data to the Statistics Canada, Canadian Centre for Justice Statistics. This process of data collection has been in effect since 1962. The data reflected in the UCR is reported crime that has been substantiated by the police. The survey collects data related to the type of incident, the victim(s), and the accused involved in the incident. This data is used for the purposes of creating policy, evaluating legislation, and comparing Canada's crime rate to other countries. Crime rate is reported based on the population. A rate is determined based on each 100,000 people living in Canada.

**Uniform Crime Reporting (UCR) Survey**
a census of crime collected by police services across Canada

The information that is collected in the UCR Survey is:

1. criminal offences known to the police;
2. unfounded offences (deemed not to be a crime following police investigation);
3. actual criminal offences (those deemed founded);

**FIGURE 2.1** Crime Rate in Canada 1952 to 2010

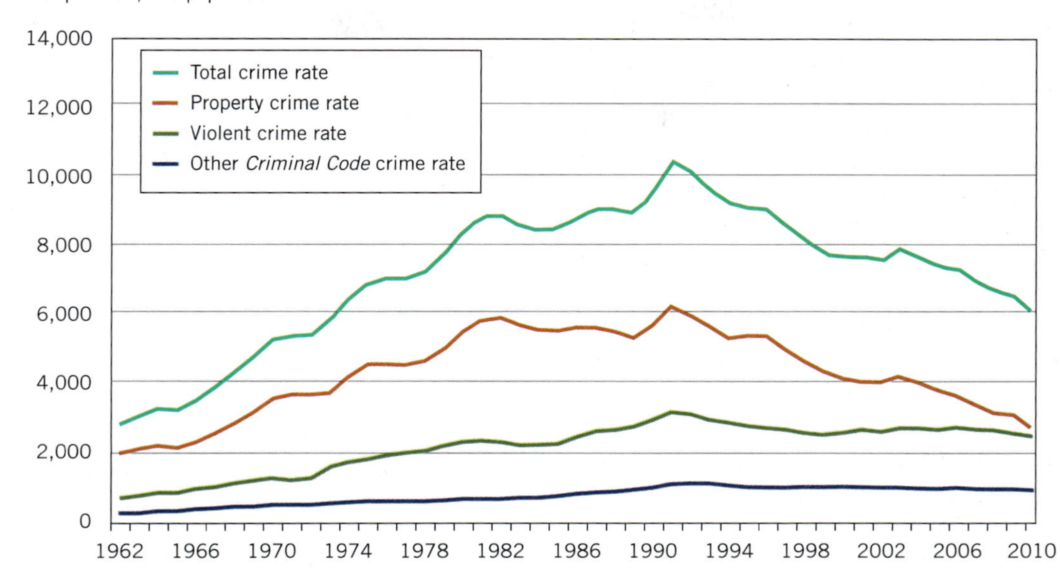


Note: Information presented in this graph represents data from the UCR Aggregate (UCR1) Survey and allows for historical comparisons to be made back to 1962.

SOURCE: Statistics Canada, Canadian Centre for Justice Statistics, Uniform Crime Reporting Survey. Crime Rate in Canada 1962 to 2010, 20 February 2012. Reproduced and distributed on an "as is" basis with the permission of Statistics Canada.

4. the number cleared by charge and cleared otherwise; and
5. the number of adults and youth charged.

(Pottie-Bunge et al., 2005)

### CANADA'S CRIME RATE

In 2010 Canada's overall **crime rate** declined by 5 percent. The crime rate has been declining steadily over the past 20 years and in 2010 it was at its lowest level since 1973 (Dauvernge and Turner, 2010). The actual rate of crime in 2010 was 6,145 per 100,000 population.

**crime rate**
measures the overall volume of crime in a population

In addition to the decline of the overall crime rate, there was also drop in violent crime, including a national homicide rate of 1.62 homicides per 100,000 population, which is the lowest homicide rate since 1966. There were 554 homicides in 2010, a drop of 56 from 2009. Nunavut had the highest homicide rate in 2010 and Prince Edward Island had the lowest by recording zero homicides in 2010. Historically, the crime rate in western and northern Canada has been higher than that in central and eastern Canada (Pottie-Bunge, Johnson, and Balde, 2005).

### 2010 Crime Rate at a Glance

- The overall crime rate in Canada is 6,145 per 100,000 population.
- The overall violent crime rate in Canada is 1,282 per 100,000 population.
- The overall property crime rate in Canada is 3,848 per 100,000 population.
- With 554 homicides reported, the homicide rate in 2010 was the lowest since 1966.
- Police reported robbery was down 7 percent from 2009, with a total of just over 30,000 robberies reported across Canada.
- The rate of theft under $5,000 is 1,572 per 100,000 population.

SOURCE: http://www.statcan.gc.ca/daily-quotidien/110721/dq110721b-eng.htm.

**FIGURE 2.2** Attempted Murder and Homicide, Police-reported Rates, Canada, 1980 to 2010

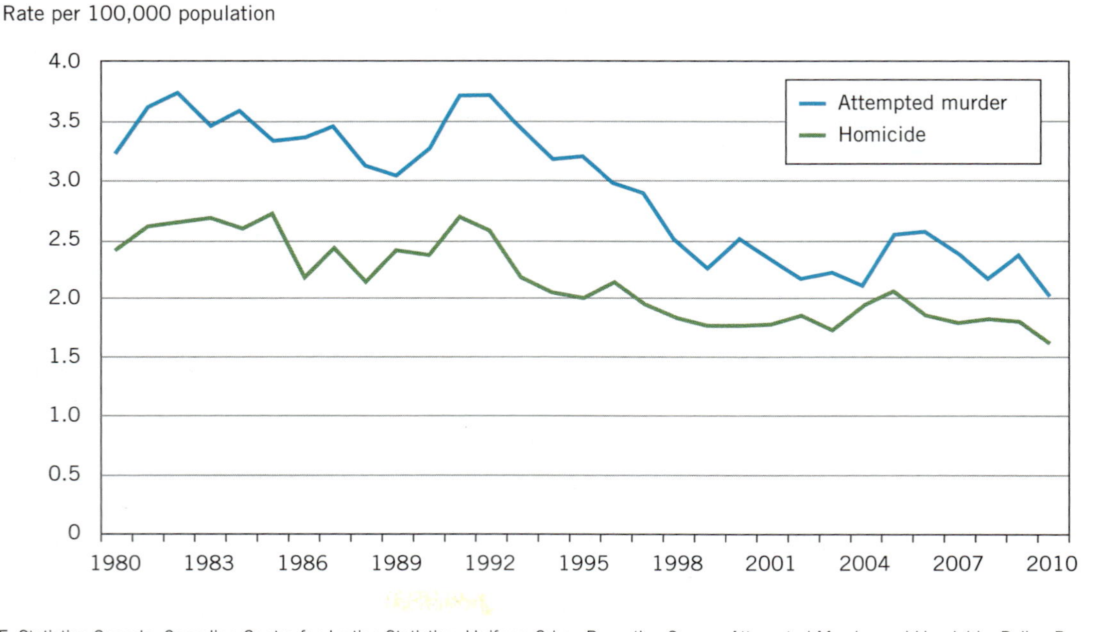


SOURCE: Statistics Canada, Canadian Centre for Justice Statistics, Uniform Crime Reporting Survey. Attempted Murder and Homicide, Police-Reported Rates, Canada, 1980 to 2010, 20 February 2012. Reproduced and distributed on an "as is" basis with the permission of Statistics Canada.

The majority of crimes reported to the police are non-violent crimes. Of the 79 percent of the non-violent crimes, the most common offences reported were theft under $5,000, mischief, and break and enter. Even with 200,000 reported incidents of break and enter in 2010, this represented a drop of 6 percent. There was a 15 percent drop of motor vehicle theft and the rate of impaired driving fell 6 percent from 2009 (though it had increased in the three previous years).

The 2010 statistics did report some increases. There was a 5 percent increase in the rate of sexual assault, the first such increase since 2005. This increase is especially problematic given that sexual assaults are under-reported in Canada. Self-reported victimization data from the most recent General Social Survey indicated that almost 90 percent of sexual assaults were never brought to the attention of the police (Perreault and Brennan 2010). The most common reasons for not reporting sexual offences to police include feeling that the incident was not important enough, feeling that it was a private matter, and dealing with the situation in another way (Brennan and Dauvergne, 2011).

## FACTORS THAT CAN INFLUENCE THE CRIME RATE

LO2

The crime rate fluctuates from year to year, indicating that there are factors that may have an influence on the overall rate of crime. The following factors have been identified in recent research.

### AGE

The age composition of a population is one potential explanation of crime rate. Individuals who are 15 to 24 years of age represent a relatively small number within the general population (approximately 14 percent). However, persons in this age group account for 45 percent of those accused of property crime and 32 percent of those persons accused of violent crime (Pottie-Bunge et al., 2005). This particular age cohort is responsible for a significant amount of crime, compared to other age-identified cohorts. When this age cohort is reduced in number, it is expected that the crime rate might be reduced as well. As individuals age, especially beyond age 50, there is a reduced risk in involvement in criminal activity as indicated in Figure 2.3 (Brennan and Dauvergne, 2011).

**FIGURE 2.3** Persons Accused of Crime, by age, Canada, 2010

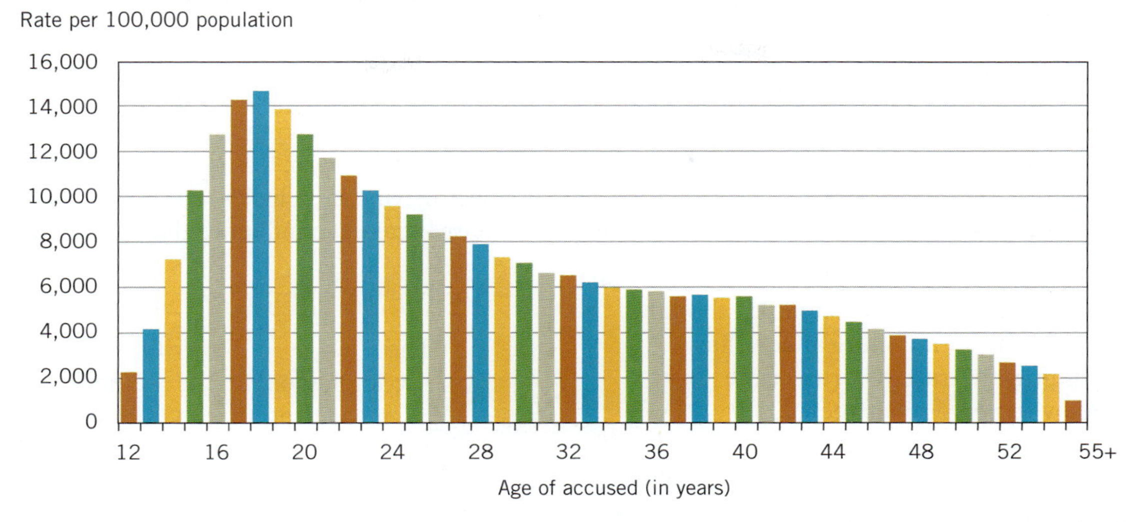


SOURCE: Statistics Canada, Canadian Centre for Justice Statistics, Persons Accused of Crime, by Age, Canada, 2010, http://www.statcan.gc.ca/pub/85-002-x/2011001/article/11523/c-g/E-11523-chart3.jpg, 20 February 2012. Reproduced and distributed on an "as is" basis with the permission of Statistics Canada.

**FIGURE 2.4** Females Apprehended by Police for Crimes Against the Person at a Rate 5 Times Lower than Males, Selected Police Services, 2005

Based on data from 122 police services, representing approximately 71 percent of the population of Canada in 2005. Rate per 100,000 population for the geographic areas policed by the UCR2 respondents, based on populations provided by Demography Division, Statistics Canada. Populations as of July 1st: preliminary post-censal estimates for 2005.

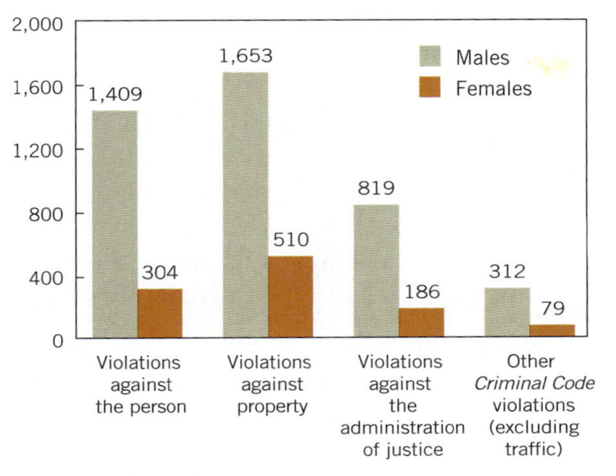


SOURCE: Statistics Canada, Canadian Centre for Justice Statistics, Incident-based Uniform Crime Reporting (UCR2) Survey. Females apprehended by police for crimes against the person at a rate of 5 times lower than males, selected police services, 2005, 20 February 2012. Reproduced and distributed on an "as is" basis with the permission of Statistics Canada.

## GENDER

Males are far more likely to commit a crime than females. Research and practise consistently indicate that males far outnumber females in committing crimes, across the country. Overall, females commit crime at about one-quarter the rate of men (Kong and Aucoin, 2006). When women do commit crime, they are most likely to commit the crime of theft (with the exception of automobiles); of the thefts, 66 percent are the result of shoplifting incidents. Fewer women are charged with criminal offences, fewer women are in the court system (16 percent of adults before the courts in 2003/4 were women) and fewer women are convicted of crime. In 2003/4, it was recorded that 51 percent of all cases against women ended in a guilty verdict, compared to 59 percent for men. In addition, 44 percent of the cases against women were stayed or withdrawn, while the same was true for 34 percent of cases against men (Kong and Aucoin, 2006). This may be attributed to the fact that women who appear before the court tend to have criminal records that are less serious than those of their male counterparts. The significantly lower representation of women within the criminal justice system has implications with regards to the resources that are directed toward correctional programming for women.

### LEGISLATION

Introducing new offences has an impact on the police-reported crime rate. Creating legislation that criminalizes an action for the first time could influence the overall crime rate. Amendments to legislation that render it harsher, resulting in more arrests, can also make an impact.

### POLICING POLICY AND DATA COLLECTION METHODS

Implementing a new policing policy can have an effect on crime rate. For example, though the overall crime rate in Canada has been declining, the rate of drug crime increased by 10 percent between 2009 and 2010. This increase is determined to be specific to the increase of cannabis offences, which rose by 13 percent between 2009 and 2010 (Brennan and Dauvergne, 2011). This increase in crime rate may be influenced by police practise that has been focusing more police resources on law enforcement of cannabis offences (Dauvergne, 2009).

Another potential factor that influences the crime rate is regional differences that may exist in the manner in which police are directed to report crimes. One study compared the way in which police in Calgary and Edmonton reported crime data related to calls to police. It was determined that police in Calgary completed occurrence reports in 80 percent of calls to police, compared to Edmonton police, who completed occurrence reports in 94 percent of the calls (Pottie-Bunge et al., 2005). This illustrates a difference in the way in which crime rate data is collected.

It has also been suggested that as the rise of private policing increased in Canada, crimes that were detected by private security may not have been reported to the police and therefore are excluded from crime rate data collection (Pottie-Bunge, et al., 2005).

**Crime Severity Index (CSI)**

complements the crime rate by measuring the severity of the crimes that are reported in Canada

### POOR ECONOMY

A poor economy has been identified with both a spike in crime rates as well as a decrease in crime rate. Crime rates rise during prolonged periods of unemployment and economic weakness (Siegel et al., 2006). However, a poor economy also means that more people are making sacrifices, which result in less social interaction, less consumption of alcohol, and less driving of vehicles. These lifestyle choices, on a large scale, can influence the crime rate.

## THE CRIME SEVERITY INDEX

The **Crime Severity Index (CSI)** complements the crime rate by measuring the severity of the crimes that are reported in Canada. The CSI, which categorizes crimes based on their seriousness, has been in place since 1998. The CSI is important because it measures crime based on its severity as opposed to an overall crime rate, which includes all crimes. The CSI is calculated by giving each crime a weighting that is calculated by using the sentence that is imposed for the crime (Wallace et al., 2009). Though they cannot be compared directly, we can see trends that are consistent between the overall crime rate and the CSI. For example, Figure 2.5 shows both the overall crime severity index rate and the traditional crime rate in Canada from 1998 to 2008. Both measurements show a decline, where the crime rate decreased by 15 percent and the CSI decreased by 21 percent.

### THE GENERAL SOCIAL SURVEY: VICTIMIZATION

The General Social Survey (GSS) on Victimization is a national survey, conducted every five years, designed to provide us with an understanding of the perceptions of Canadians related to the criminal justice system as well as their experiences with victimization. Unlike the crime rate data, this survey is based on self-reported data, presenting us

"For many years, most Canadians held the view that crime rates were increasing, regardless of the trends in crime statistics recorded by the police or victimization surveys. There is evidence that this view is now changing; members of the public appear to have begun to absorb the reality that crime rates are declining."

JULIAN V. ROBERTS, FEAR OF CRIME AND ATTITUDES TO CRIMINAL JUSTICE IN CANADA: A REVIEW OF RECENT TRENDS. REPORT FOR THE MINISTRY OF THE SOLICITOR GENERAL CANADA.

**FIGURE 2.5** Overall Crime Severity Index and Traditional Crime Rate, Canada, 1998 to 2007

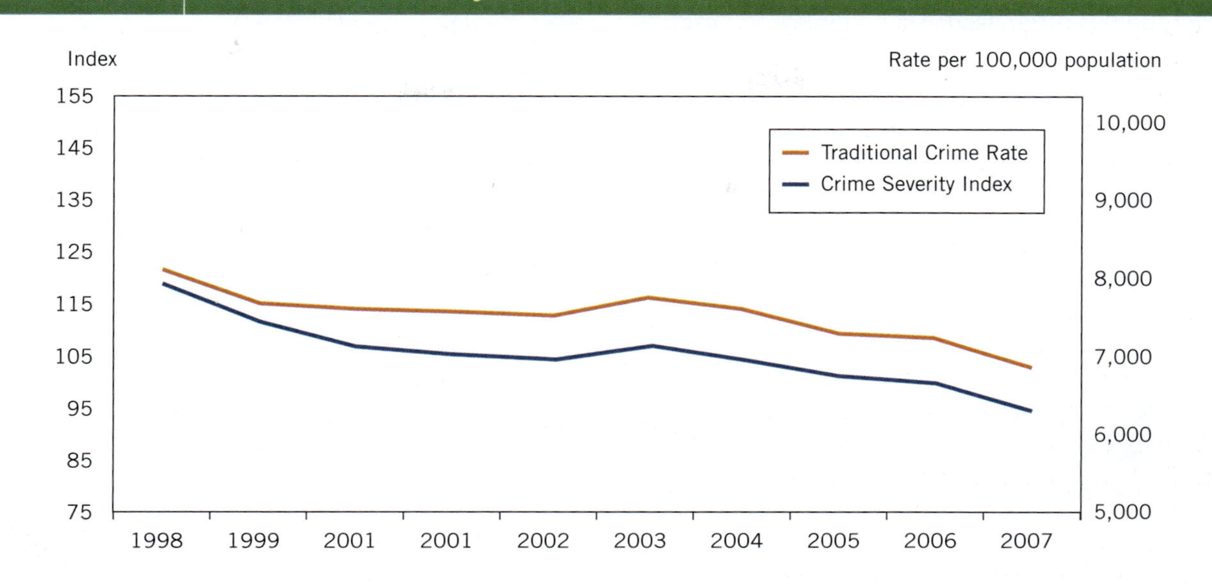


SOURCES: Statistics Canada, Canadian Centre for Justice Statistics, Aggregated Incident-based Uniform Crime Reporting Survey. Overall Crime Severity Index and traditional crime rate, Canada, 1998 to 2007, http://www.statcan.gc.ca/pub/85-004-x/2009001/ct001_en.gif, 20 February 2012. Reproduced and distributed on an "as is" basis with the permission of Statistics Canada.

with an opportunity to capture criminal incidents whether or not they were reported to the police. This data is important because it gives us a profile of victims of crime, with a view to learning more about victimization in general. In 2009, the GSS surveyed 19,500 respondents over 15 years of age, across the country.

### VICTIMIZATION ACROSS THE COUNTRY

In 2009, the GSS indicated that certain demographic factors increased the likelihood of victimization (Brennan, 2011). With regards to violent victimization, the most common form of violent crime reported was physical assault. The rate of self-reported violent victimization:

- was highest among single people and lowest among those who are married,
- was higher for people living in common-law relationships than those who are married,
- was higher for those who identified themselves as Aboriginal than those who are non-Aboriginal,
- was lower for visible minorities than for non-visible minorities, and
- was highest among individuals from the ages of 15 to 24.

Consistent with the crime rate statistics, victimization rates for both violent and household crimes were higher in western Canada than in central and eastern Canada. In 2009, the highest rate of violent victimization in a metropolitan area was reported in Regina and the lowest was in Toronto.

## MYTH VS FACT

Both the incidence rate of crime and the severity of crime are falling. However, when asked about crime in their own neighbourhoods, many Canadians do not believe this to be an accurate reflection. The 2009 General Social Survey on Victimization indicates that when asked about the level of crime in their neighbourhoods, 26 percent of those surveyed said that they believed crime had increased, while 62 percent said that they thought it stayed the same (Brennan, 2011). Only 6 percent said that they believed crime had decreased in their neighbourhood. This represents a disconnect between the reality of the falling crime rate and the perception of the crime rate.

## LO3 The Criminal Justice Funnel

The funnel is often used as a metaphor to describe the way in which crimes are processed within the criminal justice system. Just as a funnel is wide at the top and narrow at the bottom, so too are crimes as they progress through the criminal justice system. The funnel refers to the reduction of crimes from the total number of crimes that occur in our society down to those that result in a conviction. Like a funnel, the criminal justice system works like a sieve "filtering" the number of cases as they move through the criminal justice system. The funnel, as it relates to the crime of break and enter, is shown in Figure 2.6.

The criminal justice funnel begins with unreported crime. According to the 2009 GSS on Victimization published by Statistics Canada, Canadians reported 31 percent of the crime that they experienced to police. Though each crime varies in terms of the rate at which it is reported to police, it is estimated that overall 69 percent of crime is unreported. In 2009, there were 2.2 million crimes reported to police. The GSS indicated that the 2.2 million crimes represent only 31 percent of the crimes that were actually committed in Canada. This unknown number is often referred to as the **dark figure of crime**, because we really do not know exactly how much crime occurs in Canada. We only know what is reported to police and we know what Canadians say they don't report to police.

**dark figure of crime**
the unknown amount of true crime that is committed

**FIGURE 2.6 | The Criminal Justice Funnel of Break and Enter, 2002**

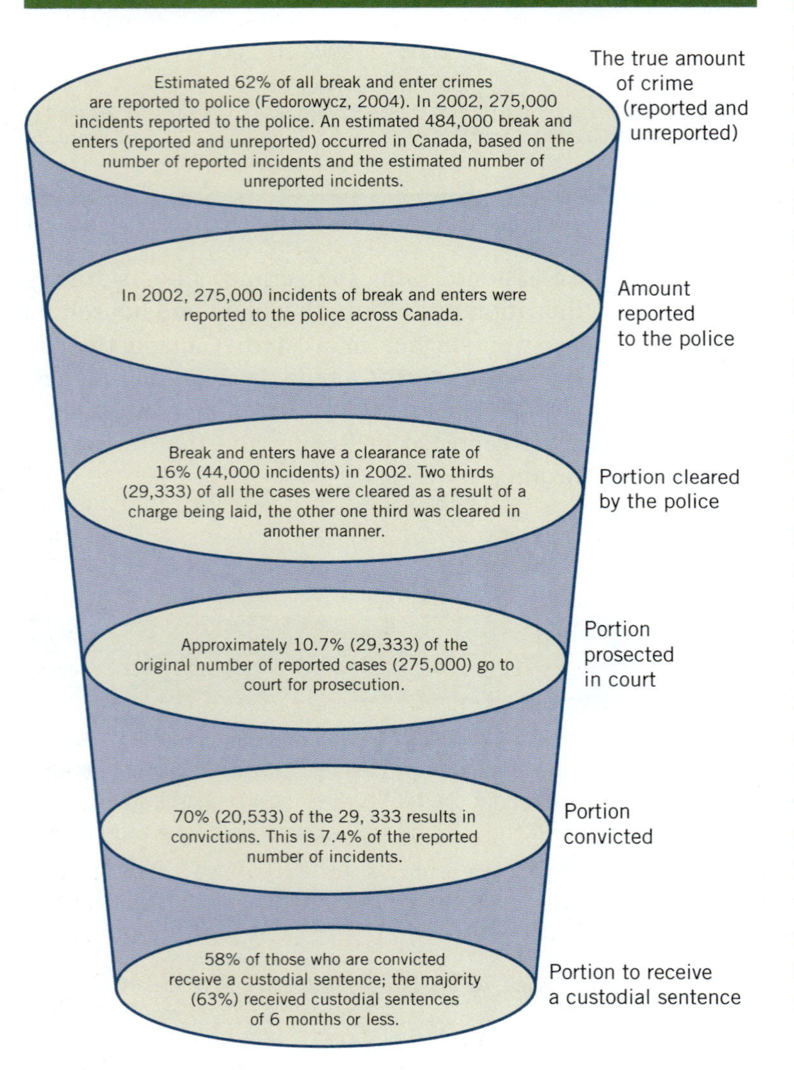


SOURCE: Canadian Centre for Justice Statistics Breaking and Entering in Canada—2002, 20 February 2012. Reproduced and distributed on an "as is" basis with the permission of Statistics Canada.

The funnel effect is not good or bad, it merely reflects the way in which cases within the criminal justice system progress. It is expected that charges will be eliminated naturally as they progress through the system. For example, it is important to note that not all reported crime is valid. Some crimes are reported in error or maliciously; such cases would not proceed to criminal charges. There are offenders who are responsible for more than one crime. It is common for an offender to be charged with more than one offence, which contributes to the funnel effect. It is important to recognize that we do not know exactly how much crime exists in Canada, we can only be aware of that which is reported. We do track the progress of reported crime and can see that it results in a funnel-like representation of data.

The "Tough on Crime" agenda was introduced in Canada by the Conservative majority government in 2011, via Bill C-10. This omnibus crime

## JUST or BUST?

Is this appropriate when statistics clearly indicate that our crime rate is falling? Is this a reflection of the Canadian experience when the most recent GSS on Victimization indicated that 93% of Canadians surveyed said they felt satisfied with their level of personal safety (Perreault & Brennan, 2010)? Should our focus be on tougher crime laws?

bill includes a legislative agenda that targets mandatory minimum sentences, youth crime, statutory release, and conditional sentences. The new laws are harsher and will inevitably be very costly to the Canadian taxpayer.

## LO4 Laws and Values

Our society is bound by laws that reflect our values and beliefs. These laws serve to guide us through our daily lives. Our laws are intended to protect us and to provide order and a sense of security. Laws are not only designed to protect society from individuals, but they are also required to protect society from the abuse of power by government or agencies of the government. The primary function of the law is to provide society with a way of resolving disputes and a way of ensuring that our rights and freedoms are protected.

Perhaps the most difficult challenge faced by our society related to the administration of law is determining which laws should be enacted or repealed as the values of our society change. Most laws are accepted unconditionally. We all agree that murder, robbery, assaults, and other violent offences belong in Canada's *Criminal Code*. There are other areas that are not so clear. For example, there are many people who believe that our laws on cannabis are too harsh. There are others who believe that euthanasia should be legal or that capital punishment should still be in effect. There are even a few who believe that polygamy should be legal. As a country we struggle with these issues, usually through the court system. The lack of collective acceptance of a law is an indication that we do not all share the same values. As a free and democratic society we debate laws and we struggle with differing views and opinions. It is important to be able to engage in this form of societal discourse in order to arrive at a legal decision that reflects the values of the majority of Canadians. Our laws are a reflection of the way in which our society views the world.

### WHAT IS A CRIME?

A **crime** is an act or an omission that is prohibited by law because it contravenes a society's values and morals. A crime is only a crime if it is prohibited by law. In a democratic society, laws are dynamic—as our society changes, so too do our laws. There are a number of offences that have been created, repealed, or amended because of changing societal attitudes and values. Examples of laws that have been modified in recent history are as follows.

**crime**
an act or an omission that is prohibited by law

### IMPAIRED DRIVING

Since being introduced to the *Criminal Code* in 1921, as 'driving while intoxicated,' the penalty and perception of impaired driving has become increasingly severe. As the prevalence and the personal and financial cost of impaired driving became more apparent, there was a growing consensus in society that supported increased penalties. Tougher penalties and clearer detection methods were introduced to support the police in apprehending impaired drivers. Advocacy groups engaged the public with media campaigns and research; the most well known group is MADD (Mothers Against Drunk Driving). The public campaigns and the enhanced enforcement netted positive results. Prior to 2007, the rate of impaired driving declined for 25 years (Dauvergne and Turner, 2011). In 2010, police reported a 6 percent decrease in impaired driving, which followed three years of an increase in the rate of impaired driving. In 2008, new legislation was introduced enabling mandatory roadside testing and assessment of suspected drug-impaired drivers. Drug-impaired

drivers represent approximately 2 percent of all impaired drivers. According to MADD, 1,200 Canadians lost their lives in impairment-related traffic crashes in 2008, while a further 68,000 were injured (MADD Canada, 2011).

### RELATIONSHIP BETWEEN BLOOD ALCOHOL LEVEL AND FATAL CRASHES

Even drivers with little alcohol in their systems are more likely to be involved in a crash causing death than the average sober driver. Beginning at the legal alcohol limit of .08, the risk rises a lot. At a level of .15, your likelihood of being in a collision where somebody dies increases by more than 65 times. If you are 35 years old and driving with an alcohol limit of between .08 and .099, you are four times more likely to die in a crash than if you were sober. If you are 19 years old and driving with the same level of alcohol in your system, you are 20 times more likely to be killed. Several jurisdictions in Canada have amended their laws pertaining to young drivers and the legal level of alcohol in their systems in response to this statistic.

Dr. Henry Morgentaler made Canadian history in his fight for a woman's right to choose abortion.

## ABORTION

Historically, abortion has been a contentious issue that has led to a number of legal challenges. Prior to 1988, a woman's right to an abortion in Canada was severely restricted. There were a number of doctors who performed abortions in clinics prior to 1988, risking their own safety and criminal prosecution. The most well-known crusader for abortion rights in Canadian history is Dr. Henry Morgentaler, who defied the law when he opened an abortion clinic in Montreal in 1969. Dr. Morgentaler was charged with the criminal offence of performing abortions on several occasions. On January 28, 1988, the Supreme Court of Canada ruled Canada's abortion laws unconstitutional, by violating section 7 of the *Canadian Charter of Rights and Freedoms* (the right to life, liberty and security of person). Chief Justice Brian Dickson said, "Forcing a woman, by threat of criminal sanction, to carry a fetus to term unless she meets certain criteria unrelated to her own priorities and aspirations, is a profound interference with a woman's body and thus a violation of her security of the person." (R. *v.* Morgentaler [1988] 1 S.C.R. 30)

## LURING A CHILD VIA THE INTERNET

Our society has experienced a surge of access to technology in recent years, and access to the Internet is now almost universal. As a result, a number of new offences have been created to respond to the potential misuse of the Internet. One crime that has emerged is luring a child, via the Internet. This crime was introduced in Canada in 2002. In 2007, there were 464 incidents of child luring reported by police services across Canada, representing an increase of 31 percent over 2006 (Loughlin and Taylor-Butts, 2009). Men in the age range of 18 to 34 were the highest represented group accused of child luring in 2006/7. In 87 percent of child luring cases, the accused was charged with other related sexual crimes, such as invitation to sexual touching, child pornography, sexual assault, and sexual interference. Most court cases involving an accused who is charged with luring a child result in a finding of guilt. When an offender is convicted solely of child luring, the offender is most likely to be sentenced to a conditional sentence or probation. When convicted of child luring and other related offences, the offender is most likely to receive a custodial sentence (Loughlin and Taylor-Butts, 2009).

The *Criminal Code* defines Luring a child as:

172.1 (1) Every person commits an offence who, by means of a computer system within the meaning of subsection 342.1(2), communicates with

(a) a person who is, or who the accused believes is, under the age of eighteen years, for the purpose of facilitating the commission of an offence under subsection 153(1), section 155 or 163.1, subsection 212(1) or (4) or section 271, 272 or 273 with respect to that person;

(b) a person who is, or who the accused believes is, under the age of 16 years, for the purpose of facilitating the commission of an offence under section 151 or 152, subsection 160(3) or 173(2) or section 280 with respect to that person; or

(c) a person who is, or who the accused believes is, under the age of 14 years, for the purpose of facilitating the commission of an offence under section 281 with respect to that person.

Punishment

(2) Every person who commits an offence under subsection (1) is guilty of

(a) an indictable offence and liable to imprisonment for a term of not more than ten years; or

(b) an offence punishable on summary conviction and liable to imprisonment for a term not exceeding eighteen months.

Presumption re age

(3) Evidence that the person referred to in paragraph (1)(a), (b) or (c) was represented to the accused as being under the age of eighteen years, sixteen years or fourteen years, as the case may be, is, in the absence of evidence to the contrary, proof that the accused believed that the person was under that age.

No defence

(4) It is not a defence to a charge under paragraph (1)(a), (b) or (c) that the accused believed that the person referred to in that paragraph was at least eighteen years of age, sixteen years or fourteen years of age, as the case may be, unless the accused took reasonable steps to ascertain the age of the person.

2002, c. 13, s. 8; 2007, c. 20, s. 1; 2008, c. 6, s. 14.

## CRIMINAL HARASSMENT (STALKING)

Criminal harassment, commonly referred to as stalking, was introduced into the *Criminal Code* in August, 1993. This criminal offence was introduced in response to a number of cases where high profile victims where stalked by perpetrators. Criminal harassment involves a person repeatedly following or communicating with another person, repeatedly watching someone's home or workplace, or directly threatening another person or member of that person's family causing that person to fear for his or her safety or the safety of someone he or she knows. The most common form of stalking behaviour is obscene and harassing phone calls. In

2009, criminal harassment represented 5 percent of all violent crimes, and police services reported an increase of 7 percent from 2008 to 2009. Females represented 76 percent of all victims of criminal harassment in 2009. Female victims of criminal harassment are more likely to be harassed by a former or current intimate partner, while male victims are more likely to be harassed by a casual acquaintance than by a former or current intimate partner. Most women know their stalkers, and a woman is more likely to be a victim of violence when the stalker is a former intimate partner. The jurisdiction with the highest rate of criminal harassment in Canada is Prince Edward Island (82 incidents per 100,000 population) while Manitoba has the lowest rate at 22 incidents per 100,000 population (Milligan, 2011). Probation is the most common sentence imposed upon persons convicted of criminal harassment.

Criminal harassment is explained in section 264 of the *Criminal Code:*

264.(1) No person shall, without lawful authority and knowing that another person is harassed or recklessly as to whether the other person is harassed, engage in conduct referred to in subsection (2) that causes that other person reasonably, in all the circumstances, to fear for their safety or the safety of anyone known to them.

Females are far more likely to victims of criminal harassment than males.

Prohibited conduct

(2) The conduct mentioned in subsection (1) consists of
- (a) repeatedly following from place to place the other person or anyone known to them;
- (b) repeatedly communicating with, either directly or indirectly, the other person or anyone known to them;
- (c) besetting or watching the dwelling-house, or place where the other person, or anyone known to them, resides, works, carries on business or happens to be; or
- (d) engaging in threatening conduct directed at the other person or any member of their family.

Punishment

(3) Every person who contravenes this section is guilty of
- (a) an indictable offence and is liable to imprisonment for a term not exceeding ten years; or
- (b) an offence punishable on summary conviction.

## Classification of Offences

LO5

Offences in Canada are identified in the *Criminal Code*. Each offence is defined and classified based on the severity of the crime. The classification of an offence is important because it determines the way in which a criminal case proceeds within the criminal justice system. Criminal offences can be classified as either a summary conviction, indictable, or a dual procedure offence. A **summary conviction offence** is the least severe type of offence and an **indictable offence** is the most severe type of offence. A **dual procedure offence**, often referred to as a **hybrid offence**, is an offence that can be either an indictable or a summary conviction offence. It is the role of the Crown attorney's office to determine whether a dual procedure offence will proceed as a summary conviction offence or as an indictable offence.

**TABLE 2.1** Offences by Classification

| Offence Classification | Definition | Example of Offence |
|---|---|---|
| Summary Conviction Offence | The least severe type of criminal offence. | Section 364: Obtain food or lodging by fraud.<br>Penalty: Maximum of six months jail and $5,000.00 fine. |
| Dual Procedure (Hybrid) Offence | An offence that can be prosecuted as a summary offence or an indictable offence (decision is made by the Crown Attorney). | Section 342: Theft or forgery of a credit card.<br>As summary: Penalty is a maximum of six months jail and $5,000.00 fine.<br>As indictable: Penalty is a maximum of 10 years in jail. |
| Indictable Offence | The most severe type of offence. | Section 382: Theft over $5,000.00<br>Penalty: Maximum of 10 years in jail. |

A charge related to a summary conviction offence must be laid within six months from the time that the offence occurred. This is referred to as a **statute of limitations**. It is not possible to hold a person accountable for a summary conviction offence if the individual is not charged within the six months. Indictable offences generally do not have a time limitation, unless identified in the *Criminal Code*.

**statute of limitations**
a time period after the commission of an offence within which a charge must be laid

## The *Criminal Code of Canada*

The *Criminal Code of Canada* is a piece of federal legislation that identifies criminal law and procedure in Canada, and is applicable across the country. It identifies behaviour and conduct that is prohibited, and identifies the processes that the criminal justice system will follow.

New Canadian laws were created in response to the tragedy that unfolded on September 11, 2001.

At the time of Confederation in 1867, Canada's first Prime Minister, Sir John A. Macdonald was the driving force behind the creation of a federal criminal code, rather than the decentralized system that had existed where each province had its own criminal laws and processes. The first criminal code in Canada was introduced in 1892 (Verdun-Jones, 2010). It is regularly updated to reflect laws that are created, repealed, and amended.

## CATEGORIES OF CRIMINAL OFFENCES IN CANADA

The *Criminal Code* is divided by categories offences based on the type of offence. The categories include those listed in Table 2.2.

The following pieces of legislation regulate crimes outside of the *Criminal Code*.

### CONTROLLED DRUGS AND SUBSTANCES

The *Controlled Drugs and Substances Act* regulates the possession of certain dangerous drugs and narcotics, known in law as "controlled substances." The legislation defines the substances and the offences, including possession, trafficking, exporting, and production of a substance. Like the *Criminal Code*, it also classifies the offences and identifies the penalties.

### CRIMES AGAINST HUMANITY AND WAR CRIMES

The *Crimes Against Humanity and War Crimes Act* holds Canadians accountable for crimes committed within Canada and in certain circumstances, outside of Canada.

## ELEMENTS OF THE OFFENCE: *MENS REA* AND *ACTUS REUS*

LO6

**mens rea** — guilty mind and/or criminal intention

**actus reus** — a guilty action or omission

In order to be found guilty of committing a crime in a court of law, it must be determined that the accused person engaged in two elements: **mens rea** and **actus reus**. *Actus reus* refers to the prohibited act itself. The *actus reus* is the guilty action or omission. It is the physical action that defines the offence. *Actus reus* includes physical actions, as well as times when the accused is in a state of being, such as possession of an illegal substance or item. In order to be found guilty of a criminal offence, it must be proven that the accused actually committed the act or omission.

*Mens rea* refers to the accused's criminal intention. The *mens rea* is the guilty mind of the accused. It is the intention that led to the act or omission. In order to be found guilty of a criminal offence, it must be proven that the accused had the intention to commit the act or omission.

**TABLE 2.2 Categories of Criminal Offences in Canada**

| Offence Category | Example of Offences |
|---|---|
| Offences against public order | Treason—Unlawful assembly and riots |
| Terrorism | Financing terrorist activity |
| Firearms and other weapons | Possession of illegal weapon |
| Offences against the administration of law and justice | Bribery of a public officer |
| Sexual offences, public morals and disorderly conduct | Sexual offences, disorderly conduct |
| Invasion of privacy | Interception of communications |
| Disorderly houses, gaming and betting | Gaming and betting |
| Offences against the person and reputation | Murder, manslaughter, and infanticide |
| Offences against the rights of property | Theft, robbery, extortion |
| Fraudulent transactions relating to contracts and trade | Fraud |
| Wilful and forbidden acts in respect of certain property | Mischief, arson, cruelty to animals |
| Offences relating to currency | Trafficking in counterfeit money |
| Instruments and literature for illicit drug use | Manufacture literature for illicit drug use |
| Proceeds of Crime | Laundering proceeds of crime |

## FOCUS ON Hate Crime in Canada

**Hate crimes** refer to criminal offences that are motivated by hate towards an identifiable group. A group may be targeted based on national or ethnic origin, language, race, religion, sex, age, mental or physical disability, or sexual orientation. Police services across Canada reported a 35 percent increase in hate crimes between 2007 and 2008. Of those, most (55 percent) were motivated by race or ethnicity, followed by religion (26 percent) and sexual orientation (16 percent) (Statistics Canada, 2010). The crimes that were motivated by hate included violent crimes such as assaults and uttering threats (42 percent) and vandalism to property (47 percent). The most violent crimes were those motivated by sexual orientation. Of those crimes, the victim was male in 85 percent of the cases. The most commonly targeted racial/ethnic group was Blacks, followed by South Asians. The most commonly targeted religion was the Jewish faith, with a rise of 42 percent in 2008 over the previous year. Hate crimes against the Catholic faith and the Muslim faith followed. The highest rates of hate crime were in Vancouver, British Columbia and Hamilton, Ontario. Hate crime differs from crime in general, in that most hate crimes are perpetrated by strangers. The victim seldom knows the perpetrator, implying that the victims are random subjects chosen strictly because they are a member of the targeted group.

**hate crimes**

criminal offences that are motivated by hate towards an identifiable group

A hate crime: Jewish graves are vandalized.

### TABLE 2.3 Hate Crime in Canada's Cities

**Hate crimes reported by police, by type of motivation, by 10 largest census metropolitan areas**

| | 2008 | | | | | |
|---|---|---|---|---|---|---|
| | Race/ ethnicity | Religion | Sexual orientation | Other or unknown | Total | |
| | | | | | number | rate[1] |
| Vancouver | 61 | 40 | 34 | 8 | 143 | 6.3 |
| Hamilton | 29 | 2 | 2 | 0 | 33 | 6.3 |
| Kitchener | 16 | 15 | 0 | 0 | 31 | 6.1 |
| Ottawa[2] | 26 | 19 | 3 | 3 | 51 | 5.6 |
| Toronto | 127 | 93 | 43 | 8 | 271 | 5.4 |
| Calgary | 43 | 8 | 6 | 0 | 57 | 5.3 |
| Edmonton | 20 | 3 | 4 | 0 | 27 | 3.4 |
| Winnipeg | 7 | 5 | 1 | 1 | 14 | 2.1 |
| Québec | 6 | 2 | 4 | 3 | 15 | 2.0 |
| Montréal | 18 | 5 | 7 | 8 | 38 | 1.0 |

1. Populations have been adjusted to follow policing boundaries and to reflect missing coverage from the Royal Canadian Mounted Police outside of British Columbia. Rates are calculated per 100,000 population.

2. Ottawa refers to the Ontario portion of the Ottawa–Gatineau census metropolitan area.

SOURCE: Statistics Canada, Hate crimes reported by police, by type of motivation, http://www.statcan.gc.ca/daily-quotidien/100614//t100614b1-eng.htm, 20 February 2012. Reproduced and distributed on an "as is" basis with the permission of Statistics Canada.

## TABLE 2.4 Hate Crime and Motivation

**Hate crimes reported by police, by type of motivation**

| Type of motivation | 2007 | | 2008 | | 2007 to 2008 |
|---|---|---|---|---|---|
| | number | %[1] | number | %[1] | % change in number |
| **Race or ethnicity** | | | | | |
| Black | 158 | 33.5 | 205 | 37.3 | 30 |
| South Asian | 53 | 11.2 | 64 | 11.7 | 21 |
| East and Southeast Asian | 57 | 12.1 | 44 | 8.0 | -23 |
| Arab or West Asian | 34 | 7.2 | 37 | 6.7 | 9 |
| Caucasian | 50 | 10.6 | 22 | 4.0 | -56 |
| Aboriginal[2] | 14 | 3.0 | 20 | 3.6 | 43 |
| Multiple races or ethnicities | 75 | 15.9 | 115 | 20.9 | 53 |
| Other | 31 | 6.6 | 42 | 7.7 | 35 |
| Unknown | 18 | ... | 14 | ... | -22 |
| **Total** | **490** | **100.0** | **563** | **100.0** | **15** |
| **Religion** | | | | | |
| Jewish | 116 | 68.6 | 165 | 64.2 | 42 |
| Catholic | 15 | 8.9 | 30 | 11.7 | 100 |
| Muslim (Islam) | 29 | 17.2 | 26 | 10.1 | -10 |
| Other | 9 | 5.3 | 36 | 14.0 | 300 |
| Unknown | 4 | ... | 8 | ... | 100 |
| **Total** | **173** | **100.0** | **265** | **100.0** | **53** |
| **Sexual orientation** | **71** | **...** | **159** | **...** | **124** |
| **Other motivation** | **14** | **...** | **33** | **...** | **136** |
| **Unknown motivation** | **17** | **...** | **16** | **...** | **-6** |
| **Total** | **765** | **...** | **1,036** | **...** | **35** |

SOURCE: Statistics Canada, Hate crimes reported by police, by type of motivation, http://www.statcan.gc.ca/daily-quotidien/100614/t100614b1-eng.htm, 20 February 2012. Reproduced and distributed on an "as is" basis with the permission of Statistics Canada.

... not applicable

[1]. Percentages exclude unknowns.

[2]. The number of hate crimes against Aboriginals may be under-reported due to the unavailability of data from police services in the territories and the northern part of the Prairie provinces where the proportion of the Aboriginal population is highest.

Not only must there be the presence of both *actus reus* and *mens rea*, but they must coincide. It must be proven that both *actus reus* and *mens rea* occurred at the same time. If they did not coincide, then a criminal offence did not occur.

**acquittal**

being found or proved not guilty

*Mens rea* can take one of several forms, as outlined in the Table 2.5.

## LO7 DEFENCES IN CANADA

A criminal defence is an answer to a criminal charge. Though not required to offer a defence, all accused persons are entitled to a defence in Canadian law, and there are various types of defences available to defendants. A successful complete, or full, defence results in a complete **acquittal**, while a successful partial defence results in a conviction of a lesser offence.

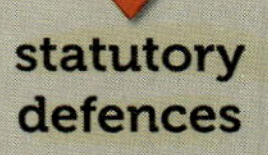

**statutory defences**

defences that are codified in the *Criminal Code*

**Statutory defences** are defences that are codified in the *Criminal Code*. Statutory defences are defined in the *Criminal Code* and their limits are identified. **Common law defences** are defences that have been created through case law and they are authorized in section 8 of the *Criminal Code*. Section 8 says:

**common law defences**

defences that have been created through case law and authorized in the *Criminal Code*

**TABLE 2.5** Forms of *Mens Rea*

| Form of *Mens Rea* | Definition | Example |
|---|---|---|
| **Specific intent** | Exists when the accused is fully aware of his or her actions and their consequences. | Accused picks up a beer bottle and throws it at the victim, hitting him in the head. |
| **General intent** | Exists when the accused may not have planned to commit the offence. The accused need only to commit a wrongful act. | Accused is in a fist fight with the victim. A punch in the neck proves to be fatal and the victim dies. |
| **Recklessness** | The accused person knows the potential consequences of an action but did not take into consideration the potential for the injury that the action might inflict on others. | Accused is driving very fast on a busy highway, changing lanes quickly while talking on a cellphone. Accused crashes into an emergency vehicle stopped on the side of the highway. |
| **Wilful blindness** | The accused chooses not to consider the potential of his or her actions being criminal because he or she does not want to know the truth. The accused chooses not to see the truth. | Accused is in a mall parking lot when she is approached by a man who says he has a very expensive watch to sell. The price of the watch is a fraction of what it retails for. The accused purchases the watch anyway; she doesn't want to know where it really came from. |

8 (3) Every rule and principle of the common law that renders any circumstance a justification or excuse for an act or a defence to a charge continues in force and applies in respect of proceedings for an offence under this Act or any other Act of Parliament except in so far as they are altered by or are inconsistent with this Act or any other Act of Parliament.

R.S., 1985, c. C-46, s. 8; 1993, c. 28, s. 78; 2002, c. 7, s. 138.

The common law allows for creating new defences to be included in Canadian law. For example, entrapment is a relatively new defence that was introduced in 1988. Defences are categorized based on their classification. A number of the common defences are as follows.

## ALIBI

An **alibi** is a defence whereby the accused denies the facts of the case as presented by the Crown. The accused has an alibi for the day, date, and time of the offence. An alibi is defined as:

> "a defence that places the defendant at the relevant time in a different time in a different place than the scene involved and so removed therefrom as to render it impossible for him to be the guilty party" (Black's Law Dictionary, 2009)

An alibi is proven through some form of objective evidence, usually an eye witness or documentation. It is a common law defence and if it is used successfully it results in a full acquittal.

## ACCIDENT

**Accident** is a common law defence that argues that the accused did commit the *actus reus*, but denies that there was *mens rea*, as the accused did not intend for the consequences of the actions to occur. This is a complete defence, which results in an acquittal if used successfully in court.

***autrefois acquit***

the Latin phrase meaning "formerly acquitted" and refers to a rule that a person cannot be tried for the same offence more than once

## *AUTREFOIS ACQUIT* AND *AUTREFOIS CONVICT*

This is a procedural defence codified in section 607 of the *Criminal Code*. The Latin phrases mean "formerly acquitted" and "formerly convicted" (Black's Law Dictionary, 2009) and they refer

***autrefois convict***

the Latin phrase meaning "formerly convicted" and refers to a rule that a person cannot be tried for the same offence more than once

## IN THE NEWS

### Honour-Based Violence

**Honour-based violence** is violence that occurs when family members kill or commit a violent act against another family member because they believe that the victim has dishonoured the family name and reputation. There is not a specific offence related to honour-based violence. Offenders are charged with the relevant criminal code offence, while honour is the motivation for committing the crime. A recent Ontario case highlighted honour-based crime when the Shafia family—father Mohammad, second wife Tooba, and son Hamed—were convicted of first degree murder in the deaths of four family members. Mohammad Shafia's first wife, Rona Amir, and Tooba and Mohammad Shafia's three daughters were found dead in a vehicle at the bottom of a Kingston canal in 2009. According to the accused, the daughters rebelled by engaging in what others in Canadian society might describe as typical behaviour of young girls—wearing makeup, dating boys, refusing to wear traditional clothing. During the trial, evidence was presented showing that the girls and Rona Amir were subjected to threats of violence and difficult living conditions (Freeze, 2012); however, they were unable to access help or services, although there were numerous signs of their distress.

Mohammad Shafia, 58, his second wife Tooba Mohammad Yahya, 42, and their son Hamed, 21, were found guilty of first-degree murder after a jury found them guilty of murdering four other family members. They were each sentenced to life imprisonment. Photograph by: Stringer, Reuters

> *"This jury found that four strong, vivacious and freedom-loving women were murdered by their own family in the most troubling of circumstances. We all think of these four, wonderful women now who died needless deaths. This verdict sends a very clear message about our Canadian values and the core principles in a free and democratic society that all Canadians enjoy and even visitors to Canada enjoy."*
>
> -CROWN attorney Gerard Laarhuis, after the verdict

Though they represent a small number of homicide cases overall, honour killings are high profile cases because of the message that they send. In honour killings, the life of the family member is far less important than the shame the family perceives. This is a strong and disturbing message for most people, making honour-based crime difficult to understand. It is estimated that there have been at least 15 honour killings in Canada since 2002 (Keeping, 2009). After the Shafia verdict, a number of Muslim leaders made it clear that honour killing is not faith-based. Several Islamic religious leaders denounced honour killings publicly, and recognized the need to educate Muslims about gender equality. Imam Syed Soharwardy, the founder of the Islamic Supreme Council of Canada, explained that such violence is clearly condemned in the Qur'an but can be present in remote regions of Muslim countries as a result of the misinterpretation of religious doctrine (CBC, 2012).

The court found that first wife Rona Amir, 54, and daughters Zainab, 19, Sahar, 17, and Geeti, 13, were victims of their father's distorted perception of honour.

SOURCES: CBC News (2012, January 12). Muslim community grapples with Shafia verdict. Retrieved from http://www.cbc.ca/news/canada/story/2012/01/30/shafia-trial-verdict-reaction.html; Keeping, J. (2009, November 20). Honour killings—premediated executions—must be stopped in Canada. Retrieved from http://www.chumirethicsfoundation.ca/main/page.php?page_id=261; Freeze, C. (2012, January 31). Canada looks for ways to prevent honour killings in wake of Shafia trial. Retrieved from http://www.theglobeandmail.com/news/national/canada-looks-for-ways-to-prevent-honour-killings-in-wake-of-shafia-trial/article2322016.

to a rule that is commonly referred to in criminal law as double jeopardy. This defence assures that a person cannot be tried for the same offence more than once. If it is determined that the accused has been previously convicted or acquitted of an offence, then he or she must be acquitted of the offence before the court.

**entrapment**

occurs when police go beyond what is permitted by law

### ENTRAPMENT

**Entrapment** is a common law defence, and has been recognized as such since 1988. There is an effort to be clear about the scope of entrapment, limiting the actions of the police. In a decision, Chief Justice Lamer articulated the scope of entrapment:

> "The police must not, and it is entrapment to do so, offer people opportunities to commit crime unless they have a reasonable suspicion that such people are already engaged in criminal activity or, unless such an offer is made in the course of a bona fide investigation."
>
> SOURCE: R. *v.* MACK [1988] 2 S.C.R. 903

Entrapment exists when the police go beyond what is permitted in law. They cannot offer opportunities to commit crime to persons whom they do not have a reasonable suspicion are already engaged in criminal activity.

### *DE MINIMUS*

This procedural defence comes from the Latin phrase *de minimus curat non lex*. This phrase means that the law does not concern itself with trifle matters. The ***de minimus*** defence accepts the fact that the accused did technically commit an offence, but it is so minor that a penalty for same would be too severe (Stansfield, 1992). An example is a person who steals an item valued at one dollar.

### UNDER AGE 12

Section 13 of the *Criminal Code* states that no person under the age of 12 shall be convicted of a criminal act or an omission in Canada. The age of criminal responsibility begins at 12 years of age.

### MISTAKE OF FACT

**Mistake of fact** is a common law defence whereby an accused person makes an honest and genuine mistake, in a situation where his or her actions were normally lawful. In other words, if the circumstances had been as the accused believed them to be, no offence would have been committed. This is a defence that results in an acquittal if used successfully.

### NECESSITY

The defence of **necessity** recognizes that circumstances may arise that require otherwise criminal acts to be excused if committed in order to avoid a greater injustice. This is a common law defence that results in an acquittal if used successfully. The accused must show that there was no reasonable opportunity for an alternative course of action that did not involve breaking the law, and that the harm that is inflicted must be less than the harm that is avoided (Stansfield, 1992).

### AUTOMATISM

**Automatism** is "a state of impaired consciousness in which an individual, though capable of action, has no voluntary control over their action" (R. *v.* Stone, [1999] 2 S.C.R. 290). This defence is one where the accused is in "a state of severely clouded consciousness that prevents the accused from acting voluntarily" (Verdun-Jones, 2010, p.48). It may be triggered by an external trauma, such as a blow to the head, or involuntarily through drugs or alcohol. This is a common law defence that is rarely used. This defence excuses behaviour that might normally be criminal, if the accused was in an automatic state and did not act voluntarily. The accused is not held accountable, despite committing the *actus reus*, because *mens rea* was lacking. This defence may not be used when the involuntary behaviour was caused by:

- a disease of the mind,
- the voluntary consumption of drugs or alcohol,
- loss of temper, or
- deliberate or negligent actions of the accused.

## INTOXICATION: VOLUNTARY AND INVOLUNTARY

Intoxication is a defence that applies only in certain situations. There are two types: **voluntary intoxication** (voluntarily consuming drugs and/or alcohol) and **involuntary intoxication** (a result of the involuntary consumption of drugs and/or alcohol).

**voluntary intoxication**

voluntarily consuming drugs and/or alcohol

Voluntary intoxication is a partial defence and applies only when an accused is charged with a specific intent offence, such as murder. A successful use of this defence would find the accused guilty of a lesser offence, such as manslaughter. An example of involuntary intoxication is when another person puts a drug in the accused person's drink, without the accused's knowledge. This is a complete defence that results in an acquittal if used successfully (Stansfield, 1992).

**involuntary intoxication**

involuntarily consuming drugs and/or alcohol

## DURESS/COMPULSION

**duress**

there are both common law and statutory versions of this defence whereby the accused asserts that he/she was compelled to commit the crime by threats of immediate death or bodily harm

There are two versions of the defence of **duress**; one is common law and one is statutory. This defence excuses criminal behaviour that occurs when the accused was forced to commit the act under threat of death or bodily harm. The common law version of the defence gives the courts a little more room for interpretation. The statutory defence identifies the exceptions for the use of the defence. It states:

> 17. A person who commits an offence under compulsion by threats of immediate death or bodily harm from a person who is present when the offence is committed is excused for committing the offence if the person believes that the threats will be carried out and if the person is not a party to a conspiracy or association whereby the person is subject to compulsion, but this section does not apply where the offence that is committed is high treason or treason, murder, piracy, attempted murder, sexual assault, sexual assault with a weapon, threats to a third party or causing bodily harm, aggravated sexual assault, forcible abduction, hostage taking, robbery, assault with a weapon or causing bodily harm, aggravated assault, unlawfully causing bodily harm, arson or an offence under sections 280 to 283 (abduction and detention of young persons).
>
> R.S., 1985, c. C-46, s. 17; R.S., 1985, c. 27 (1st Supp.), s. 40.

## CONSENT

**Consent** is a common law defence that only applies to certain types of offences. There are numerous rules of law that are related to using consent as a defence, most of which are related to sexual offences and also related to the age of the victim and the accused. Consent is never a defence to being killed and it is not valid when obtained by applying force to the victim, or threats, fear, fraud or the exercise of authority (Stansfield, 1992).

## SELF-DEFENCE

Defence of the person is a statutory defence whereby a defendant claims that there is legal reason that shows that the actions of the accused were permitted by law. **Self-defence** is a full defence that results in a complete acquittal if used successfully. There are various types of self-defence, based on whether or not the attack was provoked or unprovoked and based on the amount of injury received by the victim. Provocation refers to "blows, words or gestures." When self-defence is used it must be proven that the force that was used was not excessive. Each situation is considered individually, but generally the courts examine the physical stature of the persons, the type of weapons used, the nature and severity of the original aggressive act, and whether or not there were threats that accompanied the act (*Criminal Code*, s. 34 – 37).

## DEFENCE OF A DWELLING

Canadian law gives us the right to defend our homes. However, the *Criminal Code* makes it clear that the defence is limited to the use of no more force than is necessary. This is a statutory defence which, when used successfully, results in an acquittal.

> 40. Every one who is in peaceable possession of a dwelling-house, and every one lawfully assisting him or acting under his

There are legal limits on one's right to defend their property.

authority, is justified in using as much force as is necessary to prevent any person from forcibly breaking into or forcibly entering the dwelling-house without lawful authority.

R.S., c. C-34, s. 40.

41. (1) Every one who is in peaceable possession of a dwelling-house or real property, and every one lawfully assisting him or acting under his authority, is justified in using force to prevent any person from trespassing on the dwelling-house or real property, or to remove a trespasser therefrom, if he uses no more force than is necessary.

R.S., c. C-34, s. 41.

### SUDDEN PROVOCATION

**sudden provocation**
a partial defence of acts performed in the heat of passion

**Sudden provocation** is a statutory defence and applies only in situations where the accused is charged with murder. If used successfully, this defence reduces murder to manslaughter. The *Criminal Code* states:

232. (1) Culpable homicide that otherwise would be murder may be reduced to manslaughter if the person who committed it did so in the heat of passion caused by sudden provocation.

Provocation is defined as:

232. (2) A wrongful act or an insult that is of such a nature as to be sufficient to deprive an ordinary person of the power of self-control is provocation for the purposes of this section if the accused acted on it on the sudden and before there was time for his passion to cool.

### NOT CRIMINALLY RESPONSIBLE ON ACCOUNT OF A MENTAL DISORDER

The defence of mental disorder is codified in section 16 of the *Criminal Code*, which states:

16. (1) No person is criminally responsible for an act committed or an omission made while suffering from a mental disorder that rendered the person incapable of appreciating the nature and quality of the act or omission or of knowing that it was wrong.

**not criminally responsible on account of a mental disorder**
accused is determined to be incapable of appreciating the nature/quality of the act or omission, or of knowing it was wrong

Presumption

(2) Every person is presumed not to suffer from a mental disorder so as to be exempt from criminal responsibility by virtue of subsection (1), until the contrary is proved on the balance of probabilities.

Burden of proof

(3) The burden of proof that an accused was suffering from a mental disorder so as to be exempt from criminal responsibility is on the party that raises the issue.

R.S., 1985, c. C-46, s. 16; R.S., 1985, c. 27 (1st Supp.), s. 185(F); 1991, c. 43, s. 2.

This section of the *Criminal Code* demonstrates the fact that an accused person must possess the capacity to understand the nature and quality of his or her behaviour in order to be found guilty of the offence. They must understand that the behaviour was wrong.

When an accused person is found not criminally responsible on account of mental disorder by a court, the accused is not convicted nor is the accused acquitted. The accused is found not criminally responsible on account of a mental disorder (NCRMD) and falls under the control of a provincial or territorial Review Board. The Review Boards are created pursuant to section 672.38 of the *Criminal Code* and are responsible for monitoring the case of the accused (Sinha, 2009).

The Review Board is responsible for assessing the accused with a view to determining whether or not the accused continues to be a danger to the public. There are three options available to the Review Board when an accused is found NCRMD:

- absolute discharge;
- conditional discharge; or
- detention in custody in a hospital.

Section 672.54 states that the court or Review Board shall take into account "the need to protect the public from dangerous persons, the mental condition of the accused, the reintegration of the accused into society and the other needs of the accused."

If the court or Review Board orders an absolute discharge, the NCRMD accused is released from further involvement with the system for the specific offence that led to the NCRMD verdict. If the court or Review Board orders a conditional discharge, the accused is supervised in the community through the imposition of restrictions on his or her liberty. Typical stipulations ordered by a court or Review Board during a conditional discharge specify that the NCRMD accused must:

- reside in a particular place (e.g., group home);
- abstain from illegal drugs and/or alcohol;
- submit to urinalysis testing for prohibited substances;
- abide by a specified treatment plan;
- report to a designated person (e.g., psychiatrist) on a scheduled basis; and
- refrain from possessing weapons.

Although these represent some of the most common conditions, section 672.54 (b) states that the accused may be discharged subject to any conditions the court or Review Board considers appropriate.

If the court or Review Board orders detention, the accused is placed in custody within a hospital. There are still times, however, when he or she will be managed within the community under specific conditions. The court or Review Board can delegate authority to manage the accused to the hospital where the accused is detained. As such, the hospital administrator has the power to increase or decrease the restrictions on the NCRMD accused. Therefore, it is possible for an accused to leave hospital grounds with permission from the hospital administrator.

Under section 672.81, the Review Boards must hold a hearing every year in order to review the disposition. During these annual reviews, Review Boards can impose any of the three available dispositions (i.e., absolute discharge, conditional discharge, detention) and alter any of the conditions previously imposed on the accused. In addition to these annual reviews, additional mandatory reviews do occur within the year if, for example, restrictions on the liberty of an accused have been significantly increased for a period exceeding seven days or if a hospital administrator requests a review. Finally, discretionary reviews are possible upon the request of the accused or any other party.

## PARTIES TO AN OFFENCE

LO8

In Canadian law, a person can commit a criminal offence by being a party to an offence. There are a number of ways in which one may be a party to a criminal offence. The *Criminal Code* defines the concept of common intention in section 21:

21. (1) Every one is a party to an offence who
*(a)* actually commits it;
*(b)* does or omits to do anything for the purpose of aiding any person to commit it; or
*(c)* abets any person in committing it.

This section of the *Criminal Code* means that you do not have to specifically commit a crime in order to be a party to the crime. If you aid someone who is committing a crime by doing or not doing something, you are a party to the crime. For example, if you work in a restaurant and agree to leave the door unlocked so that your friend can enter and steal from the restaurant, you are a party to the offence. To abet a person is to offer encouragement or help. In order to be a party to an offence it must be proven that the accused had knowledge that the person was going to commit a crime and that the accused aided and/or abetted the person.

## COUNSEL TO COMMIT A CRIME

A person may be a party to an offence if he or she counsels another person to commit a crime. When one person counsels another to commit a crime he or she may advise, procure, solicit, or incite a person to commit a crime. The *Criminal Code* states:

22. (1) Where a person counsels another person to be a party to an offence and that other person is afterwards a party to that offence, the person who counselled is a party to that offence, notwithstanding that the offence was committed in a way different from that which was counselled.

(2) Every one who counsels another person to be a party to an offence is a party to every offence that the other commits in consequence of the counselling that the person who counselled knew or ought to have known was likely to be committed in consequence of the counselling.

To be an accessory after the fact is another way one may be a party to an offence. To be an accessory after the fact one must receive, comfort, or assist a person for the purpose of enabling that person to escape. In order to be an accessory, the accused must know that the person has committed an offence. A spouse of the principal offender is exempt from this section of the *Criminal Code*. No person can be charged with being a party to an offence for being an accessory after the fact if a spouse was the principal offender.

23. (1) An accessory after the fact to an offence is one who, knowing that a person has been a party to the offence, receives, comforts or assists that person for the purpose of enabling that person to escape.

## IGNORANCE OF THE LAW IS NOT A DEFENCE

Section 19 of the *Criminal Code* makes it clear that it is the responsibility of every person to be aware of the criminal laws in Canada, and that ignorance of the law is not an acceptable defence. This means that everyone on Canadian soil is responsible for being aware of the current laws.

19. Ignorance of the law by a person who commits an offence is not an excuse for committing that offence.

R.S., c. C-34, s. 19.

## Chapter Summary

This chapter provided an introduction to criminal law in Canada. Key concepts that were covered include:

- The Uniform Crime Reporting Survey, the Crime Severity Index, and the General Social Survey on Victimization were identified as the main sources of information related to crime measurement in Canada. Each of these instruments presents a different perspective on the extent and nature of crime in Canada.
- Canada's overall crime rate has been declining. The factors that may influence crime rate include age, gender, the economy, and legislation as well as policing policy and data collection methods.
- The funnel is a metaphor to describe the way in which criminal cases are filtered as they move through the criminal justice system. Like a funnel, the criminal justice system 'filters' criminal cases such that a small percentage of reported crime results in a criminal conviction.
- Criminal law is dynamic because it reflects the values of our society. A number of crimes that have been recently amended or created are identified.
- Crimes are classified in one of three ways: summary, indictable, or dual procedure (hybrid). Examples of each are provided.
- In order for an individual to be found guilty of a criminal offence, it must be proven that the individual had both mens rea (guilty mind) and actus reus (guilty action or omission).
- The defences that are available to defendants in Canadian courts were outlined, as well as the ways in which one may be a party to an offence.

## Relevant Legislation

*Criminal Code*, R.S.C. 1985, c C-46

*The Constitution Act, 1867*

## Key Terms

Accident
Acquittal
*Actus reus*
Alibi
Automatism
*Autrefois acquit*
*Autrefois convict*
Common law defences
Consent
Crime
Crime Severity Index (CSI)
Crime rate
Dark figure of crime
*De minimus*
Dual procedure offence
Duress
Entrapment
General intent
Hate crimes
Honour-based violence
Hybrid offence
Indictable offence
Involuntary intoxication
*Mens rea*
Mistake of fact
Necessity
Not Criminally Responsible on account of a Mental Disorder
Procedural law
Recklessness
Self-defence
Specific intent
Statute of limitations
Statutory defences
Substantive law
Sudden provocation
Summary conviction offence
Uniform Crime Reporting (UCR) Survey
Voluntary intoxication
Wilful blindness

## For Review

1. What is the difference between procedural law and substantive law?
2. What is the statute of limitation and why is it important?
3. What is Canada's crime rate?
4. What are the factors that contribute to a falling crime rate?
5. Why is important to have laws that are amended over time?
6. What is the maximum penalty for a summary conviction offence?
7. What are the various types of *mens rea*?
8. Why is it necessary that *mens rea* and *actus reus* coincide?
9. What is the difference between a statutory defence and a common law defence?
10. What are the various ways to be a party to an offence in Canada?
11. Describe when self-defence can be used as a defence?
12. Explain the difference between the outcome of a successful full defence and a successful partial defence.

## Thinking Critically

1. How realistic is it to assume that the average person is aware of all of the laws in our society? Does our government make a reasonable effort to raise community awareness of our laws, especially when they are added, repealed, or amended?
2. To what do you attribute our falling crime rate? Based on the current demographic makeup of Canada, can you make any predictions about Canada's crime rate in the next 20 years?
3. Why is it important to have access to both the crime rate and the Crime Severity Index? What are we able to learn from each and how do they differ?
4. Describe the crime funnel and explain why it exists. Is the crime funnel problematic? Should we make an effort to minimize this phenomenon? Explain.
5. Do you believe that our laws related Not Criminally Responsible due to a Mental Disorder respond to our societal needs? If you had the opportunity to amend that law, how might you do so?
6. Are there any laws that exist today that you would amend or repeal? Is there a law that does not exist that you would create? Defend your decisions.
7. Why are spouses exempt from the accessory after the fact laws? What does the exemption say about the relationship between spouses, in law?

CHAPTER 3

# Policing

## The Ex-Colonel's Conviction and "Old Fashioned" Police Work

A once-decorated career soldier who rose to the rank of Colonel pleaded guilty to a total of 88 charges—two charges of murder, two for sexual assault, and the remaining charges for theft—on October 7, 2010, in Superior Court in Belleville, Ontario. Russell Williams, a married, career soldier, was a high profile Colonel who had been stationed at various posts around the world. At the time of his arrest he was the Commander of the Canadian Forces Base in Trenton, Ontario. This "Jekyll and Hyde" case shocked both the military world and Canadians across the country.

### LEARNING OBJECTIVES

By the end of this chapter, you should be able to:

- **LO1** Describe the history of policing in Canada.
- **LO2** Identify the organization of policing in Canada.
- **LO3** Identify the legislation that governs police in Canada.
- **LO4** Describe the role and function of policing.
- **LO5** Explain the recruitment, selection, and training process.
- **LO6** Recognize the stresses related to police work.
- **LO7** Outline types of police accountability and oversight.
- **LO8** Identify ways in which policing is evaluated.
- **LO9** Describe the role of private police in Canada.

Williams was convicted of the murders of Jessica Lloyd, 27, and Corporal Marie-France Comeau, 38, a Trenton-based air attendant under the command of Colonel Williams. Both victims were asphyxiated. Comeau was found dead in her home, and Lloyd was discovered in a wooded area outside of Tweed, Ontario. The sexual assaults, for which Williams was convicted, involved home invasions near his cottage.

The police engaged in old fashioned police work in order to zero in on Williams as a suspect in this case. Tire tracks left at the scene of Jessica Lloyd's home were compared to the tires of vehicles stopped at a police roadblock. Williams was identified as a suspect when his tires proved to be a match. His boot print was also matched to the boot prints found in the yard of Lloyd's home. Jim Smyth conducted the police interview that led to Williams' confession. Smyth, a detective sergeant with the OPP's behavioural sciences unit, was praised for his superior interviewing skills.

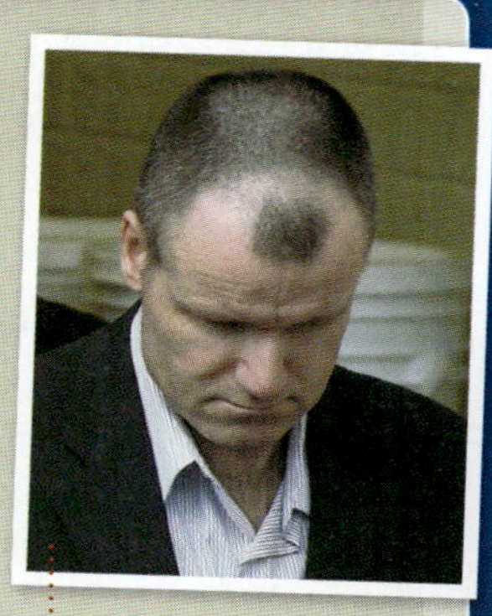

Russell Williams was interviewed by Detective Sergeant Jim Smyth.

By pleading guilty to the offences, neither a preliminary hearing nor a trial were required. Several days of evidence and victim impact statements followed Williams' guilty plea.

Police gathered evidence at the home of Jessica Lloyd.

The footprints and tire tracks of the accused were critical pieces of evidence obtained by police.

On October 18, 2010, Williams was sentenced to life imprisonment, with no possibility of parole for 25 years. Williams, who was 47 at the time of the sentencing, will be eligible for parole when he is 72 years of age.

Soon after the conviction, Williams was stripped of his rank and formally evicted from the military. In what was a profoundly symbolic act, uniforms and military apparel belonging to Williams were burned in a furnace at Canadian Forces Base Trenton where Williams once served as the Unit Commander.

## LO1 History of Policing in Canada

By tracing the history of policing in Canada we can examine the way in which Canada grew and developed as a nation. Policing in early Canada was handled primarily by the military detachments stationed across Canada, until individual communities began to identify people who agreed to be watchmen. Watchmen were responsible for holding posts and alerting the community of criminal behaviour. This form of protection was unstable and soon proved to be inadequate as the population grew.

The federal government created the Dominion Police Force in 1868, initially with the mandate of protecting federal government buildings in Ottawa. Though its jurisdiction was federal, the Dominion Police Force was primarily involved in policing central and eastern Canada. The growth of policing in Canada was influenced by the country's expansion to the west; in 1870, Canada grew to include the northwest. This growth meant that there was a need to bring law and order to the new frontier, in preparation for new settlement of the area. On May 23, 1873, an act—introduced by Canada's first Prime Minister, Sir John A. Macdonald—was passed to create a "Mounted Police Force for the Northwest Territories." (That region includes parts of present-day Saskatchewan, Alberta, the Yukon and Northwest Territories.)

The first recruitment drive to build the North West Mounted Police (NWMP) resulted in the hiring of 150 men. As the west became settled police posts were established. The early posts were determined largely by the need to control the American whisky trade and eventually the officers were deployed to the growing settlements along the new railway. By 1883, the NWMP grew to 500 men and detachments were created in new urban and rural areas. The NWMP was assigned to maintain the peace among the thousands of workers who were in the West building the railway. They maintained order when the railway workers became unruly due to excessive drinking and gambling, as well as when there were strikes. By 1885, the NWMP's strength grew to 1,000 men, many of whom were called upon to police the Klondike Gold Rush. Its jurisdiction grew to include the Yukon in 1895, the Arctic coast in 1903, and northern Manitoba in 1912.

North West Mounted Police.
Officers of the "B" Division, July 1900.

The general duties of the NWMP at that time were to:

- establish law and order;
- collect customs dues;
- enforce prohibition;
- supervise the treaties between First Nations and the federal government;
- assist in the settlement process;
- ensure the welfare of immigrants; and
- fight prairie fires, disease, and destitution.

(Origins of the RCMP, n.d.)

The federal government determined that one federal police service was required to police the entire country in 1919, likely influenced by the impact of the First World War. On February 1, 1920, after absorbing the Dominion Police, the name of the North West Mounted Police was changed to the Royal Canadian Mounted Police (RCMP) and the headquarters were established in Ottawa. At that time the role of the RCMP in Canada began to grow to include the policing of several provinces.

Provincial policing and municipal policing were also expanding in various communities across Canada. The Ontario Provincial Police (OPP) was created in 1909. Unlike Alberta and Saskatchewan, Ontario chose to police itself rather than contract policing services from the RCMP (McKenna, 2003). By 1932, the RCMP also provided policing services to Manitoba, New Brunswick, Nova Scotia, and Prince Edward Island. Ontario and Quebec continue to be the only provinces that administer their own police services.

Modern policing in Canada has been influenced by the historical relationship to Great Britain. The London Metropolitan Police was formed in 1829 and is known for the founding principles of modern day policing. Sir Robert Peel commanded the officers, who were called "Bobbies" in his honour. The London Metropolitan Service stressed the belief that a police presence could deter crime and called for police patrols rather than the fixed posts of the police in the past. This resulted in the police having an ongoing presence in the community, a critical element of modern policing. Peel's principles continue to be relevant today as they refer to a number of basic philosophical tenets of policing. Each of the principles identifies an important element; for example, Principle 7 states:

> Police, at all times, should maintain a relationship with the public that gives reality to the historic tradition that the police are the public and the public are the police; the police being only members of the public who are paid to give full-time attention to duties which are incumbent upon every citizen in the interests of community welfare and existence.

The notion that police are required to maintain a positive relationship with the public is a critical one that is manifest in many of the initiatives that drive modern policing. The first principle identifies the critical relationship between the police and crime prevention. This principle stresses the importance of the proactive role that the police play in preventing crime and their role is not restricted to reactive response.

### Then vs. Now: Hiring Qualifications for the RCMP

1873:

- Males only
- Between ages of 18 and 40
- Be of sound constitution, able to ride a horse, active, able-bodied, and of good character
- Able to read and write either French or English
- Pay was 75 cents per day for sub-constables and 1 dollar per day for constables

TODAY:

- Be a Canadian citizen
- Be of good character
- Be proficient in either French or English
- Have a valid high school diploma
- Possess a valid, unrestricted Canadian driver's license
- Be at least 19 years of age at the time of engagement
- Meet medical/health standards
- Be willing to relocate anywhere in Canada
- Be physically fit
- Pay for Regular Member Constables: $48,946. Within 36 months of service, the salary increases to $79,308 (May 2012, http://www.rcmp-grc.gc.ca/recruiting-recrutement/rm-mr/salary-avantages-eng.htm)

SOURCE: The Origins of the Royal Canadian Mounted Police, Government of Canada.

## SIR ROBERT PEEL'S PRINCIPLES

1. The basic mission for which the police exist is to prevent crime and disorder.
2. The ability of the police to perform their duties is dependent upon the public approval of police actions.
3. Police must secure the willing co-operation of the public in voluntary observation of the law to be able to secure and maintain the respect of the public.
4. The degree of co-operation of the public that can be secured diminishes proportionately to the necessity of the use of physical force.
5. Police seek and preserve public favour not by catering to public opinion, but by constantly demonstrating absolute impartial service to the law.
6. Police use physical force to the extent necessary to secure observance of the law or to restore order only when the exercise of persuasion, advice, and warning is found to be insufficient.
7. Police, at all times, should maintain a relationship with the public that gives reality to the historic tradition that the police are the public and the public are the police; the police being only members of the public who are paid to give full-time attention to duties which are incumbent upon every citizen in the interests of community welfare and existence.
8. Police should always direct their action strictly towards their functions, and never appear to usurp the powers of the judiciary.
9. The test of police efficiency is the absence of crime and disorder, not the visible evidence of police action in dealing with it.

Sir Robert Peel.

# Police in Canada Today

LO2

The number of police officers in Canada has been growing steadily since 1981. Statistics Canada indicates that in 2011, there were 69,438 active police officers in Canada. The ratio of police officers to the general population is 201 police officers for every 100,000 persons nationally, the highest it has been since 1981. This is lower than Australia (222 per 100,000), England and Wales (229 per 100,000) and the United States (244 per 100,000) (Statistics Canada, 2011). Ontario has the highest number of police officers at 26,361; a ratio of 200 officers per 100,000 population. By contrast, the Northwest Territories has the highest ratio of 462 officers per 100,000 (with a total strength of 202 police officers). These variations are related to the difference between urban and rural policing across Canada. The police in the Canadian territories are required to police large, sparsely populated areas.

We have seen steady growth in police strength across Canada over the past decade, with an increase of 2,000 officers between 2009 and 2010 alone. At the same time, we have seen a decline in the police-reported **crime rate** as well as the severity of police-reported crime.

**crime rate**
a measurement of police-reported crime

Civilian members of police services perform non-policing functions. Civilian positions include clerical, administrative, support, and maintenance functions. There are 27,000 civilian employees in police services across Canada (Statistics Canada, 2010), which is one civilian employee for every 2.5 police officers. There has been a trend toward a steady increase in the number of civilians employed in the policing sector.

## THE ORGANIZATION OF POLICING IN CANADA

The organization of policing in Canada today is multi-jurisdictional. There are three levels of policing in Canada, and each level has its own jurisdiction and responsibilities. In addition, there are First Nations policing agreements in place for Aboriginal communities across Canada.

### FEDERAL POLICING

The Royal Canadian Mounted Police (RCMP) is Canada's federal police agency and a Canadian symbol that is recognized worldwide. The RCMP polices the three territories, all of the provinces except Ontario and Quebec, and has municipal policing agreements with approximately 180 municipalities. With a mandate to police approximately 75 percent of Canada's geography, the RCMP is the largest police service in Canada. In addition, the RCMP provides services to the entire country including maintaining national databases that include fingerprints, criminal records (Canadian Police Information Centre), and ballistics identification. Specialized services include forensic sciences analysis, criminal intelligence, and police training.

The RCMP is led by a Commissioner, and is organized under the authority of the *Royal Canadian Mounted Police Act*. Under the Minister of Public Safety's direction, the Commissioner controls and manages operations from the headquarters in Ottawa.

There are 15 operations divisions, alphabetically designated, for the provinces, territories, and the National Capital Region. The RCMP Training Academy is in Regina, Saskatchewan, and the Canadian Police College, Musical Ride, and RCMP Band are all located in Ottawa, Ontario. The RCMP protects high-profile individuals, including the Prime Minister, dignitaries, and the Government of Canada overall. They have also taken on a leadership role in coordinating Canada's involvement in international policing and peacekeeping.

"The Mounties always get their man."

This famous phrase was used in numerous old Hollywood films depicting fictional Mounties. The RCMP traced the origin of the phrase to this quote from 1877:

"Thanks to the vigilance of Major Irvine and the energy of Captain Winder, of the N.W. Mounted Police, another attempt to smuggle whiskey has been frustrated by the arrest of three men, who were tried, found guilty and sentenced to pay a fine of five hundred dollars each or be imprisoned for the minor period of six months. They preferred the former. Horses were sacrificed for the arrest, but the M.P.s are worse than bloodhounds when they scent the track of a smuggler, and they fetch their men every time." (Fort Benton [Montana] Record, April, 1877)

### PROVINCIAL/TERRITORIAL POLICING

Under the *Constitution Act, 1867*, each province and territory in Canada is responsible for the administration of justice, which includes policing. All provinces and territories, except Ontario

The RCMP is the largest police service in Canada.

Sûreté du Québec is the provincial police service in Québec.

and Quebec, have agreements with the federal government whereby the RCMP police their jurisdictions. Where the RCMP is contracted for police services, the province or territory pays for 70 percent of the costs and the federal government pays the remaining amount. In Ontario, provincial policing rests with the OPP, and in Quebec with the Sûreté du Québec.

## MUNICIPAL POLICING

Municipal policing refers to policing urban centres throughout Canada. Often called city or regional police, they are assigned with policing areas with a dense population. Municipalities can choose to form their own police service, can join with a neighbouring service, or they can contract the provincial police (if in Ontario, Quebec, or Newfoundland) or the RCMP. The largest municipal police service in Canada is the Toronto Police Service with 5,588 sworn officers. The second largest service is the Montreal Police Service with 4,589 sworn officers, followed by the Peel Regional Police Service with 1,895 sworn officers (Statistics Canada, 2010). Municipal police services employ 65 percent of all police officers in Canada and provide policing services to over 25 million people (Statistics Canada, 2010). Newfoundland and Labrador, Yukon, the Northwest Territories, and Nunavut do not have municipal police services. The Royal Newfoundland Constabulary, Newfoundland's provincial police service, polices St. John's, Corner Brook, Labrador City, and Churchill Falls, while the RCMP polices the remainder of the province.

Winnipeg police on patrol.

**TABLE 3.1** Police Officers by Province/Territory 2010

| | 2007 | 2008 | 2009 | 2010 | 2011 |
|---|---|---|---|---|---|
| | | | number | | |
| **Canada** | **64,134** | **65,283** | **67,425** | **69,250** | **69,438** |
| Newfoundland and Labrador | 838 | 884 | 917 | 939 | 935 |
| Prince Edward Island | 227 | 231 | 234 | 238 | 244 |
| Nova Scotia | 1,758 | 1,864 | 1,877 | 1,912 | 1,914 |
| New Brunswick | 1,326 | 1,355 | 1,364 | 1,398 | 1,377 |
| Quebec | 15,233 | 15,403 | 15,532 | 15,586 | 15,802 |
| Ontario | 24,450 | 24,945 | 25,558 | 26,306 | 26,387 |
| Manitoba | 2,409 | 2,419 | 2,497 | 2,549 | 2,593 |
| Saskatchewan | 2,046 | 2,124 | 2,135 | 2,302 | 2,306 |
| Alberta | 5,703 | 5,734 | 6,199 | 6,608 | 6,696 |
| British Columbia | 8,075 | 8,134 | 8,809 | 9,044 | 8,966 |
| Yukon | 119 | 117 | 122 | 121 | 122 |
| Northwest Territories | 175 | 178 | 196 | 202 | 197 |
| Nunavut | 123 | 119 | 125 | 132 | 130 |
| Royal Canadian Mounted Police (RCMP) Headquarters and Training Academy | 1,652 | 1,776 | 1,860 | 1,913 | 1,769 |

SOURCE: Statistics Canada, Police officers by province and territory, http://www.statcan.gc.ca/tables-tableaux/sum-som/l01/cst01/legal05a-eng.htm, 29 March 2012. Reproduced and distributed on an "as is" basis with the permission of Statistics Canada.

### FIRST NATIONS POLICING

In 1991, the federal government introduced the First Nations Policing Policy (FNPP) in order to provide First Nations across Canada (not including the Northwest Territories and Nunavut) with policing services. Each community engages in a cost-shared agreement between the federal government, the provincial or territorial government, and First Nations. The policy applies to all Native reserves, to some First Nations communities on Crown land, and to all Inuit communities. There are several models that have been used to implement the FNPP across the country. The agreements require that all police officers must be Native, except where the First Nation agrees to the staffing of a non-Native officer. The First Nations police service must meet the same standards as other police services in the jurisdiction, and the officers are sworn peace officers, with the same rights and responsibilities.

Six Nations Police.

In addition, like other police services, each First Nations police service must be accountable to a police services board, police commission, or other formal form of oversight (Cummins and Steckley, 2003). Today there are 168 policing service agreements employing 1,240 police officers to provide services to 408 First Nation and Inuit communities across Canada (Public Safety Canada, 2011).

In *Setting the Context: The Policing of First Nations Communities*, the First Nations Chiefs of Police Association reminds us that policing in Aboriginal communities was in place long before the introduction of the current arrangement:

> Contrary to popular belief, policing in Aboriginal communities is not a new concept. The policing of First Nations communities has not merely evolved through legislation enacted by successive Crown governments over the last several hundred years. Concepts like guilt and innocence as we know them by today's legal standards were not something that existed in the language of First Nations communities. Often, Elders delivered justice within their territories by first addressing the nature of the injustice; ensuring that the punishment fit the wrong that had been done; and finally, ensuring that proper compensation or restitution was provided to the victim or to the family of the victim where more serious crimes were involved. The underlying principle of Aboriginal justice was to restore the social order within the community and to resolve conflict through conflict resolution, reconciliation and restitution. (FNCPA and Human Resources Development Canada, n.d., p. 3)

## CANADIAN SECURITY INTELLIGENCE SERVICE: CANADA'S INTELLIGENCE AGENCY

The Canadian Security Intelligence Service (CSIS) is responsible for investigating threats, analyzing information, and producing intelligence to protect Canada from threats—which include terrorism, espionage, foreign interference, and cyber-tampering—that could have a major impact on the Canadian infrastructure. Combatting terrorism in order to prevent terrorist acts in Canada and

CSIS National Headquarters, Ottawa, Ontario.

protecting Canadian assets and interests abroad is at the forefront of CSIS' priorities. The intelligence gathered by CSIS complements and supports the work being done by law enforcement agencies across Canada. CSIS collects and analyzes intelligence and shares it, as appropriate, with law enforcement agencies, government departments, and the general public.

CSIS employs 3,104 individuals (Public Report, 2009/2010) in positions including intelligence officers, analysts, surveillants, technologists, engineers, translators, and support staff. Men and women are equally represented among the staff, 67 percent of the employees are bilingual, and 27 percent speak a third language, representing over 100 foreign languages. CSIS National Headquarters is located in Ottawa, Ontario.

## LO3 LEGISLATION THAT GOVERNS THE POLICE

The police are governed by a number of pieces of legislation, many of which identify the rules and regulations that guide their duties. Each police service in Canada is governed by a Police Act, a legislative framework within their jurisdiction that identifies rules, regulations, procedures and processes. Each Act also clarifies the role and function of the police. The *Criminal Code of Canada* classifies police officers as peace officers (Section 2) and their powers emanate from various sources including both statute and common law. Statute law, which directs police activity, is federal, provincial, and municipal.

Federal statutory legislation that governs police activity across Canada includes the following:

- *The Constitution Act, 1982* (which includes the *Charter of Rights and Freedoms*)
- *Criminal Code of Canada*
- *Canada Evidence Act*
- *Controlled Drugs and Substances Act*
- *Crimes Against Humanity and War Crimes Act*
- *Youth Criminal Justice Act*

Police officers must be aware of the scope and limitations of their powers as they carry out their duties. Provincial and municipal police officers are sworn to enforce the laws within the province that employs them and their powers are limited to that province. A federal officer's powers extend across the country. Table 3.2 identifies the jurisdiction reach of each level of policing.

### THE *CHARTER OF RIGHTS AND FREEDOMS* AND POLICE POWERS

The *Canadian Charter of Rights and Freedoms* (the *Charter*) is a part of the *Constitution Act, 1982*, and it identifies rights that are guaranteed to Canadians. These basic rights are critical to the quality of life in Canada, and include rights and freedoms related to the enforcement of the law. As such, the *Charter* has a significant impact on the way in which police perform their duties. The *Charter* influences police powers by providing a safety net for Canadians to ensure that police exercise their powers as prescribed by law. It is important to note that all police powers, whether they are statute law or common law, are subject to the constitutional protection of the *Charter*. The *Charter* is the supreme law of Canada, meaning that all other laws in Canada must be consistent with it.

Since the *Charter's* inception in 1982, we have seen a considerable number of cases that have challenged the constitutionality of police powers. Once such case is R. *v.* Buhay (R. *v.* Buhay, [2003] 1 S.C.R. 631, 2003 SCC 30). The facts of the case are that Mr. Buhay rented a storage locker located in the Winnipeg bus station. When security guards detected a strong odour of marijuana emanating from the locker, they alerted a Greyhound agent,

**TABLE 3.2 Policing Levels**

| Police Service | Geographic Jurisdiction | Enforcement Authority |
|---|---|---|
| Federal (RCMP) | Throughout Canada | Federal, provincial, municipal |
| Provincial (Ontario and Quebec) | The province | Federal, provincial, municipal |
| Municipal and regional | The province, with a focus on their own jurisdiction. | Federal, provincial, municipal |

who opened the locker. They found a duffel bag of marijuana inside the locker and immediately notified the police, who seized the duffel bag, without a search warrant. On the following day, an individual arrived at the bus station and was arrested when he tried to retrieve the bag from the locker. At the trial, the judge noted that the police were in violation of Section 8 of the *Charter* which guarantees that:

> Everyone has the right to be secure against unreasonable search or seizure.

The trial judge then granted the defence motion to exclude the evidence under section 24(2) which states:

> 24. (2) Where, in proceedings under subsection (1), a court concludes that evidence was obtained in a manner that infringed or denied any rights or freedoms guaranteed by this Charter, the evidence shall be excluded if it is established that, having regard to all the circumstances, the admission of it in the proceedings would bring the administration of justice into disrepute.

With the exclusion of the evidence, the accused was acquitted. The case was then appealed to the province's Court of Appeal where the trial judge's decision was overturned and a conviction was entered. The accused then appealed to the Supreme Court of Canada, claiming that the police violated his section 8 rights and that the evidence (the marijuana) was obtained illegally and should therefore be excluded. The Supreme Court of Canada allowed the appeal and the acquittal that was entered at trial was restored. In its decision, the Supreme Court said:

> The accused had a reasonable expectation of privacy in the contents of the locker he rented. The accused had control and possession of the locker's contents through possession of the key. Moreover, the signs on the lockers made no mention of the possibility that they might be opened and searched. A reasonable person would expect that his or her private belongings, when secured in a locker that he or she has paid money to rent, will be left alone, unless the contents appear to pose a threat to the security of the bus depot. The existence of a master key does not in itself destroy the expectation of privacy. While it was not as high as the privacy afforded to one's own body, home or office, a reasonable expectation of privacy existed in the locker sufficient to engage the accused's section 8 Charter rights.... This Court should not interfere with the trial judge's decision to exclude the evidence under section 24(2) of the Charter.

This case illustrates the manner in which the *Charter* is applied to challenges related to police powers. Section 1 of the *Charter* recognizes that:

> The *Canadian Charter of Rights and Freedoms* guarantees the rights and freedoms set out in it subject only to such reasonable limits prescribed by law as can be demonstrably justified in a free and democratic society.

This section is critical to interpreting constitutional law because it recognizes that in a free and democratic society there are limits to our individual freedoms. This was illustrated in R. v. Ladouceur [1990] 1 S.C.R. 1257, when the Supreme Court of Canada determined that random traffic stops are constitutional. The appellant launched an appeal claiming that random police stops of a motor vehicle and its driver are an infringement on one's rights guaranteed by sections 7, 8, and 9 of the *Charter*, which are:

> 7. Everyone has the right to life, liberty and security of the person and the right not to be deprived thereof except in accordance with the principles of fundamental justice.

The *Canadian Charter of Rights and Freedoms* guarantees the rights and freedoms set out in it subject only to such reasonable limits prescribed by law as can be demonstrably justified in a free and democratic society.

8. Everyone has the right to be secure against unreasonable search or seizure.
9. Everyone has the right not to be arbitrarily detained or imprisoned.

The Supreme Court decision hinged on the interpretation of section 1. It was determined by the Supreme Court that random traffic stops are justified based on the deterrent aspect of the random routine check, thereby protecting society. In the decision, the Justices noted, "the random routine check does not so severely trench upon the section 9 right so as to outweigh the legislative objective" (R. *v*. Ladouceur [1990] 1 S.C.R. 1257). Today, random checks (e.g., Reduce Impaired Driving Everywhere, or RIDE) are recognized as being a reasonable infringement on our personal freedom because of this decision.

The process of *Charter* challenges as they relate to police powers will continue to provide the police with direction and reinforce our understanding of the scope of those powers in a free and democratic society.

## POLICE DISCRETION

Police officers have the **discretion** to make decisions as they carry out their duties. Though it is true that the police are bound by many laws, rules, and regulations that prescribe their actions, seldom is there a requirement for police to lay a charge when sufficient grounds exist (Carrington and Schulenberg, 2008). As such the police regularly use their own judgment to decide how they will intervene in a given situation. For example, an officer may use his or her discretion when making an arrest, issuing a ticket, or charging an individual with a particular offence. In a situation involving a minor violation, an officer may choose to warn a citizen rather than proceed with an arrest or a traffic ticket. Using discretion is highlighted in the application of the *Youth Criminal Justice Act*, where police are directed to consider the use of extrajudicial measures (as opposed to judicial measures—laying a charge) when they are faced with a youthful offender. This legislation does something that is rarely seen: it provides statutory authority for the police use of discretion and it structures that use of discretion (Carrington and Schulenberg, 2008). Again, because it is discretionary, there are variations across the country in the way in which it is applied, subject to the interpretation of each police service (and each police officer), as well as the availability of young offender resources in each jurisdiction. Carrington and Schulenberg (2008) examined the rate at which the police charge young persons, as opposed to engaging them in extrajudicial measures across Canada. They found that by 2005 there was only an 11 percent difference across the country between the province with the highest charge ratio (Ontario at 49 percent) and the lowest (Atlantic region at 38 percent). This indicates that the discretion of the police, as it applies to extrajudicial measures, is applied somewhat consistently across the country.

**discretion**
the ability to make decisions on various matters based on his/her opinion within general legal guidelines

There are situations in which a police officer has little or no discretion to act. Directives to act may be based in legislation, department policy, or by priority. Police are directed to use a pro-charge approach when responding to domestic violence calls. Another example of limited discretion is when police are in **pursuit** of a suspect. Generally, a police supervisor makes the decision about whether a pursuit will continue. Decisions on limiting police discretion are made to ensure that an individual officer's decisions are consistent with the goals and priorities of society overall.

**pursuit**
a chase

**JUST or BUST?**

**Does the use of police discretion mean that we have a system where not all people receive the same treatment by the police? Is this fair?**

## L04 THE ROLE AND FUNCTION OF THE POLICE

Effective policing is critical to the operation of a safe society. The role of the police in a democratic society is to maintain public peace and security. As our society and our communities become more complex, so too does the role of policing.

The police are the most visible of the various players within the criminal justice system. Few of us have the opportunity to sit in a criminal court to watch a judge or a Crown attorney at work. Even fewer of us will ever be incarcerated, but all of us are affected by the police at work as we go about living our daily lives. The police and their activities are integrated within our communities. We see the police directing traffic, walking, or riding bikes, securing a crime scene, or investigating a traffic accident while we go about the daily business of living our lives.

Police services are organized in a "top down" bureaucratic structure with a clear path of reporting and supervision. The rank structure is hierarchical in nature, whereby the Chief or Commissioner holds the highest rank and is the commanding officer. The organization is divided into various units, each with a different function and area of responsibility.

The paramilitary nature of police organizations is evident in their hierarchical structure. Though all police services do not identify ranks in the same manner, they all have a hierarchy that makes reporting and responsibilities clear. Police policies and procedures are written and are disseminated throughout the organization.

### MYTH VS FACT — Real Police Don't Solve Crimes in a Prime Time Hour!

The popularity of prime time entertainment-based police television shows affects the way in which the general public perceives the role, function, and success of police. There are significant differences between the way police are portrayed on television and the reality of the occupation. Police shows portray police officers in constant "crime fighting" mode, when in reality police officers spend between 10 and 20 percent of their time fighting crime and the rest of their time on other tasks (Soulliere, 2004). Police on television are far more successful than police in real life. One study indicated that on television the police have a 90 percent **clearance rate** (Soulliere, 2004), compared to real life where clearance rates are significantly lower at an average of 39 percent (Statistics Canada, 2011). An area in which there is consistency between police on television and their real life counterparts is gender and racial composition. In both, policing is a male-dominated occupation where most of the officers are Caucasian.

Crime scene analysis is a meticulous process.

**clearance rate**
the number of cases that police solve, or otherwise discharge, in a given period

The recent onslaught of crime scene investigation (CSI) shows has created a belief in viewers that not only are crimes solved in a prime time hour, but they have blurred the roles played by homicide investigators, medical examiners, and forensic scientists. In reality these are separate occupations. On television, DNA results and other complicated tests are processed instantly; in reality there is a significant delay. Police officers refer to this phenomenon as the "CSI effect," and it can lead to unrealistic expectations, which could then result in the public's decreased confidence in the real police who do not always live up to their prime time counterparts.

Policing any jurisdiction is complex and requires that police engage in different roles and functions within the organization to be responsive to the needs of the community. Though a community's size and demographics may alter the way in which police perform their duties, basic police functions are consistent. Police engage in crime prevention, they enforce the laws, and maintain order within our society. In doing so, they provide assistance to citizens and victims of crime. Policing is both proactive and reactive. It is proactive when police engage in crime prevention activities intended to reduce or eliminate crime. It is reactive when the police respond to a crime or an emergency situation. Both proactive and reactive responses are required in order to respond to the community's needs. Table 3.3 presents an overview of policing functions.

In the far north, the RCMP used sled dogs on patrol until 1969.

### POLICE PATROL

Patrol is the element of policing that is most visible to the public. Most of the police officers in Canada engage in police patrol on a daily basis, and there is a societal expectation that police

**TABLE 3.3 Police Functions**

| Police Function | Description |
|---|---|
| Assist and Inform | The police provide assistance to victims when they respond to crime. Police are usually the first to respond to a victim, and they provide emergency assistance as well as referrals to appropriate resources, as required. Police also provide information to citizens, formally and informally. Many police services offer community engagement activities such as a Citizens Academy, where they offer classes so that the citizens may learn about police and the criminal justice system overall. |
| Criminal Investigation | Criminal investigation includes a broad range of activities required to investigate a violation of the law. An investigation involves identifying, gathering, and preserving evidence. An investigator must be skilled at interviewing witnesses and suspects. The investigation involves preparing the case for trial, requiring a thorough understanding of criminal law and the court process. The investigator also prepares witnesses for their involvement in the trial process. Depending on an investigator's specialty, the responsibilities and requirements of a criminal investigator can range greatly. Some investigators specialize in certain types of crime such as fraud, domestic violence, sexual assaults, or robbery. |
| Crime Prevention | Crime prevention refers to both formal and informal actions intended to reduce the incidence of criminal activity. The police are involved in crime prevention programs and perform daily activities that deter crime. Organized crime prevention programs target specific types of crime (e.g., car break-ins in shopping mall parking lots) and specific groups (e.g., youth). |
| Law Enforcement | Police are empowered to enforce the laws by pursuing those who do not comply with them. Law enforcement is both proactive and reactive in nature and occurs on a daily basis in a random or targeted fashion. A RIDE stop is a form of targeted enforcement. |
| Maintenance of Public Order | Maintaining public order is a general requirement to ensure the safety and stability of society. This function can include a number of activities such as supervising a large crowd or responding to a noise complaint. |
| Emergency Response | Police respond to all types of emergencies including crimes in progress, medical emergencies, natural disasters, and accidents. These are high priority calls that are reactive in nature. |

Technology has had an impact on the versatility of the police on patrol.

will be visible and available to us as such. Patrol was identified by Sir Robert Peel as an essential element of policing in 1829 and it remains so today. Police patrol ensures that police are mobile and available to the public, as required. Patrol meets a number of important objectives that support the goals of crime prevention and maintaining the peace. Police patrol occurs in cars (marked or unmarked), on foot, on bike, on horseback, by helicopter, and by boat. Each type of patrol offers police a different perspective and level of engagement with the community. The relationship between police patrol and calls for service is that it is the patrol officers who respond to the calls. The time it takes to respond to a call is often used as an evaluation tool. Statistics indicate that approximately 15 percent of calls to police are of an urgent nature (crimes-in-progress or emergency), 55 percent are non-emergencies, such as minor crime that requires a police response. The remaining 30 percent are minor issues (often not criminal in nature) that do not require a police presence (Auditor General Report, 1992). As such, police departments manage their calls to maximize deployment of resources effectively.

There are a number of issues that are related to police patrol. The one-officer vs. two-officer patrol car has been the subject of debate over the years. The policy varies

### Policing Units

Police officers are initially trained to carry out the general functions and duties of a police officer. Once trained, they may be assigned to special units or divisions with the service. Many police officers have a diverse police career because of the many facets required to operate a police service. Specialized units or areas can include the following:

- Criminal Investigation
- Organized Crime
- Intelligence
- Mobile Support
- Sexual Assault and Threat Assessment
- Homicide
- Hold-Up
- Fraud
- Guns and Gangs
- Emergency Task Force
- Public Order
- Bike Unit
- Drug Squad
- Cyber-Crime
- Bomb Squad
- Mounted Unit
- Canine Unit
- Community Mobilization
- Forensic Identification
- Marine Unit
- Planning
- Education and Training
- Professional Standards
- Employment and Recruitment

Historically, dogs have supported police in various functions.

across North America, usually as negotiated in the labour agreement between police associations and the respective police service. Some police services deploy only one-officer vehicles, dispatching two or more vehicles to serious calls. Some departments will deploy both one- and two-officer vehicles, using one-officer cars up to a specific time of the night, when two-officer cars are then deployed. A study on officers killed while on vehicle patrol between 1961 and 2009 indicated that 54 percent were assigned to two-officer vehicles patrols, while 46 percent were assigned to one-officer vehicles (Dunn, 2009). Those who support two-officer cars cite concerns regarding officer safety and say that having a two-officer unit increases the efficiency of patrol (Frontier Centre, 2001), while at the same time having a positive impact on officer morale.

Foot patrol, one of the earliest forms of police patrol, has emerged as an important element of policing today. Foot patrols are now connected to community policing, enabling officers to meet community members and enhance community partnerships. Foot patrols can be engaged to support a proactive, problem-solving strategy where community relations are improved in an effort to prevent crime. Technology enables officers to engage in foot patrol with the flexibility of radio access. A successful foot patrol program is "more than just walking around. Specific planned programming and community engagement strategies must be incorporated into the process" (Craven, 2009). In addition, foot patrol is a sound environmental choice, an attractive attribute.

### COMMUNITY POLICING

Community policing is an approach that recognizes the partnership and shared responsibility for crime prevention that exists between the police and the community, and involves skills and abilities to engage communities in proactive problem solving. The police have traditionally assumed a leadership role in this area, making its success largely dependent upon their ability to provide leadership. Community policing balances reactive

## FOCUS ON Crime Stoppers: An International Success

Crime Stoppers is an international organization that facilitates a partnership between the public, the police, and the media. This proactive program encourages the general public to assist the police anonymously to solve crimes. In January, 2011, the program celebrated a total of $10 billion dollars in the value of recovered drugs and property. Crime Stoppers tips have resulted in 851,643 arrests, resulting in the clearance of 1,322,443 cases worldwide. Crime Stoppers describes the growth of this successful collaboration:

> Crime Stoppers was the brainchild of Canadian-born Greg MacAleese, a Detective with the Albuquerque Police Department in New Mexico. In 1976, Greg had run out of leads in a homicide investigation and out of frustration had appealed to the public for assistance. He went so far as to produce the first crime re-enactment, which was aired on local television, and also made available for radio and the press. Anyone providing information regarding this murder was to be eligible for a cash reward. Within hours of the broadcast, an individual called in valuable information that resulted in the arrest and conviction of two suspects who were sentenced to life in prison with no chance of parole. The growth has been dramatic with Crime Stoppers programs implemented in more than 1,300 communities worldwide. In November 1982, Calgary became the first Canadian city to start the program, followed by Edmonton in 1983. Hamilton was the first city in Ontario to implement the program and there are currently over 90 programs across Canada with over 10 programs in Ontario.

SOURCES: www.222tips.com; http://www.canadiancrimestoppers.org; http://www.opp.ca/ecms; http://crimestoppers.ns.ca/files/250362280.pdf; http://crimestoppers.ns.ca.

response with proactive problem solving that is intended to focus on the causes of crime. The Vancouver Police department defines community policing:

> Community policing is a police philosophy that involves problem solving with the assistance of the community. It has many forms: Block Watch, Citizens' Crime Watch and Community Policing Centres (CPCs) are all part of that philosophy.

Community policing projects strive to reduce crime in specific areas, with the cooperation of the community and the police. Generally, the goal of the projects is to empower communities to build the capacity to resist and prevent crime and disorder. This model sees the police and the community work together to support community-based projects that will prevent crime. Projects may be specific to certain groups within the community, such as students, newcomers, or children. The projects may target specific crimes, such as family violence, child abuse, or graffiti. The key message within the community policing perspective is the involvement of the community in problem solving that leads to crime prevention.

## LO5 POLICE RECRUITMENT, SELECTION, AND TRAINING

Police services devote a great deal of time and energy into recruiting, selecting, and training new officers. Recruitment is an on-going process, and in recent years police services have targeted areas where they could reach individuals who are not adequately represented in the current police strength. Women, Aboriginals, visible minorities, and people who speak more than one language are required to ensure that police services are able to represent the communities that they police. Once they meet basic employment qualifications, candidates are required to undergo a series of tests and assessments during the selection process, which assess their abilities based on identified police competencies required to be an effective police officer. Basic qualifications include age, fitness, moral character, driving ability, education, and eligibility to work in Canada. Though the minimum age for hire is 18, the reality is that very few new recruits are 18 years of age; in fact, the average hiring age for police constables is higher. The RCMP reports that the average hiring age of recruits is 27 years of age. (RCMP, 2012). The same holds true for education. Though the minimum educational requirement is a secondary school diploma, the reality is that most police recruits have post-secondary education. The competition is robust and police services can and do have high standards for selection that exceed the minimum requirements. Each police service is responsible for making its own hiring decisions; however, there is consistency in selection within provinces. Though the selection process may vary across the country, police services generally include testing and assessment in the following areas:

- aptitude testing,
- physical abilities testing,
- personal interview,
- psychological assessment,
- written communication abilities, and
- background assessment.

Training police officers begins at the recruit level but continues throughout their entire career. **Recruit training** is standardized training designed to ensure that all recruits meet a basic minimum requirement. Most recruit training occurs in a centralized location where new recruits have an opportunity to meet recruits from other jurisdictions. For example, the RCMP training occurs in Regina, at the Training Depot. New recruits are then given

**recruit training**

standardized, basic training for new officers

**JUST or BUST?**

Should the basic education requirement for police officers be increased to a post-secondary diploma or degree given the complex role that police play in our society?

an opportunity to engage in basic training with their home police service. This training may occur in class, in the field, or in both. A recruit who is engaged in **field training** does so under the supervision of a training officer. The training officer's role is to mentor new officers while they are involved in daily police activities with a view to providing guidance and information. Throughout their careers, police officers will engage in regular **in-service training**. In-service training refers to periodic training that officers receive in order to enhance and develop their skills. This training may prepare officers for assignment to a new unit or it may train them on new legislation or a new technology that will have an impact on their duties. A newly promoted officer may be required to develop supervisory or leadership skills. The role that training plays within a police organization is paramount because police rely on their training to deal with critical situations that can have a life or death outcome.

**field training**
training that occurs while on the job

**in-service training**
training during the course of one's career

Police services have had to adapt their recruitment strategies to meet the needs of policing within diverse communities to ensure that the services reflect that same diversity within their personnel. For example, Toronto has swelled to a population of almost 2.5 million people, many of whom are foreign-born. The 2006 Canadian census indicated that 46.9 percent of Toronto's population represents a visible minority, which translates into 1,162,630 people. Approximately 20 percent of Canada's immigrants settle in Toronto. It is projected that most of Toronto's population will consist of people who are visible minorities by the year 2012 (Census, 2006). The relationship between this kind of diversity and policing is significant and requires leadership that can overcome challenges related to communication, problem solving, and building community capacity in all areas.

Police services are no longer all Caucasian, male, and heterosexual. Managing this kind of diversity responsibly within the organization requires leadership and courage. The representation of visible minorities among Canadian police officers doubled between 1996 and 2006 (Juristat, 2008).

There has been an increase in the number of female officers across Canada. In 2010, there were 13,330 female officers; approximately 1 in 5 officers, compared to approximately 1 in 15 in 1990. The number of women in the senior ranks is 9 percent of senior officers and 15 percent of non-commissioned officers. The percentage of female constables has remained at about 21 percent since 2005 (Statistics Canada, 2010).

There have also been efforts made to attract Aboriginal people to policing. Aboriginal people represent 3 percent of the Canadian population 15 years of age and older, they represent 4 percent of police officers, and 5 percent of security personnel (Statistics Canada, 2010). Initiatives to attract more Aboriginal persons to policing include the RCMP's Aboriginal Cadet Program. This program, for Aboriginal persons from ages 19 to 29, is designed to give participants a taste of police work. It is a 17-week summer program that includes a three-week training program at the RCMP Training Academy. Once the basic training is completed, participants are posted to an RCMP detachment close to home, where they work with police on crime prevention and community policing initiatives.

## STRESS OF POLICE WORK

LO6

Police work has long been identified as a stressful occupation. Researchers have identified the sources of stress that affect police officers, and police services have make great strides in responding with ways to mitigate the stresses that police deal with on a regular basis. Police stress is often divided into two categories: **operational stresses** and **organizational stresses**. Operational stresses refers to stress that flows from officers' daily operations. In policing, the span of daily operations can vary from extreme boredom to a critical incident in a relatively short period of time.

**operational stresses**
refers to stress that flows from officers' daily operations

**organizational stresses**
refers to stress that comes from the police service itself, specifically the policies and practices of the organization

Operational stresses can include:

- dealing with difficult citizens,
- the threat of injury to self or others,

## MYTH VS FACT: Is Police Work Dangerous?

Policing is a high risk occupation, but how dangerous is it? According to Statistics Canada, the only occupation that is at higher risk of on-the-job homicide is being a taxi driver; they are twice as likely to be killed on the job as police officers (Dunn, 2009). Between 1961 and 2009, 133 police officers were murdered in the line of duty in Canada. Figure 3.1 indicates that the most dangerous situation for an officer to be in is investigating a robbery, followed by responding to a domestic dispute. Firearms were used in 92 percent of all officer homicides. Approximately one-third of officers drew or fired their weapons before being killed; the others did not have an opportunity to do so. It is also important to note that 80 percent of the slain officers were not wearing protective body armour; however, protective vests were not standard issue in the 1960s and 1970s. The slain officers were all relatively new to their police services, with an average of five years of experience, and an average age of 34. All but four of the officers were male. The clearance rate of police homicides, at 96 percent, is slightly higher than that of the general population, which is 84 percent (Dunn, 2009).

- witnessing tragic events (shootings, murder, suicide, accidents, death or injury to children, etc.),
- decisions regarding use of discretion,
- the threat of officer misconduct,
- dealing with the justice system and its imperfections,
- criticism by the public, the media, and politicians, and
- working undercover or in a specialty squad that requires personal sacrifice.

Organizational stresses refers to stress that comes from the police service itself, specifically the policies and practices of the organization. Police services are organizations that are under a great deal of stress from society overall to perform at a high level and to meet the expectations placed upon them. We expect our police services to be professional, leading-edge, efficient organizations. This pressure is passed on to every police officer who reports to work each day. Organizational stresses include living up to the expectations of one's supervisor and responding to the needs of the organization on a daily basis. In their study on police work and stress, Kohan and Mazmanian (2003) found that, overall, police officers experience more stress from organizational issues than operational ones. Patrol or front-line officers reported more operational stresses than organizational ones, while police supervisors and administrators reported feeling more stress from organizational stresses (Kohan and Mazmanian, 2003).

Shift work is an expectation for most police officers in law enforcement, corrections, and protective services, where approximately 50 percent of workers have unconventional schedules (Swenson, Waseleski and Hartl, 2008). Shift work has a negative impact on the officer, as it often results in a sleep deficit, which has an adverse affect on the officer's health, emotions, and cognition. Cumulative fatigue can affect police to the point where it impairs one's ability to engage in quality problem solving and decision making, critical skills for police officers (Swenson, Waeleski and Hartl, 2008). Some research has suggested that a lifetime of shift work may contribute to the onset of health problems such as high blood pressure, diabetes, anxiety, depression, and sleep disorders (Swenson, Waseleski and Hartl, 2008). Shift work poses a challenge not only for the officer, but also for the officer's family. Shift work means that officers are often out of sync with their families' daily schedules. It means that birthdays, holidays, and special occasions are often missed or celebrated differently. It also means that police families are required to be flexible to accommodate a shift working life. A police officer's family must adapt to the policing lifestyle in order to support the officer and to find a formula that works for them.

Police services have introduced a number of strategies to deal with police stress and to mitigate the potential impairment caused by shift work. Police services in Canada have access to employee assistance programs (EAP), which are intended to provide employees with resources to mitigate the stress of police work on both the employees and their families. The EAP includes professional guidance from psychologists and counsellors, and can also include peer counselling, where police officers are trained to support others.

**FIGURE 3.1 | Homicide Against Police Officers, by Type of Circumstance, Canada, 1961 to 2009**

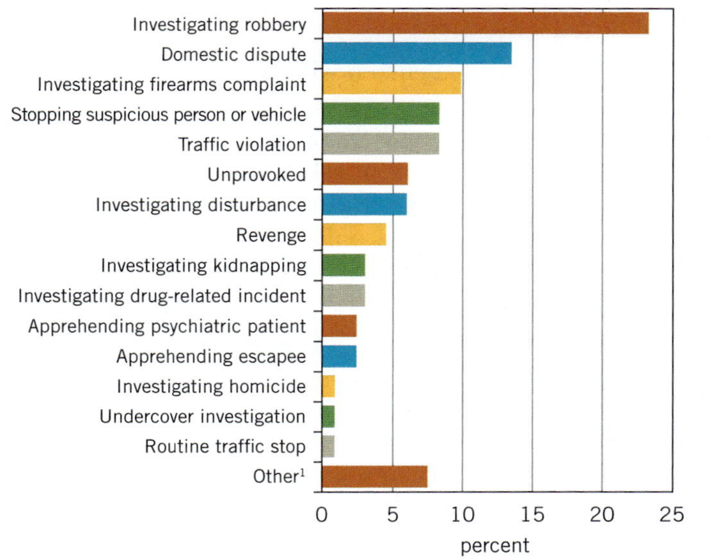


[1]. Includes all other situations not otherwise stated. For example, riot control, suicide situations, investigations of criminal incidents not listed above.

SOURCE: Statistics Canada, Canadian Centre for Justice Statistics, Homicide Survey. Homicide against police officers, by type of circumstance, Canada, 1961 to 2009, 29 March 2012. Reproduced and distributed on an "as is" basis with the permission of Statistics Canada.

## LO7 POLICE ACCOUNTABILITY AND OVERSIGHT

The oversight of police services begins with their own reporting structure. All municipal and regional police services are required to report to a **Police Services Board**. The board membership consists of both politicians and civilians. The board's size depends on the size of the municipality and can vary from three to seven members. Police boards are responsible for hiring the police chief, they create budgets, engage in collective bargaining, and they establish rules and regulations for the police service. Though they do not report to a police board, the RCMP, the Sûreté du Québec, and the OPP do report to a Cabinet Minister of the government in their jurisdiction. This Cabinet Minister is an elected official who represents the public.

Police accountability refers to the requirement of the police to provide an accounting of their ability to adhere to the laws and rules by which they are bound. Police are given extraordinary powers, unlike any other occupational group in our society. There is an expectation that these powers will be exercised in a responsible, judicious, and ethical manner. The responsibility for police oversight overlaps the community, the courts, and the police themselves. There are numerous processes and mechanisms in place that are designed to fulfill this role across Canada.

### POLICE INVESTIGATING THE POLICE

The first level of police accountability rests with the police service itself. Each police service has an internal process for dealing with civilian complaints as well as internal disciplinary matters. Civilian complaints are investigated internally by each police organization, and there are processes in place for civilians to launch complaints using processes external to the police.

Police services investigate police officer misconduct. The **Professional Standards** unit engages in internal investigations and reports its findings to the Chief of Police. The Chief of Police determines the appropriate disposition of a case, including using discipline if appropriate. There are situations where police will investigate another police service, as arranged in an agreement between the two services. This is usually in response to a specific incident. There is general criticism of the police investigating "their own," due to the lack of transparency in the process. For that reason, most jurisdictions also have a civilian model of oversight.

**Professional Standards**
a unit that engages in internal investigations and reports its findings to the Chief of Police

### CIVILIAN OVERSIGHT

Civilian oversight monitors police activities with a view to ensuring that police behaviour reflects the laws, and the rights and freedoms. The ability to address citizen complaints is a critical component of a democratic criminal justice system, and it is important that it be done in an impartial, transparent manner. In his 2005 report on the Police Complaints System in Ontario, the Honourable Patrick J. LeSage, Q.C., identified the critical nature of civilian oversight of police. He based his report on the following principles:

- the police are ultimately accountable to civilian authority;
- the public complaints system must be and seen to be fair, effective and transparent;
- any model of resolving public complaints about police should have the confidence of the public and the respect of the police; and
- the Province's responsibility for ensuring police accountability in matters of public safety and public trust must be preserved. (Lesage, 2005)

There are differences in the civilian oversight processes in each jurisdiction. However, the goal of each is to ultimately improve the relationship between the public and the police, by increasing public confidence. **Civilian review processes** offer complainants an opportunity to share their story with an independent investigator, confident that their complaint will be reviewed in an impartial manner. There are disadvantages to civilian oversight as well, including the need to train civilians on police procedure, the cost of using external experts, and the exclusion of the police, which has the potential to create a situation that undermines the police (Murphy and McKenna, 2010).

### SPECIAL INVESTIGATION UNIT IN ONTARIO

Ontario is the only province with a **Special Investigation Unit (SIU)**. The SIU is a civilian unit, established in 1990, independent of the police. The SIU investigates circumstances involving police and civilians that have resulted in serious injury, including sexual assault or death. The authority for the SIU is granted in Part VII of the *Ontario Police Services Act*. The SIU has the authority to investigate occurrences in Ontario involving municipal, regional, and provincial police officers. It has the power to investigate and to charge police officers with a criminal offence. In 2009–2010, the SIU investigated 287 occurrences, most of which involved injuries to persons while in police custody (SIU, 2010). The relationship between the police in Ontario and the SIU has been tense over the years, a fact that was highlighted when the Ontario Ombudsman released a report in 2011, entitled *Oversight Undermined*, which said that the government and the police routinely undermine the SIU. The report identifies specific examples where the SIU believes that the police did not cooperate to their satisfaction.

**Special Investigation Unit (SIU)**
a civilian unit, independent of the police, that investigates circumstances involving police and civilians that have resulted in serious injury

### CIVIL LAWSUITS

Occasionally a citizen will demand accountability of the police by launching a civil lawsuit. We have seen cases where citizens believe that the police, or other members of the criminal justice system, were negligent in the performance of their duties. In 1998, a woman, only identified as Jane Doe, launched a civil lawsuit against the Toronto Police Service. In 1986, Jane Doe was the fifth victim of a serial rapist in Toronto's downtown area. Her lawsuit was based on three grounds: negligence, a violation of her equality rights, and an infringement on her Charter right to security of the person. The facts of the case were that the police, aware of the rapes happening in the area where Jane Doe lived, did not warn women in the neighbourhood. The Judge said that the police owed the women in the area a duty of care and that the investigation into the balcony rapist was "… irresponsible and grossly negligent" (Doe *v.* Metropolitan Toronto (Municipality) Commissioners of Police, 1998). Jane Doe's lawsuit was successful; she received an award of $220,000. As a result of this case, a number of changes were made to the standards regarding the investigation of sexual assault cases.

### THE MEDIA AND POLICE ACCOUNTABILITY

The media play a significant role in exposing situations that question police accountability. We have seen a number of examples where the media have raised questions about police conduct and raised awareness and a call for further examination. Media exposure, including pictures and video, of police action during the G20 summit in Toronto in June, 2010, resulted in calls for sanctions against some police officers that were pictured in the media footage. The G20 weekend resulted in the largest

> While the police services budgets have increased, the crime rate in Canada has decreased.

number of arrests in Canadian history. There were 1,105 people arrested, 800 of whom were released without charge. The crowds consisted of peaceful demonstrators, as well as those who were engaged in vandalism that resulted in over $750,000 worth of property damage. In the aftermath of the weekend, there were complaints of police brutality, and pictures and videos surfaced that portrayed a number of officers engaging in aggressive behaviour. A number of reports resulted, including one authored by the Ontario Ombudsman.

Numerous public commissions and reviews have been created in recent history to analyze policing overall or specific elements of police activity, usually related to a problematic event or case. Such commissions are intended to examine police action with a view to making recommendations that lead to improvement. Examples of such commissions include:

- Report on the Police Complaints System in Ontario (Patrick LeSage, Q.C., 2005)
- The Missing Women Commission of Inquiry (regarding the Robert William Pickton case)
- Bernardo Investigation Review (Mr. Justice Archie Campbell, 1996)
- Royal Commission of Inquiry into Certain Deaths at the Hospital for Sick Children and Related Matters (Mr. Justice Samuel Grange, 1984)
- The Night the City Became a Stadium: Independent Review of 2011 Vancouver Stanley Cups Playoffs Riot
- Sharing Common Ground: Review of Yukon's Police Force, 2010

## COST AND EVALUATION OF POLICING

LO8

The cost of providing policing to communities in Canada is a financial challenge. In 2010, the cost of policing in Canada was approximately $12.6 billion, which amounts to about $365 per citizen (Statistics Canada, 2011). Police services budgets across Canada have increased steadily due to an increase in officer strength; the majority of budgets is spent on police salaries and benefits. While the budgets have increased, the crime rate in Canada has decreased. Given that most Canadians are content with the policing services that they receive (General Social Survey, 2004), there appears to be an acceptance, on the part of the public, that the price paid for policing is money that is well spent.

One way of measuring police service workload and productivity is by examining the number of *Criminal Code* incidents the service, and each officer within the service, processes each year. For example, in 2009, police-reported data indicated that police officers across Canada engaged in 2,161,313 criminal incidents. Each officer in Canada, on average, handled 32.1 criminal incidents. This type of reporting can be misleading because there is a large variation in the type and complexity of criminal incidents and the work that each entails.

Clearance rate is another way to measure police productivity. The clearance rate refers to the number of cases that police solve, or otherwise discharge, in a given period. A case is cleared by charge, when a suspect is charged of committing an offence. An offence may also be cleared if it is determined that the police

Julian Fantino, former Commissioner of the OPP, meets with members of the media.

have a suspect but there is not enough evidence to charge the person. Canada's clearance rate has been steadily increasing over the past five years. In 2010, the clearance rate—which is adjusted to account for the severity of the crime—was 39 (Statistics Canada, 2011). By accounting for the severity of the crime, a serious crime such as homicide or robbery receives a higher rate because of the time and effort required to clear the offence. The clearance rate of 39 indicates that 39 percent of all reported offences were cleared by charge or other form of clearance. The clearance rates vary based on the type of offence. Certain offences typically have a higher clearance rate than others. For example, violent offences tend to have the highest clearance rates. Clearance rate is affected by the number of victims and witnesses to a crime, as well as by the swiftness of the original report. The clearance rate for violent crimes in 2004 was 69 percent, while the clearance rate for property offences was significantly lower at 20 percent.

Measuring the level of fear in a community is another way of determining whether the police are doing a good job, according to the public. When a community has a high level of fear of crime, there is generally a lower level of trust and confidence in the police. According to the General Social Survey (2004), 82 percent of Canadians felt "a great deal or a lot" of confidence in the police. Overall, 94 percent of Canadians reported that they were either somewhat satisfied or very satisfied with their personal safety. When asked if they believe that local police are doing a good job of enforcing the laws, 59 percent of surveyed Canadians said yes. When asked if they believe that the police respond promptly to calls, the number drops to 52 percent support. Sixty-one percent of those surveyed said that they believe the police are doing a good job of ensuring the safety of citizens in Canada (General Social Survey, 2004).

## LO9 THE ROLE OF PRIVATE SECURITY IN CANADA

Private security officers in Canada are individuals who are hired to provide security services for privately funded businesses and organizations. Unlike public police, the private officers are hired to protect private property, much of which is used by the public. Private security officers secure areas such as sports venues, shopping malls, and businesses. Private security officers and investigators have existed in Canada for many years, meeting various needs that could not be met by their public counterparts. According to Statistics Canada, there are three people employed in the private security industry for every police officer in Canada. The private security industry continues to grow in size and influence (Statistics Canada, 2010). The appeal of private security is the fact that by using private security an organization can meet its specific needs. For example, a company can employ private security officers to focus on internal crime. Such incidents may then be reported to the public police for formal charges and movement through the criminal justice system.

Historically, the private security industry has been inconsistent with regards to standards and training. More recently there have been steps taken to move toward consistency and professionalism within the industry. Mandatory training in private security is a recent development, which aims to increase the professionalization of the field. Several provinces require that security officers and private investigators be trained, examined, and licensed in order to work.

Statistics Canada makes some of the differences between the public police and private security personnel very clear. Personnel in private security services represent greater diversity. There are more visible minorities, more women, and a greater age span among the people who work within private security. The salary and benefits within the private security industry is not standardized, but is generally significantly less than that of the

PROFILE

### Patrick Shand Inquest

In 1999, Patrick Shand, 31, died while being apprehended by two store employees and a security guard at a Loblaws store in Toronto's Agincourt Mall. Shand, suspected of shoplifting, was held on the ground, face down. An inquest into the death followed in 2004 and recommendations were made that addressed the lack of training for the security guard in this situation and the entire security industry. The recommendations made by this jury were the impetus that led to licensing and mandatory training of security personnel in Ontario. Several other provinces already required security guards to have mandatory training.

SOURCE: Shand Inquest jury recommendations, http://www.policingsecurity.ca/shand%20inquest%20rec.pdf.

public police. Public police earn about one and a half times the amount of private investigators and more than twice the amount of security guards. Police officers generally have higher levels of education than private security personnel. In 2006, 55 percent of private investigators and 37 percent of security had completed college certification, compared to 75 percent of police officers (Li, 2008).

**informed consent**

you understand what is being asked of you, and you are aware of your right to refuse.

### POWERS OF PRIVATE SECURITY OFFICERS

Private security officers must perform their duties with no more authority than an ordinary citizen. Private security officers may make a citizen's arrest when they witness a criminal on or relative to the property that they are authorized to protect. It is also possible for them to make a citizen's arrest if they see someone running from a person who has authority to make an arrest, such as a police officer. The powers of arrest that all citizens have are identified in the *Criminal Code*:

494 (1) Any one may arrest without warrant
- (a) a person whom he finds committing an indictable offence; or
- (b) a person who, on reasonable grounds, he believes
- (c) has committed a criminal offence, and
- (d) is escaping from and freshly pursued by persons who have lawful authority to arrest that person.

(2) Any one who is
- (a) the owner or a person in lawful possession of property, or
- (b) a person authorized by the owner or by a person in lawful possession of property, may arrest without a warrant a person whom he finds committing a criminal offence on or in relation to that property.

(3) Any one other than a peace officer who arrests a person without warrant shall forthwith deliver the person to a peace officer.

This section of the *Criminal Code* makes it clear that the citizen's power of arrest is limited to specific situations. It also clearly states that once a citizen's arrest is made, a police officer must intervene to conclude the process. New legislation for Reforming Citizen's Power of Arrest, Bill C-26, is currently being considered by Canadian legislators.

Private security guards have no authority to search someone without his or her permission unless they have conducted a citizen's arrest. In conducting a citizen's arrest the search must be limited to a "pat-down" search for weapons or for evidence that directly relates to the reason the person was arrested. There are a number of situations where we give our consent to be searched by private security guards. This is referred to as **informed consent** and is often required to enter entertainment or sporting events where a condition of entry is that patrons consent to being searched.

## IN THE NEWS

### Citizen's Arrest in Chinatown

Perhaps one of the most well-known citizen's arrests occurred in Toronto in May, 2009, when grocer David Chen chased down shoplifter Anthony Bennett. Chen was charged and subsequently acquitted of forcible confinement for his actions. Bennett, who served 42 days in jail before trial, received a three-year suspended sentence and he was banned from Toronto's Chinatown neighbourhood for three years.

## Chapter Summary

This chapter provided an introduction to policing in Canada. The key concepts included:

- Canadian policing evolved from our ties with Great Britain and the principles of Sir Robert Peel.
- Policing in Canada is multi-jurisdictional—there are federal, provincial, and municipal police agencies.
- The *Charter of Rights and Freedoms*, the *Criminal Code of Canada*, and other pieces of federal, provincial, and municipal legislation govern the police.
- The police engage in various functions, all of which can vary depending on the needs of the community. General police functions include criminal investigation, crime prevention, law enforcement, maintaining public order, emergency response, and providing assistance and information to victims and citizens.
- There are several forms of police accountability and oversight.
- The role of private security officers in Canada is increasing, far exceeding the number of public police. The powers of private security officers and the context within which they can be applied were identified.

## Relevant Legislation

Canadian *Charter of Rights and Freedoms. Constitution Act, 1982*, Part I.

*Criminal Code*, RSC 1985, c C-46

## Key Terms

Civilian review processes
Clearance rate
Crime rate
Discretion
Field training
In-service training
Informed consent
Operational stresses
Organizational stresses
Police Services Board
Professional Standards
Pursuit
Recruit training
Special Investigation Unit (SIU)

## For Review

1. Which of Sir Robert Peel's principles are relevant to modern day policing?
2. Why would a province or a territory choose to purchase policing services from the RCMP?
3. What powers of arrest does a security guard have?
4. What are some of the factors that contribute to the stress of policing?
5. What are the challenges that the police face with regards to recruitment and training?
6. What is the relationship between CSIS and the police services in Canada?
7. What is the significance of section 1 of the *Charter* as it relates to the application of police powers?

## Thinking Critically

1. Why is it important that our police services reflect the diversity of the communities that they serve?
2. Training police is critical—what are the implications of inadequate training?
3. Do you believe that there are sufficient safeguards to balance the powers of the police?
4. What role and responsibility do you believe individual communities should take on with regards to crime prevention?
5. If you were required to cut the police budget, where would you begin?
6. To what do you attribute the growth of private security in Canada? Do you think it will continue to grow in future?
7. How do you think advances in technology will change policing in the future?
8. How do you, as a citizen, know if your police service is doing a good job?

Mc Graw Hill connect™ | **Practise and learn online with Connect**

CHAPTER 4

# Criminal Courts

The Supreme Court of Canada was designed by Montreal architect, Ernest Cormier. There are two flagstaffs in front of the building. One is hoisted daily and the other flies only when the court is sitting.

## The Victims of Charles Smith: Re-victimized

Charles Smith, a former paediatric pathologist, worked at the Hospital for Sick Children in Toronto where he conducted approximately 1,000 child autopsies over 24 years. In 2007, an Ontario coroner's inquiry reviewed 45 of Smith's child autopsies and determined that he had made serious mistakes by concluding that criminal conduct had resulted in the deaths of 20 children, 13 of which resulted in criminal convictions. These findings led to a public inquiry that resulted in disturbing conclusions about Smith's professional conduct and abilities. The inquiry, led by Justice Stephen Goudge, revealed that Smith misled, made false statements, and often exaggerated his expertise in trials, and made mistakes by attributing the deaths of children to the criminal conduct of caregivers, usually the parents. He made decisions and expressed opinions that were not supported by evidence, seriously compromising the administration of justice. Many of these cases have been reviewed and convictions have been overturned.

### LEARNING OBJECTIVES

By the end of this chapter, you should be able to:

- **LO1** Describe the structure of the court system, and the role and significance of each level of criminal courts in Canada.
- **LO2** Identify the key players in the criminal court process.
- **LO3** Describe the basic procedure of a criminal trial and the flow of a criminal case from arrest to appeal.
- **LO4** Describe the options for diverting criminal cases from the traditional court system.
- **LO5** Identify several challenges that face the criminal court system.

Several parents were not only imprisoned as a result of the faulty autopsy conclusions, but in some cases their other children were also removed from their custody, temporarily or permanently. Tammy Marquardt was imprisoned for 14 years for the wrongful conviction of the murder of her two-year-old son, Kenneth. Smith determined that Marquardt had smothered her son, a charge that she always denied. At the time of her imprisonment she lost custody of her two other sons who were subsequently put up for adoption. She has lost contact with both of them.

Though he has not practiced since 2008, the Ontario College of Physicians and Surgeons stripped Smith of his medical license in 2011 when he pleaded no contest to charges of disgraceful conduct. The families that were affected have been offered compensation by the Ontario government. The experience of these families was tragic because not only did they lose a child, they went on to be re-victimized by being wrongfully convicted of the deaths of their children.

Tammy Marquardt.

Charles Smith, former pathologist.

## LO1 The Courts in the Criminal Justice System

It is through the courts that Canadians seek, and often find, answers to questions and resolutions to conflicts that guide us. Our courts provide leadership by making decisions that set standards regarding behaviour, societal expectations, and quality of life. They aspire for justice, search for truth, and often settle for resolution. It is in the courts that guilt and innocence are determined and where sentences are imposed. It is also the role of the court to interpret the law. Our democratic system gives the courts the right to both prosecute and protect on many different levels. In this chapter we will examine Canadian courts with a view to understanding their function, their purpose, and the obstacles that challenge their effectiveness.

### THE STRUCTURE OF THE COURT SYSTEM

The *Constitution Act, 1867*, determines the structure of Canada's court system. This piece of legislation divides the authority for the judicial system between the federal and the provincial governments.

The federal government has the authority to create "a General Court of Appeal for Canada, and for the Establishment of any additional Courts for the better Administration of the Laws of Canada." The federal government administers the Supreme Court of Canada, and appoints judges to superior courts and provincial courts of appeal.

The provinces and territories administer justice for both civil and criminal law. This includes "the Constitution, Maintenance, and Organization of Provincial Courts." The provinces and territories also have the authority to appoint judges to provincial courts, as well as authority over the constitution, organization, and maintenance of their superior courts. This federal/provincial/territorial collaboration also ensures that the administration of justice is consistent across Canada.

The court system in Canada is structured on four levels (see Figure 4.1). Each of the levels represents a different jurisdiction of law. Each court level has the authority to adjudicate certain types of cases or issues.

### PROVINCIAL/TERRITORIAL COURTS

Most of the criminal cases heard in Canada are heard in the provincial and territorial courts. Each

FIGURE 4.1 The Court System in Canada

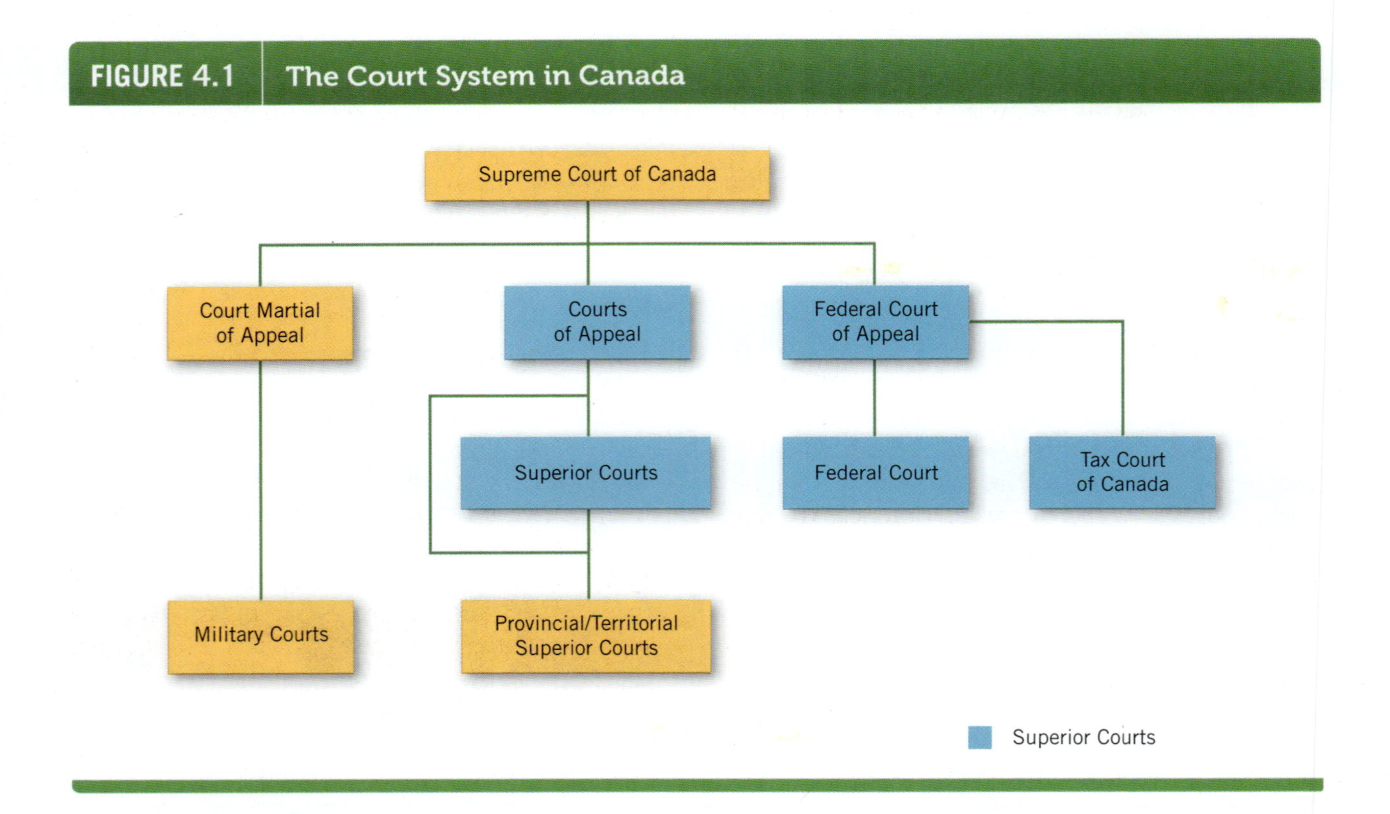

The view of downtown Vancouver from the steps of the British Columbia Provincial Court.

province and territory in Canada administers its own court system, with the exception of Nunavut where all cases are heard by a single, unified court—the Nunavut Court of Justice, a superior court. The first level, provincial and territorial courts, is often referred to as lower court as these courts make decisions related to provincial laws and those federal laws that the federal government gives them the authority to hear.

It is at this level that the process begins for all criminal cases in Canada, where all accused persons will make a first appearance whether it is a bail court, a trial court, or any other specialized court.

## SPECIALIZED PROVINCIAL/TERRITORIAL COURTS

Specialized provincial and territorial courts were created to be more responsive to offenders and victims with special needs and challenges. In the recent past we have seen specialized courts emerge that deal with cases related to mental health, substance abuse, and domestic violence. We have also seen courts emerge that deal specifically with the unique needs of the Aboriginal population. These courts are sometimes referred to as "problem solving" courts, as they are intended to not only deal with the criminal case at hand but also to work to prevent this type of offence from occurring again in the future, usually by supporting the offender with assistance of some type. Judges, prosecutors, lawyers, and clinicians are trained to deal specifically with the issues that arise in the specialized courts.

### MENTAL HEALTH COURT

Canada's first mental health court began in Toronto in May, 1998. The emergence of the mental health court was in direct response to a need to deal more effectively with the growing numbers of individuals with mental illnesses who were entering the criminal court system. The objectives of the court are identified as: to deal in an expedient manner with pre-trial issues regarding fitness to stand trial, and to make an effort to prevent the repeated reoffending and reappearance in court of mentally ill persons. In addition to providing a court that understands the issues related to mentally ill persons, this court assists offenders with discharges into the community, minimizing custodial remands.

Diversion of mentally ill offenders need not occur within a mental health court. In jurisdictions across Canada, mentally ill offenders may be diverted from the criminal court system. Such programs intend to connect the offenders with the mental health system, rather than the criminal justice system, while at the same time ensuring the safety of the offender, any victims, and the public.

### DOMESTIC VIOLENCE COURTS

Dealing with domestic violence cases in the courts has been problematic for many years.

The traditional court system has proven to be ill-equipped to deal with domestic violence cases because of the complexity of the cases. The criminal justice system is, for the most part, focused on an outcome of an isolated incident. Domestic violence is not a single-incident offence that can be remedied with a court outcome. The issues are complicated, usually long-term, and often involve collateral processes about custody of children, divorce, and financial support (Ursel, Tutty and Lemaistre, 2008). There are numerous cases of domestic violence that have resulted in serious injury or death. It became clear that the traditional approach to domestic violence cases was not enough to prevent the behaviour from being repeated nor did it protect women from being seriously injured or murdered.

In response, a number of domestic violence courts have been created across Canada. The first domestic violence court in Canada began in Toronto in 1997. An inquest into the death of Arlene May, a Collingwood, Ontario woman and mother of five, who was killed by her ex-boyfriend, Randy Isles, is believed to have been a catalyst for creating the court in Ontario (Ursel et al., 2008) which has expanded to all of Ontario's 55 jurisdictions. The goal of the court is to provide support to victims and to ensure that offenders who abuse their partners are held accountable for their actions. The court is staffed by Crown attorneys who received special training on the social, psychological, and legal issues specific to domestic violence. The court's effectiveness was assessed in 2008, and it was determined that of the 387 cases prosecuted, 81 percent resulted in a conviction, either through a trial or a guilty plea (Ursel et al., 2008).

## FOCUS ON The Use of Closed Circuit Television to Appear in Courts

Many accused persons now appear in court through the use of closed-circuit television, an innovation that saves time and money. Accused persons can appear before the court while remaining in the correctional facility.

In 2000, a dedicated domestic violence court was established in Calgary, Alberta. The HomeFront program focuses on the first-appearance court where low-risk accused persons have an opportunity to have their charges stayed with a **peace bond**. In order to qualify for the program, they must acknowledge responsibility for their behaviour and then participate in court-mandated domestic violence counselling. The goal is to intervene quickly and provide conditions that will prevent the behaviour from recurring, as well as ensure the victim's safety. Domestic violence courts also exist in Yukon and Manitoba.

**peace bond**
a written promise to the court to keep the peace

### DRUG TREATMENT COURTS

Drug treatment courts (DTC) operate across Canada with a view to reducing crimes committed as a result of drug dependency, through court-monitored treatment and community service support for offenders. The philosophy of the drug treatment courts is that by attacking the root cause of crime—in this case, drug use—we eventually reduce crime. Drug treatment court participants attend a structured outpatient program that includes individual and group counselling, and appropriate medical attention, which includes methadone if required. The participants are also subject to random drug testing. In addition, the participants must appear before the judge on a regular basis, as required. Participants who are unsuccessful in the program are returned to court and sentenced on the original offence in a traditional court.

There are now six DTCs operating in Canada: Toronto (December 1998), Vancouver (December 2001), Edmonton (December 2005), Winnipeg (January 2006), Ottawa (March 2006), and Regina (October 2006).

### COURTS FOR ABORIGINAL PERSONS

Courts for Aboriginal persons in Canada are sometimes referred to as "Gladue" courts. This is because on April 23, 1999, the Supreme Court of Canada made a decision that had an impact on the manner in which Aboriginal offenders are sentenced, in the case of R v. Gladue. The Supreme Court said Canada relied on incarceration more so than other countries, and that this over-reliance

The Gladue Court at Toronto's Old City Hall sits all day on Wednesdays and Fridays.

was a problem with the general population but was of much greater concern when sentencing Aboriginal Canadians. The Supreme Court said:

> The figures are stark and reflect what may fairly be termed a crisis in the Canadian criminal justice system. The drastic overrepresentation of aboriginal peoples within both the Canadian prison population and the criminal justice system reveals a sad and pressing social problem. (R. *v.* Gladue [1999] 1 S.C.R. 688)

The message from the Supreme Court was loud and clear—special consideration should be given to Aboriginal persons regarding sentencing. In response to the Gladue decision, the Gladue courts were created. The goal of the court is to respond to the unique circumstances of Aboriginal persons accused of criminal offences. The first Aboriginal court in Canada was the Tsuu T'ina First Nation Court in Alberta; there is a Cree-speaking court in North Saskatchewan. Gladue courts may also use traditional forms of dispute resolution, including sentencing circles.

### COURTS FOR YOUNG OFFENDERS

Courts for young offenders, which are administered under the *Youth Criminal Justice Act*, are also an example of a specialized provincial court. The youth courts are examined in detail in the Youth Justice chapter of the text.

### PROVINCIAL/TERRITORIAL SUPERIOR COURTS

The second level of courts is the provincial/territorial superior courts. The superior courts adjudicate serious criminal cases and hear appeals from the provincial/territorial courts. These courts hear civil cases as well.

### PROVINCIAL/TERRITORIAL COURTS OF APPEAL

The provincial/territorial courts of appeal hear the appeals from the superior court of that province or territory. The appeal panel usually consists of three judges, though that may be increased if it is determined that the case requires the consideration of additional judges.

## THE FEDERAL COURTS

The federal courts adjudicate only those cases that are specified in federal legislation. The federal court deals with disputes between provinces or territories as well as disputes between the provinces/territories and the federal government. Intellectual property, citizenship appeals, the *Competition Act*, and cases involving federal Crown corporations such as Canada Post are also heard in the federal court. Federal court decisions can be appealed to the Federal Court of Appeal, and then to the final court of Appeal, the Supreme Court of Canada.

## SPECIALIZED FEDERAL COURTS

There are several courts in Canada that deal with specialized areas of law. The Tax Court of Canada was established in 1983, and only hears disputes between Canadian taxpayers and the federal government related to federal taxation. An example is a dispute between a taxpayer and the Canada Revenue Agency regarding the person's annual tax return. This court is independent from the Canada Revenue Agency to ensure that it is impartial.

The Court Martial Appeal Court of Canada hears cases that originate from the *National Defence Act* and the *Criminal Code*. Military tribunals, called courts martial, are established under the *National Defence Act*. They hear cases that contravene the Code of Service Discipline, which applies to all members of the Canadian Forces and civilians on active service. The Supreme Court of Canada hears appeals from the Court Martial Appeal Court.

## THE SUPREME COURT OF CANADA

The Supreme Court of Canada is the final court of appeal in Canada. It hears cases from all areas of law including criminal, constitutional, and civil law. It is the national court of last resort and the highest court in Canada. Its mandate is "to advance the cause of justice in hearing and deciding, as the final arbiter, legal questions of fundamental importance" (www.scc-csc.gc.ca).

The Supreme Court is located in Ottawa, Ontario, and presides over cases in the fall, winter, and spring sessions. A case is heard at the Supreme Court level only when it has exhausted all appeal opportunities in lower courts. In order for a case to be heard in the Supreme Court, an application is submitted in writing, and is reviewed by three judges who will then grant or deny permission, along with their reasons for the decision. The granting of permission is referred to as "leave" to appeal. Only cases that are considered to be of significant importance are given **leave to appeal**—cases that raise important issues for Canadians. There are a number of situations where there is an automatic right to appeal, such as when a lower court of appeal has found someone guilty who had been acquitted at the original trial. In this case, the person automatically has the right to appeal to the Supreme Court. In criminal cases where a judge in the court of appeal disagrees on how the law should be interpreted, there is also an automatic right to appeal to the Supreme Court.

**leave to appeal**

the granting of permission to hear an appeal in the Supreme Court of Canada

In addition to hearing appeal cases, the Supreme Court of Canada may also be consulted by the federal government to interpret Constitutional or other legal matters. This consultation role is identified in section 53 of the *Supreme Court Act*. The Governor-in-Council may refer to the court for its opinion on important questions of law or fact concerning any matter.

Decisions made by the Supreme Court are precedent-setting and applicable throughout Canada. There is no appeal from a decision made by the Supreme Court of Canada.

The Supreme Court judges are appointed by the federal government. There is a Chief Justice and eight others, including three who, by

Supreme Court of Canada Justices Front row, left to right: Justices Morris Fish, Louis LeBel, Chief Justice Beverley McLachlin, Marie Deschamps, Rosalie Abella. Back row, left to right: Michael Moldaver, Marshall Rothstein, Thomas Cromwell, and Andromche Karakatsanis.

Should a defendant be permitted to represent himself/herself in a criminal trial?

legislation, must come from Quebec. It is usual that all nine judges will sit together when hearing cases; however, a minimum of five is required.

## LO2 The Players in the Criminal Court System

> "Law: the only game where the best players get to sit on the bench"
>
> AUTHOR UNKNOWN

### THE JUDICIARY

The judiciary preside over court proceedings with a view to ensuring that they are fair and just. It is the role of the justice in each court to ensure that the rule of law is followed. In many ways, the justice is the guardian of the legal process. The judiciary also educate the public and make laws through their decisions.

The federal, provincial, and territorial governments appoint judges. To be appointed to a Superior, Federal, or Supreme court, a lawyer must have been practising law for a minimum of 10 years. An appointment to a provincial/territorial court requires that the candidate be able to practise law in that jurisdiction. Though they have not received specific judicial training, candidates have trained throughout their legal careers by practising law.

There are two pieces of legislation that address the role that judges play in our country. They are the *Judges Act* and the *Consolidation of Constitution Acts, 1867 to1982*.

### JUDICIAL INDEPENDENCE

The Constitution clearly states that judicial independence is a critical feature of our justice system. Independence from all levels of government, and the political parties that they represent, is intended to ensure that judges are able to serve on the bench and make decisions that are free from influence of any type. This freedom allows them to make decisions based on law and fact, without political or financial consequences. A judge is eligible to serve on the bench until the age of retirement in his or her jurisdiction. This is referred to as **security of tenure**. It is important that judges be paid sufficiently to support the notion that they not be in a financial position that would subject them to pressure. Judges also have an element of administrative independence, which ensures that only judges determine how courts exercise judicial functions. This type of independence prevents outside influences from "judge shopping," since only the chief justice assigns individual cases to judges.

> **security of tenure**
>
> a judge is eligible to serve on the bench until the age of retirement in the jurisdiction

Judicial oversight happens in a number of ways. The Judicial Council in each jurisdiction promotes professional standards and develops policies and codes of conduct for judges. Councils have the power to recommend the termination of a judge's tenure, though it is a rare occurrence. The role of the Canadian Judicial Council is to oversee all federally appointed judges. The Council also investigates complaints and allegations of misconduct. Ethical principles are critical for judges, as their independence and impartiality are critical.

### ETHICAL PRINCIPLES OF JUDGES FROM THE CANADIAN JUDICIAL COUNCIL

1. Judges must exercise their judicial functions independently and free of extraneous influence.
2. Judges must firmly reject any attempt to influence their decisions in any matter before the Court outside the proper process of the Court.
3. Judges should encourage and uphold arrangements and safeguards to maintain

**FIGURE 4.2** Common Seating Arrangement in Criminal Courts

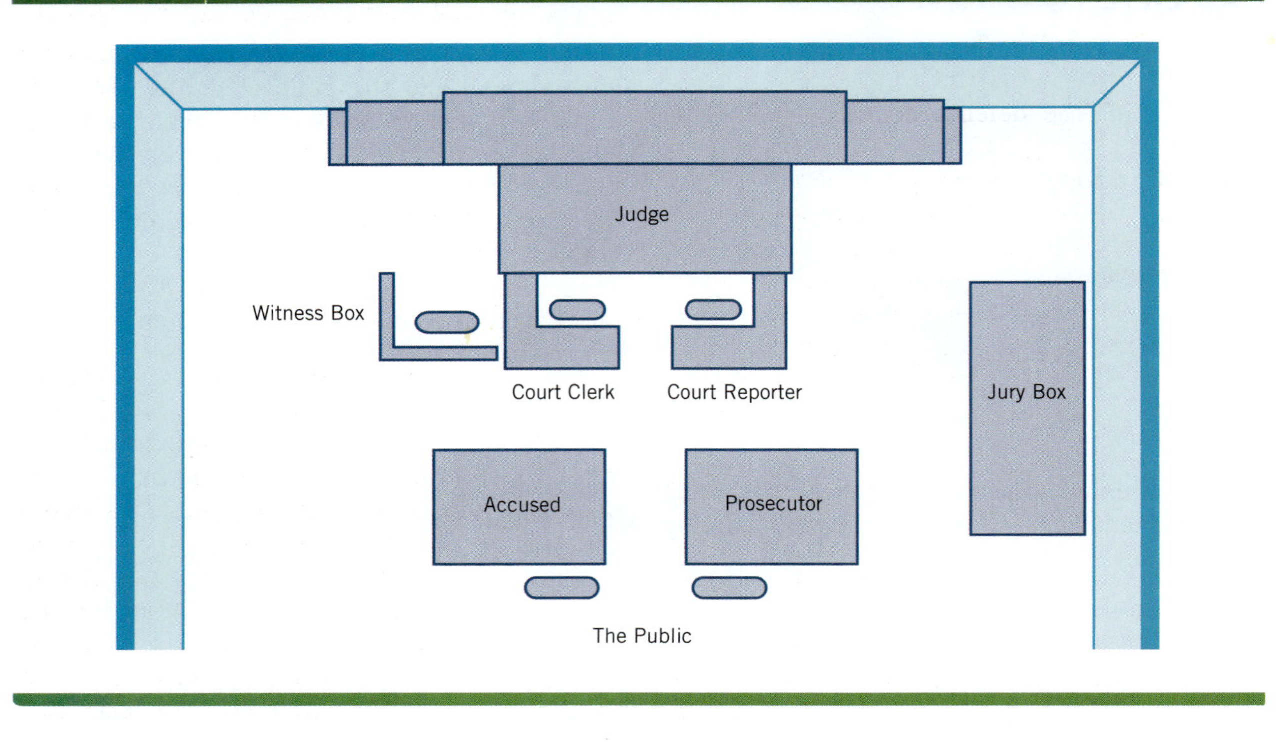


and enhance the institutional and operational independence of the judiciary.

4. Judges should exhibit and promote high standards of judicial conduct so as to reinforce public confidence which is the cornerstone of judicial independence.

(Canadian Judicial Council, 2004)

## THE LAWYERS

### THE CROWN PROSECUTOR

The lawyers that appear before the court represent the adversarial nature of our criminal justice system. The Crown prosecutor (often referred to as the Crown) represents the government, and therefore the people of Canada, in each Canadian jurisdiction. It is the role of the Crown to present the criminal case before the court. This involves working with the police to prepare a case for court and then presenting the case in court. This process includes making assessments related to evidence. Crown prosecutors are involved in interviewing and preparing witnesses for trial. They are charged with reviewing the evidence with a view to determining if a specific case should proceed to trial. It is the office of the Crown that makes final decisions about whether or not a case will proceed to trial. The Crown can make the decision before or after the police have laid charges. If the Crown decides not to pursue a criminal case then one of the following may occur:

- charges may be withdrawn;
- the case is dismissed as a result of no evidence offered in court; or
- a request is made to adjourn the case until a further date.

The decision to proceed with a criminal case is not taken lightly, because of the consequences of a case that proceeds without sufficient evidence. Not only is prosecuting a defendant costly, it is also potentially devastating for the defendant if that prosecution is determined to be wrongful or malicious.

The Crown prosecutor role is expansive. They must represent the governments' case in all courts, at all levels. In addition, they are expected to be able to prosecute a variety of types of cases, though we have recently seen some specialization through the use of specialized courts. Their caseloads are often very high, which has an impact on their ability to research and prepare cases. The people of Canada put their trust and faith in the Crown to serve with integrity while maintaining high professional standards.

### THE DEFENCE LAWYERS

Defence lawyers represent the accused in the criminal trial. The defence counsel's role is to ensure that the legal rights of the accused are protected throughout the process. Defence counsel is concerned with both the process and the substance of the case with a view to ensuring that the fundamentals of justice are upheld. Since our system is adversarial, it is often perceived that because defence counsel represents the accused there is an inherent conflict between the defence and the police. The role of the defence is to prepare a case that questions the Crown prosecutor's case. That may involve calling into question all aspects of the case, including the role and the actions of the police. If the accused is convicted, the role of defence counsel continues through sentencing. Defence may argue for a lighter sentence and may also ask for conditions that will be helpful to the accused. Lower-income Canadians who cannot afford legal counsel may qualify for provincial or territorial programs that provide legal assistance. The programs generally insist that clients meet a specific income requirement.

## THE POLICE

The police play the biggest role in the criminal court trial prior to the commencement of the trial. Through their investigation, the police collect and document most of the evidence and prepare the case to be presented to the Crown. The strength of the case is related to the diligence and integrity of the investigation. The police are in regular communication with the Crown prosecutor during the trial. The police are also often witnesses for the Crown in criminal cases in order to present the evidence that they uncovered during the investigation.

## THE VICTIM

The role of the victim within a criminal trial varies depending on the type of trial. Often the victim is called to be a witness for the Crown. In addition, victims are included in the sentencing stage of a criminal case, when they may present a victim impact statement to the court. It may be prepared in writing and submitted to the court or it may be presented in any other manner that the court deems appropriate. The impact that the crime has had on the victim is taken into consideration when the defendant is being sentenced (*Criminal Code*, s. 722).

## THE PUBLIC

There are a number of ways in which members of the community may become involved within the criminal justice system. One of the ways is by serving on a jury in a criminal or civil trial. Jury

Police gather evidence during their investigation as part of the case preparation process.

duty is one of the few legal obligations that is imposed on citizens. There is an expectation that members of the public will participate in the justice system as a jury member, even though it may be an inconvenience. Jurors are expected to represent the general population within a jurisdiction, and they are expected to be impartial and competent. Jurors are selected from a pool of juror candidates who have been randomly selected to appear in court. Being selected to join the pool of jurors does not guarantee that one will be selected to serve as a juror. There is a process for jury selection that varies by province/territory.

Members of the general public may be called on to appear as witnesses in criminal proceedings. They may be required to give evidence or appear as an **expert witness** where they speak to a specialized topic. A witness is usually summoned to appear in court by subpoena. People who do not respond to subpoenas may face a penalty imposed by the court.

**expert witness**

someone who has specialized knowledge in a given area and is entitled to provide opinion evidence during the proceedings (*Canada Evidence Act*, s. 7)

The public is involved with the criminal law simply based upon the expectation that it is aware of the laws. People are not expected to have legal expertise, but there is a duty to know the law. Laws are publicly debated and pronounced when passed. Ignorance of the law is not a defence or an excuse, which means that there is a belief that citizens "ought to know" the current laws of the jurisdiction in which they live (Department of Justice, 2005).

With few exceptions, courts are open to the public. As such, members of the public are free to be spectators in criminal proceedings. This openness ensures that there is an element of transparency and accountability. Section 11(d) of the *Charter of Rights and Freedoms* states:

> Any person charged with an offence has the right to be presumed innocent until proven guilty according to law in a fair and public hearing by an independent and impartial tribunal.

The interpretation of a public hearing has been an "open to the public" hearing.

## The Criminal Trial Procedure LO3

Before a criminal trial begins there are a number of pre-trial activities that have likely occurred. Depending on the offence, the accused may remain in the community throughout the trial process. However, the first appearance for many accused persons is in a court, where they receive a bail hearing in order to determine whether or not they will be released on a form of Judicial Interim Release, known as **bail**, until the trial date. In most cases, it is the Crown's responsibility to show that the accused is a danger to the community or is a risk to flee prosecution in order for a custodial remand to be granted. A custodial remand requires the accused to be incarcerated until the trial date. If the Crown is successful in proving that the accused should not be released pending trial, then the accused is remanded in custody. In order to detain an accused person, the Crown must justify the detention on one of the following grounds:

**bail**

to free a person arrested or imprisoned after a date and place to appear in court are set and security is taken

- to ensure attendance in court;
- for the safety and protection of the public including any victim or witness; or
- if the detention is necessary to maintain confidence in the administration of justice.

This process is referred to as a **show cause hearing**, where the Crown must show cause for why detention is warranted.

**show cause hearing**

a hearing where the Crown must state reasons why the accused should be detained in custody

If the judge decides that the accused should be released into the community to return for trial, it is one of the following ways:

- an undertaking to appear, with conditions;

**recognizance**

a document signed by an accused person indicating that he or she promises to appear in court for a trial

- a **recognizance**, a document signed by the accused indicating that he or she promises to appear in court for trial. Cash is not required; however, if the accused fails to attend court for trial then the accused is required to pay a cash amount. There may also be conditions attached;
- a recognizance with a **surety**, where the accused must bring forward friends or family who will assume the debt should the accused not show up in court. Conditions may be attached;

**surety**

one who is willing to pledge to be answerable to the court (financially) if the accused does not appear in court

- a recognizance with a deposit, where the prosecutor consents. The accused must put up a financial, or other type of valuable, deposit before being released. This is returned once the accused appears for trial. Conditions may be attached; or
- a recognizance with a deposit, with or without a surety, with or without conditions (for those accused persons reside outside the province/territory or more than 200 kilometres away from the place of custody).

Conditions that may accompany any of the release options can include:

- reporting to a peace officer or other person designated by the court;
- notifying the peace officer of any change in address or employment;
- abstaining from communicating directly or indirectly with any victim, witness, or other person identified;
- depositing a passport, as directed;
- complying with any other condition that the judge considers necessary to ensure the safety and security of any victim of or witness to the offence; or
- complying with any other conditions that the justice considers desirable.

Accused persons who do not require a bail hearing because of the nature of the offence will

**FIGURE 4.3 The Flow of a Criminal Trial**

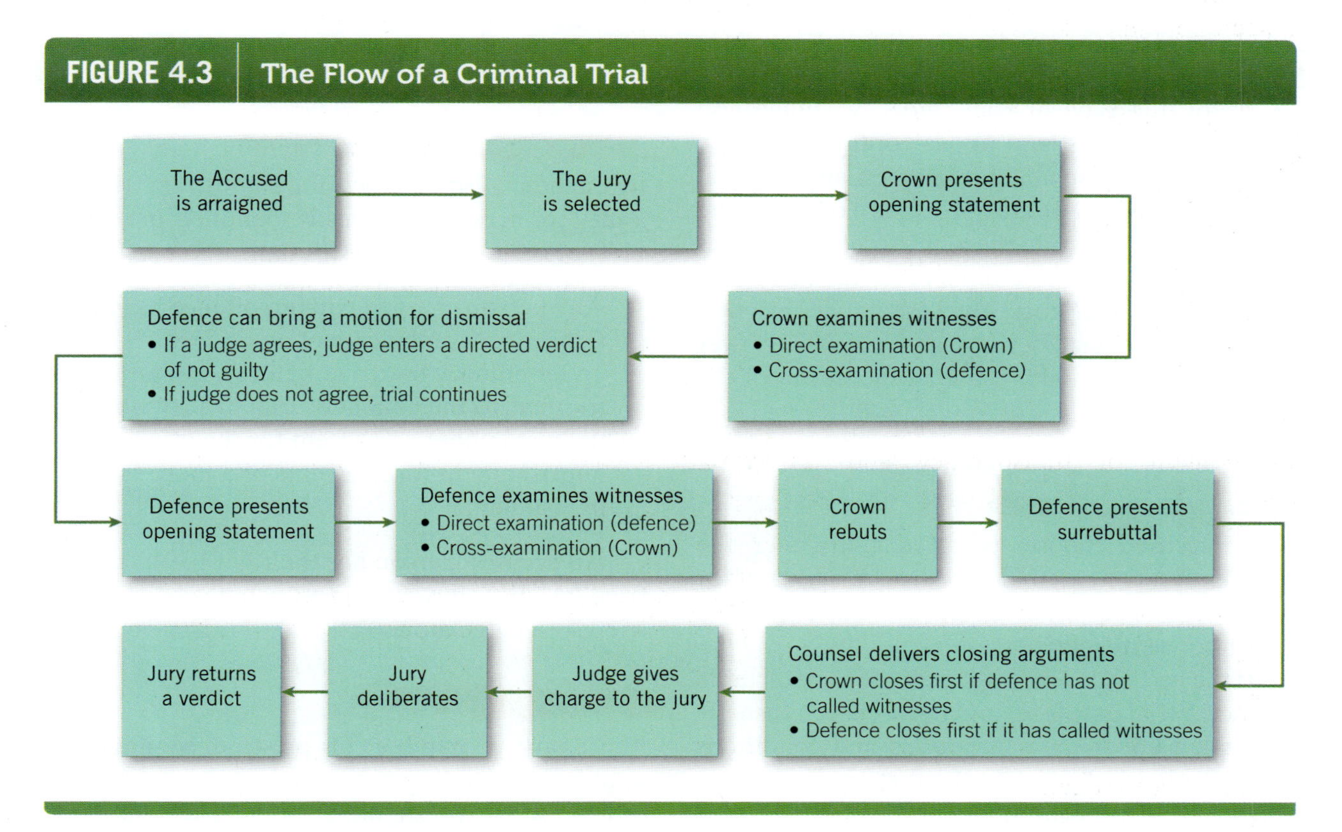

## MYTH VS FACT: Bounty Hunters Beware!

Bounty hunters appear regularly on American television; however, they do not exist in Canadian law. In fact, bounty hunters are illegal in Canada. Canadians (in Canada) are protected from being apprehended by bounty hunters. In 1993, American bounty hunter Daniel Kear came to Canada to apprehend Sidney Jaffe at his Canadian residence and return him to Florida where he was to face trial. Kear was subsequently extradited to Canada where he was convicted of kidnapping Jaffe.

make their first appearance in the provincial or territorial court. At that time, the accused chooses whether to plead guilty or not guilty. Once the initial **plea** is made, then the classification of the offence (summary conviction, indictable, or hybrid/dual procedure) will determine the next steps. It is critical to know the offence classifications in Canadian law because the offence classification determines such basic details as the court where the case will be heard, the type of trial (judge vs. judge and jury), trial process, and appeal options. Offence classification is also a factor in arrest and pre-trial release. For hybrid or dual procedure offences, the Crown prosecutor has the right to elect whether or not to proceed as a summary conviction offence or an indictable offence. The summary conviction offence is the least serious and carries a lower penalty. This election is made at the outset of the trial process.

**plea**
a defendant's response to the question, "are you guilty or not guilty?"

### THE ACCUSED IS CHARGED WITH AN INDICTABLE OFFENCE

If the accused chooses to plead guilty, then the plea is accepted and the court sets a date for sentencing. The accused is then instructed to return for sentencing.

If the accused pleads not guilty to an indictable offence, a trial date is set and the accused is usually remanded under the same terms and conditions that were in place prior to the first appearance, in custody or in the community.

### THE ACCUSED IS CHARGED WITH A SUMMARY CONVICTION OFFENCE

If the accused pleads guilty, he or she may be sentenced at the time of the plea. The sentencing may be remanded pending a **pre-sentence report**. Though accused persons may consent for a longer adjournment, the *Criminal Code* stipulates that the adjournment should not be longer than eight days.

**pre-sentence report**
a report prepared before sentencing with information concerning the offender's history and background, in order to assist the court

If the accused pleads not guilty then a date is set for a trial before a judge at some point in the future.

### DEFENCE ELECTIONS

Prior to going to trial there are a number of choices (commonly referred to as elections) that are available to the defendant, depending on the offence classification:

- A summary conviction offence can only be heard in the provincial/territorial court.
- Hybrid or dual procedure offences where the Crown elects to proceed by summary conviction are heard in provincial/territorial courts.

### ELECTION TO BE TRIED BY A JURY

In Canadian criminal law, the right to be tried by a jury for serious offences is identified in section 11(f) of the *Charter*. It states that:

> Any person charged with an offence has the right except in the case of an offence under military law tried before a military tribunal, to the benefit of trial by jury where the maximum punishment for the offence is imprisonment for five years or a more severe punishment.

An accused person has the right to elect to be tried by a jury; however, most people choose to be tried by a judge alone.

## PRE-TRIAL MOTIONS

There are a number of pre-trial **motions**, or applications, that can be made to the court by either the Crown or the accused. These motions may have a significant impact on the trial. Some of the better-known motions include the following.

### MOTION FOR CHANGE OF VENUE

In most cases, when a motion to change the venue is requested it is because there is a belief that the accused will not receive a fair trial in the city/town where the offence occurred. By changing the venue it is hoped that a new location might result in a jury pool that is not biased. A change of venue was requested in the murder trial of Michael Rafferty, who was convicted of first-degree murder in the death of Tori Stafford, a grade three student who went missing in Woodstock, Ontario, on April 8, 2009. Tori's remains were found three months later in a deserted field 130 kilometres from her home. Rafferty, through his lawyer, requested and was granted a change of venue away from Woodstock, where the crime occurred. Justice Thomas Heeney granted the change of venue from Woodstock to London, Ontario (Nguyen, 2011).

### MOTION TO DETERMINE FITNESS TO STAND TRIAL

All defendants are assumed to be fit to stand trial. This motion is used if a defendant's mental fitness is in question, and will determine if a defendant has the ability to be tried. The court may order the assessment of the issue of fitness at any point in the proceedings prior to a verdict. The case of Vincent Li required a motion to determine if he was fit to stand trial. Li was charged in the horrific case where he attacked and killed 22-year-old Timothy McLean while they were both passengers on a Greyhound bus bound for Manitoba on July 30, 2009. Published accounts say that Li decapitated and mutilated the victim with a knife without any apparent provocation. Li made a brief court appearance on August 5, 2009, and his only words to the judge were, "Please kill me." A psychological assessment was ordered to determine if Li was fit to stand trial, and it was determined that he was. Li's trial commenced on March 3, 2009, and Li pleaded not guilty by reason of a mental disorder. During the trial, a psychiatrist testified that Li had schizophrenia. The psychiatrist said that Li performed the attack because God's voice told him McLean was a force of evil and was about to execute him. The presiding judge accepted the diagnosis, and ruled that Li was not criminally responsible for the murder. Li was remanded to a high-security mental health facility (CBC, 2008).

Tori Stafford was eight years old when she was murdered in Woodstock, Ontario.

### MOTION TO BAN PUBLICATION

The court may determine that, in the interest of the administration of justice, it is necessary to ban publication of details of a trial. This is a serious decision, as it compromises the public's right to access our open court system. Such an example is the case where Mohammad Shafia, his wife Tooba Mohammad Yahya, and their son, Hamed, were each charged (and subsequently convicted) of four counts of first degree murder in the deaths of their teenage daughters and Shafia's first wife. The three sisters and Shafia's first wife were found dead inside their car, submerged in the Rideau Canal, near Kingston, Ontario on June 30, 2009. A publication ban prevented the release of any information regarding the details of the evidence in pre-trial motions and appearances (CBC, 2011).

## DISCLOSURE

**Disclosure** is the requirement for the Crown attorney and the police to provide the details (and copies) of all of the Crown's evidence against the accused, to the accused prior to the trial. The Crown attorney must also provide any new evidence as it is uncovered. This requirement is critical to the ability

The bodies of Rona Amir Mohammad, 53, and sisters Zainab, and Geeti Shafia, aged 19, 17 and 13 were found in a submerged car at a Rideau Canal lock, just east of Kingston, in June 2009.

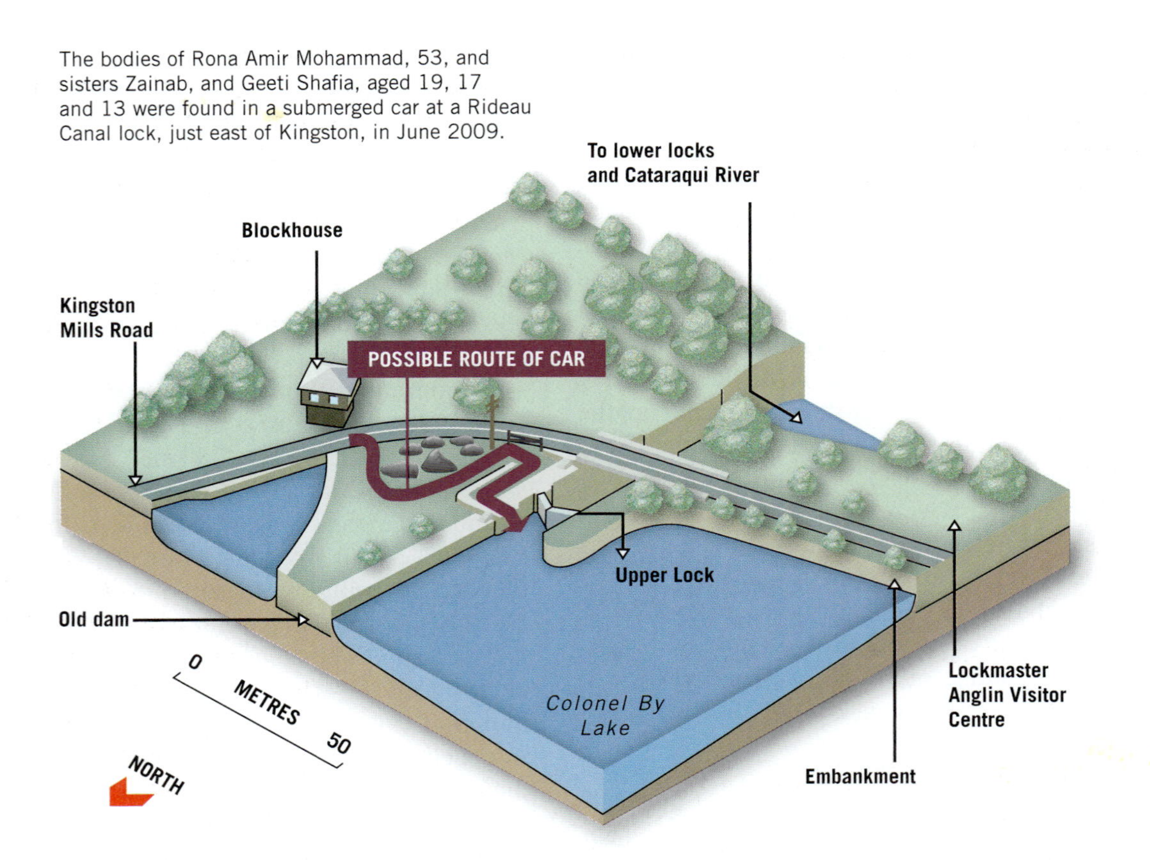


The location in the Rideau Canal where the submerged car was retrieved.

of the accused to prepare a defence and is referred to in section 7 of the *Charter*, which provides that "everyone has the right to life, liberty and security of the person and the right not to be deprived thereof except in accordance with the principles of fundamental justice." There have been issues in Canadian law regarding disclosure that has not been timely, has resulted in unreasonable delay, or has not occurred at all. In describing the critical nature of disclosure, Justice Sopinka said:

> The fruits of the investigation which are in the possession of counsel for the Crown are not the property of the Crown for use in securing a conviction but the property of the public to be used to ensure that justice is done. (R *v.* Stinchcombe, [1991] 3 S.C.R. 326, in Bajer et al.)

## PRELIMINARY INQUIRY

Also referred to as the preliminary hearing, the preliminary inquiry is designed to ensure that the Crown has enough evidence to proceed to a criminal trial, a safeguard designed to protect accused persons from unjustified prosecution. An accused person has the right to a preliminary hearing when charged with an offence that must be tried by a judge and jury, or when the accused elects to be tried by a judge and jury or by a judge alone.

At a preliminary inquiry, the onus is on the Crown prosecutors to prove that they have sufficient evidence necessary for prosecution. The evidence is presented in the same manner as it is presented during a trial; however, the Crown prosecutors need only present enough evidence to prove that they have a sound case. They are not required to present all of the evidence. Though the accused person is given an opportunity to respond to the evidence presented, there is no requirement to do so. If the accused decides to respond, that response is part of the court record and can be used in the case against the accused in the subsequent trial. The accused also has an opportunity to call witnesses. At the conclusion of the preliminary inquiry the judge makes a decision that determines the next step for the case. If the judge believes that the evidence is sufficient, the case proceeds to trial. If the judge believes that there is insufficient evidence then the judge discharges the accused, meaning he or she is then released. Unlike an acquittal, a **discharge** means that if the Crown uncovers more evidence in future, it is possible, with permission from the Attorney General, to bypass the preliminary inquiry and indict the accused directly.

Accused persons have the right to waive their right to a preliminary hearing. They might decide to do so because they have decided to plead guilty or because they want to avoid the negative publicity that may arise from the hearing. In addition, an accused person may choose to waive the right to a preliminary hearing because it will reduce the time it takes to process the case.

The preliminary inquiry is a safeguard within our criminal justice system intended to prevent a case from proceeding if there is insufficient evidence.

## PLEA BARGAINING

Plea bargaining is a term used to describe a process that occurs outside formal court proceedings where an accused person agrees to plead guilty in return for the prosecutor's agreement to reduce or amend a criminal charge or a sentence. The Law Reform Commission of Canada defines plea bargaining as "an agreement by the accused to plead guilty in return for the prosecutor's agreeing to take or refrain from taking a particular course of action" (Verdun-Jones and Tijerino, 2004). Though it is not statutory—you won't find a section on plea bargaining process in the *Criminal Code*—it is very much a part of the criminal justice system. There are a number of different types of plea bargaining that take place. The first type is charge bargaining, where the accused agrees to plead guilty in exchange for a lesser offence, withdraw or stay of charges, or a promise not to charge a family member, partner, or friend. The second type of negotiation is related to sentencing. An accused may plead guilty where the Crown promises to elect to proceed by summary conviction instead of by indictment when charged with a hybrid offence. The Crown may promise to make a certain sentence recommendation, not to appeal a sentence, or may promise to make a recommendation regarding the

**discharge**
the release of an accused without obligation

### FLASHBACK:
### THE KARLA HOMOLKA PLEA BARGAIN: "A DEAL WITH THE DEVIL"?

Perhaps the most famous plea bargain in Canadian history is the deal that Karla Homolka made with the Crown arising from her role in the deaths of Ontario teenagers Kristen French, Leslie Mahaffy, and Homolka's own 15-year-old sister, Tammy Homolka. Homolka made the deal in exchange for her testimony against her then-husband Paul Bernardo. At the time that the deal was struck, the police did not have the videotaped evidence that surfaced later. The tapes revealed that Homolka might have been more involved in the crimes than she had originally claimed. The Crown honoured the agreement and did not rescind the deal with Homolka when the tapes were found. This very public case left many Canadians with a view of plea bargaining gone bad.

place of imprisonment, type of treatment, or other details related to incarceration. The final type of negotiation is related to the facts of the case. The Crown may promise not to mention information that could lead the judge in the case to arrive at a more negative impression of the accused.

Plea bargaining supporters believe that it is required in order for the criminal justice system to function efficiently. Some believe that if every criminal case required a trial before a judge, the system would ground to a halt. They also believe that as long as both sides enter into the bargain voluntarily, then it is legal and ethical.

Many people who are opposed to plea bargaining see it as an injustice to victims. Their interpretation is that a bargain minimizes the seriousness of the crime and the victim's experience. They also believe that innocent people are more likely to plead guilty to an offence that they do not commit in order to end their experience in the criminal justice system. Others believe that plea bargaining is contrary to the sentencing principles and guidelines that exist.

## THE CRIMINAL TRIAL

Where an accused is being tried by a jury, the trial begins with the jury selection process. The process starts with the government in the jurisdiction, which is responsible for assembling a list of people who can be called upon to serve as jurors. The list of jurors, also referred to as the jury array, is a list of potential jurors in a given jurisdiction. Once a pool of jurors is summoned to the court, the in-court selection process begins. The in-court procedure is prescribed by the *Criminal Code*. The procedure is intended to ensure that the jurors who are selected are **impartial**.

**impartial**
without bias

A jury in a criminal case consists of 12 individuals chosen by both the Crown and the defence. A jury can continue with as few as eleven jurors, in the event that one of the jurors becomes ill or must be removed from the jury for other reasons. The selection process allows both the Crown and the defence to exercise their right to challenge the choice of potential jurors. The process, referred to as empanelling the jury, involves calling each juror individually. The Crown and the defence lawyer may ask questions of the potential jurors, or not. There are two types of challenges available. A challenge prevents the potential juror from being selected to sit on the jury. The pre-emptory challenge is one that occurs where there is no questioning of the potential juror and no reason for the challenge is required. The second type is a challenge for cause where either the Crown or the defence lawyer must identify the reason for the challenge. The number of challenges permitted is limited by legislation and depends on the severity of the punishment. For example, the Crown and the defence are permitted 20 pre-emptory challenges when the accused is charged with high treason or first degree murder. The number of challenges drops to 12 when the accused is charged with an offence for which the accused may be sentenced to imprisonment for a term not exceeding five years. (*Criminal Code*, s. 634(2)).

A judge has the discretion to excuse persons from duty if they are unable to serve for personal, work, health reasons, or any other cause deemed reasonable. Once the jury is selected, the individual jurors are sworn or affirmed by the court's clerk. This oath or affirmation signifies the jurors' commitment to try the case on the evidence heard during the trial. The qualifications to serve as a juror are determined by each province or territory. Generally, jurors must be at least 19 years of age and must be a resident of the province/territory that served them with the notice. Section 626(2) of the *Criminal Code* protects potential jurors from discrimination based on sex.

Once the jury is selected, the individual jurors are sworn or affirmed by the court's clerk. This oath or affirmation signifies the jurors' commitment to try the case on the evidence heard during the trial.

Police used evidence received from video footage and photography in the investigation of the rioters in Vancouver in June, 2011.

## OPENING STATEMENTS

The criminal trial opens with statements by both the Crown and the defence. The opening statement is intended to set the tone for each side and to present an overview of the evidence that will be called. It is important that only evidence that will actually be introduced is referenced at this point. The defence is not required to offer any evidence in a trial, and may choose to use the opening statement to refute the position of the Crown.

### THE PRESENTATION OF EVIDENCE

**evidence**: an assertion of fact, opinion, belief, or knowledge

The next stage in the trial process is presenting **evidence** to the court. This is a critical stage because it is the basis for the finding of the case. The Crown presents the evidence first because the onus is on the Crown to prove the case. The evidence is presented by the Crown through witnesses, documents, or physical material.

**Direct evidence** is evidence that proves a fact and does not require additional explanation or assessment. For example, a videotape of a person engaged in shoplifting an item from a store is a form of direct evidence. A storekeeper who testifies that he saw the shoplifting happen is also presenting direct evidence.

**Circumstantial evidence** is evidence that requires the court to draw inferences and make connections to the fact. For example, a witness may testify to seeing the accused leaving a room while holding a bloody knife. The witness may not have seen the accused actually stab the victim; however, the judge and jury may believe that they can conclude that the accused committed the crime because of this circumstantial evidence. Circumstantial evidence is sufficient to lead to a verdict of guilt and conviction in criminal trial.

**Real evidence** is evidence that is physical itself or is able to identify physical evidence. Real evidence includes weapons, fingerprints, ransom notes, forged documents, seized stolen goods, and spent bullets. When real evidence is presented in court, it is presented as an exhibit that, if accepted by the court, can be shared with the jury. Real evidence also includes documents such as letters, regulations, signed agreements, written confessions, and data contained in computers or other electronic devices. Real evidence may be videotaped footage or voice recordings as well.

Evidence is presented in court through witness testimony. The witnesses in a criminal trial usually include the police officers involved in the arrest and investigation, the victims, any witnesses to the offence, experts as required, and often the defendant. Before witnesses are called, they must be determined to be competent and it must also be determined that they have first-hand knowledge of that which they are testifying. A witness cannot testify based on **hearsay evidence**.

**hearsay evidence**: what a witness knows based on what was told to him or her by another person

The rule against hearsay says that our courts require that the evidence that is presented by a witness must be restricted to that which he or she knows first-hand, rather than anything learned (or heard) from someone else. First-hand knowledge is referred to as primary evidence or best evidence.

Competence can be proved based on the witness' expert knowledge or relationship to the case. For example, the competence of a shopkeeper who saw the offence take place is sound. The competence of a shopkeeper who owns the store but was not in the store at the time of the offence may not be sound. The witness must also declare the intention to and understanding of the duty to tell the truth. A witness who does not tell the truth may be charged with **perjury**, a *Criminal Code* offence.

**perjury**

a criminal offence where a person knowingly makes a false statement while under oath, as in a court of law. Perjury is an indictable offence and the penalty is a term of imprisonment not exceeding 14 years. (*Criminal Code*, s. 132)

The witness is called to the stand and is first questioned by the lawyer who called the witness. This is called **direct examination**. Witnesses called by the prosecutor are witnesses for the prosecution, and witnesses called by the defence are witnesses for the defence. Once the direct examination is completed, the **cross-examination** of the witness may begin. Cross-examination is required to test the witness' credibility to ensure that the evidence has legal integrity. At the same time, the prosecution or the defence may choose not to cross-examine a witness because they do not believe it is necessary. After the cross-examination, the initial examiner has the opportunity to question the witness again, often to clarify points made in cross-examination or to reinforce the original testimony. This is called the *redirect examination* and, again, there may be another cross-examination that follows it. The witness will only be excused once both sides believe that they have engaged in a complete examination of the witness.

Once the Crown prosecutor has presented the case, then the defence counsel has an opportunity to respond. Defendants have the right to choose whether or not they wish to testify on their own behalf in proceedings against them. Section 11(c) of the *Charter* specifies:

> Any person charged with an offence has the right not to be compelled to be a witness in proceedings against that person in respect of the offence.

This right is often referred to as the right to remain silent as defendants need not testify on their own behalf. In fact, a defendant does not have to present a defence in a trial at all. Once the Crown presents its case, it is possible for the defence counsel to indicate that it does not have any evidence to present or witnesses to call, and allow the judge and/or jury to make a decision based on the facts presented by the Crown. If this happens, the defence will often state that it does not believe that the Crown prosecution has proved its case sufficiently and that it is looking for a finding of not guilty.

### CLOSING ARGUMENTS

Before moving into the deliberation phase, both the Crown and the defence have an opportunity to provide a **closing argument** to the court. The purpose of the closing argument is to provide a summation of the evidence with a view to drawing a conclusion to the case that is consistent with the position. For example, the Crown is going to draw a conclusion that the evidence presented indicates that the defendant did indeed commit the crime and that there should be a finding of guilt. The closing argument will usually highlight the evidence and will put all of the pieces of evidence together for the judge and the jury. By contrast, the defence

**closing argument**

a statement made by counsel at the closing of a criminal trial

**JUST or BUST?**

Should the Crown prosecutor consult the victim of a crime if a plea bargain is being considered?

It is important that jurors not be pressured to change their minds or commit to a verdict because it is inconvenient for the court.

counsel will present a closing argument that looks for deficiencies in the Crown's case and will highlight evidence presented by the defence that supports the innocence of the defendant. Both the Crown and the defence will also use the closing argument to address any weaknesses in their own cases. For example, if the defendant did not testify on his own behalf, the defence might point out that this is not an indicator of guilt.

### JUDGE'S CHARGE TO THE JURY

Where a trial is heard by a jury, the judge's **charge to the jury** follows the closing argument. When the case is heard by a judge alone, the case moves directly to the **verdict**. The charge to the jury is intended to instruct the jury as it prepares to deliberate the case. The charge to the jury may include the following:

**charge to the jury**
a judge gives instructions to a jury before it deliberates with regard to the law as it applies to the case before it

- a summary of the evidence presented to refresh the jury's memory;
- a reminder of the jury's role and the court's expectation;
- a reminder that the jury is expected to review the evidence and consider it objectively;
- a reminder of the fundamental principle of the presumption of innocence and the burden of proof;
- a reminder that the principle of "proof beyond a reasonable doubt" is an essential part of the presumption of innocence; and
- the elements of the offence will be identified, which informs the jurors of how a specific offence is proven in court.

**verdict**
the finding of a jury and/or judge

### JURY DELIBERATION AND THE VERDICT

The purpose of jury deliberation is to give the jury members an opportunity to meet privately to discuss the case. The goal is to agree upon a verdict, which must be unanimous. The length of time required for deliberation varies from minutes or hours to several days; a deadline is not imposed on the jury. Once the jury arrives at a decision, the court is notified and the jury returns to the courtroom with the verdict. While deliberating, the jury may have questions of the judge or it may wish to review parts of the evidence that was presented. This must be done in open court.

If the jury is not able to arrive at a unanimous verdict the court is notified. This is referred to as a **hung jury**. A judge is permitted to provide assistance in the form of clarification should the jury reach an impasse. However, it is important that jurors not be pressured to change their minds or commit to a verdict because it is inconvenient for the court. If, after a reasonable amount of time, it is determined that the jury cannot reach a verdict, then the judge can use his or her discretion and declare a mistrial and discharge the jury. Where a mistrial is declared, there may be a new trial.

**hung jury**
a jury that is unable to reach a unanimous decision

When the jury reaches a verdict it returns to the court and advises the court of the verdict. The jurors are thanked publicly for their service and the sentencing phase of the trial remains the judge's responsibility. Sentencing may take place immediately, or the judge may set another date for a sentencing hearing.

### WHAT HAPPENS IF AN ACCUSED DOESN'T SHOW UP FOR TRIAL?

When an accused person does not appear in court as required, the court (before which the accused should have appeared) may issue a warrant for his or her arrest. The warrant may be executed anywhere in Canada (*Criminal Code*, s. 502).

## The Appeal Process

After the court has made a finding of guilt or innocence, both the Crown and the defence have the right to **appeal**. A defendant who receives a custodial sentence may request that he or she be released on bail while awaiting the results of the appeal court. An appeal can be launched based on a question of law or fact. An appeals court will assess a case before making a decision to hear an appeal. The appeal court may do one of the following:

**appeal**

examination by a higher court of the decision of a lower court

- It may decide that the appeal does not have merit and will choose not to hear it. This may mean that the appeal court agrees with the lower court decision or it may mean that the defendant does not have sufficient grounds for appeal.
- It may hear the appeal and then direct that the defendant be acquitted or order a new trial.
- If the sentence is being appealed (as opposed to the conviction) the appeals court may uphold, reduce, or increase the sentence.

## L04 Diversion from Traditional Courts

### RESTORATIVE JUSTICE

Restorative justice refers to an approach to justice that operates outside the traditional criminal justice system. Its goal is to meet the needs of both the victim and the offender with a view to restoring peace in communities after an offence has been committed. Because of the major expansion of restorative justice programs and initiatives in Canada, as well as around the world, an entire chapter has been devoted to this topic. The concepts, philosophy, and principles of restorative justice are examined in detail in the chapter entitled Restorative Justice.

### DIVERSION PROGRAMS

Diversion programs are intended to divert persons who have been charged with criminal offences away from the traditional criminal justice system. Diversion programs that are intended for young offenders are examined in the Youth Justice chapter. Diversion programs for adult offenders are offered across Canada to those who meet specific criteria. The programs are intended to minimize the strain on the court system by offering offenders an opportunity to take responsibility for their actions and resolve the legal problem in a manner that is fair and equitable. Diversion programs are often made available to first-time offenders, offenders with minor criminal records, or offenders with special needs. Most diversion programs are based on the following principles:

- all offenders must meet the criteria for each specific program;
- the Crown prosecutor (or designate) has the option of reviewing and approving each offender;
- the offender takes full responsibility for having committed the offence;
- offenders agree that should they fail to participate in or complete the program, they will be referred back to the traditional court system; and

**TABLE 4.1 The Number of Criminal Cases Heard in Adult Courts in Canada, Including the Disposition**

| Type of decision | 2005/2006 | 2006/2007 | 2007/2008 | 2008/2009 | 2009/2010 |
|---|---|---|---|---|---|
| Total decisions | 382,322 | 380,537 | 393,193 | 398,697 | 403,340 |
| Guilty | 249,141 | 247,509 | 255,487 | 263,948 | 262,616 |
| Acquitted | 14,230 | 13,591 | 12,592 | 12,548 | 13,059 |
| Stay | 112,769 | 113,684 | 120,112 | 117,289 | 122,807 |
| Other decisions | 6,182 | 5,753 | 5,002 | 4,912 | 4,858 |

NOTE: Other decisions include found not criminally responsible, waived, special plea, unfit to stand trial.

SOURCE: Statistics Canada. Table 252-0045 - Adult criminal court survey, number of cases, by type of decision, annual (number), CANSIM (database), 12 March 2012. Reproduced and distributed on an "as is" basis with the permission of Statistics Canada.

- victim involvement is voluntary.

There is a range of diversion programming across Canada. See Table 4.2 for examples of the various types of activities in which offenders might engage.

**TABLE 4.2 Diversion Programs**

| Type of Diversion Program | Description |
|---|---|
| Community Service Work | Offender performs a pre-determined number of volunteer hours in an approved agency. |
| Restitution | Offender provides payment to the victim for the cost of any loss or damages. |
| Victim/Offender Reconciliation | A mediation process that brings together the victim(s) and the offender. |
| Education Programs | Offender is required to attend an educational program related to the offence. For example, substance abuse awareness. |
| Treatment Programs | Offender is required to attend a treatment program. |
| Letter of Apology or Public Apology | Offender is required to write a letter of apology to the victim(s) and/or the community. |

## LO5 Challenges Facing the Court System

The court system is a complex arrangement of courts and processes designed to meet the needs of a large, diverse country. There are a number of challenges that it faces.

### CAMERAS IN THE COURTROOMS

One of the fundamental aspects of our court system is that it is open and accessible, enabling the public to witness the criminal justice system in operation. Though there are a number of exceptions to this open access, our court system is generally accessible to those people who are able to physically attend the court. It has been argued that this form of access does limit people who wish to observe criminal trials, because cases are heard in specific geographic areas, they are held during the workday, and only a limited number of people can actually be seated in a courtroom. In order to remedy this issue, there are those who believe that cameras should be mounted in courts so that court proceedings can be broadcast on public television. Journalists are both welcome and commonplace in courtrooms to watch and then report on proceedings. They are not permitted to transmit information using photographs, or audio or video recordings. Proceedings are often shared by media outlets in the form of court sketches, on-screen text excerpts, or a verbal summary provided by a journalist who was in the courtroom.

Proponents of cameras in the courtroom believe that having cameras will not only improve access but that they will help to educate the public. They argue that cameras will be an incentive for lawyers to be better prepared and for witnesses to tell the truth. Opponents of cameras in the courts believe that witnesses might be reluctant to come forward if they know that they will be televised, and that jurors might feel pressured when making their decisions. There is also the concern that the media would edit and focus to sensationalize the trial providing an unrealistic view of the justice system.

There have been a number of exceptions to the "no camera" rule in various courts across Canada. The Supreme Court of Canada allowed electronic access to its proceedings during a pilot project between 1993 and 1995. Three high profile cases were broadcast, one of which was the Sue Rodgriguez case, which asked the court to consider the right to assisted suicide. (The right was subsequently denied.) Since then the Supreme Court has allowed most of its proceedings to be broadcast by the Cable Public Affairs Channel (CPAC). The proceedings are also available via webcast in the archives on the Supreme Court website.

Other jurisdictions have allowed cameras for short-term experiments or for specific trials, including the Nova Scotia Court of Appeal, the Federal Court of Appeal, and the Ontario Court of Appeal. We have seen a number of royal commissions and commissions of inquiry also televised, including the Grange inquiry into the baby deaths at Toronto's Hospital for Sick Children and the Hughes inquiry into sexual abuse at Newfoundland's Mount Cashel orphanage.

At this point cameras in the courtroom continue to be hotly contested. Media outlets continue to challenge the issue. It remains to be seen if the Supreme Court of Canada, a court that televises its own proceedings, will one day make a decision that will allow electronic access to all courts in Canada.

## WRONGFUL CONVICTION

Perhaps the greatest challenge that faces the criminal justice system is the prospect of the wrongful conviction of innocent defendants. Despite all of the safeguards that are built into the system, including the commitment to fundamental principles and the many ethical codes of conduct that exist, we have learned that our system is not infallible. Mistakes have been made and innocent people have been convicted and have spent years behind bars for crimes that they did not commit. In addition, for every wrongful conviction, the actual guilty party is allowed to go free.

There have been a number of independent public commissions in Canada to examine wrongful convictions, focusing on those cases where wrongful convictions were confirmed in cases of murder. The commissions identified a number of common themes that are cause for concern, which include a belief that wrongful convictions are the result of systemic inappropriate actions of numerous people in the criminal justice system. The attitudes and actions of some are supported by a culture that tolerates their existence.

The following factors have been identified as contributing to wrongful conviction:

- tunnel vision, where police investigators do not proceed with an open mind;
- mistaken eyewitness testimony;
- false confessions;
- in-custody informers who are not reliable;
- flawed forensic and expert testimony; and
- public and media pressure to convict.

(Bajer, et al., 2008)

A number of preventative measures have been implemented into the criminal justice system related to retention of evidence, false confessions, tunnel vision, and other areas. The Association in Defence of the Wrongly Convicted (AIDWYC) was formed to advocate on behalf of persons who have been wrongly convicted (http://www.aidwyc.org/). A volunteer-based organization, it has assisted in the eventual release of a number of Canadian and international persons since its inception in 1993.

> "Rather let the crime of the guilty go unpunished than condemn the innocent"
>
> (JUSTINIAN I, LAW CODE, A.D. 535)

## COURT DELAYS

The courts have been criticized at various points for unreasonable delays in hearing criminal cases. Section 11(b) of the *Charter* assures Canadians that they will be tried within a reasonable time. There has been a great deal of speculation regarding the definition of "reasonable." In 1990, the subject of delays received a great deal of attention when the Supreme Court made a precedent-setting decision, now known as the Askov decision (R. *v.* Askov [1990] 2 S.C.R. 1199). Askov and his co-accused were charged with a number of offences, including conspiracy to commit extortion, in November, 1983. The preliminary hearing took place in July, 1984, and was concluded in September of the same year. A trial date was set for October, 1985, but could not be accommodated by the court and was therefore delayed until September, 1986. The trial date was two years after the conclusion of the preliminary hearing. At the start of the trial, the accused moved for a stay of the proceedings citing unreasonable delay. The trial judge granted the stay. The Crown appealed the stay to the Court of Appeal, which set aside the stay, disagreeing with the trial judge. The case was then appealed to the

PROFILE

## Wrongful Conviction

The names of the wrongly convicted have become well known to Canadians. Their stories are a constant reminder of the fallible nature of the criminal justice system.

### Steven Truscott

Steven Truscott was sentenced to hang for the 1959 death of Lynn Harper, a classmate. At the age of 14, Truscott was a death row inmate until his sentence was commuted to life imprisonment. He was paroled in 1969 to live an anonymous life in Ontario. Truscott always maintained his innocence and after numerous investigations into the facts of the case, the Ontario Court of Appeal overturned the conviction in August of 2007. In July, 2008, Truscott received $6.5 million in compensation.

### Donald Marshall Jr.

In 1971, at 17 years of age, Donald Marshall Jr. was convicted of murdering his friend, Sandy Seale in Sydney, Nova Scotia. He was sentenced to life imprisonment. He was released in 1982 following an RCMP review where the Nova Scotia Court of Appeal declared him not guilty. A royal commission in 1990 determined that systemic racism had contributed to the wrongful conviction. Roy Ebsary was eventually convicted of manslaughter in Seale's death. Donald Marshall Jr. spent 11 years in jail and was eventually given a lifetime pension of $1.5 million in compensation for his ordeal. Marshall died in 2009 at age 55.

### David Milgaard

David Milgaard was sentenced to life imprisonment for the 1969 murder of nursing aide Gail Miller in Saskatoon. He made several unsuccessful appeals but was subsequently cleared by DNA evidence in 1997. Larry Fisher was found guilty for the rape and stabbing of Gail Miller in 1999. Milgaard was awarded $10 million by the government of Saskatchewan.

SOURCES: Steven Truscott: CBC News (7 July 2008), Steven Truscott to get $6.5M for wrongful conviction, retrieved from http://www.cbc.ca/news/canada/story/2008/07/07/truscott-bentley.html; Donald Marshall Jr.: CBC News (6 August 2009), Wrongfully convicted Donald Marshall Jr. dies, retrieved from: http://www.cbc.ca/news/canada/story/2009/08/06/donald-marshall-wrongful-conviction-dies342.html; David Milgaard: Government of Saskatchewan (17 May 1999), Milgaard family and province settle on compensation package, news release: Government of Saskatchewan.

**FIGURE 4.4** Trend in Median Elapsed Time to Case Completion in Adult Criminal Courts, 10 Jurisdictions, 2000–2001 to 2008–2009

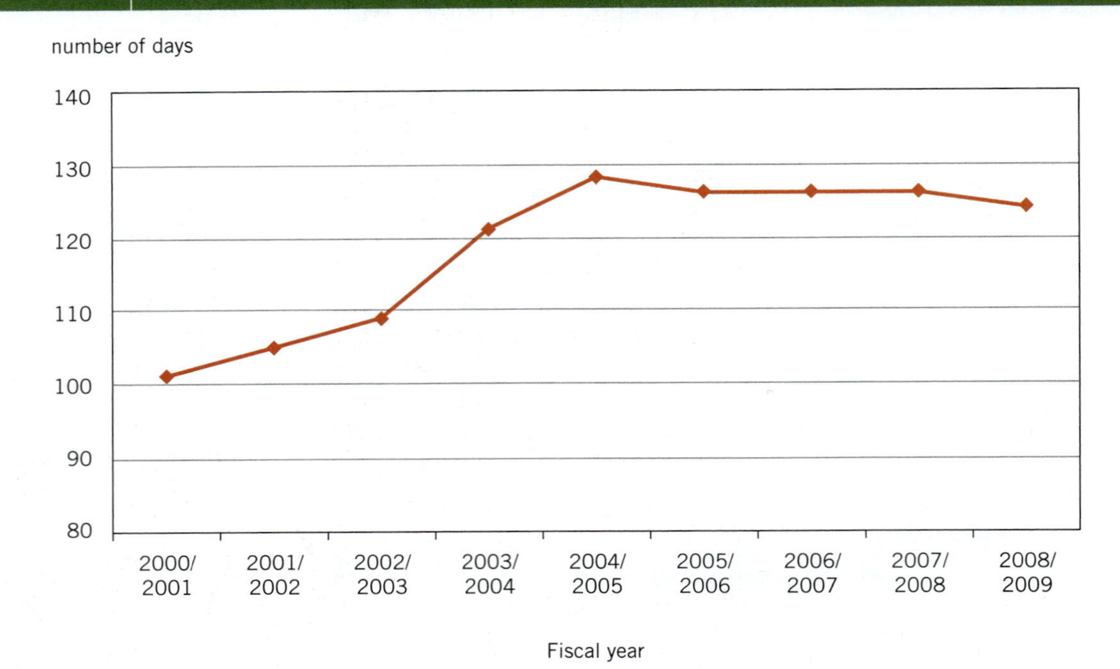


NOTES: This chart does not include data from Manitoba, Northwest Territories, and Nunavut. Coverage for Adult Criminal Court Survey data for trend analysis from 2000–2001 to 2008–2009 (10 jurisdictions) is estimated at 90 percent of adult criminal court caseload.

SOURCE: Statistics Canada,Trend in median elapsed time to case completion in adult criminal courts, 10 Jurisdictions, 2000/2001 to 2008/2009, 12 March 2012. Reproduced and distributed on an "as is" basis with the permission of Statistics Canada.

Supreme Court of Canada by the accused, where the justices sided with the accused and resulted in a stay in thousands of other cases (Goff, 2011). In doing so, the Supreme Court outlined four factors that needed to be considered when determining when a delay is reasonable. The factors are:

- the length of the delay;
- the explanation for the delay;
- a waiver exercised by the accused; and
- prejudice to the accused.

Delays continue to be a challenge for the courts. A case with multiple offences, serious offences, and many scheduled appearances will take longer. In 2008–2009, the median elapsed time for multiple-charge cases was 152 days, versus 89 days for single-charge cases (Thomas, 2010). A complex, more serious case tends to have a longer elapsed time. For example, in 2008, homicide cases were concluded with a median of 345 days, attempted murder in 274 days, drug trafficking in 223 days, and sexual assault cases had a median of 304 days. Compare that to breach of probation, which had an elapsed time of 60 days, disturbing the peace had 78 days, and theft cases had a median conclusion time of 78 days (Thomas, 2010). As would be expected, cases that went to trial took longer to conclude (median of 255 days) than those that did not go to trial (113 days). Cases where the accused entered a guilty plea had the shortest elapsed time of 97 days. In 2008–2009, a guilty plea was entered in 59 percent of all cases (Thomas, 2010). Offences that were processed under the *Youth Criminal Justice Act* were concluded in a median time of 63 days in 2008–2009.

Overall, we are seeing a modest decline in the length of time it takes to conclude a case in adult criminal courts. In 2004–2005, the median length of time was 128 days, while in 2008–2009 it fell to 124 days (see Table 4.4). Court delays continue to present a challenge, leaving the provinces and territories that administer the courts to continually search for ways to be more efficient.

## Chapter Summary

This chapter provided an introduction to the court system in Canada and the criminal trial process. Key concepts include the following:

- There are four main levels of courts in Canada; each province and territory is responsible for the administration of the court system in its respective jurisdiction.
- The Supreme Court of Canada is the highest court in Canada and it is the ultimate court of appeal in Canada.
- The key players in the court system are the judiciary, the lawyers (Crown attorney and defence counsel), the police, the accused, and the victim. Members of the public play a role that includes their ability to access the court, the need to know the law, and their role on juries.
- The flow of a criminal case from the arrest of the accused through to the appeal was described.
- Several challenges faced by the criminal courts, including wrongful convictions, court delays, and cameras in the courtroom were discussed.

## Relevant Legislation

*The Constitution Act, 1867 and 1982*
*Canada Criminal Code* (R.S.C. , 1985, c. C-46).
*Judges Act* (R.S.C. , 1985, c. J-1)
*Juries Act* (R.S.O. 1990, c. J.3)
*Canada Evidence Act* (R.S.C. , 1985, c. C-5)
Justinian I, Law Code, A.D. 535

## Key Terms

Appeal
Bail
Charge to the jury
Circumstantcial evidence
Closing argument
Cross-examination
Direct evidence
Direct examination
Discharge
Disclosure
Evidence
Expert witness
Hearsay evidence
Hung jury
Impartial
Leave to appeal
Motions
Peace bond
Perjury
Plea
Pre-sentence report
Real evidence
Recognizance
Security of tenure
Show cause hearing
Surety
Verdict

## For Review

1. What is the purpose of bail?
2. Why is the role of the jury critical to our system?
3. Why is it important that our courts be open to the public?
4. Why is the criminal trial an adversarial process?
5. What is the purpose of disclosure?
6. What is the advantage of having specialized courts? How does it benefit accused persons?
7. What role does the Supreme Court play in Canada?

## Thinking Critically

1. Should the preliminary hearing be a privilege and not a right? Does it waste time and money? Is there an easier way for the Crown to prove that it has sufficient evidence to proceed to trial?
2. Why do you think that most accused persons choose to be tried by a judge alone and not a judge and jury?
3. Do you believe that being tried by a jury can result in an appropriate judgment or should jurors be people who are educated in criminal law?
4. Should victims be consulted in the plea bargaining process? Should a victim have the right to veto a plea bargain deal?
5. Which processes exist that illustrate the belief that an accused person is innocent until proven guilty?
6. Identify ways in which we can safeguard the court system from wrongful conviction.
7. How do you think advances in technology will change courts of the future?

Practise and learn online with Connect

# CHAPTER 5
# Sentencing

Veritas, the Goddess of Truth, in front of the Supreme Court of Canada.

## Sentencing

Graham James was a hockey coach in Manitoba, where he coached junior hockey, as well as two teams in the Western Hockey League, from 1984 to 1996. In November of 1996, James was charged with two counts of sexual assault involving more than 300 incidents against two of his former players over a span of 10 years. One of the players was former National Hockey League (NHL) player, Sheldon Kennedy; the name of the second victim is protected by a publication ban. James pleaded guilty to sexual assault and he was sentenced to three and a half years in prison. He also received a lifetime ban on coaching from the Canadian Hockey Association.

In 2007, James applied for and received a pardon from the (then) National Parole Board. When it was revealed to the public in 2010, there was widespread outrage from his victims and the general public. The government admitted that it was a mistake and responded with new guidelines, making acquiring a pardon (now known as a record suspension) more difficult.

### LEARNING OBJECTIVES

By the end of this chapter, you should be able to:

**LO1** Identify the sentencing principles that guide the judiciary in Canada.

**LO2** Describe the adult sentencing options available to the courts.

**LO3** Identify the factors that are considered when sentencing decisions are made.

**LO4** Identify elements of sentencing disparity that exist in Canada.

Graham James hides his face outside the court where he was sentenced to two years in prison for the sexual assault of two of his former players.

In October 2009, Theo Fleury, a retired NHL player, released his autobiography *Playing with Fire*, in which he alleged that Graham James sexually assaulted him, beginning at age 14, while he was being coached by James. In October 2010, the Winnipeg police issued a Canada-wide warrant for James, charging him with nine new sex charges involving three boys and spanning from 1979 to 1994. James, who was in Mexico at the time, came back to Canada voluntarily and was apprehended by police at Toronto's Pearson International Airport and returned to Winnipeg. He was granted bail in December 2010, and moved to Montreal until the trial date. On December 7, 2011, he entered a guilty plea for sexually abusing Fleury and his cousin, Todd Holt. On March 20, 2012, in a Manitoba provincial court, James, 59, was sentenced to two years imprisonment. In a prepared apology, he said,

> *"I stand before you with regret… I also stand before you to apologize. I apologize to the Canadian hockey public whose interest in the national game should be found in celebration, not trouble like what I've caused… Parents expected their sons to be safe. Not all were. I apologize to the parents and the families of those most personally affected. I knew you. I liked you and I abused the trust you put in me. The fault is mine alone. Finally, and most importantly, I apologize to Theoren Fleury and to Todd Holt, against whom I have offended. I wanted the best for you but I did not give you my best. My actions forfeited our friendship. It is sad irony that it is you, being among the persons I liked the most, today like me the least. I am deeply sorry. I was wrong."* (Puxley and Edmonds, 2012)

The sentence length means that James will serve his sentence in the federal correctional system. In providing her reasons for the sentence, Provincial Court Justice Carlson stated:

*continued.*

Theo Fleury revealed that, as a teenager, he had been repeatedly sexually assaulted by James.

*"... the Court expects that no sentence it can impose will sufficiently penalize Mr. James in the eyes of his victims, or indeed in the eyes of the public. It is trite but important to note that the Canadian criminal justice system is not one of vengeance. The Court's obligation is to craft a sentence based on legal principles that must be applied to specific offences committed by a specific offender."* (R. v. James, 2012 MBPC 31)

The sentencing of Graham James in March, 2012, resulted in a wave of criticism from the victims and the public overall, in response to its perceived lenience. This case illustrates the reality that sentencing is often fraught with controversy.

# Sentencing

According to the Canadian Sentencing Commission, sentencing is defined as "the judicial determination of a legal sanction to be imposed on a person found guilty of an offence." (*Sentencing Reform, A Canadian Approach*. Report of the Canadian Sentencing Commission, 1987, p.153).

Sentencing is a critical element of the criminal trial. It is a time when the judge decides how a defendant will be penalized for committing a criminal offence. As citizens we look to the sentence to provide justice to the victim and to society at large. Sentencing requires that judges make an effort to balance the needs of society, the offender, and the victim of the crime, all within the parameters of the law. Sentencing is often controversial because we all have different views of what an appropriate sentence should be.

Sentencing occurs after there has been a finding of guilt during the criminal process. An accused person is sentenced after pleading guilty or after having been found guilty during a trial. Following a full hearing of the facts of the case, as presented by both the Crown attorney and the defence counsel, the judge determines the sentence to be applied. There are a number of sentencing options available to judges, all of which are identified in the *Criminal Code of Canada* (the *Criminal Code*). Sentencing is often limited by legal parameters; for example, the *Criminal Code* identifies maximum and minimum sentences for certain offences. The maximum sentence that can be meted out in a Canadian court is life imprisonment.

## SENTENCING PRINCIPLES

LO1

The *Criminal Code* identifies sentencing principles that guide the judiciary. These principles also speak to the purpose of sentencing and emphasize our societal beliefs related to sentencing. The *Criminal Code* states:

> The fundamental purpose of sentencing is to contribute, along with crime prevention initiatives, to respect for the law and the maintenance of a just, peaceful and safe society by imposing just sanctions that have one or more of the following objectives:
>
> (a) to denounce unlawful conduct;
> (b) to deter the offender and other persons from committing offences;
> (c) to separate offenders from society, where necessary;
> (d) to assist in rehabilitating offenders;
> (e) to provide reparations for harm done to victims or to the community; and
> (f) to promote a sense of responsibility in offenders, and acknowledgment of the harm done to victims and to the community. (*Criminal Code*, s. 718)

Section 718 of the *Criminal Code* identifies the objectives of sentencing. When a judge sentences an offender, the sentence must address one or more of these objectives, each of which addresses an important aspect of sentencing.

**A. To denounce unlawful conduct** By denouncing criminal conduct, the court is making it clear to individuals and to society at large that certain behaviours are unacceptable and will not be tolerated. It is important for the court to publicly denounce and condemn conduct, and in doing so, the court voices the community's disapproval. If the public perception is that a sentence does not fit the crime because it is too lenient, the public will often express its disapproval, usually through the media. Though most criminal offences have general support from the community overall, there are other criminal offences that do not. For example, some members of our society openly possess marijuana even though doing so is labelled a criminal act.

**B. To deter the offender and other persons from committing offences** By sentencing an offender, there is an attempt to deter the offender and society at large from committing the same crime in the future, a form of crime prevention. Deterrence is basically a reminder to the public that if we should commit the same crime, we will receive a similar fate. There are two types of deterrence. **Specific deterrence** is when a judge sentences an offender in a manner that is intended to prevent him or her from committing the same (or another) offence again in future. The deterrence is targeted specifically at the offender, hoping that he or she has been negatively affected by the sentence and will not commit the crime again. **General deterrence** is when the threat of punishment is intended to target the entire population, with the objective of preventing society overall from committing the same offence.

**specific deterrence**
sentencing an offender with a view to deterring that individual from committing another criminal offence

**general deterrence**
sentencing an offender with a view to deterring the general public from committing the same offence

**C. To separate offenders from society, when necessary** When the court imposes a sentence that removes the offender from society, the offender is incapacitated for the time that he or she is in custody. This period of incapacitation ensures that the community is protected from the offender for that period of time.

**D. To assist in rehabilitating offenders** Rehabilitation is a critical goal of sentencing. It is an effort to provide the offender with new skills, abilities, attitudes, and strengths to support the goal of remaining crime-free. Rehabilitation takes many forms and may occur in custody and/or in the community. It can include treatment programs for substance abuse, education and training courses, anger management, and personal counselling. There are also programs for specific types of offenders

Paul Bernardo, sentenced to life imprisonment in September, 1995, for the first degree murders of Kristen French and Leslie Mahaffy, has been removed from society. He was then declared a dangerous offender in November of 1995. He has been incapacitated to the full extent of the law in Canada.

such as sex offenders, impaired drivers, and those convicted of domestic violence. Each offender's needs are assessed with a view to determining the type of intervention that is most appropriate.

**E. To provide reparation for harm done to victims or the community** Reparation is an attempt to repair the damage and harm that was done to the victim and the community as a result of the offence. Sentencing options that address reparation directly are restitution and community service. Restitution is money that is paid to the victim, and community service is a form of giving back to the community through volunteer work, usually through non-profit organizations.

**F. To promote a sense of responsibility in offenders, and acknowledgment of the harm done to victims and to the community.** By promoting a sense of responsibility in the offender, the courts are requiring the offender to understand and accept how he or she has caused harm to the victim and the community. This recognition that harm goes beyond the victim and extends to the community with each crime is important. On one level, all members of the community are harmed when a criminal offence is committed.

The *Criminal Code* states that the fundamental principle of sentencing is that,

> A sentence must be proportionate to the gravity of the offence and the degree of responsibility of the offender. (*Criminal Code*, s. 718.1)

This is referred to as the principle of proportionality. It means that full consideration must be given to the gravity of the offence and the extent to which the offender is blameworthy. Attention is paid to the extent that an offender is morally responsible for his or her participation in the crime. There is often a disconnection between the court's assessment of proportionality and that of the general public.

### SENTENCING AND THE *CANADIAN CHARTER OF RIGHTS AND FREEDOMS*

The *Canadian Charter of Rights and Freedoms* (the *Charter*) applies to all aspects of the criminal justice system in general, including the sentencing phase of the trial process. However, there are specific sections that are directly related to the sentencing of defendants in Canadian courts. Section 11(i) states that:

> (i) if found guilty of the offence and if the punishment for the offence has been varied between the time of commission and the time of sentencing, to the benefit of the lesser punishment.

This section protects defendants by ensuring that if the penalty for an offence changes between the time when a defendant committed an offence and the time when that person is sentenced, he or she will be subject to the lesser penalty.

Section 12 of the *Charter* protects defendants from treatment or punishment that is determined to be "cruel and unusual." It states:

> 12. Everyone has the right not to be subjected to any cruel and unusual treatment or punishment.

If an offender believes that he or she has not been sentenced based on the **principle of proportionality** (section 78.1), the offender may use Section 12 to support the claim.

connect ONLINE ACTIVITY

## SENTENCING OPTIONS AVAILABLE TO CANADIAN COURTS

LO2

There is a wide range of sentencing options available to judges in Canada, which includes both community and institutional options. A judge chooses a sentencing option after taking into consideration the nature of the offence as well as the type of offender. The sentencing options are identified in the *Criminal Code* and they may be added to or amended in order to meet society's needs. For example, conditional sentencing was introduced in 1995, to address our high incarceration rate, by creating another sentencing option that supervises offenders in the community. There is a belief that many people who were sentenced to a period of incarceration in the past could have been supervised in the community because they did not pose a threat to public safety. This is an example of how our criminal justice system responds to changing needs and realities.

Each criminal offence identified in the *Criminal Code* is defined by its classification. The classification guides a judge in the sentencing process. For example, most summary conviction offences are punishable up to a maximum of six months in jail and a $5,000 fine. This is the maximum punishment that an offender can receive if convicted of a summary conviction offence or a hybrid offence where the Crown has elected to proceed summarily. A judge may use his or her discretion and choose to sentence the offender to a term less than the maximum.

The maximum sentence for an indictable offence, or a hybrid offence where the Crown elects to proceed by indictment, is five years' imprisonment. The exception is when the *Criminal Code* identifies a different penalty.

Canada has a wide range of sentencing options that are community-based, which speaks to our trust in community agencies and organizations that support rehabilitation. Such sentences are supervised and address the principle that offenders need not be deprived of their freedom if a less restrictive sanction is available and is effective. Community-based sentences also allow an offender to remain connected to employment, education, and family support. In addition, community-based sentencing is cost-effective.

The sentencing options available to Canadian courts, when sentencing adults, are as follows:

### ABSOLUTE DISCHARGE (*CRIMINAL CODE*, S. 730)

An **absolute discharge** is the most lenient sentence available to the courts after a finding of guilt. Judges may decide to discharge an offence if they believe that it is a sufficient response from the court and does not affect public safety. For example, a judge may deem that a first-time offender has learned a lesson simply by being charged and appearing before the court, and a greater penalty is not necessary. An absolute discharge means that the accused person is not subject to a penalty of any kind. An absolute discharge is a finding of guilt but it is not a criminal conviction in law.

### CONDITIONAL DISCHARGE (*CRIMINAL CODE*, S. 730)

A conditional sentence is similar to an absolute discharge in that it is not a conviction, it is a finding of guilt. A conditional sentence is accompanied by a probation order with terms and conditions. The offender is placed on probation for a period of up to three years for adult offenders, and two years for young offenders. This period of probation must be completed without breaching any of the conditions.

Judges are limited to when they can sentence an accused to an absolute or a **conditional discharge**. It cannot be used for offences where there is a mandatory minimum sentence, or for offences that are punishable to a maximum of 14 years or longer.

### PROBATION (*CRIMINAL CODE*, S. 731)

A **probation** order may accompany a conditional discharge, a **suspended sentence**, a fine, or a term of imprisonment.

A defendant can be sentenced to a period of probation up to a maximum of three years. All probation orders are supervised by the provincial or territorial correctional system. A person can be sentenced to probation following a period of

Probation officers meet with clients on a regular basis throughout the probation period.

incarceration, as long as the period of incarceration is less than two years in length. A judge may also sentence an individual to probation and a fine.

Probation may also accompany a suspended sentence. A suspended sentence requires the accused to comply with the probation conditions for the length of the probation order. If the accused is convicted of breaching any of the probation conditions within the probation period, then the suspended sentence may be revoked. With a probation revocation, the offender returns to the original sentencing court where he or she may be re-sentenced by the original sentencing judge. A suspended sentence is not a final sentencing order—it allows persons to be placed on probation with a view to proving themselves while under probation supervision.

**victim fine surcharge**
a charge imposed on convicted offenders that benefits victim services in the specific jurisdiction

A probation order has several mandatory and optional conditions. The mandatory conditions require the offender to keep the peace, be of good behaviour, and to appear before the court when required to do so. The offender must also notify the court of any change of address or employment. Optional conditions can include requirements to complete a community service order, observe a curfew, attend school or work, to report to a probation officer on a regular basis, or to attend various programs. A judge may also order a number of prohibitions as part of the order including: owning, possessing, or carrying weapons; driving any vehicles; or associating with certain people. If an offender breaches any of the conditions of the probation order, then he or she may be charged with a new offence of failing to comply with probation (*Criminal Code*, s. 733.1). Failing to comply with a probation order is a summary conviction offence.

The most common sentencing option used in Canadian courts for both violent crime and property crime is the imposition of a probation order.

### FINE (*CRIMINAL CODE*, S. 734)

A **fine** is a financial payment to the court, and it is a common sentencing option, especially for *Criminal Code* traffic offences and impaired driving. The maximum fine that may be imposed for a summary conviction offence is $5,000, unless the *Criminal Code* states otherwise. A judge cannot sentence a defendant to a fine without inquiring about the defendant's ability to pay a fine. Once it is determined that the defendant is able to pay a fine, the judge determines the date the fine is due to the court. If a defendant does not pay the fine on time, he or she defaults and can be imprisoned in lieu of paying the outstanding fine. Each province has a formula to determine the length of time required in custody to pay off an outstanding fine. It is not unusual to find inmates in provincial institutions as a result of unpaid fines.

Many Canadian jurisdictions have fine option programs for those offenders who are unable to pay their fines. Such programs give offenders an opportunity to engage in community work in lieu of paying the fine.

The *Criminal Code* requires that all convicted persons in Canada be subject to a **victim fine surcharge** (*Criminal Code*, s. 737). Introduced in 1989, this surcharge is used to fund victim services in the province where the offence occurred. When a fine is imposed, the surcharge is 15 percent of the fine amount. When a fine is not imposed, the surcharge is $50 for a summary conviction offence and $100 for an indictable offence. If an offender is able to prove that paying the surcharge would result in undue hardship, then the court may waive the surcharge. The court must explain the reasons for not imposing the surcharge. A New Brunswick study reviewed the imposition of victim fine surcharges in the courts between 2000 and 2005. The study determined that waivers that excused an offender from paying the surcharges were used in 66.2 percent of all cases (Law and Sullivan, 2006), meaning that the surcharge was imposed in almost 44 percent of all cases. The victim fine surcharge was more often imposed

**JUST or BUST?**

Should people be sentenced to custody for unpaid fines? What are the implications of doing so?

**TABLE 5.1** Cases in Adult Criminal Court by Type of Sentence (Canada), 2009/2010

| | Total guilty cases | Prison | Conditional sentence | Probation | Fine | Restitution | Other sentences[1] |
|---|---|---|---|---|---|---|---|
| | | | | number | | | |
| **Canada** | | | | | | | |
| *Criminal Code* (without traffic) | **183,204** | 71,417 | 8,281 | 100,956 | 28,757 | 6,699 | 88,019 |
| Crimes of violence | **50,219** | 16,135 | 2,575 | 37,815 | 3,653 | 617 | 34,270 |
| Homicide | **131** | 102 | 3 | 14 | 4 | 1 | 87 |
| Attempted murder | **38** | 28 | 0 | 6 | 2 | 0 | 14 |
| Robbery | **2,800** | 2,166 | 132 | 1,420 | 13 | 64 | 1,620 |
| Sexual assault | **1,723** | 955 | 205 | 1,132 | 47 | 6 | 925 |
| Other sexual offences | **1,429** | 903 | 70 | 1,037 | 76 | 2 | 664 |
| Major assaults | **11,883** | 5,121 | 1,042 | 8,398 | 845 | 220 | 7,407 |
| Common assaults | **19,434** | 2,752 | 591 | 15,611 | 1,704 | 237 | 15,420 |
| Uttering threats | **9,723** | 3,028 | 367 | 7,651 | 834 | 61 | 6,076 |
| Criminal harassment | **1,660** | 447 | 85 | 1,504 | 73 | 14 | 1,293 |
| Other crimes against persons | **1,398** | 633 | 80 | 1,042 | 55 | 12 | 764 |
| Property crimes | **61,289** | 23,390 | 3,833 | 36,183 | 8,707 | 5,645 | 27,495 |
| Theft | **27,408** | 10,445 | 1,387 | 14,632 | 4,945 | 1,467 | 11,639 |
| Breaking and entering | **8,042** | 4,627 | 759 | 5,221 | 273 | 593 | 2,808 |
| Fraud | **9,801** | 3,129 | 1,112 | 6,496 | 1,105 | 1,656 | 4,684 |
| Mischief | **8,538** | 1,601 | 142 | 6,047 | 1,266 | 1,631 | 5,654 |
| Possession of stolen goods | **6,106** | 2,763 | 315 | 2,985 | 1,030 | 247 | 2,290 |
| Other property crimes | **1,394** | 825 | 118 | 802 | 88 | 51 | 420 |
| Administration of justice | **60,455** | 27,679 | 1,442 | 20,945 | 14,158 | 340 | 20,304 |
| Other *Criminal Code* offences | **11,241** | 4,213 | 431 | 6,013 | 2,239 | 97 | 5,950 |
| *Criminal Code* offences (traffic offences) | **48,329** | 7,535 | 805 | 7,303 | 37,898 | 196 | 35,837 |
| Impaired driving | **39,182** | 3,580 | 270 | 4,128 | 34,408 | 84 | 30,198 |
| Other *Criminal Code* traffic offences | **9,147** | 3,955 | 535 | 3,175 | 3,490 | 112 | 5,639 |
| Other Federal Statute Total | **31,083** | 8,262 | 2,548 | 10,328 | 13,344 | 93 | 13,454 |
| Drug possession | **7,314** | 887 | 134 | 2,505 | 3,850 | 11 | 4,305 |
| Drug trafficking | **6,938** | 3,177 | 2,302 | 2,065 | 536 | 29 | 5,205 |
| *Youth Criminal Justice Act* | **1,006** | 265 | 22 | 385 | 298 | 21 | 401 |
| Residual federal statutes | **15,825** | 3,933 | 90 | 5,373 | 8,660 | 32 | 3,543 |

NOTE: The conditional sentence of imprisonment option came into effect under Bill C-41 in September 1996. When a conditional sentence is imposed, the offender serves their sentence in the community under supervision. The Adult Criminal Court Survey (ACCS) began collecting data on conditional sentences in 1998/1999 from Newfoundland and Labrador, Ontario, and Alberta. Prince Edward Island, Nova Scotia, Saskatchewan, and the Yukon began reporting conditional sentencing data to the Adult Criminal Court Survey (ACCS) from 1999/2000, and New Brunswick and British Columbia from 2001/2002. Quebec does not report conditional sentencing data at this time.

1. Other sentences include absolute and conditional discharge, suspended sentence, community service order, and prohibition order among others.

SOURCE: Statistics Canada, Cases in adult criminal court by type of sentence in Canada. CANSIM, table (for fee) 252-0046 and Catalogue no. 85-002-x, March 26, 2012. Reproduced and distributed on an "as is" basis with the permission of Statistics Canada.

when the offender was sentenced to a fine alone, at 75 percent of all dispositions. The surcharge was imposed in only 16 percent of summary conviction offences and 8.7 percent of indictable offences. The most common offence upon which the surcharge was imposed was driving under the influence (DUI), at a rate of 74 percent. Judges explained that when offenders were sentenced to a period of imprisonment, they lost the ability to pay the surcharge (Law and Sullivan, 2006). The same study indicated that the average collection rate of the victim fine surcharge was 52.8 percent across New Brunswick. An accused who does not pay the victim fine surcharge as imposed is subject to imprisonment for default of payment of the fine (*Criminal Code*, s. 734.7).

### RESTITUTION (*CRIMINAL CODE*, S. 738)

Restitution is financial compensation for any loss to the victim. Restitution requires the offender to be financially accountable for the commission of the crime. It can be ordered to compensate for property damage, stolen property, or any injuries that the victim sustained as a result of the crime. Restitution may be a stand-alone order, as indicated in section 738 of the *Criminal Code*, ordered as a condition of probation, or ordered as a conditional sentence. Restitution is ordered in approximately 3 percent of guilty cases (Canadian Resource Centre for Victims of Crime, 2009). Restitution is a form of accountability that benefits the victim directly. The use of restitution has been dropping slightly in recent years. In 1994–1995, there were 11,017 restitution orders made, which represented 4.6 percent of the total guilty cases in Canada. In 2006–2007, that number dropped to 7,490, representing 3.1 percent of the total guilty cases. Most restitution orders are made in response to property crime; in 2006–2007, that figure was 80 percent of all orders. When restitution orders are made and paid as per the order, victim satisfaction is increased. Restitution orders also serve to save taxpayers money—restitution instead of government-sponsored compensation.

The downward trend for restitution orders is likely related to the reduction in property crimes in recent years. For example, the rate of reported break-ins has been steadily declining since peaking in 1991, reaching its lowest level in over 40 years. In 2007, police reported just over 230,000 break-ins, of which about 6 in 10 were residential. The rate of residential break-ins fell 9 percent in 2007, and

**FIGURE 5.1** Percentage of Guilty Cases Receiving Restitution Orders, 1994–1995 to 2006–2007

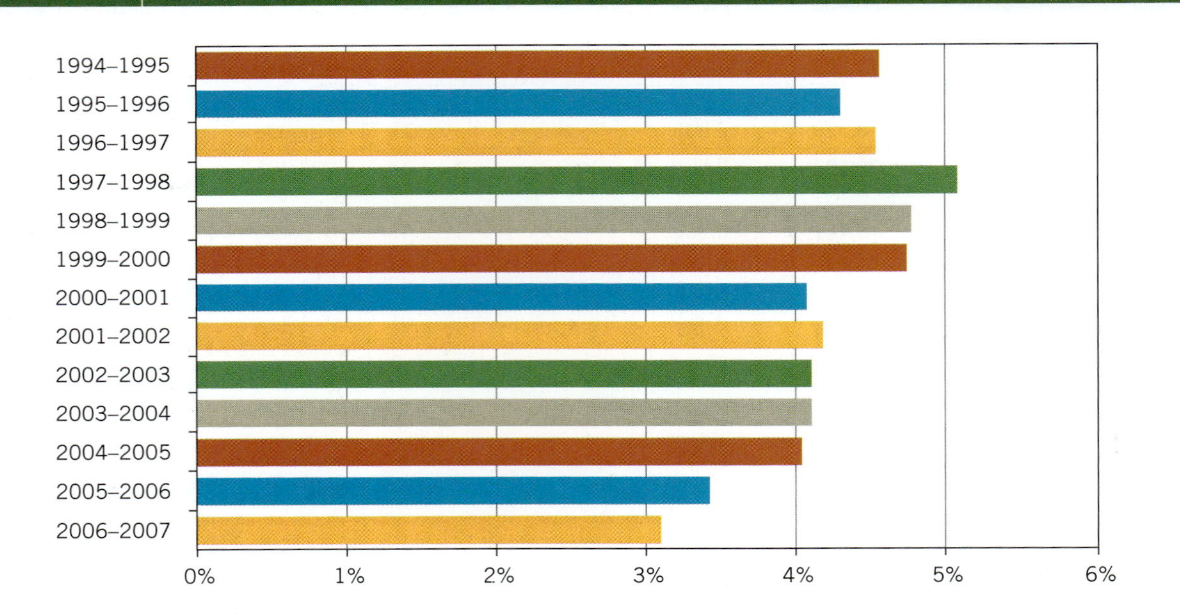


SOURCE: Statistics Canada. Crime Statistics. The Daily. July 17, 2008. http://www.statcan.ca/Daily/English/080717/d080717b.htm, accessed September 15, 2008. Reproduced and distributed on an "as is" basis with the permission of Statistics Canada.

break-ins at businesses dropped 8 percent from the previous year. The rate of motor vehicle theft has also been declining since it reached its highest level in 1996, including a 9 percent drop in 2007 from the previous year (Statistics Canada, 2008).

### CONDITIONAL SENTENCE (*CRIMINAL CODE*, S. 742)

The conditional sentence is a relatively new sentencing option, having been introduced in Canada in 1996 in response to Canada's high rate of incarceration. A conditional sentence is intended to reduce the use of incarceration, while at the same time ensuring that the offender is treated fairly and the public is protected. A conditional sentence is served in the community. It can be imposed when an offence does not carry a minimum penalty of imprisonment or has a penalty of a maximum term of imprisonment of two years or more. When an offender serves a conditional sentence, there are strict rules regarding the offender's freedom. Conditional sentences are commonly referred to as "house arrest." The offender is permitted to leave the home for specific purposes, such as medical appointments. Visits to the home may also be restricted.

### IMPRISONMENT (*CRIMINAL CODE*, S. 743)

A custodial sentence is the most severe form of sentencing available to a judge. A term of imprisonment under two years is served in a provincial/territorial correctional system. A term of two years and greater is served in the federal correctional system.

When a defendant is convicted of more than one offence, the judge may direct that the sentences be served concurrently or consecutively. A **concurrent sentence** means that all sentences are served at the same time, while a **consecutive sentence** means that the sentences follow one another. For example, a defendant may be sentenced to three one-year terms of imprisonment. If served concurrently, the defendant is imprisoned for one year. If served consecutively, the defendant is imprisoned for three years.

**concurrent sentence**
a sentence that is served at the same time as another sentence

**consecutive sentence**
a sentence that is served following another sentence

A judge also has the option, with some offences, of sentencing an individual to an intermittent period of incarceration. **Intermittent sentences** are only possible for sentences of 90 days or less. Intermittent sentences are often weekend sentences, permitting the offender to continue to work or engage in education or treatment during the week. In general, an offender reports to the institution on Friday evenings and leaves early Monday morning. This form of sentence does not interfere with employment and may prevent offenders from committing further offences because they do not lose their source of income and are also able to continue to maintain family contacts. The intermittent sentence is only an option in jurisdictions that have the capacity to detain offenders on weekends. When the offender who receives an intermittent sentence is not in custody, he or she is subject to the conditions of a probation order.

**intermittent sentence**
a sentence that has a break within it that permits the offender to leave the institution for employment or education

### LIFE IMPRISONMENT IN CANADA

Life imprisonment in Canada is for one's natural life. Offenders sentenced to life imprisonment can only be released from prison if granted parole by the Parole Board of Canada. Those convicted of first degree murder serve life as a minimum sentence, with their first parole eligibility set by law at 25 years. A person convicted of second degree murder is also sentenced to life imprisonment; however, the judge has the discretion to set the parole eligibility date between 10 and 25 years. If a **lifer** is granted parole, he or she remains subject to the conditions of parole and under the supervision of a parole officer for the rest of his or her life. Offenders who continue to pose a risk to public safety may never receive parole.

**lifer**
a person sentenced to life imprisonment

### DANGEROUS OFFENDER DESIGNATION IN CANADA

In order to protect Canadians from offenders who have been identified as dangerous and/or chronic sex offenders, the **Dangerous Offender** designation was introduced in Canada. This designation is reserved for those offenders who pose a high risk of continuing to commit violent and/or sexual offences. A dangerous offender application is launched by the Crown attorney during the sentencing phase of the trial.

Section 752 of the *Criminal Code* defines the dangerous offender designation. When a person is convicted of his or her third (or more) offence, the Crown may elect to apply to have the offender declared a dangerous offender. The Crown must receive consent from the Attorney General in order to initiate the application. In order to be declared a dangerous offender, it must be proved that the offender is at risk of re-offending and is a danger to the community. Further, there must be little hope of being able to minimize the risk the offender poses within the community. A dangerous offender is placed on an **indefinite sentence** within the federal correctional system. He or she may apply for parole after the first seven years in custody, and then again every two years afterwards. Dangerous offenders granted parole remain under federal parole supervision indefinitely.

The Dangerous Offender application provision is contained in Section 753 of the *Criminal Code*:

753. (1) On application made under this Part after an assessment report is filed under subsection 752.1(2), the court shall find the offender to be a dangerous offender if it is satisfied

(a) that the offence for which the offender has been convicted is a serious personal injury offence described in paragraph (*a*) of the definition of that expression in section 752 and the offender constitutes a threat to the life, safety or physical or mental well-being of other persons on the basis of evidence establishing

(i) pattern of repetitive behaviour by the offender, of which the offence for which he or she has been convicted forms a part, showing a failure to restrain his or her behaviour and a likelihood of causing death or injury to other persons, or inflicting severe psychological damage on other persons, through failure in the future to restrain his or her behaviour,

(ii) pattern of persistent aggressive behaviour by the offender, of which the offence for which he or she has been convicted forms a part, showing a substantial degree of indifference on the part of the offender respecting the reasonably foreseeable consequences to other persons of his or her behaviour, or

(iii) any behaviour by the offender, associated with the offence for which he or she has been convicted, that is of such a brutal nature as to compel the conclusion that the offender's behaviour in the future is unlikely to be inhibited by normal standards of behavioural restraint; or

(b) that the offence for which the offender has been convicted is a serious personal injury offence described in paragraph (*b*) of the definition of that expression in section 752 and the offender, by his or her conduct in any sexual matter including that involved in the

Millhaven Institution: home to many offenders serving life sentences in Canada.

commission of the offence for which he or she has been convicted, has shown a failure to control his or her sexual impulses and a likelihood of causing injury, pain or other evil to other persons through failure in the future to control his or her sexual impulses.

(4) If the court finds an offender to be a dangerous offender, it shall
   (a) impose a sentence of detention in a penitentiary for an indeterminate period;

As of April 2011, there were 458 dangerous offenders in Canada (Correctional Service of Canada, 2011). To date only three women in Canada have been identified as dangerous offenders—and there is only one who currently holds the designation.

### LONG-TERM OFFENDERS

The **long-term offender** designation was introduced in Canada in 1997, in an effort to provide long-term supervision to those offenders who do not qualify for dangerous offender designation.

Section 752 of the *Criminal Code* makes it possible for a Crown attorney to apply for an offender to be declared a long-term offender. The Crown attorney must have the Attorney General's permission prior to submitting the application. In order to be eligible for long-term offender status, the following criteria must be satisfied:

- it is appropriate to impose a sentence of imprisonment of two years or more for the offence for which the offender has been convicted;
- there is a substantial risk that the offender will reoffend; and
- there is a reasonable possibility of eventual control of the risk in the community.

In addition, section 753.1(2) of the *Criminal Code* provides the criteria that the court must consider to conclude that the offender poses a "substantial risk" under 753.1(1)(b):

(a) the offender has been convicted of an offence under section 151 (sexual interference), 152 (invitation to sexual touching) or 153 (sexual exploitation),... subsection 173(2) (exposure) or section 271 (sexual assault), 272 (sexual assault with a weapon) or 273 (aggravated sexual assault), or has engaged in serious conduct of a sexual nature in the commission of another offence of which the offender has been convicted; and

(b) the offender
   (i) has shown a pattern of repetitive behaviour, of which the offence for which he or she has been convicted forms a part, that shows a likelihood of the offender's causing death or injury to other persons or inflicting severe psychological damage on other persons, or

PROFILE

## A Dangerous Offender: Johnson Aziga

On August 2, 2011 Johnson Aziga, a 55-year-old resident of Hamilton, Ontario, was declared a dangerous offender. In a precedent-setting case, Aziga was convicted of first-degree murder in 2009 in the deaths of two of his sex partners through HIV transmission. Aziga was made aware that he was carrying HIV in 1996 when he was ordered by public health officials to disclose his illness to any potential sexual partners. According to the prosecutor, Aziga infected seven women with HIV, two of whom died. Along with the two counts of first-degree murder, Aziga was also convicted of 10 counts of aggravated assault and attempted sexual assault—all of which supported the dangerous offender application.

SOURCES: http://www.theglobeandmail.com/news/national/ontario-court-declares-hiv-positive-killer-a-dangerous-offender/article2117088/; http://www.cbc.ca/news/canada/story/2011/08/02/hiv-offender-aziga.html; http://www.torontosun.com/2011/08/02/hiv-murderer-faces-indefinite-prison-term.

(ii) by conduct in any sexual matter including that involved in the commission of the offence for which the offender has been convicted, has shown a likelihood of causing injury, pain or other evil to other persons in the future through similar offences.

The long-term offender designation is an attempt to minimize the long-term risk to the community through community supervision by a parole officer. Once an offender is sentenced as a long-term offender, he or she serves the prison sentence and then receives a long-term supervision order in the community of up to a maximum of 10 years. If the long-term offender breaches any of the terms of the supervision order, he or she may be charged with a separate indictable *Criminal Code* offence (*Criminal Code*, s.753.3), punishable by up to 10 years in prison.

## LO3 SENTENCING CONSIDERATIONS

Canadian law stresses that sentences should be proportionate to the offence, and reflect the degree of the offender's responsibility. This is intended to protect offenders from sentences that are too harsh or too lenient. There are a number of factors that a judge may take into consideration when sentencing a defendant. These factors provide the judge with additional information beyond the facts of the case. A judge may take the following factors into consideration when sentencing.

### GUILTY PLEA

A guilty plea often results in a reduced sentence, and the earlier in the process that the guilty plea is made, often the greater the reduction. A guilty plea is considered to be an admission of guilt, and therefore the offender is accepting responsibility for having committed the crime. In addition, a guilty plea is often connected with remorse. The second important consequence of a guilty plea is that it saves the criminal justice system significant time and resources because a trial is not required. A guilty plea also means that victims and witnesses are spared the emotional upset that accompanies testifying in court.

### PRE-SENTENCE REPORTS

The judge may choose to order a pre-sentence report in order to provide the court with more in-depth information about a defendant, after there has been a finding of guilt. A pre-sentence report is prepared by a probation officer, who interviews the offender, family members, employers, and other significant people, to provide an objective portrayal of the offender. Once completed, the pre-sentence report is distributed to the judge, the Crown attorney, and the defence attorney, prior to the sentencing date.

Pre-sentence reports are authorized under section 721 of the *Criminal Code*. The court can request that a pre-sentence report be completed

> "for the purpose of assisting the court in imposing a sentence or in determining whether the accused should be discharged pursuant to section 730."

The court can only request a pre-sentence report after the accused is found guilty or has entered a guilty plea. Each province and territory determines whether or not it permits the probation officer who writes the report to make sentencing recommendations. However, in all jurisdictions, probation officers are permitted to make recommendations regarding the offender's suitability for community supervision (Bonta, Bourgon, Jesseman, and Yessine, 2005). Generally, research indicates that there is a high agreement rate between the recommendations made in a pre-sentence report and the court's disposition of the case, especially when a community sentence is recommended by the writer (Bonta, et al., 2005).

Canadian law stresses that sentences should be proportionate to the offence, and reflect the degree of the offender's responsibility.

Pre-trial custody is taken into consideration at sentencing in many cases.

### PRE-TRIAL CUSTODY

A judge may credit a defendant for time spent in custody prior to the trial; this is referred to as "dead time." Pre-trial custody differs from custody after sentencing because the time does not earn any credit toward parole eligibility. In addition, when offenders are incarcerated in pre-trial custody, they have not been formally classified by the criminal justice system, and therefore they are not able to take advantage of education, treatment, or employment programs. There is no distinct formula that a judge must follow when giving credit for time served; however, legislation that limits the maximum credit that a judge may award is one day for every day served in pre-trial custody. In some cases, a judge can increase the one-day rule to 1.5 days if the accused meets certain criteria regarding bail history and prior convictions. Pre-trial custody does not alter a life sentence, and generally does not apply to offences with mandatory minimum sentences.

### CRIMINAL RECORD

An offender's criminal record is taken into consideration by the judge at the time of sentencing. The criminal record is introduced by the prosecution and the judge can impose a sentence that reflects the offender's criminal record. For example, if an offender has not successfully completed a period of community supervision in the past, a judge may not consider community supervision again. Generally, the longer an individual's record, the more severe the penalty imposed, up to the maximum penalty identified by the *Criminal Code*.

### THE CIRCUMSTANCES RELATED TO THE OFFENCE AND THE OFFENDER

A judge may consider the following circumstances when sentencing an offender:

- the circumstances and severity of the offence—use of violence, use of weapons, the role of the offender;
- the offender's motivation;
- the offender's relationship to the victim;
- the offender's attitude;
- the offender's previous response to sentencing options (e.g., community supervision); and
- correctional supports and programs available to the offender both in custody and in the community.

### THE PENALTY FOR THE OFFENCE

A judge considers the maximum or minimum sentence of each offence as identified in the *Criminal Code*. In addition, courts consider sentences imposed for other similar offences, committed under similar circumstances (*Criminal Code*, s. 718.2) to ensure that there is an element of consistency in sentencing.

### AGGRAVATING CIRCUMSTANCES

When sentencing an offender, the courts may take **aggravating factors** into consideration. An aggravating factor is a fact or circumstance that increases the severity or culpability of a criminal act (*Criminal Code*, s. 718.2). The aggravating factors that courts may take into consideration include:

**aggravating factors**

facts or circumstances that increases the severity of the offence

- whether or not the offence is motivated by prejudice or hate; for example, an offender who assaults someone because of his or her race, religion, or sexual orientation;
- whether or not the victim was a spouse or child of the offender; for example, an offender who physically assaults his or her spouse or child;
- whether or not the offender abused a position of authority or trust in committing the offence; for example, a coach who sexually abuses a player;
- whether or not the offence was committed for the benefit of organized crime; for example, an offender who commits a crime where the proceeds benefit an organized crime group; or
- whether or not the offence was a terrorism-related offence; for example, an offender who bombs a building to make a political statement.

### MITIGATING CIRCUMSTANCES

When sentencing an offender, the court may take **mitigating circumstances** into consideration (*Criminal Code*, s. 718.2). Mitigating circumstances are circumstances that may reduce the severity of the sentence, and can include:

**mitigating circumstances**

circumstances that may reduce the severity of the sentence

- an offender is appearing before the court for the first time;
- an offender has steady employment or is in school;
- an offender takes responsibility for his or her involvement in the offence;
- an offender has special needs or challenges;
- an offender has a good character;
- an offender has a supportive family; or
- an offender has engaged in treatment since the time of the offence.

### THE VICTIM AND THE VICTIM IMPACT STATEMENT

The impact that the offence had upon the victim is a sentencing consideration. The impact is often clear, based on the type of the offence; however, a victim has the right to provide a deeper insight to the court in the form of a victim impact statement. The statement can influence the sentencing process, as a judge may take the impact on the victim into consideration when sentencing the offender. The victim impact statement may be read by a family member or by the Crown attorney if the victim is unable to do so. When a victim chooses not to present the victim impact statement, the victim is represented by the Crown attorney.

## MANDATORY SENTENCING

Generally, when a person is convicted of an offence it is rare that he or she will receive the maximum sentence prescribed in the *Criminal Code*. The *Criminal Code* identifies the maximum length of time of imprisonment that an offender may receive; however, in practice, the courts often sentence an offender to a length of time less than the maximum. This practice often results in the public's general dissatisfaction with the criminal justice system (Edgar, 1999). In practice, the most severe prison sentences are reserved for the worst offenders. The exception to this occurs with offences that carry a mandatory minimum sentence in the event of a conviction.

Mandatory sentencing refers to the requirement to impose a minimum sentence on those who are convicted of specific offences. There are a number of offences in the *Criminal Code* that carry a mandatory minimum sentence. These are offences where judges do not have the discretion to sentence the accused as they see fit. The judge is bound by law to sentence the accused to the minimum sentence identified in the *Criminal Code*. Mandatory sentencing requires that all accused persons charged with certain offences be treated the same way, regardless of their personal

## Victim Impact Statement of Theo Fleury Read at the Trial of Graham James, March 20, 2012.

At a young and very impressionable age, I was stalked, preyed upon and sexually assaulted over 150 times by an adult my family and I trusted completely.

I was a boy with a big dream and the talent to match. I played hockey in the early morning hours, after school, on the weekends and holidays, I even dreamed of hockey. Everyone in my life knew of my passion and my talent, including convicted pedophile Graham James.

Mr. James was a well-known minor hockey coach, and he zeroed in on my family and me. He skillfully manipulated us all, and eventually my parents entrusted my care and well being to him in order to allow me to move to other towns and cities to advance my hockey dream. He was a larger than life figure with the hockey credentials and education as a teacher, to match, and it was drilled into me that he held the keys to making my dream become a reality.

I was just a kid. A child. I was completely under Graham James's control. And I was scared. I did not have the emotional skills, the knowledge, or the ability to stop the rapes or change my circumstances. I felt lost, alone, and helpless. And those feelings did not stop after I was able to get away from Mr. James; I continued to feel that way for 20+ years afterwards. I descended into years of drug addiction, alcoholism, and addictions to sex, gambling, rage.

My loved ones, including my beloved children, spiraled down with me. The pain was all encompassing. And no matter how many NHL games I won, or money I made, or fame I gained could dull the pain of having been sexually abused by Graham James. His sickness changed my life, changed the lives of everyone who was close to me, and caused more pain than can be measured.

Finally, after a night in the New Mexico desert with a gun in my mouth and finger on the trigger, I found the courage to get help and start a long process of healing. I am now reconciled with my children and family, I have been sober for 6 years and I have put the course of my professional life on an amazing path. I am fortunate to speak to victims, survivors, victors and advocates all over North America. From little boys to men as old as 82 tell me they too have been victimized. I am honoured each and every time they share with me. They shed tears, they tell me secrets they have never dared to tell anyone else, and they look for some sort of peace in the midst of their hell.

This court must know that pedophiles like Graham James do not ever change. They are devoid of anything good, and their moral compass does not exist. The statistics show 1 in 3 girls and 1 in 5 boys will be sexually abused before the age of 18. A good majority of these children will grow into angry adults who are completely stunted in their emotional growth, and are unable to contribute to healthy and loving relationships. Some will find healing, but many will not, and the after effects of sexual abuse will affect everyone close to them. They will be unable to find decent employment, they will be unable to fully commit to loving relationships, they will be unable to trust, they will be unable to parent their children, they will be unable to really contribute to society. All because a monster like Graham James preyed upon them, took advantage of their trust and their age, to commit heinous crimes on their bodies, souls and spirits. This is an epidemic and it has to stop.

Do not show leniency to Graham James, he certainly never did to me or any of his other prey. He had many opportunities to stop, to get help, to change, and he never took them. In fact, he kept going. He created situations wherein he could abuse me, he lied time and again, and he found how his authority over me could allow him to do whatever he wanted. He instilled not only physical pain, but also deep emotional pain and left scars so deep and so wide it took decades for me to sleep one night in peace. He was purposeful, he planned his assaults, he took the time and the energy to sexually abuse me every chance he got. And believe me, he will do it again and again and again if ever given the chance. He has no remorse. A monster who will sexually assault children should never be let loose in society — never.

When you consider punishment for Graham James I ask this court to think not only about the law, but also about that scared little boy who had nowhere to turn, nowhere to run and nowhere to hide each and every time Graham James raped me. Think about that little boy, his tears and his anger and his helplessness. Think long and hard about YEARS OF SEXUAL ASSAULTS, not just one or two incidents, YEARS OF SEXUAL ASSAULTS, perpetrated by Graham James on me and other children. Think about the journey to hell he sent them and me on. Think about the tears shed that could fill the oceans, rivers and streams by his victims. Think about the ruined relationships, the lost opportunities, the anguish, the fear that follows every waking moment and invades every dream. Only then should you consider punishment. And the punishment should be a lifetime removed from society in a prison where the keys are thrown away, never to be found again.

I urge this court to set an example, not only for other offenders, but to those who have been victimized — that this court and this country takes sexual abuse and assault seriously, and that you'll protect the innocent, harshly punish the guilty and encourage healing for everyone who has ever been even remotely affected by monsters like Graham James.

My name is Theoren Fleury and I am a victor over sexual abuse.

SOURCE: (Theo Fleury's victim impact statement as reprinted in *The Toronto Star*): http://www.thestar.com/sports/hockey/nhl/article/1135091.

## IN THE NEWS

### Fraud, Friendship, and a Conditional Sentence

A 23-year-old woman pleaded guilty to defrauding friends, family, and strangers of over $12,000 in 2010. Ashley Kirilow faked cancer and received thousands of dollars in donations from people who were duped by her elaborate scheme. She shaved her head, plucked her eyebrows, and constantly wore a head scarf. The court heard that Kirilow first told the lie to her boyfriend in an effort to garner sympathy from him, but the lie turned into a campaign from which she received both attention and money. She accepted personal donations from supporters, and eventually began a more public strategy by creating a Facebook page to collect donations for herself called "Change for a Cure." Kirilow received a conditional sentence of 10 months to be served under house arrest, and an additional five months under strict curfew. She was also sentenced to two years' probation and 100 hours of community service. She was prohibited from canvassing or soliciting donations for any charitable organization. The judge said he did not order restitution because the real harm to the victims was an abuse of their trust, more so than their finances.

SOURCE: CTV.ca, 2010, CBC.ca, 2011, http://www.thestar.com/news/gta/article/844614--woman-faked-cancer-to-raise-money.

Ashley Kirilow defrauded family and friends, by faking cancer.

history or circumstances. Though popular with the general public and politicians, judges do not share in the enthusiasm for mandatory sentencing, largely because it limits their ability to impose a just sentence based on the person who appears before them (Roberts, 2005). Mandatory minimum sentences are controversial because they can imply that a judge will not make a decision that is acceptable. Mandatory minimum sentences also deny a judge the opportunity to consider an accused person's individual circumstances.

The concept of mandatory minimum sentences was challenged in R. *v.* Ferguson (R. *v.* Ferguson, [2008] 1 S.C.R. 96, 2008 SCC 6). The facts of the case are that Constable M. E. Ferguson, an RCMP officer, fatally shot Darren Varley while Varley was in a police cell in the RCMP detachment in Pincher Creek, Alberta. The jury convicted Constable Ferguson of manslaughter and the trial judge imposed a conditional sentence of two years less a day, even though the *Criminal Code* states that the mandatory minimum sentence for manslaughter when a firearm is used is four years' imprisonment. Alberta's Court of Appeal overturned the conditional sentence and imposed the four year minimum sentence. Ferguson appealed to the Supreme Court of Canada, using section 12 of the *Charter*, which guarantees that everyone has the right not to be subjected to cruel and unusual treatment or punishment. Ferguson asserted that imposing the four-year minimum sentence was cruel and unusual treatment. The Supreme Court

MYTH VS FACT

## The Sex Offender Registry in Canada is Not Accessible to the General Public, Unlike the Sex Offender Registries in Other Jurisdictions.

In 2004, Canada enacted the *Sex Offender Information Registration Act*, an act that requires sex offenders to register personal information for the purpose of supporting police in preventing and investigating sexual offences. The **Sex Offender Registry** is a database that is not available to the public—it is an investigative tool that is only available to the police across Canada. It is maintained by the RCMP.

Following conviction and sentencing for one of the designated offences listed in the *Criminal Code*, the Crown can apply to the court for a Sex Offender Registration Order. The Crown can apply for registration orders not only for sexual offence convictions, but also for other offences if they were made with the intent to commit one of the designated sexual offences.

Once a court orders registration, the offender is given notice to register in person at a designated police agency (registration centre) within 15 days after the order is made, or after he or she is released from custody. The registration period begins on the day the order is made and re-registration is required once per year and within 15 days of a change of personal information, such as the name or address. If the offender is absent from his or her home address for more than 15 consecutive days, the registration centre must be notified.

Sex offenders are required to remain registered for one of three periods. The periods are geared to the maximum penalty available for the offence of which they were convicted:

- 10 years for summary conviction offences and offences with two and five year maximums;
- 20 years for offences carrying a 10 or 14 year maximum sentence; and
- Lifetime for offences with a maximum life sentence or when there is a prior conviction for a sex offence.

After 20 years and (if necessary) every five years thereafter, offenders registered for life are able to apply for a judicial review to determine the requirement to register for the remainder of the registration period.

Offenders registered for 10 or 20 years may apply for a judicial review at the 5- or 10-year mark respectively to determine if their registration requirement should be removed based on the same test as for lifetime registrants.

Sex offender information remains in the database indefinitely, except when there is a final acquittal on appeal, a record suspension under the Royal Prerogative of Mercy, or the *Criminal Code*. In these cases, information is permanently removed.

A new *Criminal Code* offence was created for failure to comply with the terms and conditions of a registration order or for providing false information. This offence is punishable by a maximum of six months in prison for a first offence, up to two years for any subsequent offence, and/or a $10,000 fine in either case.

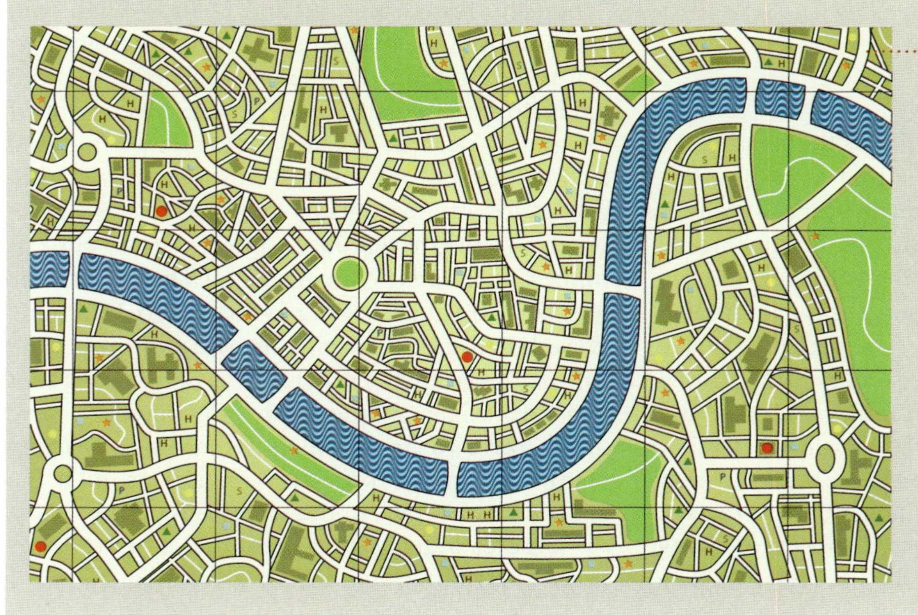

Unlike sex offender registries in other jurisdictions, information contained in the Canadian National Sex Offender Registry is not available to the public.

SOURCE: Public Safety Canada, 2004.

When asked, most Canadians say that they do not believe that our criminal justice system imposes criminal sentences that are severe enough.

of Canada found that the mandatory minimum sentence was not cruel and unusual treatment or punishment, even though as a police officer Ferguson would require protective custody, which would amount to being confined to a cell for 23 hours per day, for his own safety.

## LO4 SENTENCING DISPARITY

One of the important features of the sentencing process in Canadian courts is that in most cases, sentencing is specific to the individual offender who appears before the court. In sentencing an offender, the judge assesses the offender and the offence as a unique situation. Two persons who are charged with the same offence may leave the court with different sentences due to the specifics of each case. Even though offenders are treated as individuals, generally speaking, similar crimes receive similar sentences (*Criminal Code*, s. 718.2). When similar crimes do not receive similar sentences, this is referred to as sentencing disparity. **Sentencing disparity** occurs when a judge sentences similar persons who are convicted of the same offence, to very different sentences. It also occurs when different judges sentence similar persons who are convicted of the same offence to very different sentences.

The reality is that sentences are imposed by judges, and judges are people with personal values and personal experiences, all of which can have an impact on their assessment. Studies indicate that judges, Crown attorneys, and defence attorneys all agree that sentencing disparity does occur in Canada (Roberts, 1999). However, it is the offenders themselves who most strongly report that sentencing disparity is commonplace in our criminal justice system. Inmates were polled in a British Columbia survey, and 98 percent of them reported that they believed that some judges were more likely to send offenders to prison than others (Roberts, 1999). This means that offenders do not view judges as objective arbiters of fact; instead, they believe that judges are pre-disposed to sentence offenders in a certain way.

A sentencing study in Toronto looked at Black and Caucasian men who were charged by the Toronto police in 1989/1990. This study examined sentencing in an effort to determine whether or not the Blacks were sentenced differently than Caucasians who were convicted of the same offence. The sample included 821 Blacks and 832 Caucasians, with the same number of men in each offence category that was analyzed. The incarceration rate analysis indicated that more Blacks than Caucasians were sentenced to prison. When the researchers looked at those men who were before the court charged with drug offences, it was determined that the Caucasians were more likely to be convicted of a simple possession of drugs (90 percent) than trafficking, as opposed to 67 percent of the Blacks. Of those convicted of possession of a narcotic, 49 percent of the Blacks received a prison sentence compared to 18 percent of the Caucasians (Williams, 1999). The researchers looked at the men's criminal records to determine if the length of the criminal record was the reason for the disparity. However, it was determined that the Caucasians in the study (36 percent) were more likely to have a lengthy record, consisting of more than five previous convictions, than the Blacks (28 percent) in the study.

Studies indicate that there are certain factors that contribute to disparate sentencing. For example, offenders who are unemployed are more likely to receive prison terms than those who are employed (Williams, 1999). Perhaps the most disturbing type of sentencing disparity is when it is attributed to race, ethnicity, social status, gender, or sexual orientation.

When asked, most Canadians say that they do not believe that our criminal justice system imposes criminal sentences that are severe enough (Roberts, 1999). They also attribute this perceived leniency as leading to an increase in violent crime. In fact, most Canadians are unaware of the fact that the reported crime rate in Canada has been on a steady decline over the past decade. For the most part, Canadians gauge their opinions on the media reports of crime, most of which highlight individual offenders who commit high profile crimes.

### SENTENCING OF ABORIGINAL OFFENDERS

The *Criminal Code* provides specific direction when the courts sentence Aboriginal offenders. Section 718.2 (e) states:

> all available sanctions other than imprisonment that are reasonable in the circumstances should be considered for all offenders, with particular attention to the circumstances of aboriginal offenders.

This section is in response to the overrepresentation of Aboriginal persons in the criminal justice system, and its intention is to reduce the number of Aboriginal offenders sentenced to imprisonment. Judges are required to consider restorative options available to the courts for all offenders; however, they must pay particular attention to Aboriginal offenders in an effort to rectify what is perceived as systemic discrimination (Campbell Research Associates, 2008).

The overrepresentation of Aboriginal persons in our criminal justice system has been declared "a crisis in the Canadian criminal justice system" by the Supreme Court of Canada (R. *v.* Gladue, [1999] 1 S.C.R. 688). In its written decision of the Gladue case, the Supreme Court wrote:

The Supreme Court has determined that the "history of colonialism, displacement and residential schools…" should be taken into consideration when sentencing an Aboriginal person.

A number of restorative processes have been introduced into the courts in an effort to be sensitive to the cultural disposition of an Aboriginal offender.

> ... aboriginal offenders are, as a result of these unique systemic and background factors, more adversely affected by incarceration and less likely to be "rehabilitated" thereby, because the internment milieu is often culturally inappropriate and regrettably discrimination towards them is so often rampant in penal institutions.

As a result of the Gladue case, the Supreme Court requires all Canadian courts to accept the fact that there are serious unique issues that pertain to Aboriginal people in Canada. Courts are required to consider alternative options for Aboriginal persons before the court because incarceration is believed to be overused. **Gladue courts** have arisen in some jurisdictions, where the cases of Aboriginal offenders are heard with a view to being sensitive to their needs. Judges who sit in Gladue courts receive special training and are given access to relevant resources. There are a number of differences between the manner in which cases are adjudicated in Gladue courts. Gladue cases take much longer than traditional courts to process a case as they engage in a more detailed process of assessing the needs of the offender (Rudin, 2005), often including the preparation of a Gladue Report, which provides the court with additional information beyond that found in a pre-sentence report.

The success of the Gladue courts has received mixed reviews across the country, meaning that in some jurisdictions it has been embraced, while in others it has been ignored (Makin, 2012). This has resulted in disappointment in Aboriginal communities. In March, 2012, the Supreme Court of Canada recognized that challenges still exist in sentencing Aboriginal offenders and a Supreme Court decision was made that strengthened the need to recognize an Aboriginal offender's background during the sentencing phase. Judge LeBel of the Supreme Court said that a "Gladue report" should be prepared when sentencing Aboriginal offenders, adding that the oppressive nature of their backgrounds should be considered. LeBel added:

> When sentencing an aboriginal offender, courts must take judicial notice of such matters as the history of colonialism, displacement, and residential schools and how that history continues to translate into lower educational attainment, lower incomes, higher unemployment, higher rates of substance abuse and suicide, and, of course, higher levels of incarceration for aboriginal peoples. (Makin, 2012)

It has been suggested that there is limited information about sentencing to allow for an in-depth understanding of the differences between the sentencing of Aboriginal and non-Aboriginal offenders (La Prarie, 1999). There is research to date that suggests that federal Aboriginal offenders are sentenced to longer sentences than their non-Aboriginal counterparts (Hann & Harman, 1993; York, 1995, as cited in La Prarie, 1999). It is often difficult to compare Aboriginal and non-Aboriginal sentencing because there are often many other factors that are difficult to control. For example, it is a challenge to compare offenders when they present with varying lengths of criminal records, differences in the severity of offences, and other factors that are taken into consideration in the sentencing process.

As a result of the Gladue decision, a number of restorative processes have been introduced into the courts in an effort to be sensitive to the cultural disposition of an Aboriginal offender. The use of sentencing circles is one such example that is discussed in detail in the Restorative Justice chapter.

## Chapter Summary

This chapter provided an introduction to the sentencing of adult offenders. The following key concepts were addressed:

- The principles of sentencing were identified.
- The sentencing options available to the courts when sentencing adult offenders were identified. The most common sentencing option is probation.
- There are specific designations for very serious offenders—dangerous offender and long-term offender designations.
- The consequences of sentencing disparity was discussed, as was the need to ensure that Aboriginal defendants are given special consideration when being sentenced.

## Relevant Legislation

*Criminal Code*, RSC 1985, c C-46

*Sex Offender Information Registration Act* (S.C. 2004, c. 10)

## Key Terms

Absolute discharge
Aggravating factors
Concurrent sentence
Conditional discharge
Consecutive sentence
Dangerous offender
Fine
General deterrence
Gladue courts
Indefinite sentence
Intermittent sentence
Lifer
Long-term offender
Mitigating circumstances
Principle of proportionality
Probation
Sentencing disparity
Sex Offender Registry
Specific deterrence
Suspended sentence
Victim fine surcharge

## For Review

1. What is the difference between the dangerous offender and long-term offender designations?
2. What is the difference between aggravating factors and mitigating circumstances?
3. Why is it important for judges to pay particular attention to the sentencing of Aboriginal persons?
4. What is the most common type of sentence imposed by judges?
5. Are victims adequately represented in the sentencing phase of the criminal trial?
6. What is the purpose of sentencing?
7. Provide examples of sentencing disparity in Canada.
8. What is the purpose of the pre-sentence report? How does it inform the court?

## Thinking Critically

1. What safeguards could be put into place to ensure that sentencing is more consistent across Canada? What are the advantages and disadvantages of having consistent sentencing?
2. How can the courts ensure that they are taking the special circumstances of Aboriginal offenders into consideration? What are the consequences of not doing so?
3. Critics of the dangerous offender legislation have compared it to a form of cruel and unusual treatment. To what extent could it be interpreted as cruel and unusual punishment?
4. How might you measure whether or not the sentencing of a specific individual meets one (or more) of the sentencing objectives? Provide an example.
5. To what extent is the Sex Offender Registry a useful tool in our society? Is there anything that could be done to increase its effectiveness?
6. What is the philosophy of our court system, given that aggravating and mitigating circumstances are considered in the sentencing process?
7. Why is it important that the criminal record of a defendant be introduced in the sentencing phase?
8. The conditional sentence is a relatively new sentencing option for our courts. What are the advantages of this sentencing option, to the offender and to the criminal justice system overall?

Practise and learn online with Connect

CHAPTER 6

# Correctional Institutions

Incarcerated men play dodge ball behind the fence of the Baffin Correctional Centre in Iqaluit.

## Ashley Smith: "A Preventable Death"

Ashley Smith was a 19-year-old woman who died while in custody at the Grand Valley Institution for Women in Ontario, in 2007. Her story began many years earlier when, as a young teenager, she began to engage in disruptive and defiant behaviour. By her fifteenth birthday she had appeared in youth court 14 times for relatively minor offences. Her disruptive behaviour continued and resulted in additional criminal charges, school suspensions, and banishment from local malls. She eventually ended up in a youth treatment program, where she received a psychiatric assessment that indicated that she had ADHD, a borderline personality disorder, and narcissistic personality traits. Ongoing counselling, monitoring, and medication were recommended. Ashley spent the next three years going in and out of the New Brunswick Youth Centre, having been charged with offences such as assault, trespassing, and causing a disturbance. While in youth custody, she was the subject of over 800 incident reports for aggressive and self-harming behaviours. When she was incarcerated, she spent most of the time in a segregation unit and repeatedly looked for ways to harm herself. In January, 2006, Ashley turned 18 and she was warned repeatedly that subsequent criminal offences would result in an adult sentence. In July, 2006, the New Brunswick Youth Centre made an application under the *Youth Criminal Justice Act* to transfer Ashley to an adult correctional facility. Ashley fought the application but lost. She was transferred to the Saint John Regional Correctional Centre, where she remained for 26 days (most of the time was spent in segregation) and she incurred numerous institutional charges for defiant behaviour. From October 2006 to October 2007, Ashley was transferred six times within the federal correctional system, ending up at Grand Valley Institution for Women. She was held in administrative segregation the entire time yet she never received a treatment plan, because she was never in one institution long enough to have one completed. Her self-harming behaviours were not addressed adequately and she was eventually successful in ending her life on October 19, 2007, while on suicide watch. According to the correctional investigator's report:

> *Ms. Smith was identified by an institutional psychologist as being highly suicidal. Staff monitoring Ms. Smith in her cell, some of whom had been only temporarily and recently assigned to Grand Valley Institution for Women, were not formally provided with this crucial piece of information in the 48 hours prior to her death. With misinformed and poorly communicated decisions as the backdrop, Ms. Smith*

Coralee Smith, Ashley's mother.

### LEARNING OBJECTIVES

By the end of this chapter, you should be able to:

- **LO1** Describe the history of incarceration in Canada.
- **LO2** Identify the goal of the correctional system in Canada.
- **LO3** Describe correctional facilities based on their security levels.
- **LO4** Describe elements of life inside a correctional facility including the staff employed in correctional facilities.
- **LO5** Identify the characteristics and needs of Canada's prison population.
- **LO6** Describe the importance of risk assessment and the classification of inmates.
- **LO7** Indentify the types of programs available in correctional facilities.
- **LO8** Describe the inmate culture and the challenges it presents to the correctional environment.
- **LO9** Describe the importance of oversight and accountability in correctional services.
- **LO10** Explain three ways in which correctional institutions may be evaluated.

*continued.*

Grand Valley Institution in Kitchener, Ontario.

*died—wearing nothing but a suicide smock, lying on the floor of her segregation cell, with a ligature tied tightly around her neck—under the direct observation of several correctional staff.*

*(A Preventable Death: Correctional Investigator of Canada, 2008)*

Several of the correctional officers were charged with criminal negligence causing death; all of the charges were withdrawn in court a year later. In October, 2009, Ashley Smith's family launched an $11 million dollar lawsuit against the federal government.

The death of Ashley Smith is clearly a failure. Her story crossed over the youth and adult correctional systems, neither of which could provide her with the support or mental health treatment that she required.

## LO1 Correctional Institutions in Canada

When we look at the history of correctional institutions, it is clear that they were not introduced until it was determined that confining individuals was a sound way of punishing them. Prior to that, punishing offenders did not involve confining them in an institution. Punishment before correctional institutions involved hanging, banishment, or corporal punishment. Local jails did exist; however, they were not intended to be used for long term custody—they were simply holding places for offenders. Jails were a place for offenders to remain until they received their punishment.

The introduction of the penitentiary in the late 1700s marked a change in the way in which offenders were treated in society. The penitentiary was introduced, and imprisonment was identified as a form of punishment and a place to repent and reform. Initially, penitentiaries were intended to be a place where offenders could silently meditate and reflect on their indiscretions. As penitentiaries were built in the eastern United States, they were based on two distinct models. The **Pennsylvania system** was designed to keep inmates separate and apart from each other, day and night, encouraging solitary confinement. Inmates were not permitted to speak or to socialize with one another. This was referred to as the "separate and silent" system (Griffiths, 2010).

**Pennsylvania system**

a penitentiary model designed to keep inmates separate from each other day and night

**Auburn system**

a penitentiary model where inmates are together during the day, but separated at night

The **Auburn system**, named after the New York State Prison at Auburn, referred to a penitentiary style that permitted inmates to work and eat together during the day, and retire to separate cells at night. Like the Pennsylvania system, the inmates were not permitted to speak or communicate with one another. Most of the penitentiaries that were built in Canada and the United States were based on the Auburn system.

The first penitentiary built in Canada was the Kingston Penitentiary, based on the Auburn model. Located on the shore of Lake Ontario and built in 1835, the site was chosen largely because it permitted water transport. The penitentiary was built to respond to a belief that the current local jails were no longer sufficient, and the other types of punishment were no longer feasible, humane, or adequate. Kingston Penitentiary had a central rotunda with a number of cell blocks located off of it. The penitentiary was built to house men, women, and children, and they were expected to exist in complete silence. Life inside the penitentiary was reportedly very difficult for

Kingston Penitentiary, scheduled to close by 2014.

**corporal punishment**

physical punishment

**cat-o-nine tails**

a multi-tailed whipping device, usually made of leather

the inmates. **Corporal punishment** was meted out on a regular basis to both adults and children. It usually consisted of lashings with a **cat-o-nine-tails**. The food was substandard and the critics soon began to question the actions of the penitentiary administration. The strict system of neglect and corporal punishment was not reforming prisoners, as the recidivism rate was high (Griffiths, 2010).

About one hundred years after the Kingston Penitentiary opened, a Royal Commission was struck to examine the state of prisons in Canada. In 1938, the *Royal Commission to Investigate the Penal System of Canada* made a critical statement that prisons should not only protect society, but should also rehabilitate inmates. (Griffiths, 2010). The recommendations made by Archambault had a significant impact on the treatment of offenders, including improvements related to training, education, food, and health care. The changes were modest, but there was an acknowledgement that change was required. Corporal punishment continued to be a form of discipline for inmates until 1972. Correctional services in Canada have grown to include institutional and community services in each province and territory. Correctional institutions have evolved, as have the ways in which we treat inmates. Incarceration continues to be the harshest form of punishment available within our criminal justice system; however, today's goal for incarceration goes beyond punishment.

## THE GOALS OF THE CORRECTIONAL SYSTEM LO2

The goal of the correctional system today is often the subject of debate. By legislation, the goal of the correctional system in Canada is to:

> 3. …contribute to the maintenance of a just, peaceful and safe society by
>    a) carrying out sentences imposed by the courts through safe and humane custody and supervision of offenders; and
>    b) assisting the rehabilitation of offenders and their reintegration into the community as law-abiding citizens through the provision of programs in penitentiaries and in the community.

(SOURCE: *Corrections and Conditional Release Act*, s. 3)

The provision of correctional services in Canada is significant in that it touches the lives of many people. In 2009, there were approximately 371,768 persons who were admitted to a form of correctional supervision in Canada (Statistics Canada, 2010). There are approximately 14,000 people employed by the federal correctional system alone. Canada's system is a **split-jurisdiction** system, meaning the responsibility for administering correctional services is divided between the federal and provincial/territorial governments. An offender who is sentenced to a term of imprisonment of two years or more will serve his or her sentence in the federal correctional system, administered by the Correctional Service of Canada (CSC). The provinces and territories are responsible for providing correctional services to those offenders who receive custodial sentences under two years, as well as those offenders who receive community sentences, including probation. Most offenders fall within the jurisdiction of the provincial/territorial system.

**split-jurisdiction**

responsibility for providing a service falls to two different departments

The federal correctional system operates under the authority of the *Corrections and Conditional Release Act*, 1992. Each province and territory has a corresponding piece of legislation for the provincial or territorial administration of correctional services. The *Corrections and*

## Global Comparison: Canada's Incarceration Rate Compared to International Rates

Canada's incarceration rate (including adults and youth) is 116 per 100,000 population, which is higher than the incarceration rates in most of the western European countries, and lower than the United States (which has an incarceration rate of 756 per 100,000 people in the general population).

SOURCE: *Corrections and Conditional Release Statistical Overview, Annual Report 2010.*

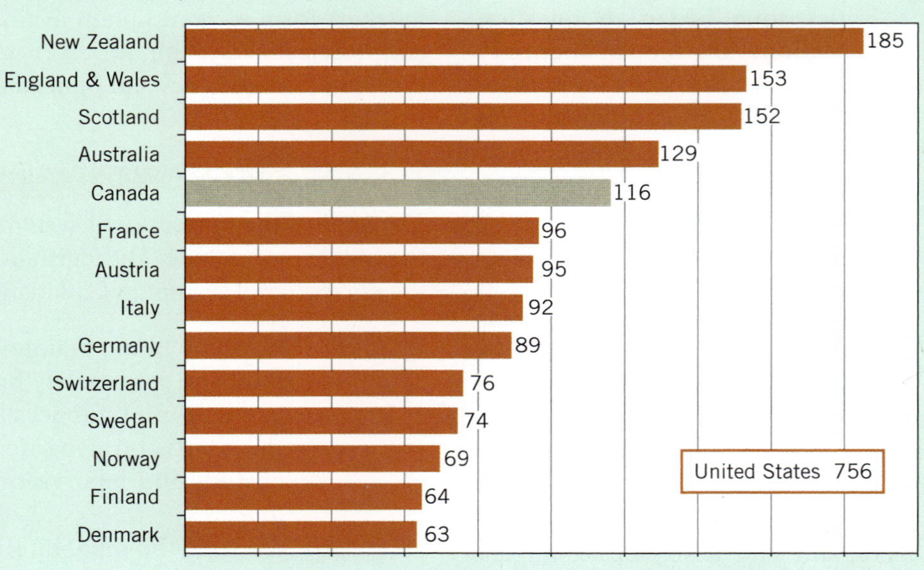


SOURCE: Corrections and Conditional Release Statistical Overview, Annual Report 2010. URL: http://www.publicsafety.gc.ca/res/cor/rep/_images/ccrso2010/ccrso-img-a3-eng.jpg. Public Safety Canada, 2010. Reproduced with the permission of the Minister of Public Works and Government Services Canada, 2010.

*Conditional Release Act* states that it is the CSC is reponsible for:

(a) the care and custody of inmates;
(b) the provision of programs that contribute to the rehabilitation of offenders and to their successful reintegration into the community;
(c) the preparation of inmates for release;
(d) parole, statutory release supervision and long-term supervision of offenders;
(e) maintaining a program of public education about the operations of the Service.

SOURCE: *Corrections and Conditional Release Act*, s. 5

## LO3 CORRECTIONAL INSTITUTIONS TODAY

There are several types of correctional institutions operating in Canada. They vary, based on the security level that they provide and the length of inmate sentence that they accommodate.

Federal institutions house inmates for two years or longer. Due to the high number of males in the correctional system, there are more institutions for men than for women. In addition to traditional prisons, the federal system has several Aboriginal healing lodges to address the needs of Aboriginal inmates who meet the entrance requirements.

There are several different types of institutions that are operated by the provinces. They vary by the security level that they provide, as well as by the type of sentence that the inmate is serving.

Jails and detention centres are facilities that provide short-term custody to inmates who are on remand awaiting trial or those who have been sentenced to short sentences (usually less than 90 days). Provincial correctional centres confine inmates who have been sentenced for up to two years less a day. The provincial system is also responsible for facilities for young persons sentenced under the *Youth Criminal Justice Act*.

### SECURITY LEVELS

One of the ways in which correctional institutions are identified is based on the level of security that they provide. Inmates are classified based on their security level and they are placed in an institution that provides the level of supervision that they require. An inmate is assigned a security level at

PROFILE

### The Don Jail—A Toronto Landmark and Movie Set

The Toronto Jail is infamous for several reasons—it hosted over 70 hangings in its history, housed hundreds of inmates, and is now used for movie shoots and special events. The original prison was built in the 1860s and a new section was added in the late 1950s. Once the home of a number of notorious criminals, there are plans to close the jail permanently in 2012, replacing it with a new facility in Toronto.

SOURCE: Behind Bars: Inside Ontario's Heritage Gaols. Copyright © Ron Brown, 2006. Printed with permission of Dundurn Press Limited.

The Don Jail, circa 1860s.

The new Don Jail, 2007.

admission and this level may change throughout the period of incarceration. An inmate's security level may go from maximum to medium to minimum as he or she prepares for reintegration into the community. A lower security level means more mobility and generally more access to programs that support re-integration into the community. Security status may increase during the period of incarceration if inmates engage in behaviour that indicate that they present a greater security risk. The following factors are taken into consideration when determining an inmate's security classification:

(a) the seriousness of the offence committed by the inmate;
(b) any outstanding charges against the inmate;
(c) the inmate's performance and behaviour while under sentence;
(d) the inmate's social, criminal and, if available, young-offender history, and any dangerous offender designation under the *Criminal Code*;
(e) any physical or mental illness or disorder suffered by the inmate;
(f) the inmate's potential for violent behaviour; and
(g) the inmate's continued involvement in criminal activities.

SOURCE: *Corrections and Conditional Release Regulations*, s. 17.

## FOCUS ON Inmate Security Classification

For the purposes of section 30 of the Act, an inmate shall be classified as

(a) maximum security where the inmate is assessed by the Service as
  (i) presenting a high probability of escape and a high risk to the safety of the public in the event of escape, or
  (ii) requiring a high degree of supervision and control within the penitentiary;
(b) medium security where the inmate is assessed by the Service as
  (i) presenting a low to moderate probability of escape and a moderate risk to the safety of the public in the event of escape, or
  (ii) requiring a moderate degree of supervision and control within the penitentiary; and
(c) minimum security where the inmate is assessed by the Service as
  (i) presenting a low probability of escape and a low risk to the safety of the public in the event of escape, and
  (ii) requiring a low degree of supervision and control within the penitentiary.

SOURCE: *Corrections and Conditional Release Regulations*, s. 18.

The Grierson Centre is a medium security facility in Edmonton, Alberta. It opened in 1990 and has the capacity to house 30 male inmates.

There are three security levels in Canadian correctional institutions. Some institutions have one security level only and some are multi-level institutions where there is more than one type of supervision within the institution. Each security level provides inmates with different types of supervision, programming, and mobility within the institution. Most federal offenders are classified as medium security risk (Corrections and Conditional Release Statistical Overview, 2010).

### MINIMUM SECURITY

Minimum security institutions permit inmates to have unrestricted movement within the institution.

Stony Mountain Institution is a medium security institution located 25 kilometres north of Winnipeg. It opened in 1976 and has the capacity to house 546 male inmates.

### MEDIUM SECURITY

Medium security institutions grant inmates limited movement within the facility, and the perimeter of the grounds is fenced.

### MAXIMUM SECURITY

Inmate movement is highly controlled within maximum security institutions. The perimeter of the institution is surrounded with high fencing and the institution is monitored by video surveillance both internally and externally.

### SPECIAL HANDLING UNIT (SHU)

Intended to be a place of last resort, the Special Handling Units are super-maximum security units designed to secure inmates who have engaged in aggressive, predatory, or self-injurious behaviour. The inmates are those who cannot be managed in a maximum security setting. Introduced in 1977, these units have evolved from mere holding areas to areas where inmates can receive psychiatric assessment, programming, and are monitored with a view to determining when they can return to a regular maximum security setting (Winterdyk, 2001).

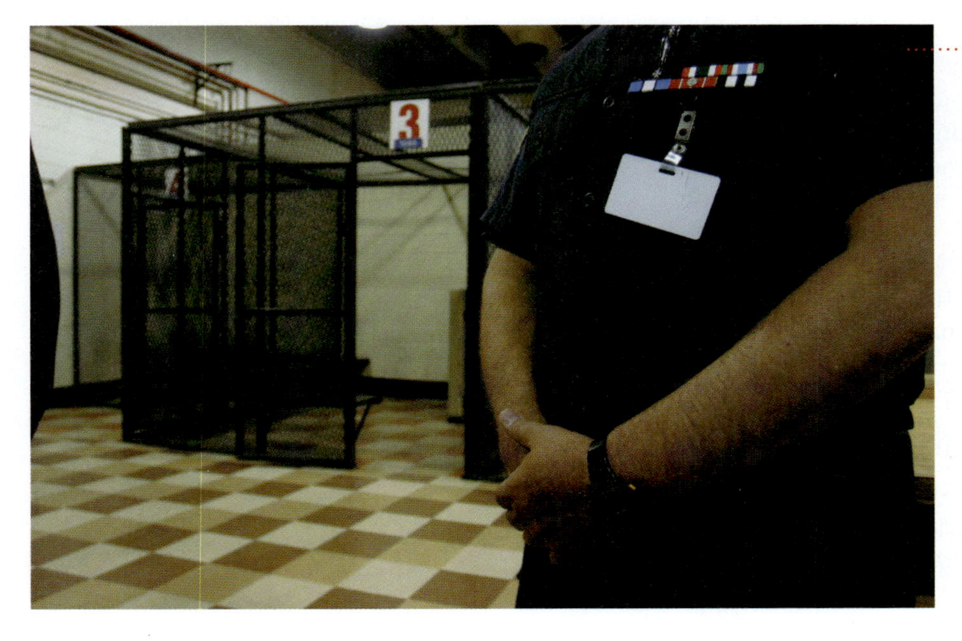


The interior of Millhaven Penitentiary, located in Bath, Ontario. It is a maximum security institution that opened in 1971 and has the capacity to house 413 male inmates.

## Life Inside a Correctional Institution

### LO4 STAFF WITHIN CORRECTIONAL FACILITIES

Numerous staff members are required to ensure that the environment inside a correctional facility is safe, secure, and meets the needs of the inmates. The head of the institution is the warden or the superintendent, and a management team supports him or her. Remaining staff include administrative support, health care workers, parole officers, psychologists, social workers, instructors, and program staff. The largest staffing group is correctional officers, who are critical to the safety and security of the institution. They perform a number of functions, all of which have an impact on the stability of the correctional facility. Correctional officers are responsible for the supervision of the inmates within the institution.

There has been considerable evidence to indicate that correctional officers are subject to great amounts of stress. Sources of stress include working in a prison environment, which is often tense with the threat of violence (Gillan, 2001), and role conflict, where correctional officers are responsible for the security of the institution as well as maintaining a working relationship with offenders. Correctional officers must deal with issues such as overcrowding, conflict among inmates, and the challenges of living within the inmate subculture where officers are often disrespected. Correctional officers are required to adapt to the climate of the correctional institution, while remaining professional. Correctional officers also work shifts, and are subject to the stresses that shift work places on individuals and families.

Working in an environment where violence is prevalent is another major stress on the working lives of correctional staff. Correctional officers work in an environment that is conducive to violence, and has the potential for hostage taking, riots, and other volatile situations. Violence does occur in correctional institutions, though it is difficult to quantify the amount of violence and the psychological impact it has on the officers. Corrections Canada reports that there are between two and ten major assaults on staff each year (Forum, 1992). Inmate violence is prevalent in correctional institutions and is also a source of stress for the staff.

One of every four admissions to the federal correctional system has a mental health illness.

### THE PRISON POPULATION LO5

The prison population presents challenges from the perspective of providing programming and security. At the time of admission, over 70 percent of the federal penitentiary population has an unstable work history, four out of five inmates have serious substance abuse problems, and one of every two inmates committed the crime while under the influence of drugs or alcohol. Mental health issues are prevalent among offenders—one of every four admissions to the federal correctional system has a mental health illness (Sapers, 2010). Fifty percent of incarcerated female offenders have a mental health illness, as do 37 percent of male offenders. Over 60 percent of offenders have histories of violence, and one in six has a known gang and/or organized crime affiliation. There has been a 100 percent increase in the proportion of offenders who are classified at the maximum security level in the past 10 years (CSC Review Panel, 2007). These facts are alarming in that they describe a very vulnerable inmate population that requires multiple types and levels of intervention. The challenge to deliver effective programming is further complicated by the special learning needs of offenders, by the special needs presented by females and Aboriginal offenders, and by the nature of the correctional client and the correctional environment overall.

#### ABORIGINAL INMATES

The over-representation of Aboriginal offenders in the Canadian correctional system has been a long-standing concern for Canadians in general, and clearly presents a challenge to the CSC. According to the 2006 Canadian Census, approximately 4 percent of the population identified themselves as Aboriginal. However, in 2006–2007, 18 percent of adults admitted to federal custody were Aboriginal (20 percent of those admitted to

## MYTH VS FACT

### Clifford Olson: Not a Typical Inmate

Clifford Olson is likely the most well-known and detested offender in Canadian history; fortunately, he was not a typical inmate. Olson was serving a life sentence for killing 11 teenagers and children (aged 9–18) in British Columbia. Olson, who spent most of his life incarcerated, confessed to the killings. However, he struck a very controversial deal with the investigators: to have them pay Olson's family $100,000 after he led them to the victims' bodies. Olson's tyranny did not end there. Once incarcerated, Olson wrote a letter to the family of one of the victims detailing how he killed their son. Fifteen years into his sentence, Olson applied for parole under the now-repealed "faint-hope clause," which once allowed convicted murderers to seek early release. He was denied, but not after requiring a full hearing that included victim impact statements from the families. In July, 2006, Olson appeared before a parole board again, and was denied parole. Olson died of cancer while still serving his sentence, in September, 2011.

An aging Clifford Olson.

SOURCE: The *Toronto Star*, September 30, 2011.

provincial or territorial custody were Aboriginal). Correctional institutions must respond to this over-representation of Aboriginal adults in custody in their programming. Aboriginal offenders present challenges in the areas of employment training and education. For example, of the offenders admitted to custody in 2006–2007, 44 percent of non-Aboriginal adults were employed, while only 29 percent of Aboriginal adults were employed. Four in ten non-Aboriginal offenders had completed high school compared to two in ten Aboriginal adults (Babooram, 2008). In addition, 65 percent of Aboriginal offenders were classified as having five or more treatment needs, compared to 41 percent of non-Aboriginal offenders. The average age at admission is lower for Aboriginal offenders than for non-Aboriginal offenders. In 2008–2009, 45.2 percent of newly-admitted Aboriginal offenders were under the age of 30, compared to 38.6 percent of non-Aboriginal offenders (Public Safety Canada, 2010). The incarceration rate of Aboriginal peoples has increased steadily over the past 30 years. Aboriginal offenders enter the correctional system as a more vulnerable client based on their skills, abilities, and treatment challenges.

The crisis in the over-representation of Aboriginal peoples within correctional custody has resulted in an acknowledgement that focused strategies are required to reduce the incarceration rate of Aboriginal peoples. There is a commitment by the CSC to work with the Aboriginal community to create programs that respond directly to the needs of Aboriginal offenders (*Corrections and Conditional Release Regulations*, s. 82). The National Aboriginal Advisory Committee has been created to provide advice and guidance to the CSC. Aboriginal spiritual leaders and elders play a significant role within institutions to provide guidance to Aboriginal offenders.

In response to a 1990 task force on federally-sentenced women, healing lodges were introduced for federal offenders in 1995 (Barrett, Allenby and Taylor, 2010). Healing lodges offer Aboriginal offenders an opportunity to incorporate Aboriginal teachings, traditions, and philosophies into their programming. The inmates are mentored by elders and other community members, who focus on their eventual release. There is an expectation that the healing lodge will decrease the recidivism rate among Aboriginal offenders. Offenders identify goals with their caseworkers, often referred to as a "healing contract or plan," that will guide them through to re-integration into the community.

PROFILE

### The Okimaw Ohci Healing Lodge for Women

In 1995, The Okimaw Ohci Healing Lodge opened its doors to federally-sentenced women. It is a facility for 28 female offenders; most of the inmates are sentenced to less than 40 months. The Lodge is located in the Necaneet First Nation, near Medicine Hat, Alberta. The Lodge can accommodate women and children, as required. The goals of the Lodge are to:

- restore pride and dignity in the inmates, as women and as mothers;
- restore a sense of worth, dignity and hope;
- rebuild their families and their communities; and
- build bridges between Aboriginal and non-Aboriginal societies.

The women receive a healing plan and benefit from the guidance of elders and native liaison workers, in addition to the staff of the Lodge.

SOURCE: Correctional Service of Canada: Report on the Evaluation of Okimaw Ohci Healing Lodge (2002), http://www.csc-scc.gc.ca/text/pa/ev-oohl-294-2-020/oohl_eval-eng.shtml#a2_1.

## FEMALE INMATES

The history of providing custodial supervision to women in Canada has been a controversial one.

Female inmates have long posed a challenge for the correctional system largely because of their small numbers, compared to the numbers of males within the prison population. The crime rate of females is significantly lower than that of males, a statistic that means that ultimately there are fewer females incarcerated. Females are responsible for 21 percent of *Criminal Code* offences in Canada (Kong and AuCoin, 2008). Females are more likely to commit property crimes and less likely to commit violent crimes. Female offenders are less likely than their male counterparts to have multiple charges and extensive criminal histories. Research indicates that conviction rates are lower for females; they are more likely to have their cases stayed or withdrawn, and are less likely to be found guilty. Because many women are first-time offenders, they are often eligible for diversion programs where they avoid conviction. Adult women who are found guilty are less likely than men to be sentenced to a period of incarceration; they are more likely to be placed on probation. Women who receive custodial sentences typically receive shorter sentences than men, likely attributed to the fact that women tend to have a less extensive criminal history than men (Kong and AuCoin, 2008).

Though the number of women being sentenced to a period of incarceration has been steadily increasing, women still represent a small number compared to men. In 2009, women represented 6.5 percent of all newly admitted federal inmates, up from 4.8 percent in 2003 (Public Safety Canada, 2010). Women make up a larger portion of the provincial/territorial inmate population than their federal counterparts, at about 7 percent. Historically, critics believed that this discrepancy in the male/female prison population resulted in fewer resources and less of an emphasis being placed on the needs of incarcerated women. Recently, there have been a number of incidents that have resulted in changes to the manner in which women are treated while incarcerated.

Construction of the Kingston Prison for Women (P4W)—within walking distance of the Kingston Penitentiary—started in the 1920s; the building accepted its first female inmate in 1934. It was the only facility for women who were sentenced to a federal custodial sentence. Women

## The Mother-Child Program for Female Inmates

PROFILE

The Mother-Child Program was created to offer incarcerated women, who are mothers, the chance to develop their parenting skills and to continue building a relationship with their young children. This program is available only at federal institutions for women. Two thirds of incarcerated women are mothers of children under five years of age, and many of them are single parents. The decision to bring a child into the correctional institution is made based upon the best interest of the child. The program allows for the following types of engagement between mothers and their children:

1. Full-time residency of the child with his or her mother in the facility.
2. Part-time or occasional residency of the child in the facility (weekends and holidays).
3. Visits of the child in the context of family visits and of the program of private family visits at the facility.
4. Exchanges of visits at the facility and outside it in the neighbourhood, between the mother and child (when the child lives in a foster home or placement house).

SOURCE: Correctional Service of Canada, Commissioner's Directive 768, http://www.csc-scc.gc.ca/text/plcy/cdshtm/768cd-eng.shtml.

Mother-child programs allow for critical engagement between female inmates and their children.

from across Canada were sent to the P4W, usually separating them from their home communities and their family members. The facility itself was antiquated, and several investigations conducted over the years indicated that it was a sub-standard institution. Just four years after it opened, the P4W was criticized by the Archambault Report, and numerous other crticial commissioned reports followed. One parliamentary report in 1977 declared that P4W was "unfit for bears, much less women" (Tadman, 2001). An incident that highlighted the inadequacies of the facility and the treatment of women in custody in general, occurred in April, 1994. The incident involved a violent confrontation between six inmates and several of the correctional staff, which spanned several days. The incident included cell extractions, strip searches, and offensive language, and it was videotaped and viewed on a Canada-wide television show. An inquiry led by the Honourable Louise Arbour followed, which resulted in a number of changes to the way female inmates were treated while in custody. One of the recommendations was to close the P4W (Arbor, 1996). This same recommendation had been made several times in the past, but this time it resulted in change. A number of federal institutions for women were opened across Canada so that women could be closer to their home communities; the last inmate left P4W in 2000. These institutions are newer and their construction better reflects the needs of female offenders. The new facilities are:

- Nova Institution for Women; Truro, Nova Scotia,
- Joliette Institution; Joliette, Quebec,
- Grand Valley Institution for Women; Kitchener, Ontario,
- Edmonton Institution for Women; Edmonton, Alberta, and

P4W: The Prison for Women was once declared "unfit for bears."

- Okimaw Ohci Healing Lodge; Maple Creek, Saskatchewan.

Though male and female inmates have similar concerns, there are a number of distinct differences that indicate that female offenders require programming and treatment that is different from what their male counterparts receive. The differences include the following:

- women are more likely to be parents, and often are single parents;
- women, by nature, have more complicated health needs than men;
- Aboriginal women are more over-represented than Aboriginal men;
- women have criminal histories that are less violent;
- women are more likely to have a history of abuse;
- overall, women have less education, fewer skills, higher levels of poverty, and welfare dependence; and
- women have a higher rate of mental illness than men, upon admission (Sapers, 2010).

In addition, **self-harm** is an increasing problem among female offenders. It is believed that approximately 25 percent of female offenders have engaged in some form of self-harming behaviour, such as head banging and cutting. This behaviour is often chronic and can result in permanent harm to the inmate (Sapers, 2010).

**self-harm**
self-injurious behaviour

Recognizing the special needs of female inmates has resulted in the implementation of specialized programming. Examples of programs designed specifically for women include parenting programs, programs for survivors of abuse and trauma, substance abuse programming, family violence prevention programming, and treatment programs to address self-harming behaviours.

### LIFERS

In 1976, Canada abolished the death penalty and replaced it with long-term sentencing. The maximum sentence in Canada is **life imprisonment**. In 2009, lifers made up 22 percent of the federal inmate population, an increase of 4 percent since 1998 (Olotu, Luong and Brews, 2010). Lifers are likely to have committed fewer, yet more serious, offences than non-lifers and are generally older, single, less educated, and more likely to have been employed at admission. Lifers present a challenge because they are long-term inmates, most of whom will eventually be released into the community. In 1991, the LifeLine Program was introduced across Canada to assist long-term offenders (10 years or longer)—lifers and offenders with indeterminate sentences—

**life imprisonment**
the maximum sentence in Canadian law

to adjust to long-term custody and to prepare for their eventual release. The LifeLine Program is voluntary and responds to the needs of long-term offenders as they transition through the stages of their incarceration experience: adaptation, integration into prison, preparation for release, and re-integration into the community. One of the program components is called "in-reach," where former lifers and long-term offenders who are now successfully integrated into the community provide motivation and support to the program participants. The program also guides the inmates through pre-release planning and exposes them to community resources and support, a proven determinant of successful reintegration. The program increases an offender's ability to adapt to both life on the inside and life on the outside.

**JUST or BUST?**

**Should elderly inmates be released on compassionate grounds once they reach a certain age, even if their sentence is not completed?**

A typical cell in a federal, maximum-security institution.

### THE ELDERLY INMATE

Elderly offenders (age 50 and older) represent about 18 percent of the federal inmate population (Sapers, 2011). The challenge of dealing with elderly offenders is that they often have chronic health conditions that must be accommodated throughout their period of incarceration. The cost of incarcerating an elderly offender can be as high as three times that of a younger prisoner (Morton, 2005), due to the extra health care they require as well as the additional support they require from others to assist them in day-to-day activities.

### INMATES AND THEIR FAMILIES

Maintaining a relationship with a family member who is incarcerated presents many challenges. There are geographic, emotional, and financial implications for family members. It is important to help inmates sustain relationships with family members while they are incarcerated, as research indicates that maintaining links with family members does reduce the risk of reoffending (Clarke et al., 2005). Efforts are often made to include family members in an offender's correctional plan. Family members may be involved in treatment decisions or programs, visits from family members are encouraged, and inmates with young children are often afforded extended visits in private spaces within the institution. Inmates who are incarcerated in federal institutions are eligible for private family visits. Private family visits are intended to encourage

## Tattoos in Prison

In 2005, the CSC introduced a controversial program whereby they were offering inmates "clean" tattoos in prison-run tattoo parlours. The harm reduction plan was adopted to prevent inmates from using dirty needles to give themselves tattoos, with a view to preventing the spread of HIV and hepatitis C. Inmates were charged $5.00 for a two-hour tattoo session; however, the annual cost of the program was $611,000 per year. The program was cancelled by the federal government one year after it began, citing the excessive cost as the reason for the decision. Tattoos have long had symbolic meaning to inmates, and many inmates will mark milestones behind bars with specific tattoo markings.

SOURCES: CBC, December 4, 2006; http://www.thebody.com/content/art24770.html; http://canadianharmreduction.com/blog/needle-exchange-in-prisons.

offenders to develop and maintain their ties with family members in preparation for their return to the community. In some instances, family members can join the inmate in special two-bedroom units with cooking and living areas, for a 72-hour visit. Correctional staff closely monitor the visits, and visitors are advised of items that are prohibited by the facility. As one inmate stated:

> "The hardest part about being in prison is that you're taken away from your family. You're not there. There's so many things. My daughter just turned 16 when I was arrested, so she pretty well had to live on her own. I missed that time of her life, a mother and daughter. All my kids went through a hard time. It's very hard to cope with being in prison. Like talking to them on the phone. It hurts really bad. They're hurting and all you've got is the phone to communicate." (Tadman, 2001, p. 60)

## LO6 RISK ASSESSMENT AND CLASSIFICATION

From the time an inmate enters an institution through to any eventual form of community release, the correctional service is engaged in a risk management process ensuring the safety of all persons who may come into contact with a particular inmate. There is a requirement to balance the needs of the inmate, the general public, crime victims, correctional staff, and other offenders. In addition, the correctional service strives to use measures that do not restrict an inmate's life more than necessary. This process of managing and assessing risk is continual as an offender's risk potential may change. Risk assessment influences an offender's security **classification**, the programming he or she receives while incarcerated, eligibility for temporary absences, and an eventual release date.

**classification**

a process to determine an inmate's security level and individual program needs

There are two main types of risk assessment—actuarial and clinical (John Howard Society, 2000). An actuarial assessment involves collecting historical data about the offender. It includes, but is not limited to, details about the offender's criminal record and previous criminal behaviour (including age of onset, number of convictions), substance abuse, interpersonal skills, community support, details about the offence(s), basic life skills, and motivation to change. This information is gathered to determine the risk of the offender continuing to engage in criminal behaviour. There are numerous tools that are used in actuarial risk assessment.

Another method used to assess an offender's level of risk is through the use of clinical assessments. A clinical assessment is based on the professional opinions of psychologists and psychiatrists, who assess the offender by examining personality traits, mental illness, as well as biological, social, and psychological factors that are related to offending (John Howard Society, 2000). It is important to stress that risk assessment is ongoing through an offender's involvement with the correctional system.

An element of the classification process involves identifying an inmate's needs and security requirements when he or she is admitted to the institution. The security classification results in the inmate's eventual placement in an institution. It is possible that during the period of incarceration an inmate's security level may change. All inmates are notified in writing of the reasons for the security level that is determined, and should their level change during their period of incarceration they are entitled to receive the reasons for the change in writing (*Corrections and Conditional Release Act*, s. 30).

Early in the sentence, staff will engage the inmate in a process that results in the creation of a **correctional plan** that will guide the inmate's rehabilitation throughout the period of incarceration through to community supervision. This plan is designed to ensure that inmates receive effective programming to prepare them for a successful return to the community as law-abiding citizens. An accurate assessment is critical because it ensures that inmates are classified in a fair and ethical manner, and that resources are used efficiently. Throughout the period of incarceration an inmate continues to be monitored with a view to modifying the plan as required. For the purpose of determining their needs, inmates are assessed based on their strengths and challenges in the following areas:

**correctional plan**

a plan of care designed to support an inmate's reintegration into the community

- employment and education;
- marital/family;
- associates/social interaction;
- substance abuse;
- community functioning (including basic life skills);
- personal/emotional functioning; and
- attitude.

Each inmate's correctional plan is designed to address his or her needs related to these areas.

## INMATE PROGRAMS

LO7

Rehabilitation is a primary goal of incarceration and correctional programming is intended to support an inmate's rehabilitation plan. Programming for inmates is a critical component of incarceration as programs address the needs of offenders and are critical to their successful reintegration into the community. The *Corrections and Conditional Release Act* clearly states that there is a requirement for a range of programs designed to "address the needs of offenders and contribute to their successful reintegration into the community" (*Corrections and Conditional Release Act*, s. 76). The reality is that most incarcerated inmates will one day be released. Inmates are expected to engage in programming that assists their progress toward a successful release. The manner in which they are treated and the supports that they receive while incarcerated may have a significant impact on the person they are when they leave the institution. The intention of correctional programming is to reduce the rate at which offenders reoffend and in doing so, ensuring that our communities are safer.

Correctional programming is implemented by program facilitators who not only deliver programming but also evaluate the offenders and the program itself. There are several categories of prison programs across Canada. There are treatment programs that address specific issues such as mental health conditions, substance abuse, anger management, domestic violence, and conflict resolution. In addition, there are cognitive or other therapeutic programs designed to address the holistic needs of the inmate. There are recreational, religious, cultural, life skills, health promotion, and hygiene programs. Specialized programming is offered for specific groups including women, Aboriginal inmates, inmates serving life terms, and sex offenders. Though the programs differ, the ultimate goal for all is to provide the offenders with the ability to realize a successful return to the community.

Perhaps one of the biggest challenges of providing programming to inmates in a correctional setting is the fact that the inmates enter the institution as multi-problem individuals, many of whom have experienced a lifetime of social problems and educational neglect.

### INMATE WORK

The opportunity for inmates to work while incarcerated is a privilege. Work detail within correctional institutions includes working in various departments such as the laundry, kitchen, library, grounds maintenance, or cleaning. The rate of inmate pay ranges from $5.25 to $6.90 per day, an amount that has not changed since 1999 (Commissioner's Directive, 1999). Inmates engage in work outside the institution, escorted or unescorted, as well.

The CSC supplements the vocational training component of their programming with an innovative work experience program for inmates called CORCAN. One of their most recognized programs, it consists of four business lines: construction, manufacturing, services (such as printing and laundry), and textiles. CORCAN provides offenders with work experiences and training that replicate private sector work environments as closely as possible. CORCAN programs are in place in 31 federal institutions across Canada, creating the equivalent of 2,000 full-time trainee positions. Each year, approximately 4,000 offenders receive employment and employability skills training in CORCAN. On any given day, approximately 15 percent of the total offender population is working and learning in CORCAN shops. Most offenders have little or no work experience and a low level of skill when they begin working with CORCAN. Offenders receive training in the manufacture and provision of a wide range of products and services such as office furniture, clothing, shelving, metal fabrication, data entry, digital imaging, and telemarketing. CORCAN products are marketed to the public sector: governments, non-profit organizations, and educational and health care institutions. CORCAN also offers community-based short-term employment, job counselling, and placement programs. It also implemented a follow-up program for inmates once they return to the community (Correctional Service of Canada, CORCAN). In the annual report, the CEO of CORCAN states:

> We work hard at our core mission—giving offenders the chance to succeed and successfully reintegrate back into society. The true measure of our success—our real "product"—is not a table or chair but a successfully employed productive member of society who has broken the cycle of criminal behaviour.
>
> SOURCE: CORCAN Annual Report, 07/08.

The CORCAN program allows inmates to take the next step—not only do they receive vocational training but they are also given an opportunity to apply the training while incarcerated.

### EDUCATION IN PRISONS

Educational programs are available to inmates, to varying degrees, across Canada. The educational program categories reflect the classification of

**MYTH VS FACT** | **Prisoners and Their Pensions**

In 2010, a new law came into effect that prevents prisoners who are incarcerated in federal institutions from receiving their pensions while in custody, with the exception of the final month of custody. The new law was initiated after the public became aware of the shocking reality that Clifford Olson, the notorious serial child killer, was receiving both Old Age Security and the Guaranteed Income Supplement payments while incarcerated. Critics of the new law explained that the $1,100 per month was necessary for those pensioners who would be released to the community without the security of some financial savings that the pension provides, jeopardizing their success at reintegration by forcing them into criminal activity to survive. A 2010 poll conducted by EKOS concluded that most Canadians concur that federal prisoners should not be entitled to government pensions.

SOURCES: http://www.cbc.ca/news/canada/story/2010/04/08/ekos-poll-inmates-pensions.html; http://www.ekospolitics.com/index.php/2010/04/canadians-agree-with-prime-minister-on-restricting-pensions-for-federal-prisoners-april-8-2010; http://www.torontosun.com/news/columnists/greg_weston/2010/03/24/13348051-qmi.html.

education that exists in the community, enabling an inmate to acquire the same credentials (and perhaps complete that credential) in the community. The intention is to offer prison education that will equip inmates with skills required to be successful when they return to the community. On a broader scale, the role of correctional education is intended to function as a change agent for the inmate as well as for the correctional system as a whole (Stevens and Ward, 1997).

Prison education has focused largely on the area of adult basic skills, primarily literacy and numeracy. In 1987, the CSC made Adult Basic Education (ABE) a priority in educational programming. At the time, the CSC identified a training goal that all inmates attain certification in both literacy and numeracy at the grade 8 level during their incarceration. In 2001, this goal was reassessed due to market trends and the realities of society, which indicated that 84 percent of new jobs in Canada require at least a high school diploma. In response, the CSC made grade 12 the minimum standard for its ABE program. In view of the link between illiteracy and criminality (Hrabowski and Robbi, 2002), it is understandable that the educational priority for offenders is adult basic education.

At any given time, over 10 percent of the total federal inmate population in Canada is engaged in ABE, approximately half are full-time participants, and the other half are part-time students who engage in work or other types of programming (CSC, 2009). All offenders are assessed in language and mathematics during the offender classification process. Those who score below the grade 10 level are offered the opportunity to enrol in ABE programs. The average inmate who enrols is at a grade 4 level in reading, writing, and math skills. (Forum, 1991). A 1994 study conducted by Frontier College indicated that 70 percent of inmates score below a grade 8 level and 86 percent test below a grade 10 level. Despite the onset of the information age, inmates' literacy skills had not improved according to a comparison study done between 1987 and 1994. Statistically, the initial enthusiasm to enrol in the ABE programs is encouraging; approximately one third of all inmate students are enrolled in ABE programs. Unfortunately, research indicates that less than half of the inmates who enrol in the program complete it (Forum on Corrections Research, 1991). There are a number of reasons that are identified for the poor completion rate. They include a lack of motivation on the part of the inmate, inmate transfer to another institution, or inmate release, as well as a lack of support for the inmates while engaged in the courses. This low completion rate is problematic because of the importance of literacy in the crime prevention equation. Basic literacy programs are critical due to the link between illiteracy and crime, as well as the link between literacy and employment.

Educating prisoners can take many forms, from basic literacy to post-secondary education.

Inmate subculture develops as a way of engaging in social control among the inmate population.

Those inmates who attain a basic literacy level are offered an opportunity to enrol in a secondary education program. These courses lead to graduation at a grade 12 level. Approximately 25 percent of inmates enrolled in educational programming are involved in secondary school training (Forum on Corrections Research, 1991). Vocational training programs are available to inmates across Canada. These education programs prepare students for jobs that are trade-specific. Vocational programs can be, but are not limited to, apprenticeship offerings. Approximately 25 percent of inmate students are enrolled in these programs. The types of trades offered include:

- welding and metal trades,
- hairdressing,
- small engine repair,
- auto mechanics and auto body repair,
- electronics,
- carpentry and cabinet making,
- upholstery,
- plumbing,
- cooking, and
- computer programming.

Post-secondary education is an option for qualified inmates. Fewer than 10 percent of inmates in education programs are enrolled in post-secondary programs at a college or university level. Generally, inmates are required to finance their own post-secondary courses, unless they are able to demonstrate that the education addresses a specific need. Many inmates qualify for Government of Canada student loans while incarcerated (Duguid, 1998). Inmates can be taught within the institution by visiting professors, study via online delivery or correspondence, or they can attend classes on campus.

The effective delivery of correctional education presents significant challenges for institutions. The correctional student comes with a great deal of baggage often acquired during a lifetime of dealing with the consequences of social problems and educational neglect. In addition, the education is provided in a correctional environment complete with a prison subculture that includes challenges related to security and supervision. The correctional culture creates numerous challenges for implementing educational programming of any type. Programming in the correctional facility comes second to security, which often means it is compromised.

## The Inmate Culture

LO8

**Inmate culture** refers to the values, beliefs, attitudes, and actions of incarcerated individuals. A knowledge and understanding of inmate culture is required in order to work effectively within an institution, and to be able to provide meaningful programming to inmates in a secure environment. Inmate culture pertains to the nature of the relationship between inmates and correctional officers, as well as the relationship between the inmates themselves. Generalizations are often made when describing inmate culture and there are exceptions to the generalizations, often related to the type of institution in which the inmate is confined. The inmate subculture is a function of the confinement, meaning that the subculture develops as a way of engaging in social control among the inmate population (Cooley, 1992). Inmates band together in opposition to the prison administration (represented by the correctional officer). In opposing the prison order that they must live by, inmates regulate their own behaviour and create rules of social control for each other. The rules and regulations give them an opportunity to have control over their behaviour. Dennis Cooley (1992) writes that there are rules of social control that appear to be universal, which include:

- do your own time (mind your own business—do not rat on anyone);
- avoid the prison economy (there are consequences for engaging in trades for drugs/cigarettes);

- don't trust anyone (a fellow inmate or staff); and
- show respect (for your fellow inmates).

Correctional administrators and officers must learn to live and work within and around the prison culture.

## DRUGS IN PRISONS

One of the biggest challenges faced by correctional administrators is controlling drugs within the institutions. There is a continued effort to stop drugs from entering institutions, and there are numerous programs intended to help inmates with their substance abuse issues. The reality is that drugs still find their way into the institutions. Drugs are smuggled in with visitors, with inmate work crews, and by dropping drugs on prison property to be retrieved by inmates. There are a number of creative ways in which drugs make their way into institutions, requiring correctional staff to be extra vigilant. Drugs in prisons pose a risk for both inmates and staff. According to the CSC, 80 percent of all inmates are assessed upon arrival as having a substance abuse problem. This results in increased assaults, transmittable diseases, and hinders the rehabilitation process. There are a number of strategies in place to eliminate drugs in prisons. Drug detector dogs are used to search visitors and inmate accommodation and activity areas, vehicles and individuals entering the prisons are searched thoroughly, and there is an emphasis on intelligence gathering and an increased use of technology (CSC, Review Panel, 2007).

"The idea of drug-free prison does not seem to be any more realistic than the idea of drug-free society."

SOURCE: SCOTTISH REPORT ON DRUG USE AND PRISONS.

**harm reduction**

an approach designed to reduce harm of a specific behaviour

Several Canadian correctional institutions have made a commitment to engage in **harm reduction** strategies, in an effort to minimize the transmission of disease both within the institution and in the community. HIV levels, and hepatitis B and C levels, are higher among the prison population than the general population (Kerr et al., 2004). The transmission occurs when inmates share syringes and other injection aids. The harm reduction programs provide inmates with items that that will minimize the harm that is done when drug use and sexual activity occur behind bars. Condoms, dental dams, and lubricants are provided to inmates, as are bleach kits and methadone. The bleach kits are used to clean the needles used to inject drugs, the condoms and dental dams are intended to promote safe sex, and methadone is a drug designed to help inmates overcome their addiction to drugs. The challenge in offering harm reduction programs is that they contradict the institutional regulations that prohibit drug use and sexual activity. The harm reduction program recognizes that the activity is restricted, while acknowledging that in spite of the regulations and efforts made by the correctional staff to stop them, drug use and sexual activity continue to occur. Harm reduction is a way in which the institution takes some responsibility to prevent the spread of disease, which protects the inmates, the correctional staff, and, ultimately, the community.

**JUST or BUST?**

**Should the public taxpayer be supporting harm reduction strategies that allow inmates to engage in illegal activity, such as drug use, behind bars?**

## INMATE CONDUCT AND DISCIPLINE

The conduct of inmates within an institution has a tremendous impact on the safety and security of the institution. There are a number of incentives for inmates to abide by the rules and to conduct themselves in an orderly manner. An inmate who is cooperative is more likely to be granted conditional release when eligible, as the institution is required to provide the parole board with an assessment of the inmate's behaviour during the period of imprisonment. When an inmate does not abide by the rules there is a disciplinary system that is invoked. There are a number of offences that have been identified by legislation that warrant disciplinary action within correctional institutions:

40. An inmate commits a disciplinary offence who

(a) disobeys a justifiable order of a staff member;
(b) is, without authorization, in an area prohibited to inmates;
(c) wilfully or recklessly damages or destroys property that is not the inmate's;
(d) commits theft;
(e) is in possession of stolen property;
(f) is disrespectful or abusive toward a staff member in a manner that could undermine a staff member's authority;
(g) is disrespectful or abusive toward any person in a manner that is likely to provoke a person to be violent;
(h) fight with, assaults or threatens to assault another person;
(i) is in possession of, or deals in, contraband;
(j) without prior authorization, is in possession of, or deals in, an item that is not authorized by a Commissioner's Directive or by a written order of the institutional head;
(k) takes an intoxicant into the inmate's body;
(l) fails or refuses to take a urine sample when demanded pursuant to section 54 or 55;
(m) creates or participates in
 (i) a disturbance, or
 (ii) any other activity
 that is likely to jeopardize the security of the penitentiary;
(n) does anything for the purpose of escaping or assisting another inmate to escape;
(o) offers, gives or accepts a bribe or reward;
(p) without reasonable excuse, refuses to work or leaves work;
(q) engages in gambling;
(r) wilfully disobeys a written rule governing the conduct of inmates; or
(s) attempts to do, or assists another person to do, anything referred to in paragraphs (*a*) to (*r*).

SOURCE: *Corrections and Conditional Release Act*, s. 40.

An inmate who is accused of breaching the code of conduct is entitled to a hearing, where guilt must be proven beyond a reasonable doubt. If it is determined that there was a breach, then the inmate may be disciplined in one or more of the following ways:

(a) a warning or reprimand;
(b) a loss of privileges;
(c) an order to make restitution;
(d) a fine;
(e) performance of extra duties; and
(f) in the case of a serious disciplinary offence, segregation from other inmates for a maximum of thirty days.

SOURCE: *Corrections and Conditional Release Act*, s. 44 (1).

## WHAT IS CONTRABAND?

**Contraband** refers to any object that is not permitted within the institution. It includes the following:

(a) an intoxicant,
(b) a weapon or a component thereof, ammunition for a weapon, and anything that is designed to kill, injure or disable a person or that is altered so as to be capable of killing, injuring or disabling a person, when possessed without prior authorization,
(c) an explosive or a bomb or a component thereof,
(d) currency over any applicable prescribed limit, when possessed without prior authorization, and
(e) any item not described in paragraphs (a) to (d) that could jeopardize the security of a penitentiary or the safety of persons, when that item is possessed without prior authorization.

SOURCE: *Corrections and Conditional Release Act*, s. 2(1).

Pierre Mallette, a federal correctional officer, displays homemade weapons seized in federal prisons in Canada. Paul Chiasson/CP

It is critical to be vigilant, as contraband can jeopardize the safety and security of the institution.

### DISCIPLINARY SEGREGATION

Disciplinary segregation is a punitive measure where inmates can spend up to 30 days alone in a cell, and it involves the loss of additional privileges such as recreation, work or other programs, or visits. Inmates commonly refer to this form of punishment as being in "the hole." It is intended to be used for the most serious of offences and its use is limited in law.

### ADMINISTRATIVE SEGREGATION

Administrative segregation is different than disciplinary segregation. It refers to placing an offender in a unit that is separate from the general population of the correctional institution. There are two types of administrative segregation—voluntary and involuntary. For voluntary administrative segregation, an offender chooses to be removed from the general population, usually for his or her own protection. Involuntary administrative segregation is when the institution makes the decision for the inmate's placement. The *Corrections and Conditional Release Act* identifies criteria that are used to justify the placement of an inmate into administrative segregation:

> (3) The institutional head may order that an inmate be confined in administrative segregation if the institutional head believes on reasonable grounds
>
> (a) that
>
> (i) the inmate has acted, has attempted to act or intends to act in a manner that jeopardizes the security of the penitentiary or the safety of any person, and
>
> (ii) the continued presence of the inmate in the general inmate population would jeopardize the security of the penitentiary or the safety of any person,
>
> (b) that the continued presence of the inmate in the general inmate population would interfere with an investigation that could lead to a criminal charge or a charge under subsection 41(2) of a serious disciplinary offence, or

(c) that the continued presence of the inmate in the general inmate population would jeopardize the inmate's own safety,

and the institutional head is satisfied that there is no reasonable alternative to administrative segregation.

SOURCE: *Corrections and Conditional Release Act*, s. 31 (3).

Administrative segregation is intended to be a last resort used as a preventive, not punitive, measure that precludes "altercations, harm or interference with certain investigations" (CSC, 2008, Task Force). Statistically, approximately half of the inmates who are in administrative segregation are there voluntarily, and half are there involuntarily (CSC, 2008, Task Force). Inmates who are voluntarily segregated are more likely to have a sexual offence history and to have been victimized in the past. In general, segregated inmates present higher risks and have greater needs. In addition, they are more likely to reoffend upon release.

Though inmates in administrative segregation are entitled to the same rights, privileges, and conditions as the general inmate population, it is clear that the use of administrative segregation is controversial in that it can have a profound effect on the inmate. There are limitations related to programming, visits, phone calls, and socialization within administrative segregation. The Task Force report on administration segregation states, "Administrative segregation is one of the most intrusive forms of interference with inmates' rights of freedom, liberty, and association. The social isolation and sensory deprivation associated with administrative segregation not only are potentially harmful to inmates' mental and physical health, but can seriously interfere with their ability to reintegrate safely and successfully into the community."

### FOCUS ON Segregation of Inmates

"We are primates, we are made to socialize, but in segregation you have no contacts, you can't speak to anyone. My friend died three months ago, he hung himself in the hole. Now I am in the hole. Sometimes you look at what you got and take it from there. If all you have is boredom, sometimes just getting excited and creating commotions is better than nothing. I am starting to crack... I am so bored and so cut off from interaction I can't take it anymore. I can't even see another man's eyes when I speak to him, can you imagine what that feels like?"

A segregated maximum security offender in his own words, November 2009.

SOURCE: Office of the Correctional Investigator Annual Report 2009-2010, http://www.oci-bec.gc.ca/rpt/annrpt/annrpt20092010-eng.aspx.

## LO9 Oversight and Accountability of Correctional Institutions

Each province and territory has an Ombudsman responsible for investigating inmate or third party complaints related to correctional services. The Office of the Correctional Investigator was established on the recommendation of an inquiry into the 1972 riot at the Kingston Penitentiary, designed to investigate and resolve offender complaints and issues in the federal correctional system. The Correctional Investigator adjudicates individual offender complaints with a view to examining systemic issues. The office receives its mandate from the *Corrections and Conditional Release Act*, entitling the office to determine if a situation was "unreasonable, unjust, oppressive or improperly discriminatory, ... [or] based wholly or partly on a mistake of law or fact" (Sapers, 2011).

There are a number of complaints that are consistent among inmates. The most common complaint is in the area of health care, followed by issues related to institutional transfers. Other areas of concern include cell property and the use of administrative segregation (*Corrections and Conditional Release Statistical Overview*, 2010). An inmate who has a complaint and wishes to contact the Ombudsman or the office of the Correctional Investigator can do so by telephone, letter, or through an interview process within the prison.

### DEATHS IN CUSTODY

It is troubling when an individual dies while in correctional custody. According to the Correctional Investigator of Canada there were nine in-custody deaths between April 2008 and April 2010, three of which were suicides (Sapers, 2011). Suicide is the number one cause of death for inmates in

Canada (Centre for Prevention of Suicide, April 1998). Prisoners are three times more likely to commit suicide than the general population, and first-time prisoners and those on remand have the highest risk. Violent offenders, sex offenders, lifers, and those with a psychiatric history tend to be more vulnerable. Approximately 20 percent of the offenders who die by suicide are Aboriginal, which is comparable to the proportion of Aboriginal offenders in custody in CSC (Power and Riley, 2010). Research indicates that the following are identified as contributing factors to inmate suicide:

- recent excessive drinking and/or use of drugs,
- recent loss of resources,
- severe guilt or shame over the offence,
- current mental illness,
- poor physical health or terminal illness,
- prior suicide attempt, or
- emotional breakdown.

SOURCE: Centre for Prevention of Suicide, April 1998.

Correctional institutions strive to maintain active monitoring systems with a view to preventing suicide among the prison population overall, as well as those who have been identified as higher risks. Correctional staff are trained to be aware of suicidal risk factors; however, they are not mental health professionals, and suicides do occur. Institutions may isolate inmates at risk of committing suicide by placing them in a special observation area where they are monitored around the clock. Inmates who commit suicide are most likely to use a ligature, slash, or overdose (*Twenty Years Later…*, CSC, 2010).

Howard Sapers, the Correctional Investigator, identified a number of areas that present challenges to correctional staff in an effort to prevent inmate deaths. The need to share information between clinical and front line staff, the need to monitor suicide pre-indicators, and the management of mentally ill offenders were among the areas in need of improvement.

Howard Sapers, the Correctional Investigator, has focused on the prevention of deaths in custody.

> Preventing deaths in custody is challenging work. There are no shortcuts. Even the slightest of errors or omissions – failure to record or communicate a change in an offender's behaviour, for example – can lead to tragic if unintended consequences. Despite appropriate policy, a legal duty of care and the best efforts of staff, a prison is not a hospital. Security is always a factor. Managing health care emergencies is complex, precarious and demanding even in the most technologically sophisticated and advanced emergency departments. In a custodial setting, it is all the more complicated by the constant necessity to balance security concerns against a legal duty of care.
>
> SAPERS, OCI—FINAL ASSESSMENT, SEPTEMBER 2010: HTTP://WWW.OCI-BEC.GC.CA/RPT/OTH-AUT/OTH-AUT20100908-ENG.ASPX.

## LO10 Evaluation of Correctional Institutions

### RECIDIVISM

The **recidivism** rate is often thought of as the main measurement used to evaluate the success of a correctional institution or program. The recidivism rate refers to the rate at which offenders reoffend and it is one indicator of success in the correctional system. Determining the recidivism rate is often difficult as there are numerous studies that attempt to identify it, and these studies may define recidivism in different ways. Recidivism can refer to the rate of rearrest or re-conviction. An individual may offend, but may not be convicted. Recidivism may also be measured based on the rate of readmission to a correctional facility, as opposed to a conviction that may not have resulted in a custodial sentence. Some studies assess recidivism based on specific characteristics or criteria. For example, the recidivism rate of a specific type of offender, or offenders who engaged in a specific type of program, may be studied. Correctional researchers struggle with being able to identify the recidivism rate in a way that can be generalized to a simple statistic.

**recidivism**
the rate at which an offender reoffends

In one study, federal offenders were assessed based on their re-conviction rates. The offenders were released between April 1, 1994, and March 31, 1995. They were followed for two years and were determined to have a re-conviction rate of 44 percent. The non-violent re-convictions represented 30 percent of the offenders, while violent re-convictions represented 14 percent. The study also found that females had a lower re-conviction rate than males, and that Aboriginal male offenders had a higher re-conviction rate than non-Aboriginal males. (Bonta, J., Rugge, T, Dauvergne, M. 2003). It was determined that this re-conviction rate was comparable to that in other countries and that considering the high-risk nature of the offenders being studied, this was a finding that the federal correctional system was working well (Bonta et al., 2003).

### THE COST OF INCARCERATION

The increasing cost of incarceration is a difficult challenge to manage. The annual average cost of incarcerating a male federal inmate in 2009–10 was $117,700 per year, or $323 per day (Public Safety Canada, 2010). This is compared to the cost of incarcerating a female federal inmate, which is $180,000 per year. The cost of supervising an offender in the community is about one eighth the cost of incarceration (Sapers, 2010). The cost of incarcerating an offender in the provincial correctional system is lower, at just over $161 per day, or $59,100 per year (Public Safety Canada, 2010). The federal correctional system amounts are higher than their provincial and territorial counterparts because of the higher level of security required, and the specialized programming that is required for the longer-term inmates. The cost of community supervision is significantly less than that of incarceration, which means that it is costly to confine offenders who do not require incarceration. In addition, the higher the inmate's security level, the more expensive it is to confine him or her. It is critical to ensure that an inmate's security level is not higher than required, not only because it is unfair to the inmate, but also because it is more expensive.

### RESPECTING THE RIGHTS OF INMATES

Another way in which we can evaluate our correctional institutions is based upon the manner in which we respect inmates' rights. Canada has the legal justification to incarcerate individuals, where they are denied of their right to liberty and freedom. Offenders retain the rights and privileges of all members of society, except those rights and privileges that are necessarily removed or restricted as a consequence of the sentence (*Corrections and Conditional Release Act*, s. 4e). Inmates have the right to essential health care and to reasonable access to non-essential mental health care that will contribute to their rehabilitation and reintegration (*Corrections and Conditional Release Act*, s. 86). An inmate has the right to refuse treatment or withdraw from treatment at any time. Canada's record for the treatment of female inmates and Aboriginal inmates has been challenged in the recent past.

The rights of prisoners are championed by the United Nations as declared in the *Basic Principles for the Treatment of Prisoners*:

1. All prisoners shall be treated with the respect due to their inherent dignity and value as human beings.
2. There shall be no discrimination on the grounds of race, colour, sex, language, religion, political or other opinion, national or social origin, property, birth or other status.
3. It is, however, desirable to respect the religious beliefs and cultural precepts of the group to which prisoners belong, whenever local conditions so require.
4. The responsibility of prisons for the custody of prisoners and for the protection of society against crime shall be discharged in keeping with a State's other social objectives and its fundamental responsibilities for promoting the well-being and development of all members of society.
5. Except for those limitations that are demonstrably necessitated by the fact of incarceration, all prisoners shall retain the human rights and fundamental freedoms set out in the Universal Declaration of Human Rights, and, where the State concerned is a party, the International Covenant on Economic, Social and Cultural Rights, and the International Covenant on Civil and Political Rights and the Optional Protocol thereto, as well as such other rights as are set out in other United Nations covenants.
6. All prisoners shall have the right to take part in cultural activities and education aimed at the full development of the human personality.
7. Efforts addressed to the abolition of solitary confinement as a punishment, or to the restriction of its use, should be undertaken and encouraged.
8. Conditions shall be created enabling prisoners to undertake meaningful remunerated employment which will facilitate their reintegration into the country's labour market and permit them to contribute to their own financial support and to that of their families.
9. Prisoners shall have access to the health services available in the country without discrimination on the grounds of their legal situation.
10. With the participation and help of the community and social institution, and with due regard to the interests of victims, favourable conditions shall be created for the reintegration of the ex-prisoner into society under the best possible conditions.
11. The above Principles shall be applied impartially.

SOURCE: United Nations General Assembly, Forty-fifth Session.

In addition, the *United Nations Universal Declaration of Human Rights* indicates that all people, including those who are incarcerated, have the right to full and equal recognition and protection before the law. Our own *Canadian Charter of Rights and Freedoms* guarantees that Canadians will not be subjected to cruel and unusual treatment or punishment. The punishment for sentenced offenders consists of depriving them of their freedom. Inmates are not to be subjected to punishment while incarcerated, they are entitled to be treated fairly and humanely.

"One must resist the temptation to trivialize the infringement of prisoners' rights as either an insignificant infringement of rights or as an infringement of rights of people who do not deserve any better."

JUSTICE LOUISE ARBOUR, THE ARBOUR COMMISSION, 1996.

## Chapter Summary

This chapter provided an introduction to correctional institutions in Canada. The key points included:

- Providing correctional services in Canada is split between the federal government and the provincial/territorial governments. Inmates sentenced to prison for two years or more are incarcerated in federal institutions; inmates sentenced to less than two years are incarcerated in provincial/territorial institutions. Correctional institutions are categorized based on the level of security that they provide—minimum, medium, and maximum.
- Canada's prison population presents numerous challenges including unemployment, illiteracy, substance abuse issues, and mental health problems. There are many programs designed to address these issues.
- The inmate culture consists of a number of informal rules, which are generally adhered to in correctional institutions.
- Each province/territory has an Ombudsman and the federal government has a Correctional Investigator to investigate and respond to individual complaints and systemic issues.
- There are a number of ways to evaluate correctional institutions including cost, recidivism, and the way in which inmates are treated.

## Relevant Legislation

*Corrections and Conditional Release Act* (S.C. 1992, c. 20)

*Corrections and Conditional Release Regulations* (SOR/92-620)

## Key Terms

Auburn system
Cat-o-nine tails
Classification
Contraband
Corporal punishment
Correctional plan
Harm reduction
Inmate culture
Life imprisonment
Pennsylvania system
Recidivism
Self-harm
Split-jurisdiction

## For Review

1. What is the goal of correctional services?
2. What are the security levels in Canada?
3. What correctional programs exist for inmates in Canada?
4. How do the needs of male inmates differ from the needs of female inmates?
5. What is contraband and why is it important that it be monitored?
6. How does the correctional service support inmates in their relationships with their families?
7. How do we measure success in correctional institutions?

## Thinking Critically

1. Given the challenging nature of the offender population, what are the ways that we can measure success?
2. To what extent do you believe that prisons represent the society in which we live?
3. What is the impact of the inmate culture on the operation of a correctional facility?
4. Correctional budgets are significant—how would you save money on correctional spending?
5. How would you prepare a person who was about to enter a correctional institution as an inmate? How would you prepare a person who was about to enter the profession of correctional officer?
6. Do you believe that harm reduction strategies should be increased behind bars? If so, what would you suggest?
7. Should every Canadian visit a prison? How do you think this would benefit Canadians?
8. How do you think advances in technology will change prisons of the future?
9. To what extent should inmates have the same rights as non-incarcerated persons? Should inmates have the right to vote in elections? Should inmates have access to the same materials/magazines everyone else in Canada?

CHAPTER 7

# Community Corrections

## The Tragic Death of Tema Conter

Most parolees complete their sentences in the community successfully. When one parolee commits a crime while in the community, the entire system is called into question. Tema Conter, a 25-year-old woman who lived in Toronto, was murdered by Melvyn Stanton on January 27, 1988. Stanton, 31, had been granted a temporary release from an Ontario federal penitentiary. Within hours of arriving at a Toronto community halfway house, he raped and murdered Tema Conter in her Toronto apartment. Stanton was serving a life sentence for murder and three rapes when he came upon Conter in the corridor of her apartment building, as she was on her way to work. Paramedic Vincent Savoia and his partner Barrie Martin were the first responders and both experienced the trauma of the crime scene in Ms. Conter's apartment where she was bound, gagged, and stabbed 11 times. This tragedy provided a wake-up call to the community and resulted in outrage. The inquest that followed produced 38 recommendations designed to improve parole procedures, case management, and the way in which halfway houses are managed. Stanton fled the scene and was eventually arrested in Wawa, Ontario, for driving under the speed limit. He pleaded guilty to first degree murder in June, 1988, and is currently serving a life sentence. He is eligible for full parole on January 30, 2013. Vincent Savoia went on to found the Tema Conter Memorial Trust, designed to assist emergency services personnel to better understand and cope with the physical, psychological, and emotional stressors of acute trauma. The trust was founded to improve the understanding of acute and post traumatic stress disorder through research and public education.

### LEARNING OBJECTIVES

By the end of this chapter, you should be able to:

- **LO1** Define community corrections and discuss its role in the criminal justice system.
- **LO2** Describe the following types of community supervision: pre-trial, and conditional release.
- **LO3** Identify community treatment programs available to offenders and the challenges of supervising offenders in the community, including those with special supervision considerations.
- **LO4** Describe the role of community residential facilities.
- **LO5** Explain the importance of community acceptance to the success of community correctional programs.
- **LO6** Describe the role that community agencies play in supporting the reintegration of offenders into the community.

First responders to crime scenes may experience life-altering trauma.

## LO1 Community Corrections in Canada

Community-based correctional services include a range of programs where offenders and accused persons are supervised in the community. Community correctional programs exist at various points within the criminal justice system, from pre-trial to post-sentence. Some community correctional services are an alternative to incarceration, while others are intended to provide supervision to support offenders while they are reintegrated into the community. Generally, community-based correctional services are in place to support individuals with a view to assisting them to live crime-free, in the community.

The success of community corrections largely depends on the involvement of the community itself. Communities are required to take responsibility for integrating and supporting offenders while they are in the community. As a result, there are numerous agencies that have been created to support offenders in the community—recognizing that their support is a critical element for success.

When considering the role that community correctional services play, it is important to recognize that at the core rests the need to balance risk and the rights of the community, the offender, and the victims of crime. Risk is assessed through a process that is intended to predict an offender's ability to succeed in the community. The community has the right to be safe and not to be harmed by offenders who are violent or present any other type of risk. The victims of crime are owed respect and recognition of the challenges that they have faced. The community is a partner in community corrections in that there is a need for offenders to be supported and accepted into the community. There is an expectation on the part of the public that the correctional services—federal and provincial/territorial—will do their part to ensure that inmates who are released pose a minimal risk and that every effort has been made to mitigate that risk.

Correctional facilities are given the responsibility of ensuring that offenders who are incarcerated are adequately prepared for their return to the community. Section 3 of the *Corrections and Conditional Release Act* states:

> 3. The purpose of the federal correctional system is to contribute to the maintenance of a just, peaceful and safe society by
>    a) carrying out sentences imposed by the courts through the safe and humane custody and supervision of offenders; and
>    b) assisting the rehabilitation of offenders and their reintegration into the community as law-abiding citizens through the provision of programs in penitentiaries and in the community.

This requirement to prepare offenders to return to the community is addressed when they are first admitted to custody. There is a focus on preparing offenders for release that continues throughout custody. While they are incarcerated, offenders are continually assessed based on their level of risk and problem areas, which are addressed in a Correctional Treatment Plan. The Correctional Treatment Plan is intended to provide a rehabilitation plan that follows the offender through both the institutional and community phases of supervision. In addition to a treatment plan it is critical that, when inmates are released into the community, the risk factors that lead to recidivism are addressed. These risk factors may include a lack of accommodation and/or employment, poor support systems, lack of family ties, and lack of programming to address issues such as addiction and sexual offending (Berinbaum, 2009).

As is the case with institutional corrections, the responsibility for delivering correctional services within the community is shared by both the federal and provincial/territorial correctional systems. The federal correctional system is responsible for the conditional release of all inmates who have been sentenced to custody for two years or longer. This includes parole, statutory release, and all temporary absences. The provincial/territorial

Communities are required to take responsibility for integrating and supporting offenders while they are in the community.

### The Commitment of the Correctional Service of Canada Towards the Public

The commitments of CSC community corrections toward the public are to:

1. Assess each offender to determine the level of risk to the public and problem areas to be addressed.
2. Prepare a Correctional Treatment Plan with each offender to ensure that he or she has the supervision, training, and programming needed to reduce the risk to reoffend.
3. Suspend the release of any offender believed to be at risk of criminal involvement.
4. Ensure that information about particular offenders is made available (within the limits of legislation) to police, victims and other legitimate partners in the supervision area.
5. Supervise each offender by seeing him or her at home and in CSC offices at a frequency that complies with CSC standards for supervision.
6. Document each offender's case according to CSC policy.

SOURCE: Correctional Service of Canada: Protecting Society through Community Corrections, http://www.csc-scc.gc.ca/text/pblct/protect/broch-eng.shtml.

system is responsible for providing **probation** services and supervising conditional sentences in each jurisdiction, as well as parole and temporary absences for those inmates who received custodial sentences of less than two years.

Community supervision programs must be accessible to every community across the country. In 2009, there were 8,716 federal offenders in the community on day parole, full parole, statutory release, or long-term supervision orders (Parole Board of Canada, 2010). In the same year, there were approximately 84,281 offenders in the community under probation supervision plus 19,000 under another form of conditional release in the provinces and territories across Canada (Statistics Canada, 2010). These numbers are a clear indication of the commitment to community corrections both federally and provincially/territorially.

Community correctional programs are offered at three points within the criminal justice system. At the pre-trial phase, bail supervision programs are available to qualified accused persons. At the point of sentencing in the criminal justice system, **fine option programs**, probation, and conditional sentences are available to judges as alternatives to custodial sentences. And finally, there are several types of conditional release available to offenders who have been convicted of an offence and have been sentenced to a term in custody. In this chapter, we will examine pre-trial and conditional release options that are offered following a custodial sentence.

## PRE-TRIAL SUPERVISION

LO2

### BAIL SUPERVISION PROGRAMS

There are a number of provinces and territories across Canada that have elected to create pre-trial supervision programs for accused persons who lack the financial resources or suitable sureties to give them access to pre-trial release (bail). These **bail supervision programs** provide accused persons with an alternative to interim detention, and usually involve reporting to a bail supervisor while adhering to a number of identified conditions. The intention is to ensure that being without financial means does not result in being incarcerated before trial. In most jurisdictions the trend is an increase in bail supervision. For example, in Saskatchewan there were 2,214 new admissions to bail supervision in 2010, with an average of 985 people under bail supervision daily (Government of Saskatchewan, 2010). In order to provide the court with adequate information to make a decision regarding bail supervision, staff will prepare reports on an offender's situation. In a two-year Saskatchewan study conducted between 2003 and 2005, half of all bail supervision admissions were for violent crimes, while 22 percent were for property crimes (Juristat, 2006).

## CONDITIONAL RELEASE PROGRAMS

**Conditional release** refers to the supervision of offenders who have received a custodial sentence and have qualified for a form of release into the community. **Community release** includes day parole, full parole, statutory release, as well as those who are under temporary release programs and long-term supervision orders. All forms of community release include conditions that the

**conditional release**

a general phrase encompassing all forms of release from custody with conditions attached offenders must adhere to while in the community and if the conditions of the release are not met, the release will be revoked.

Long before offenders are released from custody, they are prepared for their eventual release—the successful reintegration into the community begins long before their release date. Successful reintegration begins during the inmates' classification process and is a part of their correctional plan. During their period of incarceration, inmates engage in programs that prepare them for eventual reintegration into society by identifying and addressing high risk areas. Program involvement is voluntary; however, there is a relationship between involvement in programs and eventual release. The parole board will consider an inmate's involvement in programs when making a decision regarding parole or statutory release. Involvement in institutional programs can have a dramatic impact on an offender's success. For example, offenders who complete substance abuse programs while in custody have recidivism rates decreased by up to 50 percent (Griffiths, Dandurand & Murdoch, 2007).

**escorted temporary absence**

a temporary release from custody with an escort for administrative, medical, community service, socialization, personal development, or humanitarian reasons

**unescorted temporary absence**

a temporary release from custody without an escort for administrative, medical, community service, socialization, personal development, or humanitarian reasons

Offenders who return to the community after a period of incarceration have a number of obstacles to overcome, depending on their circumstances. The challenges can be significant. We know that many offenders enter custody with issues related to substance abuse, mental health challenges, education, literacy, abuse, violence, poor social skills, social isolation, limited supports, and financial deficiencies. These issues may be addressed while in custody, but they will remain a challenge upon release. In addition, the offender returns to society with a new label: an offender.

### TEMPORARY ABSENCE PROGRAMS FROM CORRECTIONAL FACILITIES

Incarcerated individuals may apply for an escorted or unescorted temporary absence. The purpose for the absence could be personal, medical, educational, or for employment. They are often used to support the reintegration process. Inmates are eligible for an **escorted temporary absence** any time during their sentence. Inmates are eligible for an **unescorted temporary absence** once they have served one-sixth of the sentence or six months, whichever is later. They come with conditions and expectations, and are limited in length and time. Work release

**FIGURE 7.1** Conditional Release Timeline

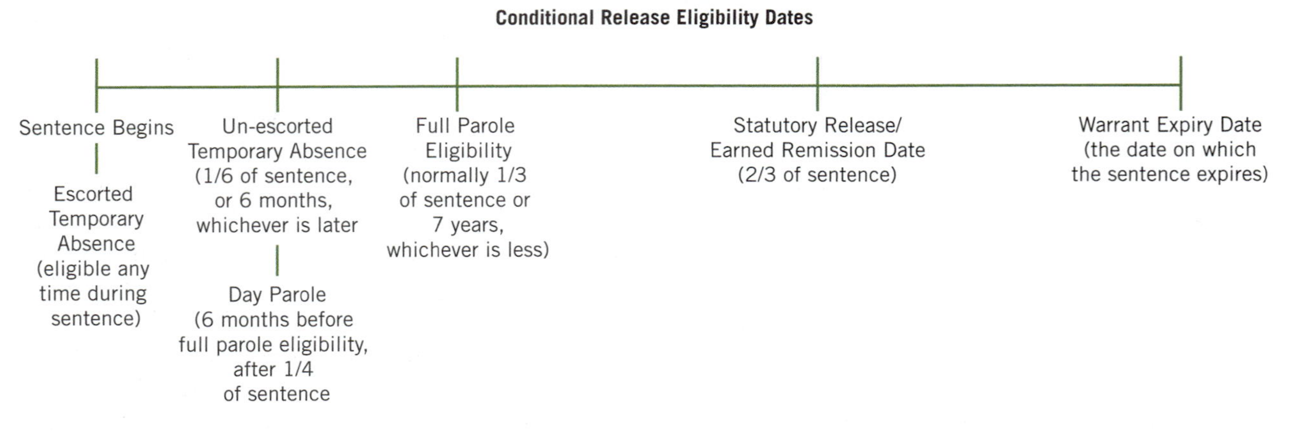

programs are structured, unescorted release programs that permit penitentiary inmates to work in the community, under supervision, allowing them to prepare for their eventual reintegration into society.

## Parole

Parole supervision provides offenders with an opportunity to make a transition from custody to the community. The transition approach ensures that the inmate is supported throughout the process, and that the inmate is supervised throughout the process in order to identify any problems or challenges that can be addressed. Offenders who are on parole, whether day parole or full parole, are still serving their sentence, just in the community under the supervision of a parole officer instead of in a correctional facility. Parole is available to both federal and provincial/territorial inmates. There are two types of parole supervision: day parole and full parole.

**day parole**

a form of conditional release generally granted for up to a six-month period to prepare inmates for full parole or statutory release; they must return to the penitentiary, community-based residential facility, or provincial/territorial correctional facility each night

**Day parole** is releasing offenders into the community, in order to prepare them for eventual full parole or statutory release. An offender on day parole is required to return to the institution, community resource centre, or provincial/territorial correctional facility each night. Federal offenders are permitted to apply for day parole six months before their full parole eligibility date or after they have served one-sixth of their sentence. Inmates who are serving a sentence for first or second degree murder are eligible for day parole three years before they are eligible for full parole. Accelerated parole review is available to first time, non-violent offenders only, and allows them to apply for day parole after serving one-sixth of their sentence.

**full parole**

full-time conditional release under supervision normally at one third of the sentence

**Full parole** is releasing offenders into the community to serve the remainder of their prison sentence. During this time, they are supervised by a parole officer and are required to abide by terms and conditions established by the parole board that granted the release. Federal offenders are eligible to apply for parole after serving one third of their sentence or seven years after admission, whichever is less. There are exceptions to this; for example, offenders sentenced to life imprisonment for first degree murder are not eligible to be considered for parole until they serve 25 years. Those sentenced to life imprisonment for second degree murder have their parole eligibility date determined by the sentencing judge, between 10 and 25 years. Offenders who are serving life sentences while granted parole are required to remain under parole supervision for the rest of their lives. All other offenders remain on parole until the warrant expiry date, which is the entire length of their sentence. Judges have the option to delay parole eligibility for violent and serious drug offenders from one third to one half of the sentence completion. Provincial/territorial offenders are eligible to apply for parole after serving one third of their sentence.

Parole is not a statutory right—it is a privilege that is earned by the inmate. The Parole Board of Canada grants approximately 69 percent of day parole applications and 44 percent of full parole applications (Parole Board of Canada). An inmate must prove that he or she is responsible and understands the challenges that parole can present. The inmate must have a parole plan that supports his or her release and minimizes the risk of engaging in criminal conduct or other types of behaviour that will jeopardize his or her success. Parole allows an offender to reintegrate into the community on several levels. It is based on a belief that supervised release will help to ensure that offenders will become law-abiding citizens. Parole enables offenders to reconnect with family, friends, and support networks. It allows them to work or attend school and it gives them an opportunity to reintegrate while under the supervision of a parole officer. The parole board that releases the offender identifies the conditions that the parolee must abide by throughout the parole period. Conditions are directly related to the type of support the parolee requires and often include a requirement to continue the correctional plan that began in the institution. The plan may include treatment for drugs or alcohol use and may require an employment or education condition.

There continues to be evidence to support the fact that when Canadians are provided with adequate information about the criminal justice system, they are more supportive of correctional services.

An inmate who is not granted parole has the right to appeal the decision. The appeal must be sent to the Appeal Division of the Parole Board of Canada within 60 days of the date of the decision. The Appeal Division will review the case to ensure that the decision was made based on relevant and reliable information.

### SUCCESSFUL COMPLETION OF PAROLE

There are approximately 8,400 offenders on federal conditional release on any given day in Canada (Juristat, 2006). A 2007 study indicated that the overwhelming majority of them successfully complete their conditional release. There were 1,310 offenders released on full parole: 70.5 percent completed their full parole, 19.8 percent **breached** their conditions, 9.2 percent committed a new, non-violent offence, and 0.5 percent committed a new violent offence (www.victimsofviolence.on.ca). The same study indicated that day parole was more successful than full parole, as 83.5 percent of 3,025 offenders released on day parole completed successfully. These successful statistics are often overshadowed by the tragic, rare, cases where a parolee commits a serious crime such as murder while under community supervision. Each of these cases creates understandable panic and fear in the community. Such events lead to the misconceptions by the general public regarding both the parole grant rate as well as the rate of successful completion of parole. When polled, Canadians consistently overestimated the recidivism rate of offenders while on parole (Roberts, 2005). A survey conducted in 2004 asked Canadians to estimate the percentage of federal parolees that commit another crime while on parole. The correct response is 10 percent; however, 65 percent of the respondents said that they believed the answer to be over 30 percent (Roberts, 2005). This attitude results in a general apprehension regarding parole supervision though there is research to suggest that Canadians support parole under certain conditions. A 2002 study conducted by Leger Marketing indicated that 84 percent of respondents in Ontario and Quebec fully agreed with the statement, "It is safer to gradually release offenders into society under supervision and control than to release them without conditions at the end of the sentence" (Roberts, 2005). This support of conditional release does appear to have some limits. When asked if "all offenders should be considered for parole" in the same poll, 55 percent said that parole should be abolished for all violent offenders (Roberts, 2005).

**breached**
violated

There is a clear connection between public knowledge of the criminal justice system and public support of conditional release options. Numerous studies indicate that when persons receive accurate information about conditional release, they are more supportive of it. This hypothesis was tested by Roberts et al., (2000) when they asked a sample of Canadians if they would support releasing a specific offender on parole. In the first, low information condition, Canadians were asked the following question: "John Smith is serving a 3-year sentence for break and enter. He has served one year in prison and is now applying for parole. Should he get parole?"

A second sample of Canadians was asked the same question; however, they were provided with additional information about parole. Their question was asked in the following manner:

"Parole is a programme by which some inmates are allowed to spend part of their sentence in the community. If the Parole Board is convinced that the offender is not a risk to the community, parole is granted. This means that for the remainder of the sentence, the offender has to report to a parole officer and follow a number of rules imposed by the National Parole Board. If the offender breaks the rules he can be returned to prison. Now that you know what parole is about, here is an actual case. John Smith is serving a three year sentence for break and enter. He has served one year in prison and is now applying for parole to help him adjust to life once his sentence is completed. Smith will be supporting his family when he leaves prison. Should he be released from prison to serve the rest of his sentence in the community, reporting to a parole officer and following the conditions laid down by the Parole Board?"

Only 42 percent of those who were selected to respond to the short version favoured granting parole to this inmate, while 75 percent of those who responded to the long version of the question favoured granting parole to the inmate (Roberts, 2005). Providing additional, accurate information about the parole process in Canada resulted in reassurance and, therefore, support of the process. There continues to be evidence to support the fact that when Canadians are provided with adequate information about the criminal justice system, they are more supportive of correctional services. In 2004, an Environics poll asked Canadians, "About 10% of all federal offenders released on parole commit another crime while on parole. Do you find this very, somewhat, not very or not at all reassuring?" Half of the sample said that they were reassured by this information (Roberts, 2005).

Public support of community corrections is critical to its success. Community corrections relies on the community to provide programming, employment, and residential facilities for offenders upon release. A lack of information contributes to the perpetuation of stereotypic beliefs and unfounded fears that can have an impact on community corrections overall and on individuals specifically.

### RECENT LEGISLATIVE CHANGES THAT AFFECT PAROLE ELIGIBILITY

On December 2, 2011, two new pieces of legislation came into force in Canada, both of which impose greater restriction on parole eligibility for those serving life sentences having committed first or second degree murder. On February 15, 2011, the Canadian Parliament passed Bill S-6, *Serious Time for the Most Serious Crime Act*. This bill repealed the **"faint hope clause,"** which was a section of the *Criminal Code of Canada* that permitted those convicted of first degree murder to apply for parole after serving 15 years of their sentence, even though they had been sentenced to life imprisonment without parole eligibility for 25 years. It was called the "faint hope clause" because it was determined to be a clause that most inmates would not likely use successfully. However, they did have a right to apply for parole at this point in their sentence. This resulted in a full parole hearing, which involved victims undergoing the trauma of repeatedly appearing before the Parole Board. As a result of the new law, parole eligibility for first degree murder is 25 years and parole eligibility for second degree murder is up to 25 years, as determined by the court.

On March 9, 2011, the Canadian Parliament passed Bill C-48, the *Protecting Canadians by Ending Sentence Discounts for Multiple Murders Act*. Under this legislation persons convicted of more than one murder are no longer able to serve their parole eligibility period concurrently, if imposed by the court. A judge now has the power to impose consecutive parole eligibility periods on individuals convicted of more than one count of first or second degree murder. Prior to the passing of the legislation, an offender who was convicted of two murders and received two life sentences

Parole board hearings are conducted in correctional facilities.

would be eligible for parole at the same time as a person who received one life sentence. Critics said that this concurrent counting devalued the lives of victims and it did not reflect the seriousness of multiple murder. Judges are now required to state their reason for imposing or not imposing the sentence discount to offenders. This change affects roughly 5 percent of convicted murderers, as 95 percent of homicides involve a single victim (Mackay, 2011).

### THE ROLE OF THE PAROLE BOARD

Each jurisdiction that offers parole does so under the authority of a parole board. Offenders are released under the authority of the parole board in the jurisdiction within which they serve their sentence. The parole board has the authority to grant, deny, terminate, or **revoke** parole, to terminate or revoke statutory release, detain offenders past their statutory release date, and grant unescorted temporary absences.

**revoke**

withdraw privileges

Parole for federal offenders is administered by the Parole Board of Canada. The Parole Board of Canada is legislated under the *Corrections and Conditional Release Act* where its mandate is identified as:

> To contribute to the maintenance of a just, peaceful and safe society by means of decisions on the timing and conditions of release that will best facilitate the rehabilitation of offenders and their reintegration into the community as law-abiding citizens (*Corrections and Conditional Release Act*, s. 100).

The Board bases its policies and decisions on the following principles:

- Protection of society is the paramount consideration of any conditional release decision.
- Supervised release increases the offender's potential for successful reintegration and, thereby, contributes to the long-term protection of society.
- Restrictions on the freedom of the offender in the community must be limited to those necessary and reasonable to protect society and to facilitate reintegration.

The Parole Board of Canada can have a maximum of 45 full-time members and 40 part-time members who hear cases across Canada. Provinces and territories administer their own parole boards. Parole boards make decisions about releasing offenders into the community, balancing the issue of public safety with successfully reintegrating the offender into the community. Parole boards meet on a regular basis in correctional institutions to decide the fate of those inmates who have applied for parole. When making a decision, the parole board reviews the risk that an offender may pose to society. The parole board takes the following factors into consideration when making the decision to release an offender:

- the offence;
- the offender's criminal history;
- the offender's history of violent behaviour, including use of weapons;
- suicide attempts and other types of self-harming behaviour;
- drug or alcohol use;
- mental status;
- progress in the institution (behaviour, involvement in treatment programs);
- relationship to co-accused persons and other negative influences;
- success of previous community release;
- employment (previous and future);
- family relationships and supports;
- psychological and psychiatric reports;
- information supplied by police, judges, Aboriginal elders;
- victim information; and
- the offender's release plan (including address, employment, supports, relationships, programming in the community).

The parole board convenes a hearing with the offender, at which point the members decide whether or not to grant parole. If parole is granted, then the board may identify conditions for the parole period. The conditions must be related to the offender's criminal behaviour with a view to minimizing the risk of reoffending. Throughout the parole period, a parole officer supervises the parolee. If the parolee violates any of the parole conditions, the parole board may revoke the parole and the parolee is returned to custody.

## RECORD SUSPENSIONS

A person who has been convicted of a federal offence may apply for a **record suspension** (formerly known as a **pardon**), after a waiting period that is based on the severity of the original offence. Waiting periods vary from five years (for a summary conviction offence) to 10 years (for an indictable offence), a period where the person must remain crime free. The application to the Parole Board of Canada is followed by an investigation. A record suspension results in all information pertaining to convictions being removed from the Canadian Police Information Centre (CPIC), and it may not be disclosed without permission from the Minister of Public Safety Canada.

There are limitations to the record suspension, as it does not erase the fact that the person committed a criminal offence. A record suspension generally makes international travel easier; however, it does not guarantee that another country will grant the offender entry or a visa. Persons convicted of sexual offences will have their name flagged on the CPIC. Individuals convicted of sexual offences against minors (with certain exceptions) and those who have been convicted of more than three indictable offences, each with a sentence of two or more years, are now ineligible for a record suspension. If a sex offender does receive a record suspension, his or her record is still available to future employers as part of a criminal record check for persons who wish to work with vulnerable persons. A record suspension will not cancel a prohibition order (such as a driving or firearms prohibition) that may have been a part of an original sentence.

### MYTH VS FACT

There is a general belief that the Canadian criminal justice system is more lenient than its international counterparts. The following chart identifies the average time spent in custody by an offender with a life sentence for first degree murder. You will note that next to the United States, offenders serving a life sentence in Canada serve the longest time in custody.

**Average Time Spent in Custody**

| Country | Time in Custody (years) |
|---|---|
| New Zealand | 11.0 |
| Scotland | 11.2 |
| Sweden | 12.0 |
| Belgium | 12.7 |
| England | 14.4 |
| Australia | 14.8 |
| United States | |
| Life with parole | 18.5 |
| Life without parole | 29.0 |
| Canada | 28.4[a] |

NOTE: [a] Department of Justice Canada, "Fair and Effective Sentencing: A Canadian Approach to Sentencing Policy," Backgrounder, October 2005.

SOURCE: Legislation Summary of Bill C-36: An Act to Amend the Criminal Code (Serious Time for the Most Serious Crime Act), Table 1 —Average Time Spent in Custody. URL: http://www.parl.gc.ca/About/Parliament/LegislativeSummaries/bills_ls.asp?lang=E&ls=c36&Parl=40&Ses=2&source=library_prb. Department of Justice Canada, 2005. Reproduced with the permission of the Minister of Public Works and Government Services Canada, 2012.

The Parole Board of Canada makes decisions about clemency, or Royal Prerogative of Mercy.

Records indicate that over 400,000 Canadians have received record suspensions since 1970, and 96 percent of these people continue to live in the community, crime-free (Parole Board of Canada, 2010).

The Parole Board of Canada also makes recommendations to the Minister of Public Safety Canada regarding **clemency**, or Royal Prerogative of Mercy. Only considered under exceptional circumstances, this is reserved for those individuals who have suffered excessive hardship as a result of a court imposed penalty. In 2009, there were 21 requests for clemency and four were granted (Parole Board of Canada, 2010).

### THE ROLE OF THE VICTIM IN THE PAROLE PROCESS

The victim's role in the parole process is very important as it gives victims a voice in the parole board's decision-making process. Victims are encouraged to provide the parole board with a written statement indicating information about the continuing impact that the crime has had on their lives. Impact on physical, emotional, and financial issues is often relayed in the statement. Victims comment on the impact of the offender's release as it relates to their own safety and the safety of the community overall. If the direct victim of the crime is deceased, then the family members attend the hearing. Until recently, it was often difficult for a victim to attend parole hearings that were held in another province or territory or across the country. This concern was addressed in 2005, when the Victims' Travel Fund was established to provide financial assistance to enable victims to travel to Parole Board of Canada hearings.

Victims of criminal offences have the right to be informed of an offender's status, if they so choose. These rights are guaranteed under the *Corrections and Conditional Release Act*. The information includes details about where the offender is detained, parole hearing dates, the granting of parole, and whether or not an offender has appealed a parole decision. It has been determined that the victim's right to be advised of these details outweighs the offender's right to privacy.

Observers who wish to attend Parole Board of Canada hearings may apply to do so as indicated in the *Corrections and Conditional Release Act*. In addition to victims, family members and supporters, the media, and the general public may also attend in order to facilitate an open and accountable system and enhance the public's knowledge and understanding of the parole process. There are approximately 1,900 observers of Parole Board of Canada hearings each year (Parole Board of Canada, 2010). Those interested in details related to decisions may access the registry of Parole Board of Canada decisions. The registry is maintained and members of the public are permitted access to it. A written application to the Parole Board of Canada is required for access to the content, for personal and research purposes.

## STATUTORY RELEASE

**statutory release**

legal entitlement to release under supervision after completing two thirds of a sentence

**Statutory release** refers to releasing federal offenders into the community after they serve two thirds of their sentence. The Parole Board of Canada reviews the cases of federal inmates who are eligible for statutory release, and may detain offenders if it does not believe that they are ready to be released into the community because they pose a risk to the public. Offenders may choose to waive their statutory release while incarcerated and remain in custody until the end of the sentence. The success rate of statutory release is lower than both day parole and full parole, at 60 percent (The Parole Board of Canada, 2011). It is not surprising that the rate of success for statutory release is lower because, generally speaking, inmates who pose a lesser risk are released on parole prior to their statutory release date. Inmates released on statutory release are, by category, at greater risk of reoffending.

## EARNED REMISSION

**earned remission**

an incentive for provincial/territorial inmates to earn "good time" of 15 days for every month served

**Earned remission** is the provincial/territorial equivalent of statutory release. Provincial/territorial inmates can be released after serving two thirds of their sentence with earned remission. Earned remission is an incentive designed to promote positive behaviour while in custody. Once inmates are released at the earned remission date, they are not supervised in the community. Their release is unconditional, unlike offenders in the federal system who are supervised when released on statutory release. Inmates can earn 15 days of earned remission for each month served, which means that they serve approximately two thirds of their sentence in custody. By violating institutional rules or regulations, an inmate may be placed on misconduct. This may result in a loss of a portion of earned remission time, requiring the inmate to remain in custody longer.

Though referred to as "earned" remission, inmates are actually given credit for their earned remission time upon admission to a correctional facility. If they do not abide by institutional rules and regulations then they may lose a portion of their "good time."

## ELECTRONIC MONITORING

Electronically monitoring offenders enables them to live in the community while under electronic surveillance. Advanced technology has permitted the use of **electronic monitoring**, which allows the offender to remain in the community while ensuring that there is an element of surveillance to protect the public. It is an attempt to control offender risk while at the same time ensuring a degree of public safety (Bottos, 2007). In addition, electronic monitoring is reported to be potentially cost-effective if it is used as an alternative to custody.

Electronic monitoring was first introduced in the 1960s by Dr. Robert Schweitzgebel, an American psychologist. It took about 20 years before his idea was put into practice. British Columbia was the first province to use it, in 1987 (John Howard Society of Alberta, 2006). Its use has increased since then and is now used extensively.

Electronic monitoring restricts an offender's movement and also allows for the movement that does occur to be tracked. An offender must wear a transmitter on his or her body, which is usually in the form of an ankle bracelet or a wrist bracelet. That bracelet is connected to a monitoring centre, which tracks the offender's behaviour. If the device is tampered with, the monitoring centre is alerted as well.

To date, electronic monitoring has been used as an added level of offender accountability. Electronic monitoring is used in the pre-trial phase (while an offender is on bail) as well as post-trial, as an alternative to custody. Each jurisdiction that uses electronic monitoring chooses at what point an offender is eligible for the program. Electronic monitoring is designed for offenders who present a moderate to high risk of reoffending; it is not intended for use for offenders who present a low risk. Numerous studies have looked at participant success rates. In a study that examined the success rate of participants in a Newfoundland electronic monitoring program, the success rate was 87.5 percent. It was also determined that the recidivism rate of the offenders one year after completing the electronic monitoring was 32.1 percent (John Howard Society of Alberta, 2006).

The use of electronic monitoring has raised numerous ethical issues about the invasion of privacy and the potential humiliation of wearing an electronic device. This has been argued and it was determined that an offender must consent to being involved in the program. Another issue is the fact

Offenders who are subject to electronic surveillance wear a transmitter.

that an offender must pay for using the equipment and the monitoring. This could potentially prevent some people from having access to the program. Overall, the positive aspect of being able to remain in the community appears to overshadow the negative aspects of electronic monitoring. A British Columbia study that measured the attitudes of offenders who were under electronic surveillance indicated that 86 percent of the respondents said that the benefit of electronic monitoring was the ability to remain in close contact with family members, employment, and treatment programs (John Howard Society of Alberta, 2006). That same study noted that there are sources of stress related to the hardships of electronic monitoring, but again the benefits outweighed the negative aspects. Another study found that offenders believed that electronic monitoring allowed them to improve their relationships with their family members (Rubin, 1990).

The Correctional Service of Canada introduced a one-year electronic monitoring pilot program in 2008, designed to measure the effectiveness of the program (Olotu, Beaupre & Verbrugge, 2009). The study involved 46 federal parolees who volunteered to take part. The results of the study were disappointing, as there were numerous technical malfunctions related to the anklet and the anklet global positioning system, in that it often failed to identify a parolee's position accurately. The device emitted false alarms and continually required personal follow-up from correctional personnel, calling into question its future use.

## LO3 Community Treatment Programs

There is a clear indication that providing supervision is not enough to support offenders in the community. Effective treatment programs are required to help offenders in an effort to minimize the risk of reoffending. Many of the programs are designed to maintain treatment and skills that are introduced while offenders are incarcerated, while others are for offenders who have never been incarcerated but are under probation or other types of community supervision. Some of the programs are a mandatory element of the community supervision and are supervised by a parole officer.

The Correctional Service of Canada identifies the needs of inmates at admission as well as upon release. A profile of federal inmates being released into the community in 2002 indicated that the highest needs of the offenders were related to personal/emotional orientation, social interaction/associates, and substance abuse (Trevethan and Rastin, 2009). These needs are the basis of treatment programs that are required to support the inmates. Treatment programs that are offered reflect the needs and focus on five main areas: substance abuse, violence prevention, family violence, sex offender programming, and community maintenance. Often there is a direct connection between the type of offence that the offender committed and the program. For example, there are specific programs for offenders who have been convicted of family violence as well as programming for offenders who have been convicted of sexual offences.

Treatment programs are often offerred in group settings.

PROFILE

## Tragic Events: Hard Lessons Learned

There have been several tragic events in which an offender on conditional release committed a serious offence. In recent history, we have seen changes made to correctional processes and/or legislation because of tragedies that occurred when an individual under community supervision commits a murder. Each of the tragic events identified in the following chart resulted in a number of changes to processes and procedures, intended to improve community safety.

| Tragic Event | Legislative Change or Response |
| --- | --- |
| **1985 Death of Celia Ruygrok**<br>Celia Ruygrok, a recent university graduate, was a 21-year-old employee with an Ottawa halfway house. Alan Sweeney was a convicted sex offender/murderer on parole, living in the house. On July 5, 1985, he sexually assaulted and stabbed Ms. Ruygrok when she was working a midnight shift at the house. Sweeney was convicted of first degree murder and sentenced to life imprisonment without parole for 25 years. | This tragedy resulted in the creation of new legislation that allowed the detention of individuals beyond their mandatory release dates if there were reasonable grounds to conclude that they were likely to commit an offence causing death or serious harm.<br>SOURCE: Brodeur, (1990). |
| **1988 Death of Tema Conter**<br>Tema Conter, a 25-year-old woman who lived in Toronto, was murdered by Melvyn Stanton on January 27, 1988. Stanton, 31, had been granted a temporary release from federal penitentiary in Ontario. Within hours of arriving at a Toronto community halfway house, he raped and murdered Tema Conter in her Toronto apartment. Stanton was serving a life sentence for murder and three rapes when he came upon Conter in the corridor of her apartment building as she was on her way to work. | The inquest that followed produced 38 recommendations designed to improve parole procedures, case management, and the way in which halfway houses were managed.<br>SOURCE: www.tema.ca. |
| **1988 Death of Christopher Stephenson**<br>Christopher Stephenson, an 11-year-old boy from Brampton, Ontario, was abducted, raped, and murdered by Joseph Fredericks, a long-time sex offender who was under mandatory intensive supervision. He was convicted of first degree murder without parole for 25 years. | The trial of Joseph Fredericks and the subsequent inquest resulted in an increased awareness of several problems within community corrections. A number of recommendations were made by the inquest jury that have had a significant impact on criminal justice policy. Christopher's Law created a sex offender registry in Ontario, which required all sex offenders to register with their contact information.<br>SOURCE: Petrunik & Weisman, 2002. |
| **2002 Death of Gillian Hadley**<br>Gillian Hadley was murdered by her estranged husband, Ralph Hadley, while he was on bail for charges related to domestic violence, where Gillian Hadley was the victim. Ralph Hadley killed his estranged wife in her home, the same home they once shared. | One of the jury recommendations that came out of the inquest into Gillian Hadley's death was the development of a domestic violence bail program to increase the safety of victims of domestic violence. These programs involve an interview with the victim to identify risk factors, and to educate the victim on supports and resources available to them. The accused person is assessed based on risk, and bail conditions are determined based on the risk posed.<br>SOURCE: Toronto Star, 2001. |
| **2004 Death of Louise Pargeter**<br>Louise Pargeter was a community parole officer in Yellowknife, NWT, who died in the line of duty on October 6, 2004. Ms. Pargeter made an appointment to meet with parolee Eli Ulayuk at his apartment on October 6 at 10:00 am. When Ms. Pargeter did not return to the office that morning, her colleagues alerted the RCMP, who found her dead body later that day in Ulayuk's apartment. Ulayuk was arrested the following day. He pled guilty to second degree murder on February 22, 2006, and was sentenced to life imprisonment without parole for 25 years. Ms. Pargeter was the first parole officer to die in the line of duty in the Correctional Service of Canada. | As a result of this tragedy, the Correctional Service of Canada implemented improvements to strengthen community staff safety. These include:<br>• All community staff must have the capacity to communicate by phone while carrying out their duties in the community.<br>• All community officers must have reliable sign in/out systems that ensures the means to verify the location and safety of community staff.<br>• All community offices must have contingency plans that include a plan to deal with situations where a staff member cannot be located.<br>• All program and parole officers, psychologists, and sections supervisors to receive the Community Personal Safety training and annual safety refresher training.<br>SOURCE: Correctional Service of Canada, *Investigation Report into the Case of Eli Ulayuk*. |

Research conducted by the Correctional Service of Canada indicates that participation in correctional programming reduces the risk of recidivism and decreases violent, general, and sexual reoffending (CSC National Evaluation, 2009 as cited in McDonough, 2010). Specifically, offenders who participated in Violence Prevention Programs were 41 percent less likely to return to custody for a new offence, and 52 percent less likely to return to custody for a new violent offence (McDonough, 2010). Other evidence to support the success of programming is the Family Violence Prevention Program, where offenders who participated were 36 percent less likely to be readmitted for a new offence, and 57 percent less likely to be readmitted for a new violent offence (McDonough, 2010).

There have been significant challenges related to offering the programs in the community (Annual Report of the Correctional Investigator, 2007). For example, many programs have long waiting lists, postponing treatment for some offenders. Offenders who live in remote areas are often unable to access services (Yazar, 2009), and historically there has been a void in the availability of Aboriginal-specific programming.

## SPECIAL SUPERVISION CONSIDERATIONS

### FEMALE OFFENDERS

As is the case while in custody, female offenders represent a small number of offenders who are supervised in the community. Women who serve sentences in the federal system leave custody and are dispersed across the country to their home communities. Even though their numbers are sparse compared to male offenders, it is important that the range of care be continued into the community to help female offenders remain crime-free. Research indicates that female offenders have a high need for support in the following areas, upon release:

a) Employment needs are substantial: 71 percent of federally-incarcerated female offenders have unstable employment histories (compared to 67 percent of male offenders). Criminal records and a lack of training are the major obstacles in this area (Kong and AuCoin, 2009).

b) About one third of federally-incarcerated female offenders were convicted of drug offences, indicating a need for drug treatment (Kong and AuCoin, 2009).

c) The number of female offenders diagnosed with a mental health condition has increased, indicating a need for continued health care.

d) Over half of female offenders in the federal system are serving time for a violent offence (Revised National Community Strategy for Women Offenders, 2010).

e) The prevalence of physical, sexual, and emotional abuse among the female offender population is higher than that of non-offenders and male offenders (National Parole Board, 2005).

Even though as a group they present with many challenges to reintegration, women demonstrate greater success than men, upon release. In addition, the proportion of releases on day parole is higher for women than for men (Revised National Community Strategy for Women Offenders, March 2010). The percentage of successful full paroles for women in 2007–2008 was 78.8 percent, compared to 72.2 percent for men (Corrections and Conditional Release Statistical Overview, 2008).

In order to better meet the needs of female offenders, programs and their mode of delivery must be flexible. Programs for women must be gender-responsive and must address the significant challenges that they face. A focus on the special needs of female Aboriginal offenders is also required. Because there are fewer female offenders, programs need to be adjusted to maximize their benefit. For example, the standard minimum group size has been lowered, enabling smaller numbers of women to enrol in programs. Because many female offenders are mothers and primary caregivers, it is critical to ensure that programs are sensitive to their family responsibilities.

### SEX OFFENDERS

Sex offenders present a significant challenge to correctional officials. There are a number of programs and processes put into place with the intention of minimizing the risk that sex offenders pose to the community. The Correctional Service of Canada provides programming to sex offenders

"Women are Persons," Parliament Hill, Ottawa.

while they are engaged in community supervision. The programs are intended to continue the treatment that began while they were in custody and to prevent relapse. Programs involve individual and group counselling, and address problematic issues. Research into the effectiveness of such programs is promising: a 2000 study indicated that sex offenders who participate in the individualized treatment services along with parole supervision had lower rates of recidivism (Griffits, Danduand, Murdoch, 2007).

There have been a number of community initiatives designed to provide support to sex offenders. Circles of Support and Accountability are volunteer-based efforts that support high-risk sex offenders. Involvement is voluntary on the part of the offender as well. The "circle" is a group of volunteers who assist the offender in the community by providing guidance and assistance for accommodation, employment, budgeting, worship, and personal support. The offender is essentially embraced by the volunteer group with a view to preventing relapse and involvement in criminal behaviour. The Circles do have an effect on recidivism. One study indicates that offenders who participated in this program had a 70 percent reduction in sexual recidivism and a 57 percent reduction in all types of violent recidivism (Griffiths, Dandurand, Murdoch, 2007). The Circles require commitment from community volunteers who are willing to support a sex offender, a type of offender who is generally shunned and abhorred in our society.

The **long-term supervision order** was introduced into the *Criminal Code* to provide long term supervision and support to sex offenders who are at risk of reoffending. When an individual charged with certain sex offences appears before the court for trial, the Crown attorney can apply to the court to have the individual identified as a long-term offender requiring a long-term supervision order. The application is heard by a judge alone. This designation provides for the supervision of sex offenders after a prison sentence expires. The Parole Board of Canada has the right to impose a period of community supervision not longer

"Mental health problems are up to three times more common among inmates in correctional institutions than among the general Canadian population. More than 1 out of 10 male inmates and 1 out of 5 female inmates have been identified at admission as having significant mental health problems, an increase of 71 percent and 61 percent, respectively, since 1997. A recent snapshot of federally incarcerated offenders in Ontario indicated that 39 percent of the Ontario offender population were diagnosed with a mental health problem – a staggering challenge for any correctional authority."

-HOWARD SAPERS, CORRECTIONAL INVESTIGATOR OF CANADA, JUNE, 2009

than 10 years following the completion of the original sentence and that supervision includes a number of conditions that the offender must abide by. There are approximately 300 long-term supervision order offenders in Canada. In 2005, 187 of them were incarcerated and 113 were in the community being supervised by the Correctional Service of Canada (Trevethan and Rastin, 2009). There are approximately 24 long-term supervision orders designated each year in Canada (Trevethan, Crutcher and Moore, 2002).

The Sex Offender Registry (as discussed in Chapter 5, Sentencing in Canada ) also provides a form of accountability.

### OFFENDERS WITH MENTAL HEALTH DISORDERS

For offenders diagnosed with mental illnesses, reintegration into the community is especially challenging because of the requirement to ensure that the care that was provided in custody is continued in the community, ideally through a case management approach. There is a need to connect soon-to-be released offenders with community mental health services prior to release to ensure that there is not a gap that can result in a period of instability in the community. Offenders who are released to community-based residential facilities have the benefit of accessing available resources through the staff within the facility. The staff can make residents aware of mental health services that are available in the community and may escort them to appointments as required. There are barriers to receiving adequate mental health care in the community, as there is a limited number of mental health professionals and programs, many of which have long waiting lists. Community mental health facilities require that their patients volunteer for help, while correctional clients are often mandated to engage in treatment. This clash in philosophy can result in challenges to receiving treatment on an on-going basis (Desai, 2010). The number of offenders identified with mental health disorders has increased, as have the challenges to provide adequate services to them in the community.

Substance abuse programs are critical to the successful reintegration of offenders.

### MANAGING OFFENDERS WITH ADDICTIONS IN THE COMMUNITY

In response to the large number of inmates who present with substance abuse problems, there are numerous programs that exist to help them deal with substance abuse when in the community. Approximately 70 percent of inmates released from federal custody are assessed as having substance abuse needs (Murray, Gates, Hansen, 2009). Upon release, offenders face a number of challenges, including the need to find and sustain adequate housing, secure and maintain employment, as well as engage with family and social situations. These issues have the potential to result in stresses that may result in a relapse of substance abuse addiction. There are several community-based programs designed to respond to the need to prevent relapse, by increasing an offender's knowledge of the effects and consequences of drug and alcohol abuse. In addition, the programs teach skills that strengthen the ability to abstain from and control substance abuse.

## LO4 Community-Based Residential Facilities

There are various types of **community-based residential facilities** that are available to offenders who are being reintegrated into the community. The facilities are designed to provide the offenders with a place where they can adjust to life beyond the correctional institution in a supportive, supervised setting. These facilities, often referred to as **halfway houses**, are owned and operated by the federal correctional service, provincial and territorial services, and by private agencies operating under government contract. The government enters into a contractual arrangement with private agencies to provide supervision and accommodation to the residents in some jurisdictions. In addition to their provincial/territorial counterparts, there are 16 federal Community Correctional Centres (CCC) with the capacity to accommodate 449 people. There are an additional 2,000 federal spots available through about 200 contracts that the government has with private agencies across Canada (Correctional Service of Canada, 2009). Residents of the facilities are supported while they engage in employment, education, or treatment programs throughout the reintegration process. It is believed that by providing the basics—such as accommodation, food, and services—an offender will be better able to make the transition from custody to community.

Residential facility staff provide guidance, supervision, and programming. They also ensure that the residents abide by the conditions of their release. The facilities are classified by the type of resident (gender) and there may be exclusions based on certain types of crimes or resident challenges, such as substance abuse. Most residential facilities seek out those residents who are motivated to succeed by following through on their correctional plan. It costs an average of $60,656 annually to maintain one offender in a CCC compared to $23,030 for each offender living in the community (Olotu, Beaupre & Verbrugge, 2009).

The success of community residential facilities is reflected in the 80 percent success rate of day parole (Correctional Service of Canada, 2001), as many of the individuals on day parole return to community residential facilities in the evenings.

### THE CHALLENGE OF COMMUNITY CORRECTIONS: COMMUNITY ACCEPTANCE LO5

One of the biggest challenges faced by community corrections is achieving community acceptance. Community correctional programs and activities happen on residential streets and in all types of neighbourhoods. Community residential facilities are located on streets in city neighbourhoods. Probation and parole offices are located in commercial buildings along side other commercial enterprises, and offenders are paroled to residences in all neighbourhoods. The news of a community correctional facility opening in an area often results in residents organizing with the intention of blocking the facility from locating there. Concerns that are often raised relate to fears regarding community safety issues. The potential of an increased crime rate where offenders frequent or live, and the potential that house values will decrease, are often identified as concerns. This attitude is contrary to surveys done in areas where such facilities currently exist in Canada. For example, Kingston, Ontario, is home to nine correctional facilities and numerous community residential facilities. When residents of that city were asked if the halfway houses that existed there made their city more or less safe,

One of the biggest challenges faced by community corrections is achieving community acceptance.

Many people are unaware of the existence of community residential facilities in their neighbourhoods.

only 16 percent said that the area was less safe, two thirds said it made no difference, and 12 percent said that they believed the city to be safer as a result of their presence (Environics Research Group, 2000). A later study done by Environics in 2004 provided respondents with the statement, "The halfway houses program is a good way to help offenders reintegrate into society." Approximately two thirds of the sample agreed with the statement (Roberts, 2005).

There is no evidence to suggest that community correctional residential facilities result in lower property values; several studies confirm that there is no relationship (John Howard Society, 2002). In 1995, the British Columbia government studied the changes to property values in communities that included "non-market housing," which includes halfway houses. The study showed no evidence that the non-market housing had an impact on the sale prices of homes in the area. In addition, homes in the areas were not on the market for extraordinary lengths of time nor was there any evidence of panic selling (British Columbia, 1995). The concern about deflated property values is often based on speculation, rather than fact.

Correctional agencies strive to include the community by increasing awareness of correctional programs and the correctional process. Raising awareness about public safety and the truth about the amount of crime (or lack thereof) related to the existence of a correctional residence is critical. Studies show that Canadians have a positive attitude about rehabilitating offenders. In a survey conducted by Environics in 2002, 80 percent of respondents said that they believe that "a significant number of offenders can become law-abiding citizens through programs, education and other support." When asked if most offenders could be rehabilitated, 63 percent said yes (Roberts, 2005). That confidence in rehabilitation drops considerably when Canadians are asked if they believe that "inmates who have committed violent crimes and sexual offences can be rehabilitated." Only 18 percent of those polled said that these offenders could be rehabilitated, while 71 percent said they could not be rehabilitated. It is important to recognize that the public perception of a violent offender and a sex offender is usually based on media reports of high profile crimes, and is not an accurate reflection of most offenders.

## THE ROLE OF THE COMMUNITY IN COMMUNITY CORRECTIONS

LO6

It has been stressed that the community is a partner in providing community correctional programming. The success depends on a variety of types of involvement by individuals, neighbourhoods, and community agencies across Canada. Individuals are sought to engage as volunteers to assist in community programs or as members of a Citizen Advisory Committee.

Community agencies play a significant role in reintegrating offenders and they engage in several functions, which include:

- performing in an advisory capacity to the government,
- supervision to offenders in the community through local contracts,
- providing support to newly released offenders as they become integrated within the community,
- providing treatment programs that complement programs that the offenders started while in custody, and
- advocating for the rights of offenders and their families.

The following community agencies have a solid history of providing long-term support to persons who have been involved in the correctional system.

### ELIZABETH FRY SOCIETY

The Elizabeth Fry Society offers various programs for women in courts, institutions, and in the community. Its goals include the following:

- To increase public awareness and promotion of decarceration for women.
- To reduce the numbers of women who are criminalized and imprisoned in Canada.
- To increase the availability of community-based, publicly funded, social service, health and educational resources available for marginalized, victimized, criminalized and imprisoned women.

SOURCE: http://www.elizabethfry.ca/egoals.html.

Like many community agencies, the Elizabeth Fry Society began with the belief of one person.

> Elizabeth Fry (Gurney) was born into a family of Quakers in 1780 in England. Her mother's father, the Scottish theologian Robert Barclay, played an important role in defining early Quaker beliefs.
>
> It was fortunate for all concerned that Quakers believed in the equality of women (250 years before they won the vote), otherwise Elizabeth Fry's unusual talents in the area of prison reform might never have been realized.
>
> Her insight, persistence, organizational ability and her willingness to see a "divine light" in every person resulted in striking reforms taking place in the manner in which women and children were treated in London's Newgate Prison.
>
> She was a strong proponent of humane treatment for prisoners and regarded by many as a leading expert in prison reform.
>
> Most of her life was spent in England, although she did visit Ireland and continental Europe. She also offered advice to the Americas, Russia and Australia. She died in

Elizabeth Fry.

1845 at the age of 66 years.

The first Canadian Elizabeth Fry Society was established in Vancouver in 1939. The Canadian Association of Elizabeth Fry Societies (CAEFS) was originally conceived of in 1969 and was incorporated as a voluntary non-profit organization in 1978.

Today there are 26 member societies across Canada.

SOURCE: http://www.elizabethfry.ca/ehistory.html.

### JOHN HOWARD SOCIETY

The John Howard Society of Canada is an organization of provincial and territorial Societies comprised of and governed by people whose goal is to understand and respond to problems of crime and the criminal justice system. Their mission is to offer effective, just, and humane responses to the causes and consequences of crime. The John Howard Society:

- works with people who have come into conflict with the law,
- reviews, evaluates and advocates for changes in the criminal justice process, engages in public education on matters relating to criminal law and its application, and
- promotes crime prevention through community and social development activities.

The Canadian history of the John Howard Society began in 1867 with a group of church workers seeking to bring spiritual help to prisoners in the Toronto jail. In 1874 this small group became known as the "Prisoners Aid Association of Toronto." They soon came to recognize that more than spiritual aid was needed by prisoners, but interest dwindled during World War I (1914-1918). In 1929 a citizens' group led by Toronto's Chief of Police, General Draper, reactivated their cause as the "Citizens Service Association." Chief Draper understood that police work was undermined by the circumstances facing people upon release from prison. The Citizens Service Association—an organization of volunteers—set itself the task of providing practical help to ex-prisoners with housing, clothing and employment. In 1931 Reverend J. Dinnage Hobden formed a similar group in British Columbia under the name of the John Howard Society. John Howard was a great prison reformer who lived from 1726 to 1790 and whose pioneering studies of the conditions of English and European prisons established the modern English-speaking prison reform movement. The John Howard Society—established to carry Howard's mission—aided prisoners and ex-convicts in rehabilitation and re-integration following their sentence.

John Howard, Prison Reformer.

More specifically, the Society engages in the following:

- Advocacy, which includes active, planned and frequent contact with the media, key government policy analysis, advisors and politicians and committees with respect to the promotion of the objectives of the John Howard Society of Canada;
- Research related to the development and dissemination of briefs and positions on matters of national importance which incorporates positions of member societies

Refocusing and redefining justice expectations of the criminal justice system is a priority of the Salvation Army's correctional and justice program.

in the furtherance of the objectives of the John Howard Society of Canada;

- Communication with members societies to promote a coordinated consultative process which allows the national society to monitor and respond to the needs of members and facilitate joint projects between the John Howard Society of Canada and its members;
- Community Education which focusses on the sharing of information among members and the promotion of the objectives of the John Howard Society of Canada to the members through board development activities and broad based community education initiatives which enhances the role of the John Howard Society throughout Canada;
- Coalition building through a coordinated process of information sharing and the dissemination of materials with other like-minded national organizations;
- Resource development initiatives to strengthen the ability of the national office to further the objectives of the John Howard Society of Canada.

SOURCE: http://www.johnhoward.ca.

The John Howard Society is a non-profit charity governed by a volunteer board of directors. It offers many different services across Canada, many of which are under contract with the federal or provincial/territorial correctional services.

### SALVATION ARMY

Since 1883, the Salvation Army has been a leader in correctional services. Still busy in the traditional environments of prison cell and courtroom, the Army now provides facilities for adult and young offenders, attendance and community resource centres, drug and alcohol facilities and undertakes supervision of offenders in the community program. Its vast experience and wide resources, coupled with its ability to change and be innovative, set the Army apart as uniquely equipped to fulfil this challenging and demanding work within the community.

From the inception of the Canadian Federal Parole System, when a Salvation Army officer was the first official chaplain in a correctional institution, to management of the first juvenile detention centre in Canada, the Army has been identified with more than 250 adult and youth programs. You'll find them involved in community service orders, pre-charge diversion, family group conferencing, pre and postrelease planning, chaplaincy, substance abuse counselling, music therapy, life skills and literacy training, as well as providing circles of support and aftercare.

Today, refocusing and redefining justice expectations of the criminal justice system is a priority of the Army's correctional and justice program. Restorative justice, for example, rooted in indigenous spirituality and Christian scripture, focuses on identifying what needs to be done to reduce the possibility of persons being harmed again, often by rebuilding relationships and by addressing underlying social problems which led to the crime.

The Army's correctional and justice services are provided by 44 Army officers, supported by approximately 350 staff and 557 volunteers. Statistics recorded last year confirm that the Salvation Army conducted 62,054 interviews, made 31,291 visits and provided 47,723 residential bed days, encompassing almost 600,000 work hours. In addition, we held more than 1,600 worship services attended by more than 28,000 people. As impressive as statistics can be, the true value of this service is best seen in terms of lives restored and of people helped during times of great stress and anxiety.

More than 80 years ago, Doctor Gilmour, Parole Commissioner for Ontario, said that there would always be a great need for some moral and spiritual force within the criminal justice system. The Salvation Army's criminal and justice services remain as committed today as they were then to be such a force. This is well expressed in the department's mission statement, "to minister to offenders, victims, witnesses and other persons affected by, and serving in, the system, by practical assistance and through a demonstration of Christian love and concern."

SOURCE: http://www.salvationarmy.ca/britishcolumbia/correctionaljusticeservices/.

Community correctional programs offer a number of advantages to the criminal justice system and society overall. The programs reduce the prison population, which saves taxpayer money and prevents offenders from spending time in prison when they could be contributing to society in a positive manner. By offering community alternatives to incarceration, the number of days that offenders spend in custody is reduced. The cost of incarcerating an individual in a federal institution was almost $285 per day in 2009. The cost of supervising an offender in the community varies depending on the type of supervision, ranging between $5 and $75 per day (Statistics Canada, 2009). Community corrections produces an overall financial savings for Canadians as long as the programs are indeed alternatives to incarceration, or if they provide supervision services that ultimately prevent an individual from being incarcerated. If that is not the case, then we are in danger of creating additional ways to supervise offenders in the community, who may not require supervision. This danger of "widening the net" is something that policy makers must be aware of.

Community correctional programs support individuals as they transition to a crime-free life in the community. The research is clear that offenders who are released into the community gradually are more likely to complete their sentences and are less likely to reoffend than those who are released without any period of community supervision (John Howard Society/HalfwayHouses, 2001). Parole (both day and full) and statutory release contribute to the successful release of offenders, and they do so in a cost-effective manner. The successful reintegration of offenders is complex and requires the cooperation and involvement of many. The success of one offender can involve professionals in several sectors including criminal justice, health and education, the general public, community and faith-based agencies, and the offender's own friends and family. The success of an offender transitioning to a crime-free life (or a life with less crime) is often the cumulative result of many years of perseverance and commitment by many people.

## Chapter Summary

This chapter provided an introduction to community corrections in Canada. Key concepts included:

- Community corrections includes a range of programs where offenders and accused persons are supervised in the community. There is a requirement to balance risk with the needs of the offender, the victim, and the community overall.
- At the pre-trial stage, accused persons who do not have the financial means to receive interim release (bail) may qualify for a bail supervision program.
- Conditional release programs include:
  - temporary absence programs,
  - parole (day and full),
  - statutory release, and
  - earned remission.
- Offenders in the community require ongoing supervision and programs to meet their needs related to employment, education, literacy, substance abuse, mental health issues, and other areas of vulnerability.
- A community's cooperation and support are required to ensure the success of community correctional programs.

## Relevant Legislation

*Corrections and Conditional Release Act*, S.C. 1992, c. 20

*Criminal Code*, R.S.C. 1985, c. C-46

## Key Terms

Bail supervision programs
Breached
Clemency
Community release
Community-based residential facilities
Conditional release
Day parole
Earned remission
Electronic monitoring
Escorted temporary absence
"Faint hope clause"
Fine option programs
Full parole
Halfway houses
Long-term supervision order
Pardon
Probation
Record suspension
Revoke
Statutory release
Unescorted temporary absence

## For Review

1. Identify the various forms of conditional release in Canada.
2. What is the difference between day parole and full parole?
3. What is the difference between statutory release and earned remission?
4. What are the eligibility dates for each of the following:
   a) escorted temporary absence
   b) unescorted temporary absence
   c) parole
   d) earned remission
   e) statutory release
5. What are the benefits of receiving a record suspension?
6. Identify three agencies that provide community support to offenders.
7. What role can the victim play in the parole process?

## Thinking Critically

1. Do you believe that it is advantageous to have a system of earned remission where inmates must "earn" their way out of custody?
2. What are the implications of the new laws that impose greater restrictions on parole for offenders convicted of a single murder and multiple murders?
3. To what extent is the government responsible for sharing information about released offenders to the community?
4. Does the community have the right to be made aware of parole board decisions?
5. Do you support the changes to the law that remove the discount for multiple murderers?
6. How will technology affect the future of community corrections?
7. Is conditional sentencing (house arrest) a viable alternative for non-violent offenders?
8. Should people who work in community residential facilities have special skills or abilities? What should they be?
9. Why is it problematic if we "widen the net" of correctional services? How can we safeguard our communities when doing so?

Practise and learn online with Connect

CHAPTER 8

# Youth Justice

## The Shocking Murder of Kimberly Proctor

The brutal murder of grade 12 student Kimberly Proctor, of Langford, British Columbia, shocked the community as the horrific details unfolded in court. Kimberly Proctor was lured to her death by two fellow students, Cameron Alexander Moffatt and Kruse Hendrick Wellwood, on March 18, 2010. Kimberly went to meet them at Wellwood's home under the pretense that the boys were going to explain to her why they had been mean to her. At Wellwood's home, they reportedly duct taped her mouth, hands, and ankles, and they took turns sexually assaulting her and eventually they mutilated her body. They then placed her dismembered body in a freezer in the garage and the following day transported it in a duffel bag (using public transit) to the Galloping Goose Trail in Victoria, where they set her body and the duffle bag on fire. Her body was found the following day under a bridge where it was buried, and an autopsy revealed that Kimberly Proctor died of asphyxiation due to the duct tape that covered her mouth.

Their scheming to lure and murder their victim was documented in text messages and online chats, prior to the murder. The messages included details about the brand of fuel they would use to burn her body, the bus they would take, a description of their plan to bind and sexually assault her, as well as a discussion of the site at which to dispose of her body.

The two boys, who were 16 and 17 at the time of the murder, pleaded guilty to first degree murder and indignity to a dead body. Their identities were protected under the *Youth Criminal Justice Act* until British Columbia Supreme Court Judge Robert Johnston lifted the ban when it was determined that they would be sentenced as adults. Both were sentenced as adults to life in prison with no

### LEARNING OBJECTIVES

By the end of this chapter, you should be able to:

- **LO1** Describe the evolution of youth justice legislation in Canada.
- **LO2** Describe the philosophy of the *Youth Criminal Justice Act.*
- **LO3** Define extra-judicial measures and identify their significance in the *Youth Criminal Justice Act.*
- **LO4** Identify the sentencing options available under the *Youth Criminal Justice Act.*
- **LO5** Identify the rate of youth crime in Canada.
- **LO6** Examine issues related to young female offenders, Aboriginal young offenders, and youth gangs in Canada.

Friends mourn the loss of Kimberly Proctor.

*continued.*

possibility of parole for 10 years. Youths sentenced as adults receive a mandatory life sentence without the possibility of parole for 10 years for a first degree murder conviction, compared to adults who, when convicted of first degree murder, receive a mandatory life sentence without the possibility of parole for 25 years. If Moffat and Wellwood had been sentenced as youths, they would have received the maximum penalty, which is a 10-year sentence, six of which are served in custody and the remaining four years served in the community under supervision. Moffat and Wellwood will eventually be transferred to serve their sentence in the adult federal system where they will have access to treatment programs. Though they are eligible for parole in 10 years, their release is not guaranteed.

## LO1 The Evolution of Youth Justice Legislation in Canada

When a young person commits a criminal act, it is important to ensure that every effort is made to prevent that young person from one day becoming an adult offender. Youths in conflict with the law become involved with the criminal justice system at an important time in their growth and development. They are vulnerable and effective intervention is required with a view to preventing them from becoming adult offenders. The Youth Criminal Justice System in Canada makes an effort to rehabilitate youths who have been in conflict with the law. The legislation aims to balance both the needs of youths at this critical point in their lives and to protect society. Legislation responding to youth crime has evolved since the introduction of the ***Juvenile Delinquents Act***, the first piece of legislation to address the criminal behaviour of youths in Canada. Introduced in 1908, the *Juvenile Delinquents Act* took a social welfare approach to crime, apparent in the manner in which young offenders should be treated:

> This Act shall be liberally construed in order that its purpose may be carried out, namely, that the care and custody and discipline of a juvenile delinquent shall approximate as nearly as may be that which should be given by his parents, and that as far as practicable every juvenile delinquent shall be treated not as a criminal, but as a misdirected and misguided child, and one needing aid, encouragement, help and assistance. (*Juvenile Delinquents Act*, s. 38).

Under the *Juvenile Delinquents Act*, young offenders were not charged with a *Criminal Code* offence. Instead, they were charged with the generalized status of "delinquency"—offending youth were commonly referred to as "juvenile delinquents." Criminal accountability began at age seven; however, the upper age limit varied across the country, anywhere from 15 to 18 years old. Judges had enormous discretion with sentencing options for juvenile delinquents. A child could be placed in foster care, pay a fine, or be institutionalized until the age of 21. There were few safeguards in place to ensure that there was consistency across the country.

The *Young Offenders Act* replaced the *Juvenile Delinquents Act* in 1984. This resulted in a policy shift from the social welfare approach to an approach that required young people to take responsibility for their actions. One of the contributing factors to the creation of the new legislation was that Canada had recently introduced human rights legislation that called into question several aspects of the *Juvenile Delinquents Act*, including the paternalistic treatment of the children and youth.

The ***Young Offenders Act*** did not label young offenders as delinquents. Instead, young offenders were charged with specific offences under the *Criminal Code*. They were no longer charged with being "delinquent." The *Young Offenders Act* raised the age of criminal responsibility from 7 to 12, and it also established a consistent upper age limit for young offenders of 17. Youths who committed a criminal offence while under the age of 12 were not criminally responsible for their actions. The *Young Offenders Act* also protected the identity of young offenders from the media and limited the penalties available to the court.

The guiding principles of the *Young Offenders Act* included the following:

- youths who commit offences must take responsibility for their actions; however, youths have special needs and cannot be held accountable for their illegal actions in the same way as adults;
- society has a right to be protected from offences committed by youths; however, where possible, it is in society's best interest to address youth crime through social and community-based solutions, rather than incarceration;
- youths have legal rights and freedoms, including those outlined in the *Canadian Charter of Rights and Freedoms;* and
- parents have the right to be notified of all court proceedings affecting their child.

The *Young Offenders Act* required that young offenders be kept separate and apart from adult offenders. They were considered to need protection from the negative influence of adult offenders and therefore had to be detained in separate facilities and units.

There were a number of criticisms of the *Young Offenders Act* "for being too soft on the offender; for lacking a clear philosophy on youth justice in Canada; for inconsistent and unfair sentences; for not properly addressing serious and violent offences; for an overuse of the court system; and for not giving enough recognition to the victims." The reality is that under the *Young Offenders Act* there was an overreliance on custodial sentences (Statistics Canada2007). There were far more youths imprisoned under the *Young Offenders Act* than the current *Youth Criminal Justice Act* (Statistics Canada, 2007). In fact, it was determined that Canada's youth **incarceration rate** under the *Young Offenders Act* was higher than many other countries in the world. According to the 1997 Standing Committee on Justice and Legal Affairs, Canada's youth incarceration rate was higher than that of the United States and 10 to 15 times greater than a number of other countries including New Zealand and Australia (Standing Committee on Justice and Legal Affairs, 1997). Much of the public criticism of the *Young Offenders Act* was based on the high profile cases where young people committed serious crimes and received penalties that were perceived as lenient. These cases received a great deal of publicity and they led the general public to believe that the *Young Offenders Act* was soft on crime.

The following table shows the rate (per 1,000 youths age 12 to 17 in the jurisdiction) of sentencing youths to custody in 1998–9. The use of custody varied considerably across the provinces. For example, Saskatchewan sentenced youths to custody at a rate of 24.1 per 1,000 youths, while Quebec sentenced youths at a rate of 4.8 per 1,000 youths.

There was little evidence to support the belief that the high incarceration rate resulted in a lower rate of youth crime. There is evidence to support the assertion that detention has a negative impact on young offenders' mental and

**FIGURE 8.1 Rate of Youths Sentenced to Custody 1998–1999**

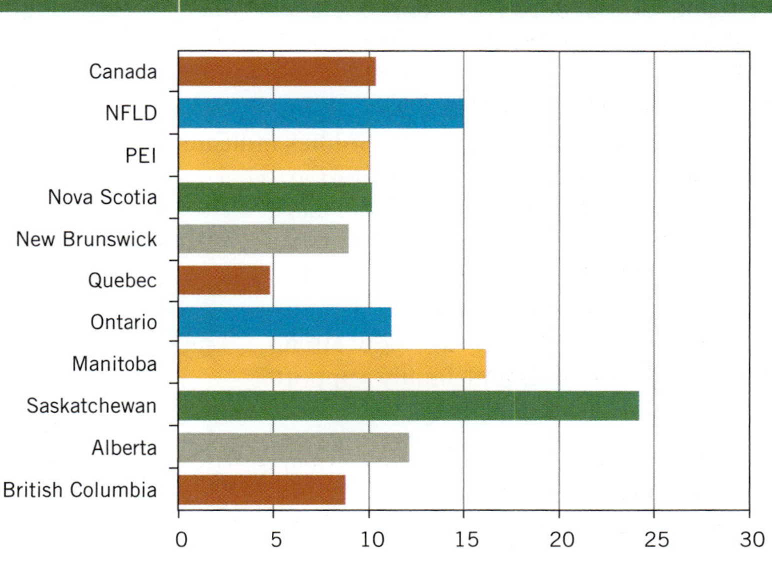


NOTE: Rates per 1,000, ages 12 to 17, sentenced to custody.

SOURCE: Background for YCJA, Part B: Use of Custody, Figure B1: Rate of youths sentenced to custody. URL: http://www.justice.gc.ca/eng/pi/yj-jj/res-rech/back-hist/partb.html. Department of Justice Canada. Reproduced with the permission of the Minister of Public Works and Government Services Canada, 2012.

**FIGURE 8.2 | Youth Custodial Sentences: A Comparison Between Canada and the United States**

The overall rate (per 100,000 youth age 12 to 17) of youth court judges imposing custody in Canada and the US (1997)

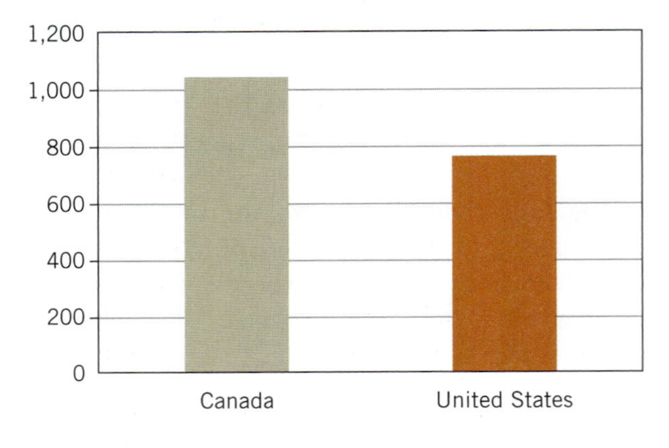


SOURCE: Statistics Canada, Youth Court Statistics 1997-1998. Ottawa: Canadian Centre for Justice Statistics, accessed March 26, 2012. Reproduced and distributed on an "as is" basis with the permission of Statistics Canada.

physical well-being, as well as their education and employment prospects. Incarcerated youth are at risk of being depressed, committing suicide, and engaging in self-harm. In addition, it has been shown that incarcerating a young person may make it more likely that he or she will continue to engage in criminal behaviour upon release (Holman and Ziedenberg, 2006). Studies indicate that the experience of incarceration is the most significant factor in increasing the odds of **recidivism** among youths (Holman and Ziedenberg, 2006). While youth are incarcerated they are denied normal engagement with education, employment, friends, and family supports. Instead, they are connecting and identifying with other offenders. They are learning from other young offenders instead of healthy, positive role models, during this critical stage of adolescent development.

**recidivism**
the rate of reoffending

## LO2 The *Youth Criminal Justice Act*

In 1998, the federal government, under then Liberal Prime Minister Jean Chrétien, announced a new strategy for youth justice, based in part on the recommendations of the Standing Committee on Justice and Legal Affairs. After several years of delay, the ***Youth Criminal Justice Act*** was introduced in 2001 and passed in the House of Commons in 2002. It came into effect in April, 2003, replacing the *Young Offenders Act*. The new legislation attempted to incorporate the best elements of both the *Young Offenders Act* and the *Juvenile Delinquents Act*. It includes the legal framework that was introduced in the *Young Offenders Act* and maintains the focus on social needs as identified in the *Juvenile Delinquents Act*.

The following principles apply in the *Youth Criminal Justice Act:*

> (a) The youth criminal justice system is intended to
> (i) prevent crime by addressing the circumstances underlying a young person's offending behaviour,
> (ii) rehabilitate young persons who commit offences and reintegrate them into society, and
> (iii) ensure that a young person is subject to meaningful consequences for his or her offence,
>
> in order to promote the long-term protection of the public.
> (*Youth Criminal Justice Act*, s. 3 (1))

The *Youth Criminal Justice Act* stresses that the criminal justice system for young persons should emphasize:

> (i) rehabilitation and reintegration,
> (ii) fair and proportionate accountability that is consistent with the greater dependency of young persons and their reduced level of maturity,
> (iii) enhanced procedural protection to ensure that young persons are treated fairly and that their rights (including the right to privacy) are protected,
> (iv) timely intervention that reinforces the link between the offending behaviour and its consequences, and
> (v) the promptness and speed with

which persons responsible for enforcing this Act must act, given young persons' perception of time

(*Youth Criminal Justice Act*, s. 3 (1) (b))

(c) within the limits of fair and proportionate accountability, the measures taken against young persons should
   (i) reinforce respect for societal values,
   (ii) encourage the repair of harm done to victims and the community,
   (iii) be meaningful for the individual young person given his or her needs and level of development and, where appropriate, involve the parents, the extended family, the community and social or other agencies in the young person's rehabilitation and reintegration, and
   (iv) respect gender, ethnic, cultural and linguistic differences and respond to the needs of aboriginal young persons and of young persons with special requirements.

(*Youth Criminal Justice Act*, s. 3 (1) (c))

Special considerations were identified that apply in respect of proceedings against young persons such as:

(i) young persons have rights and freedoms in their own right, such as a right to be heard in the course of and to participate in the processes, other than the decision to prosecute, that lead to decisions that affect them, and young persons have special guarantees of their rights and freedoms,
(ii) victims should be treated with courtesy, compassion and respect for their dignity and privacy and should suffer the minimum degree of inconvenience as a result of their involvement with the youth criminal justice system
(iii) victims should be provided with information about the proceedings and given an opportunity to participate and be heard, and
(iv) parents should be informed of measures or proceedings involving their children and encouraged to support them in addressing their offending behaviour.

(*Youth Criminal Justice Act*, s. 3 (1) (d))

The *Youth Criminal Justice Act* provides a clear philosophy and solid principles that provide direction to the youth criminal justice system. There is a vital focus on protecting youths, as well as the significance of the victim. Young offenders are protected by keeping them separate from adults, and by protecting their privacy and rights. The victim is given information about the proceedings and is given an opportunity to be involved in several of the sentencing options, if appropriate. The legislation also directs the youth criminal justice system on the way in which victims should be treated—with courtesy, compassion, and respect. Involving parents is also a key element of the legislation, intended to provide the young person with ongoing support by keeping the parents informed and supportive of the sentencing options, where possible. Emphasis is placed on providing appropriate service to Aboriginal youths as well as those who require special attention, helping to ensure that the criminal justice process results in meaningful consequences for the young person and his or her community.

### CRIMINAL OFFENCES BY YOUNG PEOPLE UNDER THE AGE OF 12

Children under the age of 12 who commit a criminal act are not criminally responsible for their actions in Canada. When a child commits a criminal

There is a vital focus in the *Youth Criminal Justice Act* on protecting youths, as well as the significance of the victim.

act, the authorities may refer to the relevant child protection legislation in their province or territory. Under the authority of child protection legislation it is determined whether the child is adequately supervised or is in need of protection. There are provisions under the legislation to begin proceedings to determine whether a child protection agency needs to be involved. If a child under the age of 12 commits a criminal act, it may also be determined that the child and his or her family requires support, which may be available through social service or health agencies.

## HIGHLIGHTS OF THE *YOUTH CRIMINAL JUSTICE ACT*

- The statement of principle removes any uncertainty about how the *Youth Criminal Justice Act* should be interpreted and it expresses the philosophy that the needs of society and the offender are not in conflict.
- There is a focus on the number of extrajudicial measures available, such as police warnings, referral to restorative justice agencies in which the offender must face his or her victim and the victim's family, and deferred custody orders, whereby a young person can avoid incarceration by demonstrating good behaviour.
- There is a clear statement that the court process is reserved for more serious offences. Police must consider all other options, such as a warning or making restitution, before laying charges.
- There is clarity regarding the conditions for sentencing youths into custody, and custody is reserved for violent or repeat offenders.

### FLASHBACK:
### JUVENILE JUSTICE PRIOR TO THE *JUVENILE DELINQUENTS ACT*

Prior to the passing of the *Juvenile Delinquents Act,* young people were treated the same way as adults. They were charged with offences and treated like adults at trial, and were held in custody with adults. Children in conflict with the law were treated similar to adult criminals, often receiving harsh sentences for relatively minor crimes. The treatment of children while incarcerated was documented in the Brown Report, a Royal Commission report created to examine accusations of abuse at Kingston Penitentiary in 1848. In the report, Brown describes the case of Peter Charboneau, a 10-year-old child who was admitted to Kingston Penitentiary for seven years in 1845. He received 57 lashings within eight and half months for committing the offences of staring and laughing (Curtis, Graham, Kelly and Patterson, 1985).

Children were once imprisoned in Kingston Penitentiary.

- There are provisions for integrating youths in custody back into society. The *Youth Criminal Justice Act* introduces a graduated sentence, where youths spend two thirds of their time in custody, and one third in the community under supervision.
- There is an opportunity for intensive treatment while in custody, and community supervision for those youths who require it.
- Youths may not be transferred to adult court; however, they may be sentenced as adults if they are found guilty of committing certain offences and have reached the age of 14.
- This legislation gives the provinces and territories the discretion to determine the various types of custodial arrangements they can arrange for their youth.

## RIGHT TO COUNSEL

Section 25 of the *Youth Criminal Justice Act* makes it clear that youths should be advised of their right to counsel at any stage of their involvment in the justice system. Critical times include at the time of the arrest, before making a statement, and when making an appearance in court.

## THE ROLE OF THE PARENT

The *Youth Criminal Justice Act* makes it clear that parents are expected to play an active role when their child is involved in the criminal justice system. Police are required to notify parents when youths are arrested or if they have received a summons or appearance notice that requires them to appear in court (*Youth Criminal Justice Act*, s. 26). The parents may be advised verbally and in writing. If their child is in custody, the parents must be advised of the specific location. Youths have the right to confer with their parents at any point in the court process. If the parents cannot be reached, another adult may be contacted who can provide assistance to the young person. The *Youth Criminal Justice Act* also gives a judge the power to require a parent to attend court, if required (*Youth Criminal Justice Act*, s. 27).

### THE FLOW OF A CASE UNDER THE YOUTH CRIMINAL JUSTICE SYSTEM

The flow of a case through the youth criminal justice system is similar that of a case through the adult system with some exceptions (see Figure 8.3).

**FIGURE 8.3** A Young Offender Case as it Flows Through the Court System

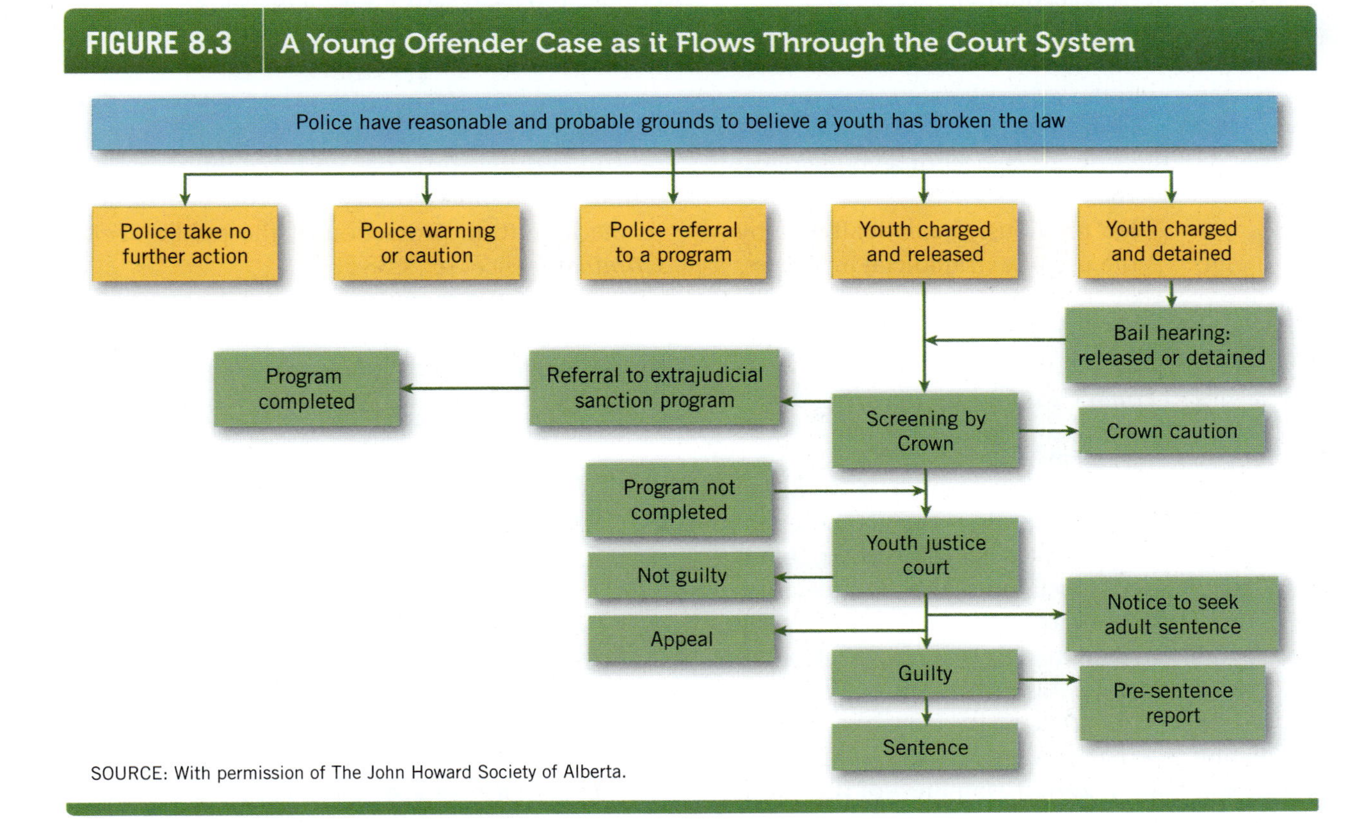


SOURCE: With permission of The John Howard Society of Alberta.

## LO3 EXTRAJUDICIAL MEASURES

An important feature of the *Youth Criminal Justice Act* is the inclusion of extrajudicial measures, in section 4.

**Extrajudicial measures** are designed to provide young offenders with a variety of options that divert them from the traditional criminal justice system. The *Youth Criminal Justice Act* identifies the principles that form the foundation of extrajudicial measures. They are:

> a) extrajudicial measures are often the most appropriate and effective way to address youth crime;
> b) extrajudicial measures allow for effective and timely interventions focused on correcting offending behaviour;
> c) extrajudicial measures are presumed to be adequate to hold a young person accountable for his or her offending behaviour if the young person has committed a non-violent offence and has not previously been found guilty of an offence; and
> d) extrajudicial measures should be used if they are adequate to hold a young person accountable for his or her offending behaviour and, if the use of extrajudicial measures is consistent with the principles set out in this section, nothing in this Act precludes their use in respect of a young person who
> i) has previously been dealt with by the use of extrajudicial measures, or
> ii) has previously been found guilty of an offence.
> (*Youth Criminal Justice Act*, s. 4)

Extrajudicial measures are intended to be both timely and effective. Unlike a traditional trial experience, extrajudicial measures can be implemented quickly. The objectives behind introducing extrajudicial measures are restorative in nature; as such there are a number of measures that are defined as restorative justice programs. The *Youth Criminal Justice Act* states that youths should be encouraged to acknowledge the harm that has been done to the victim and the community. In addition, families of the young person and victims of the crime are encouraged to become involved in the extrajudicial measures process.

The *Youth Criminal Justice Act* requires the police and the prosecution to consider using extrajudicial measures before proceeding with traditional judicial proceedings. Extrajudicial measures include **warnings, cautions**, and referrals to community social service agencies and programs. If it is determined that a warning or a caution is not appropriate in a given situation, then an extrajudicial sanction may be appropriate. A young person must consent to his or her participation in an extrajudicial sanction and must accept responsibility for the act or omission that forms the basis of the offence. If a young person does not consent to participating in an extrajudicial measure, then the charge is dealt with in the traditional youth justice court (*Youth Criminal Justice Act*, s. 6).

## SENTENCING UNDER THE *YOUTH CRIMINAL JUSTICE ACT* LO4

Sentencing under the *Youth Criminal Justice Act* occurs when a young person is charged and the case is processed through the youth court, as opposed to using extrajudicial measures.

The purpose of the *Youth Criminal Justice Act* is to hold the young person accountable for committing an offence using just sanctions that have meaningful consequences to the young person and that promote both rehabilitation and reintegration into society, thereby contributing to the long-term protection of the public (*Youth Criminal Justice Act*, s. 38 (1)).

The *Youth Criminal Justice Act* identifies a number of sentencing principles intended to guide the judiciary. The principles include the following:

- A young person cannot receive a harsher sentence than an adult would receive for a similar offence and the sentence should be comparable to that imposed on other young persons in the area (*Youth Criminal Justice Act*, s. 38 (2)).
- All available sanctions other than custody that are reasonable in the circumstances should be considered for all young persons, with particular attention to the circumstances of Aboriginal youth (*Youth Criminal Justice Act*, s. 38 (2)).

- Sentences should be the least restrictive to achieve the purposes set out in section 38 (1) of the *Youth Criminal Justice Act*, and be the most likely to rehabilitate and reintegrate the young person into society.

The legislation is unique (*Youth Criminal Justice Act*, s. 39 (1)) in that it directs the youth justice court to ensure that a young person is not committed to a custodial sentence unless:

- the young person commits a violent offence,
- the young person fails to comply with a non-custodial sentence, or
- the young person has a pattern of findings of guilt for indictable sentences that would have more than two-year sentences for adults.

A fundamental sentencing principle of the *Youth Criminal Justice Act* is that custody is to be viewed as a last resort for youths, and that a court must ensure that other options are considered before sentencing a young person to custody. Youth court justices must provide reasons for the sentence in the record of the case, and provide them to the young person, his or her counsel and parents, the **provincial director**, and the prosecutor.

**provincial director**
a person, group, or class of persons or a body appointed by the provinces to take responsibility for the administration of the *Youth Criminal Justice Act*

## MYTH VS FACT High Profile Youth Crime is Rare Youth Crime

High profile cases that receive a great deal of attention from the media represent the rarest form of youth crime. The 2006 case of the 13-year-old Alberta girl who was found guilty of murdering her parents is such an example. After just three hours of deliberation a jury found the youth guilty of murdering her parents and her 8-year-old brother. She was 12 years of age when she committed the crime in the family's Medicine Hat home. During the trial, the girl testified that her 23-year-old boyfriend, Jeremy Steinke, broke into her home, and attacked and killed her mother and father. She said that Steinke ordered her to stab her brother, which she did. Steinke then slit her brother's throat. The girl said that she was in a "zombie" state of mind at the time of the killings and could not stop her boyfriend or get help. She did say that she and her boyfriend often discussed killing her parents, but she explained that she was only joking. Police testimony revealed that the attack was brutal, as the girl's father was stabbed 24 times, the mother was stabbed 12 times, and the brother, who died from a severed jugular vein, was strangled and he had four stab wounds on his face and chest.

Courtroom sketch of Jeremy Steinke.
SOURCE: CBC, 2007.

The girl was sentenced to 10 years, the maximum allowed under the *Youth Criminal Justice Act*. Jeremy Steinke, her boyfriend, received a life sentence at his trial in adult court in December, 2008.

SOURCES: http://www.cbc.ca/news/canada/calgary/story/2008/12/15/cgy-steinke-sentencing.html; http://www.thestar.com/news/canada/article/549476--boyfriend-guilty-of-murders; http://m.theglobeandmail/com/news/national/alberta-girl-sentenced-in-murders/article796110/?service=mobile.

## Sentencing Options for Youths

The *Youth Criminal Justice Act* contains a variety of sentencing options for the court to apply to youths. The range of sentencing options exists so that the unique needs of each individual appearing before the court can be addressed. The youth court can impose one or more of the sentence options, as long as they are compatible with each other. The sentencing options are as follows:

### REPRIMAND

The **reprimand** is the mildest sentence available to the court. It involves a verbal reprimand from the court and it remains on the young person's record for two months. This sentence is used for minor offences and usually when the young person has not been found guilty of a criminal offence in the past. (*Youth Criminal Justice Act*, s. 42 (2) (a))

### ABSOLUTE DISCHARGE

An **absolute discharge** is not accompanied by a sanction of any kind. The young person does not need to fulfill any requirement or obligation. An absolute discharge remains on the young person's record for one year. (*Youth Criminal Justice Act*, s. 42 (2) (b))

### CONDITIONAL DISCHARGE

A young person who receives a **conditional discharge** must abide by specific conditions identified by the youth court judge. Conditions may include probation, restitution, or community service. A conditional discharge remains on the young person's record for three years. (*Youth Criminal Justice Act*, s. 42 (2) (c))

### FINE

A fine up to a maximum of $1,000 may be imposed on a young person. The judge must inquire about the young offender's ability to pay before imposing a fine and conditions. In addition, the fine includes a fine surcharge up to 15 percent, which is used to fund government programs for victims. (*Youth Criminal Justice Act*, s. 42 (2) (d))

### RESTITUTION

Restitution is a financial payment paid directly to the victim. If it is possible to determine the financial harm that was done to the victim, then the court may impose financial restitution to the victim. A judge must inquire about the young offender's ability to pay before imposing a restitution order. (*Youth Criminal Justice Act*, s. 42 (2) (f))

### COMMUNITY SERVICE

A youth court may impose a sentence of **community service**, to a maximum of 240 hours. The young offender must perform volunteer service for an agency or community member for a specific number of hours. It must be determined that the young person is a suitable candidate for a community service order and that the order would not interfere with normal hours of work or school for the young offender. The performance of the

Community service gives youthful offenders an opportunity to give back to the community.

community service is monitored by a probation officer or a community agency. (*Youth Criminal Justice Act*, s. 42 (2) (i))

### MANDATORY PROHIBITION ORDER

A prohibition order may be ordered for prohibition, seizure, or forfeiture that may be imposed under any Act or Parliament or any regulation made under it if an accused is found guilty or convicted of that offence (other than under *Criminal Code* section 161). Examples include prohibiting the use of firearms, seizing weapons, forfeiting proceeds of a crime. (*Youth Criminal Justice Act*, s. 42 (2) (j))

### PERFORMANCE OF A PERSONAL SERVICE

Similar to a community service order, a young offender may be ordered to perform a **personal service** for the victim. This type of order requires consent from the victim. Such orders include personal services such as cutting grass, painting, shovelling snow, gardening, and other similar chores. (*Youth Criminal Justice Act*, s. 42 (2) (h))

### PROBATION

A probation order can be imposed on a young offender, up to a maximum of two years. The probation order can be extended to three years for offences where the maximum sentence for an adult is a life sentence. The probation order will have a number of conditions as determined by the court. A mandatory condition is to keep the peace and be of good behaviour. Other conditions may include reporting to a probation officer, attend school or work, reside at a specific address, observe a curfew, or attend treatment programs. The probation order may also have prohibition orders attached related to alcohol, drugs, driving, or associations with specific persons or groups. Probation orders are specific to the circumstances and needs of the individual offender. If a young offender does not successfully complete the probation order, the probation officer may initiate a charge of failure to comply with a probation order. (*Youth Criminal Justice Act*, s. 42 (2) (k))

**TABLE 8.1 Sentencing Maximums For Young Offenders**

| Custody and Supervision Sentence Type | Type of Crime | Maximum Sentence |
|---|---|---|
| Order made under 42(2)(n)<br>Custody and supervision order | If adult could not get life sentence for this crime | 2 years |
| | If adult could get a life sentence for this crime | 3 years |
| Order made under 42(2)(o)<br>Custody and supervision order given for a presumptive offence that is NOT murder | Attempted murder<br>Manslaughter<br>Aggravated assault | 3 years |
| Order made under 42(2)(q)<br>Custody and supervision order given for a presumptive offence that is murder | First degree murder | Up to 10 years, with a maximum of 6 years in custody, followed by community supervision |
| | Second degree murder | Up to 7 years, with a maximum of 4 years in custody, followed by community supervision |
| Order made under 42(2)(r)<br>Intensive rehabilitative custody and supervision order | If adult could not get a life sentence for this crime | 2 years |
| | If adult could get a life sentence for this crime | 3 years |
| | First degree murder | Up to 10 years, with a maximum of 6 years in custody, followed by community supervision |
| | Second degree murder | Up to 7 years, with a maximum of 4 years in custody, followed by community supervision |

SOURCE: With permission from The John Howard Society of Alberta.

Burnaby Youth Justice Services Centre has 84 beds for young offenders.

### COMMUNITY SUPERVISION OR SUPPORT PROGRAMS

The young offender may be ordered to participate in a community-based program of intense community supervision or support, or attend a community-based non-residential program (an attendance centre) for up to 240 hours. (*Youth Criminal Justice Act*, s. 42 (2) (m))

These programs are imposed with the consent of the provincial/territorial director and are offered in select jurisdictions across Canada. Each jurisdiction in Canada has the freedom to create these programs and they are intended to assist youths in specific areas of their lives. For example, they may be programs that address life skills, substance abuse, conflict management, or other relevant areas.

### CUSTODY AND COMMUNITY SUPERVISION

A young person can be sentenced to custody for up to two years, and up to three years for more serious offences, with the last third served in the community. This form of graduated sentencing is unique to the *Youth Criminal Justice Act*. When a young person is sentenced to a period of custody, the *Youth Criminal Justice Act* requires that one third of the sentence must be served in the community, where the community supervision is guided by a **reintegration plan** that was developed while he or she was in custody. This focus on community reintegration is intended to support the young offender upon release to prevent him or her from reoffending. While in custody, a young offender may apply for a reintegration leave, under section 91. The leave is intended to provide an opportunity for the young offender to prepare for his or her reintegration into the community. The leave can be granted for up to 30 days and can be used for educational, employment, or treatment opportunities. (*Youth Criminal Justice Act*, s. 42 (2) (n))

**reintegration plan**
used to plan a young person's release into the community

The *Youth Criminal Justice Act* imposes limits on the length of custodial sentences, and the limits are based on the type of offence and type of custody being imposed. Table 8.1 identifies the sentencing maximums.

### DEFERRED CUSTODY AND SUPERVISION ORDER

**Deferred custody** provides young offenders with an opportunity to prove themselves before they are required to be sentenced to custody. When a young person is found guilty of an offence that is not a serious violent offence, a sentence of up to six months deferred custody and supervision may be imposed. The young offender is permitted to continue to live in the community, under specific conditions, with the understanding that any breach in the conditions will result in serving the rest of the sentence in custody. If conditions are breached, the young offender returns to the youth court and may be ordered to serve the rest of the order in custody. (*Youth Criminal Justice Act*, s. 42 (2) (p))

### INTENSIVE REHABILITATIVE CUSTODY AND SUPERVISION

When a young person appears before the court and is convicted of a third serious violent offence or one of the most serious presumptive offences, a sentence of intensive custody and supervision may be imposed. This sentence is reserved for those youths who require an alternative to regular custody due to a mental illness, disorder, or other type of emotional disturbance. The treatment in the secure environment is followed by a period of intense supervision in the community. (*Youth Criminal Justice Act*, s. 42 (2) (r))

### YOUTH JUSTICE COMMITTEES

Under section 18, the *Youth Criminal Justice Act* introduced **youth justice committees**. The committees are comprised of citizens who are empowered to work toward identifying community solutions to dealing with young offenders. Such solutions may involve creating extrajudicial measures or arranging for community support for the young offender and/or the young offender's family. Youth justice committees also provide advice to the federal and provincial governments on policies and procedures related to the youth criminal justice system and provide information to the public.

### APPEALS AND REVIEWS

Like adults, young offenders have the right to appeal a sentence imposed by the court. Youth court cases are appealed to the Appeal Court in each jurisdiction. The *Youth Criminal Justice Act* allows for sentence reviews to ensure that the sentence that was imposed is still meeting the needs of the young offender. All custodial sentences are automatically reviewed each year and can be reviewed sooner with permission from the youth court. If the young offender is sentenced to less than a year in custody, the sentence may be reviewed earlier. A sentence that is non-custodial can be reviewed after six months, or earlier with the permission of the youth court. The young offender, his or her parents, or the provincial director can initiate a review. There are grounds that must be satisfied in order to permit a sentence review, such as:

- the circumstances that led to the sentence have changed,
- the young offender is unable to comply with or is facing serious problems with the sentence that was imposed,
- the young offender has breached one of the conditions of the order, without reasonable excuse,
- the sentence is adversely affecting the opportunities available to the young offender to obtain services, education, or employment, or
- any other grounds that the court considers appropriate.

The outcome of the review of a non-custodial sentence can:

- confirm the existing sentence,
- terminate the youth sentence and discharge the young person from any further obligation of the sentence, or
- vary the sentence by imposing a new sentence under section 42, other than a committal to custody, for any period of time not exceeding the remainder of the period of the earlier sentence.

The outcome of the review of a custodial sentence can:

- confirm the existing sentence, or
- release the young offender from custody and place him or her under conditional supervision for a period not exceeding the remainder of the sentence that the young offender is currently serving.

A young offender's sentence cannot be extended, unless he or she has committed another crime. Unlike the adult system, the youth system does not allow for parole. As such, the court must make any changes to the custody length. A sentence that is under appeal cannot be reviewed.

Young offenders who do not comply with the conditions of their sentence can be charged with a new offence—failure to comply with sentence or disposition (*Criminal Youth Justice Act,* s. 137). This is a summary conviction offence.

### CONDITIONAL SUPERVISION OF YOUTHS

The *Criminal Youth Justice Act* permits, in section 96, the provincial director of each jurisdiction to make a recommendation to the youth court that a young offender be released from custody and placed under conditional supervision. This decision is based on the belief that "the needs of the young person and the interests of society would be better served" by releasing the young person, and requiring him or her to engage in a period of conditional supervision in the community. A conditional supervision order has mandatory conditions and the court may impose additional conditions if the young offender had been convicted of a presumptive or other serious offence. A young offender who breaches a conditional supervision order, or who is about to breach the order, can be apprehended by the police. The offender will appear before the youth court to determine if the order will be rescinded.

## ADULT SENTENCES FOR YOUTHS

The most punitive aspect of the *Criminal Youth Justice Act*, in section 62, is the option for a court to sentence a young offender who has been found guilty of an offence to any sentence that could be imposed on an adult who has been convicted of the same offence. An adult sentence applied to a young offender is rare and is limited to certain circumstances where it is determined that a youth sentence would not hold the youth accountable. In order to be sentenced to an adult sentence, the young person must be at least 14 years of age and the circumstances must be consistent with one of the three following scenarios.

**Category 1:** The young offender was convicted of one of the following offences:

i) First degree murder or second degree murder (*Criminal Code*, s. 231 or s. 235)
ii) Attempt to commit murder (*Criminal Code*, s. 239)
iii) Manslaughter (*Criminal Code*, s. 232, s. 234, or s. 236)
iv) Aggravated sexual assault (*Criminal Code*, s. 273)

**Category 2:** The young offender was convicted of a serious violent offence, combined with at least two previous judicial determinations of a serious violent offence in previous cases. (A serious violent offence is one where the youth has caused or attempted to cause serious bodily harm to another, and must have happened after the youth turned 12 years of age; however, the third offence, before the court, must have occurred after the youth turned 14 years of age).

The third way in which a young offender may receive an adult sentence is when he or she is convicted of an indictable offence for which an adult is liable to imprisonment for a term of more than two years.

If the Attorney General seeks an adult sentence for a young person, the young person must be notified prior to the trial (*Youth Criminal Justice Act*, s. 64(2)). Young offenders who receive a custodial sentence serve their time in a youth facility. Young offenders sentenced after turning 18 years of age will usually serve their time in an adult facility unless the court believes it is not in the best interest of the young offender. The Attorney General must prove that an adult sentence is appropriate, as opposed to the accused having to prove that one is not.

**levels of restraint**
the extent to which a young person's freedom is limited

## YOUTH CUSTODY

The *Youth Criminal Justice Act* defines a custodial sentence as one that provides protection for society while providing young offenders with "safe, fair and humane" restraints that will assist them in their rehabilitation and their eventual reintegration into the community (*Youth Criminal Justice Act*, s. 83).

There are two forms of custody identified in the *Youth Criminal Justice Act*, and they are identified based on the **level of restraint** available. They are referred to as being "the least degree of restraint" and "a higher degree of restraint." Under the *Young Offenders Act*, which preceded the *Youth Criminal Justice Act*, there were two levels of custody as well. They were referred to as open custody and closed custody. Open custody represented the least degree of restraint, as it usually referred to a home or facility located in the community where a young offender could continue to work or attend school during the day. Closed custody represented a higher degree of restraint, where young offenders were sentenced to locked institutions with perimeter fencing. The *Youth Criminal Justice Act* gives each province and territory the ability to determine which type of custodial arrangement will best meet the needs of each jurisdiction.

Since the introduction of the *Youth Criminal Justice Act*, Canada has experienced a significant reduction in the incarceration rate among sentenced youth (Statistics Canada, 2010). This is believed to be due to the fact that a young

**FIGURE 8.4** Average Daily Count of Youth in Remand and Sentenced Custody, 2004/2005 to 2008/2009

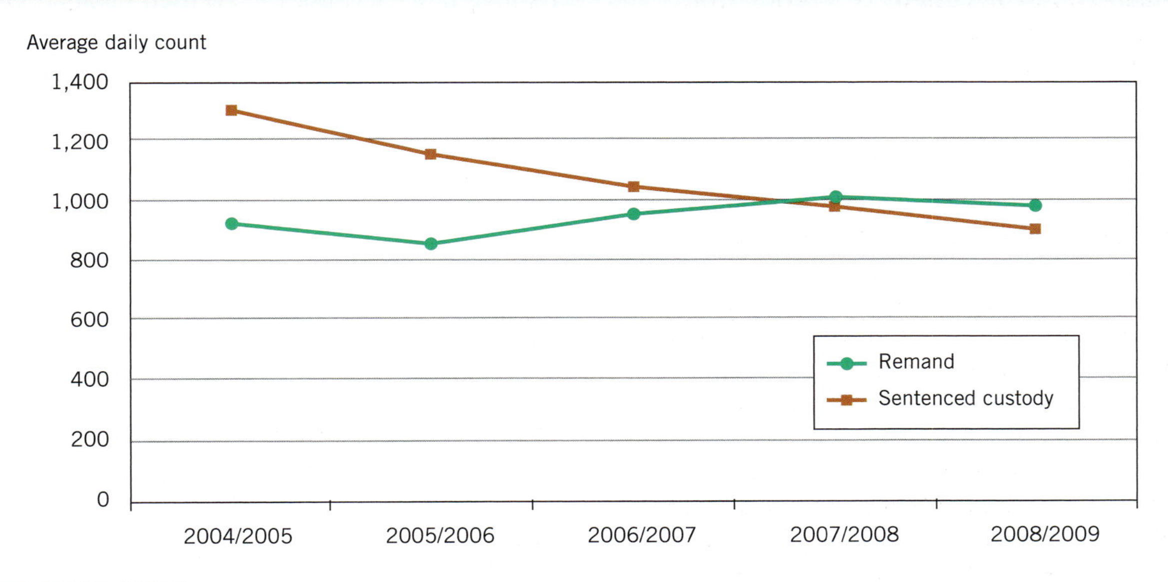


NOTE: Excludes Nunavut.

SOURCE: Statistics Canada, Canadian Centre for Justice Statistics, Youth Key Indicator Reports. http://www.statcan.gc.ca/pub/85-002-x/2010001/article/11147-eng.htm, accessed March 26, 2012. Reproduced and distributed on an "as is" basis with the permission of Statistics Canada.

The Manitoba Youth Centre at 170 Doncaster St. in Winnipeg.

person can only be sentenced to custody under certain circumstances, reserving custodial sentences for those who have committed the most serious offences. Statistics Canada indicated that in 2008/09, 7 of 10,000 youth in the general population were in custody (Calverley, Cotter and Halla, 2010). This is a decrease of 4 percent from the previous year and a decrease of 15 percent from 2004/2005. In 2008/09, there were more youth in remand than those serving custodial sentences, with up to 52 percent of incarcerated youth being held on remand on any given day in Canada (Calverley, Cotter and Halla, 2010). This statistic is alarming because when youth are held in remand they are not classified, generally not receiving much programming (if any), and are legally innocent.

There are a number of challenges to detaining youth in custody. Many of the challenges that plague the adult system are also a factor in the youth system, such as problems with security and drug use. In November, 2009, a Winnipeg teen who was serving time in the Manitoba Youth Centre set his room on fire, causing $5,000 in damages. The 18-year-old youth pleaded guilty and was sentenced to the maximum youth sentence available, three years of custody and community supervision. The accused admitted to taking prescription pills prior to setting the fire and then refused to leave the room once it was ablaze. Firefighters had to smash a window and forcibly remove him. Because the accused pleaded guilty, the Crown attorney in the case agreed not to seek an adult sentence. The young person has been in and out of youth custody since age 13.

## PROTECTION OF YOUNG OFFENDER IDENTITY AND RECORDS

Section 110 (1) of the *Youth Criminal Justice Act* prohibits the media from identifying youths involved with the *Youth Criminal Justice Act*, in order to protect the young person. There are a number of exceptions to this rule, listed in section 110 (2), including:

- when a young offender receives an adult sentence,
- when identification is made within the justice system, enabling the system to operate,
- once the young person reaches the age of 18 and is not in a youth custody facility,

## FOCUS ON Roy McMurtry Youth Centre

The Roy McMurtry Youth Centre in Brampton, Ontario, opened in May, 2009, with the promise of creating a positive environment for rehabilitating young offenders. Almost immediately, the Office of the Provincial Advocate for Children and Youth for Ontario began receiving complaints from the youth in custody there, including:

- uncooked and small portions of food,
- a lack of access to medical care,
- unable to call the Provincial Advocate,
- a lack of programming,
- staff shortages, preventing movement, resulting in a lack of access to school, spiritual centres, washrooms, and recreation,
- locked in rooms for long periods of time,
- staff using physical interventions to manage behaviour,
- staff using excessive force,
- excessive violence, and
- peer-to-peer violence.

Responding to the complaints, the Government of Ontario hired and trained new officers, increased staff, opened a new library, introduced a new complaint procedure, and established a new youth advisory committee.

SOURCE: The Roy McMurtry Youth Centre: A Summary of Advocacy Activities and Issues, August 2009 to February 2010 – Office of the Provincial Advocate for Children and Youth for Ontario.

- when the police apply for a court order, that lasts five days only, with the belief that identifying a potentially dangerous young person who is at large will help them apprehend the person; once the young person is apprehended, the media can no longer identify the young person by name, and
- when the young person applies to the court to identify himself or herself, and if the court is satisfied that such identification is not contrary to his or her best interests or the public interest.

Youth records are protected under the *Youth Criminal Justice Act*. Law enforcement officials can access the records for a limited period of time, depending on the type of penalty that the young offender received. If the offender was found guilty of a summary conviction offence, the record can be accessed for a period of three years from the date of the conviction. If he or she was convicted of an indictable offence, the record can be accessed for a period of five years from the date of the conviction.

Once a young person reaches the age of 18, his or her fingerprints are held in a special repository, then destroyed five years later.

**JUST or BUST?**

**Should youths who are convicted of committing serious violent offences be identified in the media?**

The *Youth Criminal Justice Act* requires that the identity of young offenders be protected.

## LO5 Youth Crime in Canada – A Statistical Overview

Like our overall crime rate, the rate of police-reported youth crime in Canada is falling. In 2010, Canadian police reported that 153,000 persons from 12 to 17 years of age were accused of committing a criminal offence (Statistics Canada, The Daily, July 21, 2011). This represents a decline of 7 percent (and 15,000 fewer) from the year before. Like the overall trend, youth crime rates for homicide, serious assaults, motor vehicle thefts, and break-ins declined; however, robbery showed an increase of 2 percent. The youth crime rate was at the same level as it was 10 years earlier, but the youth violent crime rate in 2009 was 11 percent higher than it was in 1999 (Statistics Canada: Police-reported crime statistics 2009). The rate of youths committing homicide, the most serious criminal offence, increased steadily between 2001 and 2009, and fell slightly in 2010. Of those youths charged with homicide in 2009, 22 were charged with gang-related homicide, which is 28 percent of the total number of accused.

Youths and young adults in Canada commit a disproportionate amount of crime, based on the population. In 2009, the age group that committed the highest number of crimes was comprised of those aged 15 to 22, the highest of which was those aged 17.

Police data indicates that youth crime most commonly occurs in private residences (32 percent), followed by commercial establishments such as stores, malls, office buildings, service centres, and other commercial properties at 23 percent, and in outdoor public spaces (also at 23 percent) such as streets, parks, and parking lots. Youth violent crime and drug violations were more likely to occur on school property than any other location. Weapons were present in 7 percent of school crimes, with less than 1 percent of school crimes involving firearms. Violent offences such as physical assault, sexual assault, and robbery occurred more often on weekdays than weekends. Drug offences were more likely to occur on Fridays, and traffic violations were higher on weekends.

Violent and non-violent youth crime occurred most often between the after-school hours of 3 p.m. and 6 p.m., while noon to 3 p.m. was the most common time for youth drug offences. Traffic violations happened most frequently between 9 p.m. and midnight.

Winter was the least likely time of year for youth crime, compared to spring, summer, and fall, which had a relatively equal amount of youth crime (Statistics Canada, 2010).

Youths between the ages of 15 and 19 are also at a greater risk of victimization—approximately 40 percent of youths are victimized, compared to 25 percent of the general population (Canadian Council on Social Development, 2011). The rate

**FIGURE 8.5** Police-Reported Youth Crime Rates, Canada, 2000 to 2010*

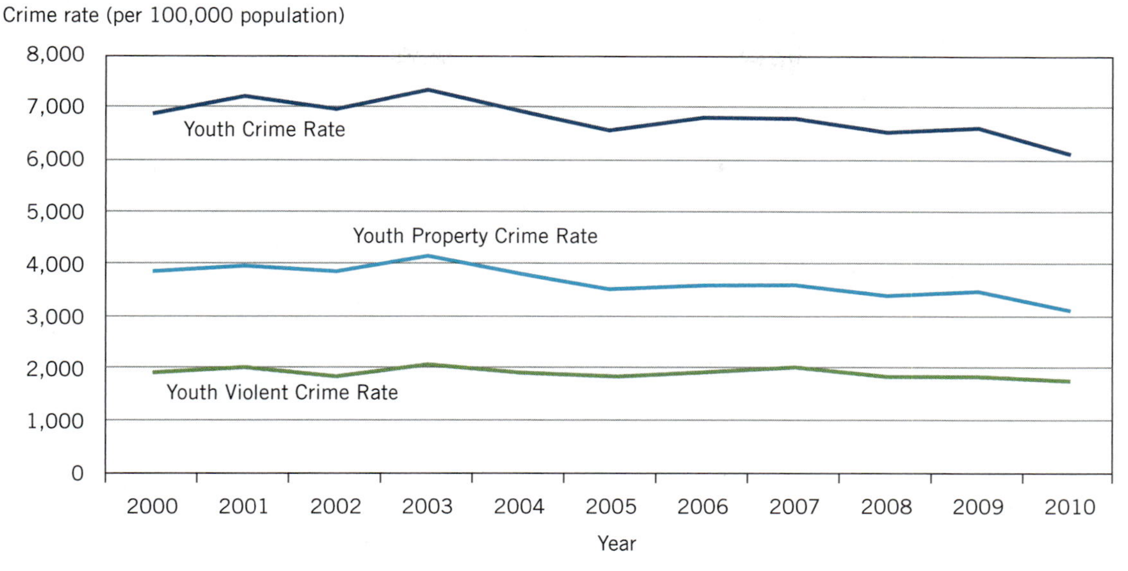


NOTE: The overall youth crime rate† has dropped from 6,914 per 100,000 population to 6,147. The youth property crime rate has dropped from 3,909 per 100,000 population to 3,155. Violent crimes committed by youth has dropped from 1,944 per 100,000 population to 1,838.

* Brennan, S., & Dauvergne, M. 2011. "Police reported crime statistics – 2010." Ottawa, ON: Statistics Canada.

† The youth crime rate is a measure of the volume of youth aged 12 to 17 accused of a Criminal Code offence.

SOURCE: National Crime Prevention Centre (NCPC). *A Statistical Snapshot of Youth At Risk and Youth Offending in Canada.* Ottawa, ON; 2012.

of victimization among youths aged 15 to 17 is 2,710 per 100,000—the highest of any age group in Canada (Statistics Canada, 2010). Youths are more likely to be victimized by other youths than by an adult. The rate of sexual assaults against children and youths was over 1.5 times higher than the rate for young adults aged 18 to 24. The victimization rate for children and youths in Canada in 2008 (police-reported violent crime) was 1,111 per 100,000. Violent crimes in Canada include murder, attempted murder, robbery, assault, and sexual assault.

Youth crime often (23 percent) occurs in outdoor public places, such as streets, parks, and school property, as was witnessed on March 17, 2012, in London, Ontario.

**FIGURE 8.6** Rates of Violent Victimization Highest Among Youths Aged 15 to 17

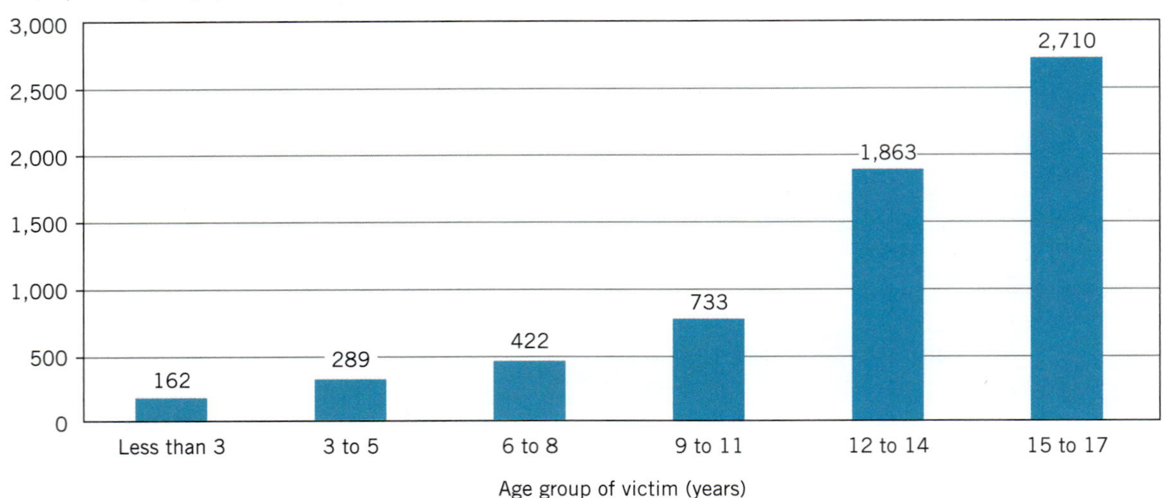


SOURCE: Statistics Canada, Rates of violent victimization highest among youth aged 15 to 17, http://www.statcan.gc.ca/pub/85f0033m/2010023/ct001_en.gif, accessed March 26, 2012. Reproduced and distributed on an "as is" basis with the permission of Statistics Canada.

## FOCUS ON Canada's Version of the International Self-Reported Delinquency Study, 2006

A survey conducted with Toronto youths highlights a number of facts regarding youth and delinquent behaviour. Youths in grades 7 to 9 in Toronto public and private schools were surveyed to measure self-reported delinquency. One out of every five students reported committing at least one delinquent act in the year prior. Thirteen percent of the students reported participating in violent delinquent behaviour in the 12 months prior to the survey. The most frequently reported violent act involved carrying a weapon such as a stick, chair, or knife. The most frequent type of property-related delinquent act was theft from a store, followed by vandalism and arson. The boys were twice as likely to report being involved in violent behaviours, and those same boys were responsible for about 72 percent of all reported violent acts in the year prior to the survey. The results indicated that 80 percent of all self-reported delinquent behaviours were committed by 25 percent of the young people who responded to the survey. About one quarter of the students admitted to delinquent behaviour online, including illegally downloading movies or music, hacking into a computer, or sending harassing email messages (Statistics Canada, The Daily, September 25, 2007).

The survey also focused on factors that may be associated with a higher likelihood of delinquency. Those factors included students who:

- reported that they consumed alcohol and drugs,
- reported having little parental supervision,
- reported having older friends, friends who were delinquent or who tolerated illegal activities,
- reported spending a lot of time with friends in public places such as malls, parks, or streets, and
- reported that they did not get along well with their parents.

This survey highlights, in middle school students, a number of critical indicators of youth crime. The higher prevalence of male offenders, the relationship between crime and substance abuse, the relationship between crime and criminal associations, and crime and family supports are all prevalent in adult crime. In addition, a small number of offenders (25 percent) were responsible for most (80 percent) of the delinquent behaviour—a fact that is evident in youth crime overall. This study is important because it addresses the need to engage youths as soon as possible with a view to intervening and preventing future criminality.

SOURCE: Statistics Canada, Study: Self-reported delinquency among young people in Toronto, http://www.statcan.gc.ca/daily_quotidien/o7l925/dq070925a-eng.htm, accessed March 26, 2012. Reproduced and distributed on an "as is" basis with the permission of Statistics Canada.

Focusing exclusively on child and youth victims of violent crime, a 2008 study found that rates of violent crime among children and youths peaked at age 17 for both girls and boys. Among these victims, reported rates of violence were slightly higher for girls than boys across age categories, with the exception of adolescents 9 to 12 years of age, where rates of violence reported to police were higher for boys than for girls. The higher rates of violent crime perpetrated against girls is primarily due to the higher rates of sexual violence (Hotton Mahoney, 2011). Rates of sexual assault victimization were highest among female youths 12 to 14 years of age (623 incidents per 100,000 population) declining thereafter with age (from 552 for ages 15 to 17, to 246 for young adults 18 to 24 years of age). Sexual violence against girls is most commonly perpetrated by someone known to the victim (75 percent), such as a male acquaintance or relative (Hotton Mahoney, 2011).

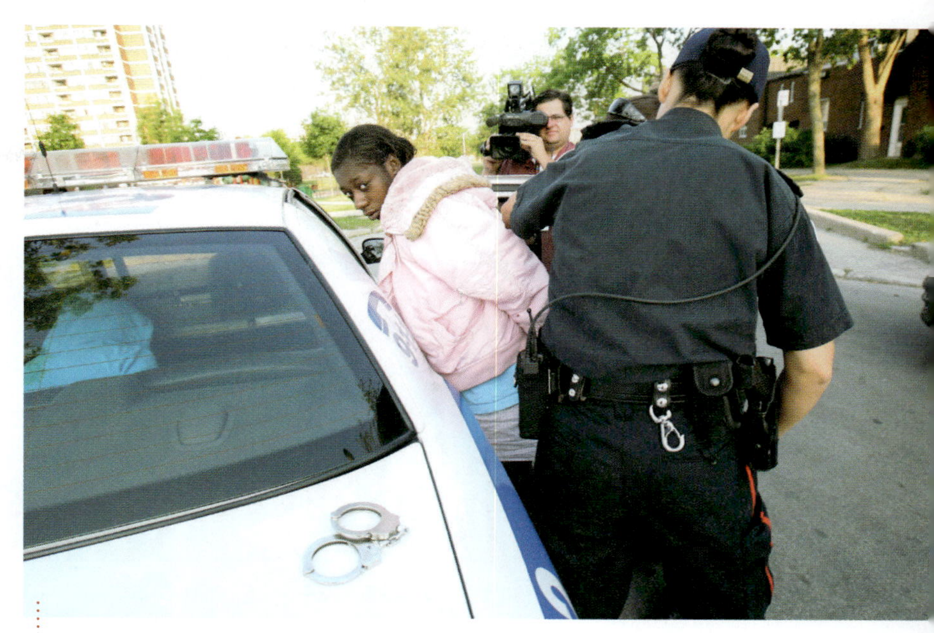

The number of young females charged with serious violent crime has risen.

Rates of police-reported violence against girls have remained relatively stable over the five year reference period (2004 to 2008) but did vary across Canada. Rates were highest in the northern territories of Nunavut, Northwest Territories, and Yukon (ranging from 5,401 to 2,444 per 100,000), and lowest in Ontario (909) and Quebec (970).

## LO6 FEMALE YOUNG OFFENDERS

Like their adult counterparts, there are far fewer female youths in conflict with the law than males. However, that number has been increasing. The number of female youths charged with serious violent crime rose from 60 per 100,000 population in 1986, to 132 per 100,000 population in 2005 (The Daily, January 24, 2008, Statistics Canada). The overall rate of offending among females is about one quarter of males (Kong and AuCoin, 2008), and is consistent across all crime categories. When examining the age at which females engage in crime, it was determined that criminal activity peaks at age 15 (Kong and AuCoin, 2008), compared to males who peak at age 17. Young females (aged 12 to 17) have a higher rate of offending than adult females, committing crimes at a rate of three and a half times higher than their adult counterparts (Kong and AuCoin, 2008).

This increase in young females involved in crime has resulted in a significant amount of media interest and has led researchers to ask why it is happening. One researcher suggests that the criminality of girls is exaggerated because of the higher expectations that we have of girls to "behave" (Gelsthorpe and Worrall, 2009). A study that examined the perspectives of professionals working in the criminal justice system revealed that some professionals expressed confusion about whether or not the behaviour of females has actually deteriorated, or whether they are being subjected to more intensive and formalized social control than ever before (Sharpe, 2009). Others have suggested that low self-esteem results in an increase in the use of drugs and alcohol, and bad decisions that have criminal consequences.

## ABORIGINAL YOUTHS IN CONFLICT WITH THE LAW

Like their adult counterparts, Aboriginal youths are over-represented in the youth criminal justice system. The incarceration rate of Aboriginal youths is 64.5 per 10,000 population, while the incarceration rate for non-Aboriginal youths is 8.2 per 10,000 population. Aboriginal youths are almost eight times more likely to be in custody than non-Aboriginal youths.

**FIGURE 8.7** Violations of Offending Females, Based on Age

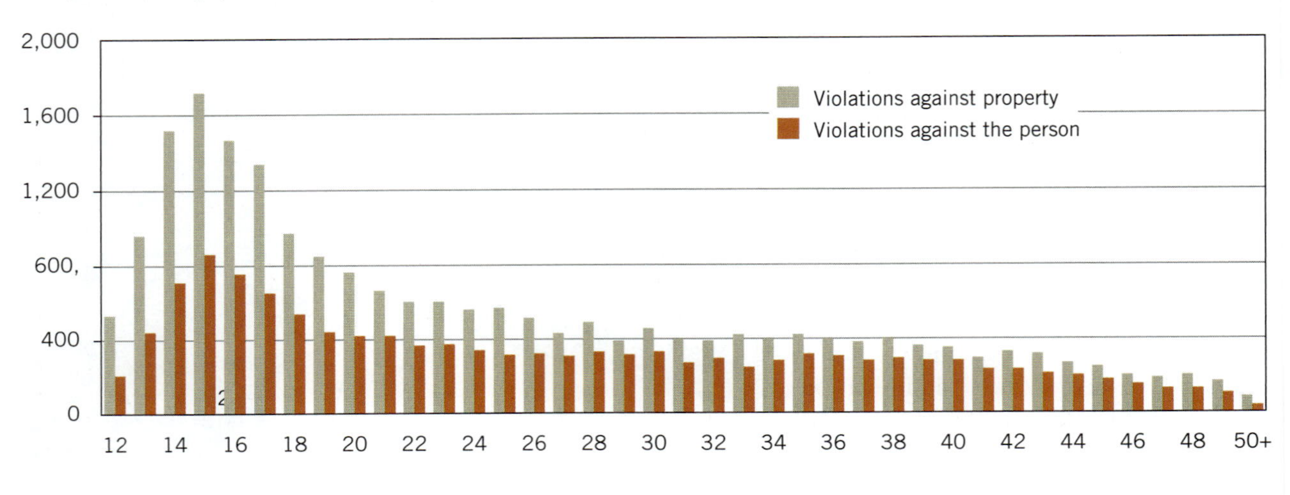


SOURCE: Statistics Canada, Canadian Centre for Justice Statistics, Incident-based Uniform Crime Reporting (UCR2), Violations of offending females, based on age, accessed March 26, 2012. Reproduced and distributed on an "as is" basis with the permission of Statistics Canada.

In general, the incarceration rates for Aboriginal youths were lower in eastern and western Canada and higher in central and northern Canada (Ontario, Manitoba, Saskatchewan, Yukon, Northwest Territories) with the exception of Nunavut. The incarceration rates for non-Aboriginal youths, in comparison, were generally lower in northern and western Canada and higher in eastern Canada.

The 2006 census indicated that 6 percent of all youths 12 to 17 years of age in Canada self-identified as Aboriginal (Calverley, Cotter and Halla, 2010). By contrast, Aboriginal youths represented 27 percent of the youths in **remand**, 36 percent of the youths sentenced to custody, and 24 percent of the youths sentenced to probation across Canada. Depending on the province or territory, Aboriginal youths were represented at a rate of 1.4 to 5.6 times higher than their representation in the general population. The number of female Aboriginal youths entering correctional services is significant and is growing.

**remand**
pre-trial custody

Aboriginal offenders are more likely to be younger, more likely to be incarcerated for a violent offence, and to have greater personal needs. In addition, 80 percent of Aboriginal offenders report early drug or alcohol use, 45 percent report that they were victims of physical abuse, 41 percent report that they came from situations of parental absence and neglect, and 35 percent indicate that they came from poverty. Aboriginal offenders have a higher incidence of health problems and 28 percent were raised in the custody of the child welfare system (The Correctional Investigator of Canada, 2010). The high rate of incarceration of Aboriginal youths and adults is complicated in itself, but is associated with a lack of social support, poverty, and substance abuse.

## YOUTH GANGS IN CANADA

A youth gang is defined as:

> An organized group of adolescents and/or young adults who rely on group intimidation and violence, and commit criminal acts in order to gain power and recognition and/or control certain areas of unlawful activity. (Montreal Police, 2004)

In 2002, the *Canadian Police Survey on Youth Gangs* determined that youth gangs are active across Canada and are not limited to urban settings. Criminal Intelligence Service Canada (CISC) confirmed that street gangs are growing in Canada (CISC, 2010). In 2006, CISC estimated that there were over 300 street gangs with about

11,000 members. Gang membership is primarily male (94 percent), though there is a growing number of female members. About half of youth gang members are under the age of 18; however, some gangs have members who are in their 20s and 30s. Gang membership is not limited by ethnicity, geography, demographics, or socio-economic status. The *Canadian Police Survey on Youth Gangs* estimated that 25 percent of youth gang members are African-Canadian, 21 percent Aboriginal, and 18 percent Caucasian. The survey also found that a growing number of females were becoming involved in street gangs (National Crime Prevention Centre, 2007a, as cited in Linden, 2010). The term "street gangs" is often used to describe gangs—a label that can include a number of different characteristics. In their 2010 Report on Organized Crime, CISC indicates:

**FIGURE 8.8** Incarceration Rates for Aboriginal and Non-Aboriginal Youths in Canada

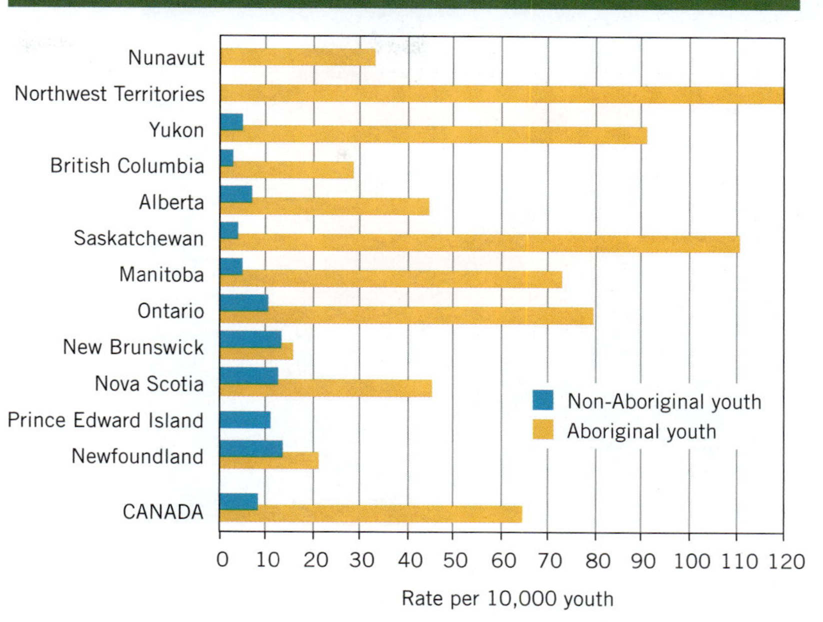


SOURCE: A One-Day Snapshot of Aboriginal Youth in Custody Across Canada: Phase II. Figure 1, Incarceration Rates for Aboriginal and Non-Aboriginal Youth in Canada, http://www.justice.gc.ca/eng/pi/rs/rep-rap/2004/yj2-jj2/p3.html, Justice Canada. Reproduced with the permission of the Minister of Public Works and Government Services, 2012.

> There is a wide variation in the structure, composition and membership of street gangs from coast to coast in Canada. Terms such as urban gangs, aboriginal gangs, rural gangs, hybrid gangs, youth gangs and ethnic gangs are all commonly used to denote some aspect of what is generally referred to as 'street gangs'.... The composition of street gangs varies in terms of total membership, gender and age and is generally determined by the demographics of the community. While some gangs are ethnically homogeneous, there are also those with a diverse multicultural base. Those from a similar ethnic background tend to operate within a fixed area and are generally found in lower income urban areas (prevalent in the Prairies, Toronto and Montreal). Further, some street gangs are based on familial relations or friendships while others are hierarchical in nature with multiple cells and more complex networks. While commonly associated with cities, street gangs are not exclusive to urban centres and are also active in rural areas, on aboriginal reserves and in correctional facilities.

SOURCE: Criminal Intelligence Service of Canada, *2010 Report on Organized Crime.*

The relationship between gangs and criminal activity is identified in even the youngest gang members. A survey conducted with Toronto middle school students indicates that the prevalence of delinquent behaviour among youths who reported belonging to a gang was over double that of youths who were not involved with gangs (The Daily, 2007).

"The drugs that steal our children and destroy their lives bring misery to families and huge profit to organized crime."

2010 REPORT ON ORGANIZED CRIME IN CANADA, HTTP://WWW.CISC.GC.CA/ANNUAL_REPORTS/ANNUAL_REPORT_2010/STREET_GANGS_2010_E.HTML. CRIMINAL INTELLIGENCE SERVICE CANADA. REPRODUCED WITH PERMISSION OF THE MINISTER OF PUBLIC WORKS AND GOVERNMENT SERVICES, 2012.

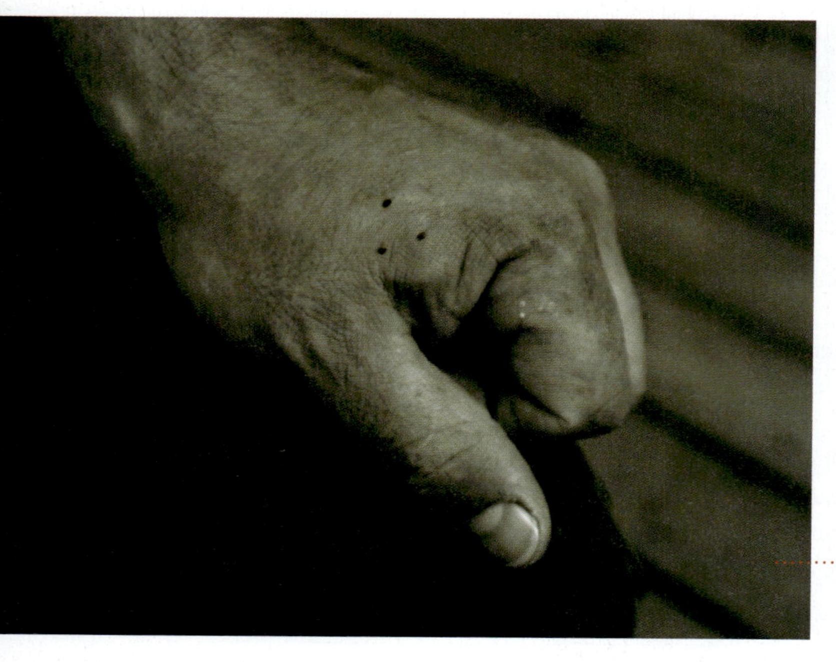

Gang-related crime is recognized as a significant problem and has been addressed by Canadian lawmakers. One response to gang violence was the introduction of new legislation in 2009 that targets gangs and organized crime. All gang-related homicides are classified as first degree, whether or not they meet the standards of planned and deliberate. In 2009, one in five homicides reported to police across Canada were determined to be gang-related, a number that was 14 fewer than in 2008 (Beattie and Cotter, 2010).

The three-dots tattoo, set in a triangle, is common and signifies gang membership.

## YOUTH JUSTICE FLASHBACK:

### STEVEN TRUSCOTT CASE

The evolution of the administration of youth justice in Canada is highlighted by examining the way in which youths were treated in the past. Steven Truscott, a 14-year-old boy from Clinton, Ontario, was charged with the murder of 12-year-old Lynne Harper in 1959. Steven maintained his innocence throughout the entire ordeal. In September, 1959, Steven was tried as an adult and a jury found him guilty of the murder and sentenced him to death. A year later, the death penalty was commuted to life imprisonment. Steven spent his time in custody in adult institutions. In 1966, a book was written that uncovered a number of the problems with the case, the most significant of which was that when the police came to arrest Steven, he was taken from his home, alone, without his parents' knowledge. Even though there was public outrage, the Supreme Court of Canada decided against giving Truscott a new trial. In 1969, he was released on bail and he assumed a new identity, married, and raised a family. Almost 30 years later, Steven's case was taken on by the Association in Defence of the Wrongly Convicted. In 2000, Steven Truscott appeared in a CBC documentary that revealed information that called into question the timing of the victim's death and the guilty verdict of the initial jury. In 2007, the Ontario Court of Appeal heard Truscott's case and overturned the conviction. The court stated that the case was "a miscarriage of justice" and would be quashed. The Attorney General offered Truscott an apology, and in 2008 Truscott was paid $6.5 million in compensation for the suffering he and his family endured.

## Chapter Summary

This chapter provided an introduction to youth justice in Canada. The key concepts that were covered included:

- The evolution of legislation related to youth justice in Canada. The *Juvenile Delinquents Act* was the first piece of legislation that responded to youth in conflict with the law. This piece of legislation was in effect from 1908 to 1984. In 1984, the *Young Offenders Act* was introduced and was in effect until 2003, when the *Youth Criminal Justice Act* was implemented. Under the *Juvenile Delinquents Act*, criminal responsibility began at age seven and had an upper limit of age 15. Both the *Young Offenders Act* and the *Youth Criminal Justice Act* raised the age of criminal responsibility to 12 and imposed an upper age limit of 17.
- The *Youth Criminal Justice Act* strives to prevent crime, rehabilitate youths, and ensure that a young person receives meaningful consequences for his or her offences with a view to promoting long-term protection of the public.
- There are numerous sentencing options available to youth court justices, designed to meet the specific needs of youths. The *Youth Criminal Justice Act* provides guidelines for youth court justices, outlining the conditions under which youths may be sentenced to custody.
- Just as the overall crime rate is declining, so too is the rate of police-reported youth crime.
- Issues related to female young offenders, Aboriginal young offenders, and youth gangs were identified.

## Relevant Legislation

*Criminal Code*, RSC 1985, c C-46

*Juvenile Delinquents Act*, R.S., c. 160, s. 1. 2. (1)

*Young Offenders Act*, R.S.C. , 1985, c. Y-1

*Youth Criminal Justice Act*, S.C. 2002, c. 1

## Key Terms

Absolute discharge
Cautions
Community service
Conditional discharge
Deferred custody
Extrajudicial measures
Incarceration rate
*Juvenile Delinquents Act*
Levels of restraint
Personal service
Provincial director
Recidivism
Reintegration plan
Remand
Reprimand
Warnings
*Young Offenders Act*
*Youth Criminal Justice Act*
Youth justice committees

## For Review

1. What impact has the evolution of youth justice legislation had on the way youths are treated in Canada?
2. What is the impact of incarceration on youths? Under what circumstances would a custodial sentence be justified?
3. What is the significance of extrajudicial measures in the *Youth Criminal Justice Act*?
4. What responsibility do the police have regarding extrajudicial measures?
5. Why is it important to protect the identity of youths?
6. Under what circumstances can a young person be sentenced as an adult?
7. What role do parents play under the *Youth Criminal Justice Act*? Why is it important that they play a significant role?
8. Why is it important to ensure that a young person is treated fairly when involved with the criminal justice system?

## Thinking Critically

1. To what extent are youths held accountable for their actions under the *Youth Criminal Justice Act*? Do you believe that the legislation sends a strong message of accountability?
2. Does the *Youth Criminal Justice Act* deter youths from engaging in criminal behaviour?
3. What are the positive and negative consequences of sentencing a young person as an adult? What goals are achieved when this happens?
4. To what extent is the community given the responsibility for the well-being of youths under this legislation?
5. To what extent does the *Youth Criminal Justice Act* meet the needs of Aboriginal youths in conflict with the law? Could there be elements added to the legislation that might better meet their needs?
6. What measures exist to ensure that youths are protected while in custody? Are there specific programs or restrictions that could be put in place to ensure their safety?
7. Should a young person be able to refuse to participate in programs while in custody or under community supervision? What are the consequences of doing so?
8. Should there be a mandatory requirement that all non-violent offences involving youths be diverted through extrajudicial measures? What would the impact of this decision be?

Practise and learn online with Connect

# CHAPTER 9
# Restorative Justice

## A Restorative Journey: The Reena Virk Case

Reena Virk was a 14-year-old student from View Royal, a suburb of Victoria, British Columbia. In November, 1997, Virk was badly beaten and murdered by a group of teenagers who lured her from her home under the pretense of being invited to a party. Eight girls took turns punching and kicking her, after which two others dragged her to a beach, held her head under water and killed her. Six of the eight girls involved in the beating were convicted of assault and the two who dragged her to the beach, Warren Glowatski and Kelly Ellard, were charged and eventually convicted of second-degree murder. The court heard that Virk's injuries were so severe that they were compared to those received by a person who had been run over by a car, adding that she would have likely died from head trauma had she not drowned. Glowatski, 16, was tried as an adult and sentenced to life in an adult prison; Ellard, 15, was tried as a young offender. While incarcerated, Glowatski approached the Restorative Justice program with a view to participating in a reconciliation process with Reena's parents, Manjit and Suman Virk. The reconciliation meeting was facilitated by Dave Gustafson and Sandi Bergen in Mission, British Columbia, and involved a conversation where Glowatski took responsibility for his participation in the crime and apologized to the family. The Virks described the devastating impact the crime had on their family, explaining, "he's been able to see how he destroyed our family" (Plouffe & Godfrey, 2011). A year after their meeting the Virks attended Glowatski's parole hearing where they indicated that they would not oppose his application. He was successful in his bid and was approved for 72 hours a month of parole.

The Virks engaged in a public process of forgiveness, demonstrating both courage and compassion, a reality that for most would be unimaginable. Though they continue to live with the profound sadness of losing a child under such tragic circumstances, the Virks are involved in public speaking engagements where they share their journey with others. In the words of Manjit Virk, "While we were going though the whole thing, I did a lot of thinking. It didn't make any sense why this happened but I realized that everyone makes mistakes and the only way we can move on is to learn from them. I am speaking from personal experience. When you hold on to anger, it can consume you." (Martin, 2011).

### LEARNING OBJECTIVES

By the end of this chapter, you should be able to:

- **LO1** Describe the roots of restorative justice.
- **LO2** Identify the philosophy and the principles of restorative justice.
- **LO3** Identify restorative justice programs that are offered in Canada.
- **LO4** Examine the differences between the traditional court system and the restorative justice model.
- **LO5** Describe the role of the victim within the practice of restorative justice.
- **LO6** Analyze the impact of restorative justice programs.

Reena Virk's parents, Manjit and Suman Virk.

Restorative justice puts the emphasis on the wrong done to a person as well as on the wrong done to the community. It recognizes that crime is both a violation of relationships between specific people and an offence against everyone—the state.

FEDERAL-PROVINCIAL-TERRITORIAL WORKING GROUP ON RESTORATIVE JUSTICE (2000).

## LO1 The Roots of Restorative Justice

Restorative justice has its roots in Aboriginal culture. The practice of addressing criminal behaviour within a community and not in a formal court is consistent with indigenous approaches around the world. New Zealand was among the earliest adopters of restorative justice, influenced by the philosophy and beliefs of the Maori people and culture. In the early 1980s, these practices were shared more broadly around the world. The philosophy of the Maori involved a recognition that the entire community was responsible for the behaviour of each person in the community. For example, when a young person committed a criminal act, the entire community took responsibility for restoring balance in the community by working together to create a solution to the problem. Restorative justice gives the entire community a voice, as well as the offender and the victim. The "circle" was the main forum for dealing with behavioural problems in the community, where all those affected by the behaviour would meet in a circle, facilitated by a community leader. The focus of the circle was to give everyone involved a voice and to identify ways to move forward and to restore and transform the community.

In 1989, New Zealand adopted the *Children, Young Persons and Their Families Act 1989*, a piece of legislation that adopted the concept of the Maori family circle for use in their national juvenile justice system (Lockhart and Zammit, 2005). This new model, which was successful in its impact on victims, offenders, and communities, quickly spread to Australia and North America.

In Aboriginal communities throughout North America, healing circles and peacemaking circles have been used for many years. They are intended to allow the community to assume responsibility for the behaviour of everyone within it. In addition, there were a number of faith-based initiatives that involved restorative practices across Canada. For example, the first victim-offender mediation program in Canada was introduced by the Mennonite church in Kitchener-Waterloo, Ontario, in 1974 (Public Safety Canada, 2002). Victim-offender mediation programs have since grown at a tremendous rate and are offered across the western world.

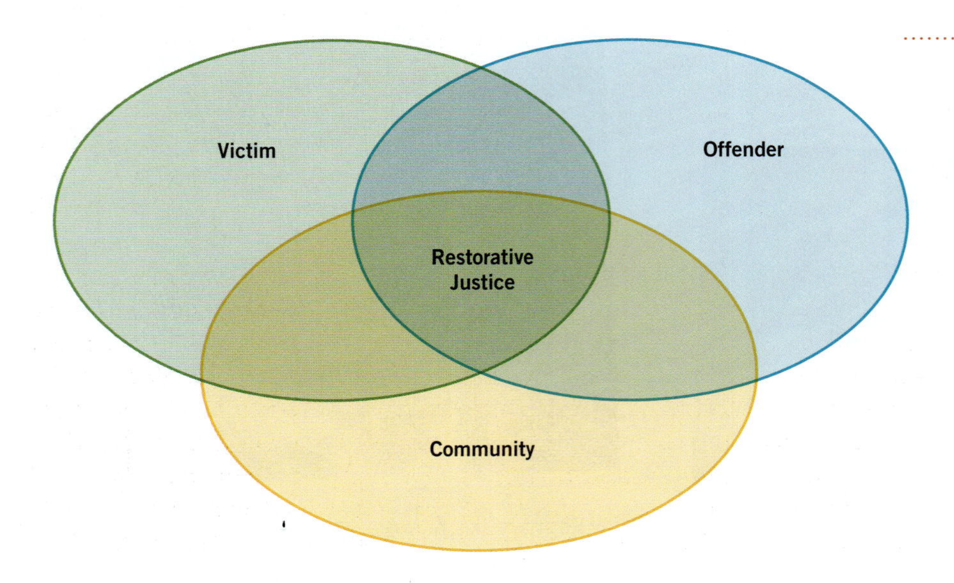


Restorative justice brings together the victim, the offender, and the community to address the needs of each.

Restorative Justice is a process whereby all the parties with a stake in a particular offence come together to resolve collectively how to deal with the aftermath of the offence and its implications for the future.

-TONY F. MARSHALL
LATIMER, DOWDEN, MUISE, 2001.

## LO2 Restorative Justice: The Philosophy

Before examining restorative justice, it is important to recognize the basic philosophy behind our traditional criminal justice system. Our traditional system is based on a model of **retribution**, where the focus is on the offender being required to "pay" for his crime. That payment is usually in the form of punishment such as time in custody, a fine, community service, or house arrest. There is a focus on preventing the offender from reoffending and protecting society.

**retribution**
punishment that is considered to be morally right and fully deserved

The traditional criminal justice system is adversarial; an offender may plead guilty or not guilty.

Critics of the traditional system say that this model does not always permit the community, the victim, and even the offender to have a voice in the process. The process is restricted by the legal limitations and formality of our criminal justice system. Critics add that the traditional system seldom requires the offender to speak or to take responsibility for his or her actions; often it is the lawyer who does the speaking. In the traditional court system, the victim may not have an opportunity to speak to the court or even be aware that the case has been tried. By contrast, restorative justice programs invite the involvement of all parties. The offender is an active participant in the restorative justice program, as is the victim. The affected members of the community are also a part of the process. Restorative justice is not adversarial in nature; in fact, the offender must plead guilty and take responsibility for the crime in order to take part in restorative justice programs.

**reparation**
making amends for a wrong or an injury done

Restorative justice is an evolving practice that provides opportunities for both victims and offenders to strive for resolution outside the traditional court experience. Restorative justice programs are generally seen as **diversion programs**, alternatives to the traditional court experience. The philosophy behind restorative justice programs recognizes that the traditional court experience does not often provide victims, offenders, or the community with an effective resolution that repairs the damage that has been caused by a criminal offence. When responding to a criminal offence, restorative justice programs involve everyone who has been affected by the crime. There is a focus on all parties, not just on the person who committed the crime.

**diversion programs**
programs that offer accused persons a community alternative to the traditional criminal justice system

Restorative justice programs take place at various points within the criminal justice system process. A **conferencing circle** may be used immediately after an offence has taken place in a school setting, rather than calling the police and moving the crime through the traditional criminal justice system. An offender and a victim may meet in a correctional setting, after sentencing, to engage in a victim-offender reconciliation process. A neighbourhood dispute may be remedied through a community justice forum where the neighbours gather and a facilitator guides them through a process of **reparation**.

Restorative justice programs are recognized globally. They are offered throughout the western world, in many different types of settings. They are used with children, adults, with criminal offences, and with differences of opinion. Ultimately, the goal of restorative justice programs is to transform the communities and the people within them, so that rather than being broken by the impact of the offence, they are empowered to receive strength from the process. Restorative justice practices aim to initiate healing by recognizing harm and identifying ways to restore balance in the people and the community affected by the crime. It is

**TABLE 9.1 Fundamental Principles of Restorative Justice**

| Crime is fundamentally a violation of people and interpersonal relationships | Violations create obligations and liabilities | Restorative justice seeks to heal and put right the wrongs |
|---|---|---|
| • Victims and the community have been harmed and are in need of restoration.<br>• Victims, offenders, and the affected communities are the key stakeholders in justice. | • Offenders' obligations are to make things right as much as possible.<br>• The community's obligations are to victims and to offenders and for the general welfare of its members. | • The needs of victims for information, validation, vindication, restitution, testimony, safety, and support are the starting points of justice.<br>• The process of justice maximizes opportunities for exchange of information, participation, dialogue, and mutual consent between victim and offender.<br>• Offenders' needs and competencies are addressed.<br>• The justice process belongs to the community.<br>• Justice is mindful of the outcomes, intended and unintended, of its responses to crime and victimization. |

SOURCES: *The Little Book of Restorative Justice*, by Howard Zehr/Good Books, 2002; *Restorative Justice: Transforming Society* [Paper back], Art Lockhart & Lynn Zammit (Authors), Production day, May 10, 2005; *Returning to the Teachings: Exploring Aboriginal Justice* (reissue) [Paperback], Rupert Ross (Author), March 4, 2009.

widely recognized that not all crimes and not all offenders are appropriate for restorative justice practice. Restorative justice is not intended to replace the criminal justice system, it is an option that complements the traditional criminal justice system. Many restorative justice programs limit involvement based on the type of crime and the type of offender. There are programs that are specific to youth or to specific types of offences. In addition, in all cases, it is only when there is agreement from the victim and the offender that a case will be referred to a restorative justice program. Restorative justice practices are used in schools (elementary to post-secondary) and communities, and as diversion programs for adults. Offences addressed can vary from bullying to vandalism to assault.

To accept restorative justice is to accept a paradigm shift in the way in which one views the concept of justice.

## LO3 Restorative Justice Programs

The prevalence of restorative justice programs was confirmed in a recent survey, which indicated that there are over 500 mediation programs in Europe, over 300 in the United States, and over 100 in Canada (Centre for Justice and Reconciliation, 2008). Restorative justice programs are defined broadly as any program that uses restorative processes and seeks to achieve restorative outcomes (United Nations, 2002). Though the types of programs are growing and continually evolving, there are a number of program models that currently form the core of restorative practice. The programs occur at various entry points within the criminal justice system or outside of the

**JUST or BUST?**

**Should restorative justice programs be restricted to non-violent offences? Canadians are much more accepting of the use of restorative justice programs to address non-violent crimes, and there is less acceptance of restorative justice programs that address violent crimes. Do you agree?**

criminal justice system all together. Entry points with the criminal justice system include:

- pre-charge—usually referred to a diversion program by police;
- post-charge—usually referred to a diversion program by the Crown attorney;
- pre-sentence—referred to a **sentencing circle** by the court/judge; and
- post-sentence—while in custody or under community supervision.

**sentencing circle**

a process whereby all persons affected by a criminal offence address the crime and arrive at an appropriate sentence

connect ONLINE ACTIVITY

## SENTENCING CIRCLES

The circle has been adopted as a symbol of restorative justice programs. Everyone who sits in a circle is equal; there is no hierarchy in a circle, as power is distributed equally around the circle. Sentencing circles and healing circles are convened to address behaviour in a community. The circle is based upon Aboriginal practices, where community members sit in a circle to speak together to address issues of conflict. Recognizing that there is tremendous diversity within the Aboriginal culture, there is a similar approach to justice among the various communities.

Sentencing circles are also referred to as peacemaking or healing circles, depending on the context. They are based upon three principles that are consistent within Aborginal culture:

1. A criminal offence is a breach of the relationship between the offender and the victim and a breach of the relationship between the offender and the community.
2. These breaches must be healed in order to restore stability within the community.
3. The community is able to address issues related to the causes of crime, because crime happens within communities. (Lilles, 2002)

Circles typically involve the victim, the offender, family and community members, and can include police, lawyers, and a judge. Everyone in the circle is provided with an opportunity to share his or her perspective, and to ultimately arrive at a consensus and appropriate sentencing plan for the offender that addresses the issues and concerns of everyone present. It often involves identifying the ways in which the offender will repair the harm that has been caused by the crime. The victim has an opportunity to express his or her feelings and perceptions and to provide input into the solution. The community members who have been affected (directly or indirectly) are also involved. These are often persons who, in the traditional court system,

The significance of the circle in Aboriginal culture is often manifest in their art.

Restorative justice is a process used to right the wrongs that may have resulted when a crime was committed. It is a type of "community healing" and recognizes that crime is wrong and should not occur but also understands that imprisonment is not an ideal solution. Therefore, it deals with crime outside of a court setting. In a restorative justice setting, both the offender and the victim are present and they both come up with a solution to rebuild the relationship that was damaged by the crime.

ISABELLE GUERTIN, A NEW WAY OF ADDRESSING CRIME: RESTORATIVE JUSTICE, 2010

may not have been consulted. In the sentencing circle they can express their views on how the crime has had an impact on their lives. A skilled facilitator will guide the participants through the process, giving each person an opportunity to contribute to the final resolution. An object of symbolic value is often passed around the circle to the person who is speaking. The symbol can be a stone, a feather, or any object that is meaningful to the community.

The goal within the circle is to engage in discussion in order to arrive at a consensus regarding the sentence plan for the offender. The plan usually involves other members of the circle, including the victim and community members. Members of the circle will engage in discussion that often goes beyond the case before them and can include:

- the extent of similar crimes in the community;
- an analysis of life in the community, past and present;
- the impact of the crime on victims, families, and community life;
- the community involvement in preventing crime;
- what needs to be done to heal the offender, the victim, and the community;
- the sentence plan;
- the details of carrying out the plan;
- support that will be available for the victim and the offender;
- goals for those involved; and
- a process to review the sentence plan.

(Lilles, 2002)

Sentencing circles are used in communities across Canada.

A number of Canadian courts have implemented sentencing circles (sometimes called circle sentencing). In 1992, Justice Barry Stuart of the Yukon Territorial Court used a sentencing circle with an offender who pleaded guilty to carrying a baseball bat with the intention of assaulting an RCMP officer. Justice Stuart convened a circle in his court and as a result of the family and friends who were in attendance, the Judge suspended sentencing and issued probation for two years, on the condition that the offender live at home and be treated for alcohol abuse. This culturally sensitive process produced the first judgment to be reported as using a sentencing circle (Leung, 1999) (R. *v.* Moses, 3 C.N.L.R. 116).

In the Supreme Court of Canada's decision in R. *v.* Gladue [1999] 1 S.C.R. 688, Canadian judges were directed to consider sentencing procedures that may be appropriate in the circumstances for the offender because of his or her particular Aborginal heritage or connection. In addition to creating courts specific to Aborginal persons, this decision resulted in a more common application of sentencing circles.

In February, 2009, a sentencing circle was convened in Rose Valley, near the Yellow Quill Reserve in Saskatchewan, to address a crime committed by Christopher Pauchay. One year earlier, on January 28, 2008, Pauchay took his two young daughters Kaydance, 3, and Santana, 15 months, out into the sub-zero weather. Pauchay, intoxicated at the time, did not dress the girls appropriately—they were wearing t-shirts and diapers. Pauchay became separated from his daughters and the girls were later found dead, as a result of hypothermia. In court, Pauchay pleaded guilty to criminal negligence causing death. He made a request to Provincial Court Justice Morgan that a sentencing circle be convened to make recommendations that would be considered in sentencing. There was some opposition to the sentencing circle from the Crown attorney and from the media who questioned the use of a sentencing circle in a case that had such a tragic outcome. Justice Morgan agreed to the circle, making it clear that the purpose of the circle was to provide recommendations, the final decision regarding the sentence would be determined in court. The circle was convened and a number of recommendations were made including:

- to allow Pauchay to return to his wife and child in the community,
- to require him to take drug and alcohol treatment, and
- to have him assist elders with cultural and spiritual activities indefinitely.

When sentencing Pauchay in March, 2009, Justice Morgan chose not to implement the recommendations made by the sentencing circle, stating that he did not agree with their recommendations (Goldbach, 2011). Instead, he sentenced Pauchay to three years in jail. The court was not obligated by law to implement the recommendations of the sentencing circle. However, by not doing so, it calls into question whether sentencing circles have a legitimate place in Canadian courts.

Christopher Pauchay, daughters Santana and Kaydance, and their mother, Tracey Jimmy.

Sentencing circles also occur as a form of diversion from the traditional court system. The diversion programs have different titles and vary by community; however, they are often led by a community justice committee (committees that deal with youth are youth justice committees). The community justice committee assesses the case to determine if it is suitable for the program, and makes a decision to accept or reject the case. Rejected cases are referred back to the traditional court system, and accepted cases are then prepared for participation in a sentencing circle. A case may be rejected if the victim is unwilling to participate, or if the offender is unsuitable or unwilling to abide by the conditions of the sentencing circle process.

After the circle is convened and a solution is proposed, the offender is required to follow through on the sentence plan. The consequences for non-compliance vary based on the program. In some diversion programs, non-compliance results in being returned to the traditional court system for trial. Non-compliance in less structured programs may result in community consequences as determined by members of the circle, at the time the sentencing circle convened.

## FAMILY OR COMMUNITY GROUP CONFERENCING

Family or community group conferencing occurs outside of the criminal justice system, offering the offender an opportunity to make amends to the victim and community, separate and apart from the criminal justice process. The process is led by a skilled facilitator and brings together the victim, offender, family, friends, and other supporters with a view to addressing the outcome of the crime that was committed. Conferencing gives the victim an opportunity to be a part of the resolution and it gives the offender an opportunity to become aware of the consequences of his or her actions. It also connects the offender to community support people and processes. Examples of strategies that flow from conferencing circles include an apology, restitution, an undertaking to change behaviour, enrolment in a program or treatment plan, or involvement in volunteer work. This commitment from the offender is not part of a court sanction and therefore not subject to any formal penalty.

## VICTIM OFFENDER RECONCILIATION PROGRAMS

Victim Offender Reconciliation Programs bring victims and offenders together with a facilitator. Victims are given an opportunity to share their feelings and their loss, and offenders are given an opportunity to listen, to speak to the victim and to attempt to repair the harm that was done. These programs require the voluntary involvement of both the victim and the offender. The participants discuss the impact of the offence and the resulting harm. They will identify strategies to repair the harm. The strategies may include restitution, volunteer work, an apology, or the physical repair of damage. A process or schedule to carry out the strategies is also identified. The programs may focus on a specific type of offender, offence, or community. For example, the program may be for youthful offenders, it may be restricted to non-violent offences, or it may be for offences that occur in a specific setting, such as a school, a long-term care facility, or a treatment facility. Victim Offender Reconciliation Programs may operate as diversions from the traditional criminal justice system or they may supplement the actions of the criminal justice system.

Community

The Correctional Service of Canada has been offering Restorative Opportunities to the victims of crimes committed by incarcerated offenders across Canada since 2004 (Correctional

Service of Canada, 2009). Victim-Offender Mediation is a program that offers victims and offenders the chance to communicate through a trained community-based facilitator in a safe, structured setting after sentencing. The focus of the program is to give interested participants an opportunity to engage in open communication consistent with the values of restorative justice. The program model varies depending on the institution and the circumstances of the offence. Victims and offenders may meet face to face, through letters, or via video. The facilitator may be used to relay messages back and forth over a considerable period of time, as appropriate. The process is confidential and cannot be used to influence, positively or negatively, Parole Board decisions. The program can be initiated by the victim or the offender; however, both must participate voluntarily.

Reconciliation—a monument dedicated to peacekeepers in Ottawa, Ontario.

Though there is not a great deal of research on the evaluation of restorative justice programs in prisons, there is some evidence that prisoners recognize the value of restorative approaches. One study recognized that prisoners generally support restorative justice approaches. It indicated that 74 percent of prisoners wanted an opportunity to make amends for the harm that had been done to their victims. A majority (65 percent) of the prisoners wanted to meet their victims and 44 percent indicated that they were willing to write letters of apology to their victims. Only 14 percent of the prisoners recognized that their crimes also harmed the wider community, which is indicative of a traditional definition of victimization (Dhami, Mantle, Fox, 2009). There has been little research to examine the effect of restorative justice programs on the rehabilitation of offenders upon release.

**community-assisted hearings**

circles administered by the Parole Board of Canada, intended to prepare Aboriginal offenders for release

## COMMUNITY-ASSISTED HEARINGS

**Community-assisted hearings** are also referred to as "releasing circles." They are administered by the Parole Board of Canada for Aboriginal offenders and they include Aborginal community members. These hearings are most popular in western Canada. They are designed to give all members of the circle an opportunity to discuss the impact of the crime and to identify supports for the offender, upon eventual release.

**healing circles**

a circle that is convened with the intention of specifically addressing or healing an individual or individuals

## HEALING CIRCLES

**Healing circles** are derived from Aborginal ceremonies that are intended to bring closure to conflict between people. All of the people involved are invited to share their experience and feelings, with a focus on the relationship between the victim and the offender. The goal of the circle is to assist in the personal healing process of the individuals involved. Healing circles are done in various settings to resolve conflict and repair relationships.

The circle brings community members together.

LO4

## Comparison Between Traditional and Restorative Justice

The following table identifies some of the key differences in the approaches between the traditional model of retribution and the restorative model.

| Traditional Criminal Justice System | Restorative Justice Model |
|---|---|
| The act is seen as a violation of a piece of legislation (e.g., *Criminal Code of Canada*). | The act is seen as a violation of a person, relationships, or the community within which it occurs. |
| The focus of the process is on the offence. | The focus of the process is on the obligation of the offender to make amends to the victim and to the entire community that has been affected by the act. |
| The punishment is decided externally (by a judge or jury). | The plan for reparation of harm is decided by those who have been affected by the incident. |
| Offenders are defined by their deficits (weaknesses that led to the commission of the crime). | Offenders are defined by their capacity to make reparation to the victims. |
| The focus is on the offender and the incident itself. | The focus is on the victim and reconciliation of all parties that were affected by the incident. |
| The focus is on removing the offender from the community. | The focus is on the reintegration of offenders, with the necessary supports, and rebuilding their relationships within the community. |

ADAPTED FROM: Lockhart and Zammit, 2005.

Restorative justice is an approach to justice that focuses on repairing the harm caused by crime while holding the offender responsible for his or her actions, by providing an opportunity for the parties directly affected by the crime—victims, offender and community—to address their needs in the aftermath of a crime, and seek a resolution that affords healing, reparation and reintegration, and prevents future harm.

DR. ROBERT B. CORMIER, SENIOR DIRECTION, CORRECTIONS RESEARCH AND DEVELOPMENT, PUBLIC SAFETY AND EMERGENCY PREPAREDNESS CANADA

## Restorative Justice and Victims

LO5

Perhaps the most significant contribution of restorative justice is providing victims with an opportunity to play a major role in an offender's outcome, as the restorative justice process offers victims options to be involved in the aftermath of a crime. The victim is central to restorative practice as the main person who has been offended by the process. This differs from the traditional criminal justice system where the "state" is the offended party and the prosecution takes place on behalf of the state. The victim is a witness in the traditional criminal justice system. Philosophically, the victim is central to restorative practice; however, there are challenges to involving victims consistently. Victims may choose not to be involved in the process because they do not wish to face the offender or they do not wish to be identified within a community. Between 20 and 60 percent of victims who are asked to participate in restorative justice programs agree to do so, depending upon the type of program (Doerner & Lab, 2008). The Canadian Resource Centre for Victims of Crime identified the following needs of victims when a restorative justice program is being considered:

1. Safety: This must be the program's highest priority.
2. Information: A clear explanation of the program's goal and the role that the victim will play within the program, including the connection to the offender through the process.
3. Choice: Options for participation at all levels.
4. Support: Providing the victim with an advocate or support person throughout the process.
5. Testimony: Providing the victim with an appropriate environment to tell his or her story and options for ways in which the story can be told (verbally, on tape, written).
6. Validation: Providing a stage where the victim is given an opportunity to hear a very clear message from the offender.
7. Restitution: Discussing the various options for reparation, including and beyond restitution.

Participating in restorative justice programs brings victims more satisfaction than participating in the criminal justice system (Sherman and Strang, 2007). Studies that measure the effects of restorative justice on victims have been fairly consistent. Most victims who participate in the programs report that they leave with less fear of the offender and less anger for the offender, as well as a greater ability to move on with their lives (Sherman and Strang, 2007). Victims who do not report a positive outcome have generally been involved in restorative programs where the offender has refused to accept responsibility for the commission of the offence or has not followed through on the strategies that were put in place during the program.

> Restorative justice is an evolving response to crime that respects the dignity and equality of each person, builds understanding, and promotes social harmony through the healing of victims, offenders and communities.
>
> UNITED NATIONS ECONOMIC AND SOCIAL COUNCIL/ BASIC PRINCIPLES ON THE USE OF RESTORATIVE JUSTICE PROGRAMMES IN CRIMINAL MATTERS, 2002

## Restorative Justice and Youth

There have been a number of changes to Canadian legislation that govern the way in which we deal with young offenders, as we strive for legislation that is effective and appropriate. The *Youth Criminal Justice Act* moved us closer to restorative practice with the inclusion of extrajudicial measures (*Youth Criminal Justice Act*, s. 5). The objectives of extrajudicial measures are consistent with the principles of restorative justice. Extrajudicial measures:

a) provide an effective and timely response to offending behaviour outside the bounds of judicial measures;
b) encourage young persons to acknowledge and repair the harm caused to the victim and the community;
c) encourage families of young persons —including extended families where appropriate—and the community to become involved in the design and implementation of those measures;
d) provide an opportunity for victims to participate in decisions related to the measures selected and to receive reparation; and
e) respect the rights and freedoms of young persons and be proportionate to the seriousness of the offence.

Engaging in community service, such as graffiti eradication, is an example of extrajudicial measures.

Extrajudicial measures programs vary across the country and include community service, restitution, attending a wilderness camp for life skills training, treatment programs, public speaking, and other creative approaches. Young offenders have also been involved in **victim-offender reconciliation programs**.

**victim-offender reconciliation programs**

programs where victims may share their feelings and describe their loss to the offender

Research into the success of restorative practices with youth has been promising. New Zealand's approach to youth crime is that every juvenile offender, between the ages of 14 and 17, who is arrested is required to attend a Family Group Conference (Consedine, 2002) and in a 14-year study, 84 percent of the youth and 85 percent of their parents expressed satisfaction with the outcomes. This policy has resulted in a significant reduction in young offenders who appear before the traditional courts in New Zealand.

In addition to being used with youth involved in the criminal justice system, restorative justice practices are also used in schools. Restorative practice has been introduced in the school setting by introducing restorative principles into the conflict resolution process. In many schools the zero tolerance policies have been challenged and replaced with restorative activities that encourage communication and problem solving (Schachter, 2010). Restorative practice gives schools an opportunity to use alternatives to traditional discipline like suspension. Alternative responses can include behaviour monitoring, counselling, community service, restitution, contracting, parent supervision in school, and alternative programming (Schacter, 2010). Schools are using conferencing circles to deal with behaviour problems and bullying as well. One Minnesota study showed that public schools that used a range of restorative responses between 1998 and 2001 experienced a reduction of suspensions from 30 to 50 percent (Zaslaw, 2010).

## MYTH VS FACT

Critics of restorative justice often express their concern that this alternative process is too lenient. The following case illustrates that participation in restorative justice can result in a meaningful sentence—it also gives the offenders an opportunity to appreciate and understand the harm and hurt they have caused.

Two young offenders were accused of knocking over 113 headstones in Eastlawn Cemetery in August, 2010. The Hamilton, Ontario, police service referred their case to the John Howard Society's restorative justice program, enabling them to participate in a sentencing circle. In the circle, the boys met the families of two of their victims. One of the family members brought in a picture of her daughter, who had died as a child. Her headstone had been knocked down. A second woman spoke about bringing her daughter's wedding bouquet to rest at her own mother's headstone, only to find it knocked down. At the circle's conclusion, the two young offenders agreed to perform 113 hours of community service work, one hour for each gravestone that they vandalized. Participating in the circle gave the victims an opportunity to speak to the offenders and explain the impact of the crime. The young offenders were given an opportunity to participate in identifying a strategy to make amends.

## LO6 Restorative Justice: The Impact

Restorative justice programs have the ability to offer a number of benefits that the traditional criminal justice system cannot. Restorative justice programs can address crime in a timely fashion, without the delays of dealing with the formal justice system. It is cost-effective: the costs are limited to the cost of having people represented at the table. Victims are provided with an opportunity to be heard and informed. The community is a part of the decision-making process in many cases, which acknowledges the impact that the crime had on it and includes it in the solution. Offenders have an opportunity to speak for themselves and to take responsibility for their actions. This is critical to being able to move forward and to repair relationships.

Restorative justice programs are also important in Canada because of their connection to Aborginal culture and beliefs. Given the overrepresentation of Aborginal people in our courts and prisons, restorative justice programs present an option, in some cases, that diverts offenders from the traditional system.

A Canadian team researched the effectiveness of restorative justice practices based on victim satisfaction, offender satisfaction, offender compliance with restitution, and recidivism. The researchers analyzed 22 studies that examined the effectiveness of 35 different restorative justice programs across the world (only three of the programs studied were Canadian). The findings were positive and found that "restorative justice programs were more effective methods of improving victim and offender satisfaction, increasing offender compliance with restitution and decreasing the recidivism of offenders when compared to more traditional criminal justice responses" (Latimer, Dowden, Muise, 2001). At the same time, it is important to note that when restorative justice programs are being evaluated, we are evaluating offenders who admitted guilt and who volunteered to be a part of the process.

The results are influenced by their willingness to be amenable and involved in a restorative process.

There are critics who caution us that it is important to recognize that there are limits to the potential of restorative practice. Some victims reported that they felt pressured to be involved in restorative justice programs, while others reported that they were not psychologically prepared for the process and as a result found it to be overwhelming (Gaudreault, 2005). Critics also point out that, even though the victim is involved, the focus is still on the offender. Restorative practice has been used primarily for non-violent offences. When asked, some victims of violent crime have said that they would be unable to meet face-to-face with their offenders because of the emotional nature of the meeting. Some likened it to a form of re-victimization (Gaudreault, 2005). Restorative justice is not appropriate for all offenders either. Many offenders have difficulty making the emotional commitment necessary to face their victims, their families, or their communities in the restorative process.

The future of restorative justice is positive. It is clear that the success of restorative practice depends on the ability to ensure that the offence committed is appropriate for the intervention and that the victim, the offender, and the community have been adequately prepared for the process. There have been restorative justice program successes in various settings and there is evidence to suggest that it provides victims, offenders, and communities with an opportunity to learn from their experiences and transform their experience.

## Chapter Summary

This chapter provided an introduction to restorative justice. Key concepts that were examined included:

- Restorative justice has its roots in Aborginal culture. In Aborginal communities throughout North America, healing circles and peacemaking circles have been used for many years. They are intended to allow the community to assume responsibility for the behaviour of everyone within it. Restorative practice has evolved to include a number of activities including sentencing circles and victim-offender reconciliation.
- Restorative justice gives a voice to the victim, the offender, and the community that is affected by the criminal offence.
- Victim agreement is required before a restorative process can take place and offenders must be willing to make an admission of guilt and take responsibility for their role in committing the offence.
- There are limitations to the use of restorative justice—it is used primarily in cases involving property offences.

## Relevant Legislation

*Youth Criminal Justice Act*, S.C. 2002, c. 1.

## Key Terms

Community-assisted hearings
Conferencing circle
Diversion programs
Healing circles
Reparation
Retribution
Sentencing circle
Victim-offender reconciliation programs

## For Review

1. What are the historical roots of restorative justice?
2. Identify the various types of restorative justice programs that currently exist.
3. What are the potential entry points for restorative justice programs in the criminal justice system?
4. What are the benefits of participating in a restorative justice program for the victim, the offender, and the community?
5. What are the differences between the traditional justice system and restorative justice?
6. What are the limitations to using restorative practice?

## Thinking Critically

1. What are the reasons that victims and/or offenders may not wish to participate in restorative justice programs?
2. What value do restorative justice programs bring to our society?
3. How can we ensure that our communities have appropriate resources to implement restorative justice programs?
4. To what extent does forgiveness play a part in restorative justice programs?
5. What role does shame play in the traditional justice system and in the restorative justice system?
6. How is community defined within the restorative justice paradigm?
7. How might the success of restorative justice programs be measured?

CHAPTER 10

# The Victim in the Criminal Justice System

## Vancouver's Missing Women—Victims in Life and Death

Between January 23, 1997, and February 5, 2002, Vancouver's downtown east side experienced an increase in the number of women who were reported missing. By 1999, there were 27 missing women, with 18 added in 2001 and five more added in 2002. Most of the missing women had something important in common—they were street-involved. Many were sex trade workers, most were engaged in substance abuse, and many were Aboriginal. The women were reported missing by friends or family, many of whom claimed that the police dismissed their concerns.

Eventually Robert Pickton, a pig farmer from Port Coquitlam, British Columbia, came to the attention of the police. Pickton lured the women to his farm, killed them, and butchered their bodies in the slaughterhouse on his farm. Eventually, the dismembered remains or DNA of 33 missing women were found on Pickton's farm, buried on the property or in plastic pails.

In 2007, Pickton was tried and convicted of the second degree murder of the first six women. He was sentenced to life with no chance of parole for 25 years. Pickton appealed the decision to the Supreme Court of Canada, which upheld the six convictions. The Crown attorney was prepared to move forward with a further 20 murder charges, but decided not to, and stayed the charges. Pickton once bragged to an undercover officer that he had in fact killed 49 women in total.

In the aftermath of the conviction, the Missing Women Commission of Inquiry was created to inquire into the police investigation. The Commission has heard about the mistakes made by the police in the investigation. There was a reported lack of cooperation between the police services, described as a "systemic breakdown in communication" between the Vancouver Police Department and the RCMP. It is believed that this lack of communication prevented Pickton from being investigated and apprehended earlier, which would have saved lives. Perhaps most disturbing are the allegations made by those who believe that the police did not respond seriously to the missing person reports that had been filed years earlier. Family and friends have attributed racism, sexism, and classism to the police inaction, believing that they did not launch a vigorous investigation early on because the victims were marginalized women, unworthy of an investigation.

Both the Vancouver Police Department and the RCMP have issued apologies for the mistakes they made during the investigation.

### LEARNING OBJECTIVES

By the end of this chapter, you should be able to:

- **LO1** Describe the role of the victim in the criminal justice system.
- **LO2** Describe the rate of victimization in Canada.
- **LO3** Identify those individuals who are most likely to be victimized in Canada.
- **LO4** Examine the impact of victimization.
- **LO5** Identify the legislation that protects the rights of victims on an international and a national level.
- **LO6** Describe the organizations and the types of support available to victims in Canada.
- **LO7** Examine the level of victim satisfaction with the criminal justice system.

Over 5,000 people marched in Vancouver's downtown east side annual Women's Memorial March. The March on February 14, 2012, included many friends and family membersof the women murdered by Pickton.

## LO1 The Role of the Victim in the Criminal Justice System

The role of the victim within the criminal justice system has been discussed and debated since criminologists began discussing the lack of victim representation in the trial process in the 1970s (Wemmers, 2008). It was formally recognized at that time that victims, particularly victims of violent offences, were expressing their discontent with the court process and their lack of involvement within it. The introduction of the **victim impact statement**—in countries such as the United States, Australia, England, and Canada—has resulted in a formal role for victims with the trial process. The victim impact statement was introduced in Canada in 1988, and is codified in section 722 of the *Criminal Code of Canada*. Persons who meet the definition of a victim have the right to submit a written statement, or to read one in court at sentencing, after there has been a finding of guilt. The statement is intended to describe the harm that has been done to the victim and the effect that the crime has had on his or her life, and the court is required to take the statement into consideration when sentencing the offender. Victims will often refer to the physical, emotional, medical, and financial impact of the crime. Some victim advocates have said that the victim impact statement occurs too late in the trial process, leaving the victim out of the process until the very end. At the same time there are those who believe that including the victim impact statement can present some problems, such as including information that is prejudicial to the accused, including sentencing recommendations. Victim impact statements are presented in a minority of cases that are before the courts, with a higher rate of submission when crimes are of a violent or personal nature. There are a number of reasons for the low rate of statement submission including the inability to provide victims with the time and assistance to complete the statement, an inability to describe the purpose of the statement, and victims' negative attitudes that exist regarding the expectations of the statement outcome (Roberts, 2008).

**victim impact statement**

a verbal or written statement delivered by, or on behalf of, the victim at the time of sentencing

Research indicates that those victims who do submit victim impact statements express more satisfaction with the sentencing process (Roberts, 2008). Judges also report a level of satisfaction with the use of victim impact statements at sentencing, particularly with violent crime, indicating that it provides them with a unique perspective that they often refer to in their reasons for the sentence (Roberts, 2008).

### Victim

A person is considered a victim of crime if:

- he or she has been harmed as a result of a criminal offence;
- he or she is a spouse, conjugal partner, relative of, or person responsible for a victim who has died or is not able to act for themselves (e.g., the victim is ill or is a child);
- the person who harmed him or her has not been prosecuted or convicted, but he or she has made a complaint to the police or Crown attorney.

Victims also have legal rights when the convicted offender is incarcerated. In 1992, the *Corrections and Conditional Release Act* was amended to provide the victims of crime with the right to obtain information related to the offender. At their request, they are entitled to the following information about the offender:

**26.** (1) At the request of a victim of an offence committed by an offender, the Commissioner:

a) shall disclose to the victim the following information about the offender:
   (i) the offender's name,
   (ii) the offence of which the offender was convicted and the court that convicted the offender,
   (iii) the date of commencement and length of the sentence that the offender is serving, and
   (iv) eligibility dates and review dates applicable to the offender under this Act in respect of temporary absences or parole; and

b) may disclose to the victim any of the following information about the offender, where in the

Commissioner's opinion the interest of the victim in such disclosure clearly outweighs any invasion of the offender's privacy that could result from the disclosure:

(i) the offender's age,

(ii) the location of the penitentiary in which the sentence is being served,

(iii) the date, if any, on which the offender is to be released on temporary absence, work release, parole or statutory release,

(iv) the date of any hearing for the purposes of a review under section 130,

(v) any of the conditions attached to the offender's temporary absence, work release, parole or statutory release,

(vi) the destination of the offender on any temporary absence, work release, parole or statutory release, and whether the offender will be in the vicinity of the victim while travelling to that destination, and

(vii) whether the offender is in custody and, if not, the reason why the offender is not in custody.

(2) Where a person has been transferred from a penitentiary to a provincial correctional facility, the Commissioner may, at the request of a victim of an offence committed by that person, disclose to the victim the name of the province in which the provincial correctional facility is located, if in the Commissioner's opinion the interest of the victim in such disclosure clearly outweighs any invasion of the person's privacy that could result from the disclosure.

(*Corrections and Conditional Release Act*, s. 26).

In order to receive this information, victims are required to register with the Correctional Service of Canada. Though it is not a right sanctioned in legislation, it is a policy of the Parole Board of Canada to encourage victims to submit a victim impact statement at parole hearings. The victim may present the statement in person or in a written or recorded format. In their statements, victims may detail the physical, emotional, or financial impact of the crime and they may also request conditions for the offender's release to be considered by the Parole Board. The Parole Board can use this information to help to assess the offender's risk in the community, particularly as it relates to proximity to the victim. The Parole Board of Canada reports that between 1996 and 2010, their contacts with victims have increased by 274 percent, most of which was with victims of violent crimes (Public Safety Canada, 2010).

It is clear that the need to educate victims about the victim impact statement process is critical to increasing their informed involvement in the criminal justice system, which may have an impact on their satisfaction with their experience.

### A VICTIM IMPACT STATEMENT

The following victim impact statement was submitted by Elaine Belanger at the trial of Robert Pickton. Belanger is the mother of Brenda Wolfe, one of Robert Pickton's victims.

> The impact the trial has had on me has been devastating and traumatizing. There is an anger within me that reacts to fear, powerlessness and pain. I've started to heal and the media opens up the wound again.
>
> And now this impact statement has again reopened up the wounds.
>
> Oh, I know that life is a healing process from the time that we are born until the time that we meet the creator.
>
> There is a hole in my heart and soul that will not ever close, the loss of my first-born child Brenda.

It is a policy of the Parole Board of Canada to encourage victims to submit a victim impact statement at parole hearings.

Friends and family gathered to mourn Brenda Wolfe, a victim of Robert Pickton.

Brenda was a mother to two beautiful little girls. As much as I try to protect (them) from the circumstances that ended their mother's life it was impossible.

There are some things that are really troubling me. I am wondering how a portion of my daughter's remains ended up on the farm. I am also wondering how my daughter Brenda's jacket ended up in Mr. Pickton's bedroom.

Even if Brenda had not been murdered like this, giving her money and drugs would only enable her addiction.

I really want to know what happened to my daughter in the final hour of her life. Only the person who murdered her knows that and can tell me that.

Brenda was not only a mother, a daughter; my first-born was loved and wanted. Brenda was a sister that was loved, wanted and respected.

Brenda was an aunt and was very proud, loved by her nephews. Brenda was also a niece and loved, adored and respected by her aunts.

There is a pain in my heart that will not heal. I have tried to forgive you as my native traditional elders have suggested me to do. This is impossible to do. The tears that I shed would fill an ocean. And knowing my granddaughters are growing up without a mother is heartbreaking and devastating. The dreams I have of my daughter Brenda are so real and she is alive. And then I wake up and the emptiness in my stomach realizes Brenda is gone but not forgotten.

If the teardrops I shed made a pathway to heaven I would walk all the way and bring you home again and hold you in my arms again Brenda and never let you go.

SOURCE: (Elaine Belanger's victim impact statement as reprinted on CTVnews.ca): http://www.ctv.ca/CTVNews/Canada/20071211/victim_impactstatements_071211/#ixzz1np7qijhw.

## THE RATE OF VICTIMIZATION IN CANADA

LO2

The Canadian government collects information related to the victimization of Canadians with the **General Social Survey** (GSS) on Victimization. It is conducted every five years on a sample of Canadians across the country. It asks them to disclose their personal accounts of criminal victimization for the following crimes:

**General Social Survey**

a survey that collects data related to victimization, conducted every five years

1. Sexual assault
2. Robbery
3. Physical assault

4. Break and enter
5. Motor vehicle/parts theft
6. Theft of household property
7. Vandalism
8. Theft of personal property

In 2009, the GSS indicated that in the previous 12 months, 7.4 million Canadians (approximately 25 percent of the population over age 14) reported that they had been a victim of a criminal incident. The rate of violent victimization across Canada in 2009 was 118 per 1,000 population. (Note: The rate of victimization is generally measured per 1,000 population). Provincially, there were variations in Manitoba, and Saskatchewan reported the highest levels of violent victimization and Prince Edward Island reported the lowest level.

The rate of household victimization in Canada in 2009 is a reported 237 per 1,000 population. The offences that were most often reported to the police in 2009 were break and enter and motor vehicle theft, followed by robbery, vandalism, physical assault, theft of personal property, and theft of household property. The break and enter rate of crime was highest for those households that are rented, and those persons who lived in

The connection between drug use and victimization is evident in the research.

**FIGURE 10.1** Self-Reported Violent Victimization Incidents, by Province, 2009

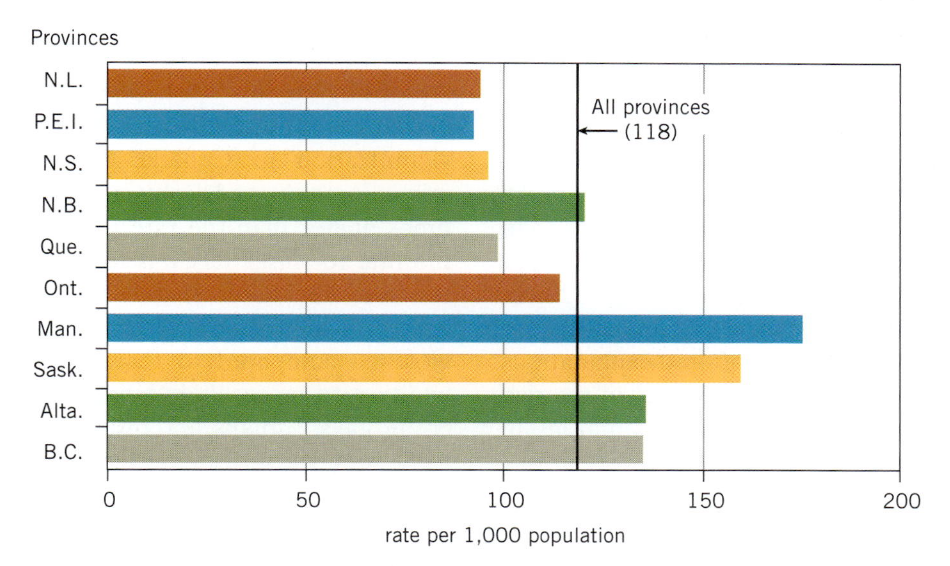


NOTE: Violent victimization includes sexual assault, robbery, and physical assault. Caution should be used in making comparisons between provinces as not all differences between provincial estimates are statistically significant. Excludes data from the Northwest Territories, Yukon and Nunavut which will be published at a later date.

SOURCE: Adapted from Statistics Canada, Statistics Canada, General survey 2009. March 1, 2012. Reproduced and distributed on an "as is" basis with the permission of Statistics Canada.

**TABLE 10.1 Risk Factors Influencing Victimization**

| | |
|---|---|
| **Age** | Younger people (ages 15–24) are 15 times more likely to be a victim of a violent crime than persons over age 65. |
| **Marital status** | Single people are more likely to be a victim of violent crime than married people. People in common law marriages are more likely to be a victim of violent crime than those in traditional marriages. |
| **Aboriginal status** | Aboriginal persons are more likely to be a victim of violent crime. |
| **Immigration status** | Immigrants are less likely to be a victim of crime than non-immigrants. |
| **Involvement in evening activities** | The more evening activities in which a person is involved the more likely the person will be a victim of crime. |
| **Sexual orientation** | People who are homosexual are more likely to be a victim of violent crime. |
| **Student status** | Students are more likely to be victims of crime than those who are employed workers. |
| **Drug use** | People who use drugs are more likely to be a victim of crime than those who do not. |

SOURCE: Adapted from Statistics Canada, Criminal victimization in Canada, 2009. March 1, 2012. Reproduced and distributed on an "as is" basis with the permission of Statistics Canada.

their homes for a shorter period of time were more likely to be a victim of crime than those who were long term residents.

LO3 When we examine the results of the GSS on Victimization (2009), it is clear that there are a number of risk factors that influence victimization, as listed in Table 10.1.

### ABORIGINAL PEOPLE AS VICTIMS OF CRIME

Just as they are overrepresented as offenders, research also indicates that Aboriginal persons are more likely to be victimized than non-Aboriginal people. The 2009 GSS indicated that Aboriginal persons were two times more likely to be a victim of violent crime (assault, sexual assault, or robbery) than non-Aboriginal persons. The homicide rate for Aboriginal persons is 8.8 per 100,000 population, significantly higher than that of non-Aboriginal persons, which is 1.3 per 100,000 population (Statistics Canada, 2008). The reasons for this high rate of victimization are complex but researchers have offered explanations that include recognizing that a number of the risk factors for victimization are highly apparent in the Aboriginal population in Canada. These risk factors include living in a single-parent family situation, a common-law marriage, high levels of unemployment, and the consumption of alcohol (Scrim, 2010). Another risk factor relates to age, as younger people are more likely to be victims of crime. The Aboriginal population in Canada has a median age of 27, while the rest of Canada has a median age of 40 (Statistics Canada, 2008). Aboriginal women are more likely to be victims of violent victimization—24 percent of Aboriginal women in Canada report having been assaulted by an intimate partner, compared to 7 percent of non-Aboriginal women. Aboriginal women are also overrepresented as sex trade workers (Scrim, 2010). There is a continuing need to engage in research to understand and respond to the overrepresentation of Aboriginal persons within the criminal justice system, as victims and as offenders.

### SEXUAL ORIENTATION AND VICTIMIZATION

According to the 2004 GSS, gays, lesbians, and bisexuals experience higher levels of violent victimization in Canada. The rate of violent crime for gays and lesbians was two and a half times higher than the rate for heterosexuals, and the rate for bisexuals was four times higher than the rate for heterosexuals. Gays, lesbians, and bisexuals also reported higher rates of spousal violence compared to that of heterosexuals. In addition to more likely being a victim of violent crime, gays, lesbians, and bisexuals are more likely to be victims of discrimination as well. The 2004 GSS reported that 44 percent of gays and lesbians and 41 percent of bisexuals believed that they had experienced some form of discrimination in the previous five years, compared to 14 percent of heterosexuals. The discrimination was most likely to occur in the workplace or when applying for a job (Beauchamp, 2008).

## IN THE NEWS

### Gay Basher Sentenced to Imprisonment

Gay bashing is a hate crime that targets individuals based on their sexual orientation. Michael Kandola, from British Columbia, was convicted and sentenced to 17 months in jail for the aggravated assault of Jordan Smith. In September, 2008, Smith was walking down a Vancouver street, holding hands with another man when Kandola beat Smith, while uttering homophobic slurs. Smith suffered serious injuries, including a fractured jaw.

SOURCES: http://www.cbc.ca/news/canada/british-columbia/story/2010/04/30/bc-kandola-sentence.html; Man "begged for mercy" in suspected gay bashing, by: Darcy Wintonyk, ctvbc.ca, Tuesday, Jan. 25, 2011, 3:55 PM PT, http://www.ctvbc.ctv.ca/servlet/an/local/CTVNews/20110125/bc_gay_assault_110125/20110125?hub=BritishColumbiaHome; http://www.canada.com/vancouversun/news/westcoastnews/story.html?id=67fd2ced-e7f0-4ef0-8068-935b61814478.

The rainbow flag honours the lesbian, gay, bisexual, transgender (LGBT) community.

When we compare Canada's victimization rate to that of other countries, it appears that we are similar to the average of countries polled. The International Crime Victimization Survey measures 10 offences in 30 countries to arrive at an **international victimization rate**. They then compare the data. Figure 10.2 indicates that 16 percent of all persons aged 16 and older in the reporting countries had reported being a victim of at least one of the measured crimes in the year preceding the survey. Canada reported that 17 percent of Canadians aged 16 and older had been victims of at least one crime in the same period (Sauve and Hung, 2008). The country with the highest reported rate of victimization was Ireland and the country with the lowest rate was Spain.

## How Much Crime is Reported to the Police?

It is estimated that only one out of every three victims contacts the police after being victimized (Wemmers and Cyr, 2006). The 2009 GSS polled respondents for reasons that a crime victim may or may not choose to report an incident to the police. The most common reason that victims do report crime is a sense of duty, and the second most common reason is because the victims want the offender to be arrested and punished. Victims of household crimes reported the crime in order to make an insurance claim. Victims of violent crime reported crimes because they sought protection from the criminal justice system. Perhaps the reasons that victims do not report a crime are more important than the reasons that they do (Figure 10.3). Fear and lack of confidence in the police and criminal justice system are among the reasons that victims do not report crime to the police. The fact that the number one reason that victims do not report crime is because they do not believe that the offence was important enough implies that victims generally do not expect any police response to minor crime. The second most common reason—that the police could not do anything about it—implies that the police do not have the ability, or perhaps the resources, to respond to certain types of crime. There was a 63 percent satisfaction rate with the actions of the police among victims of violent and household crimes.

## FIGURE 10.2 Canada's Rate of Victimization Compared to Other Countries

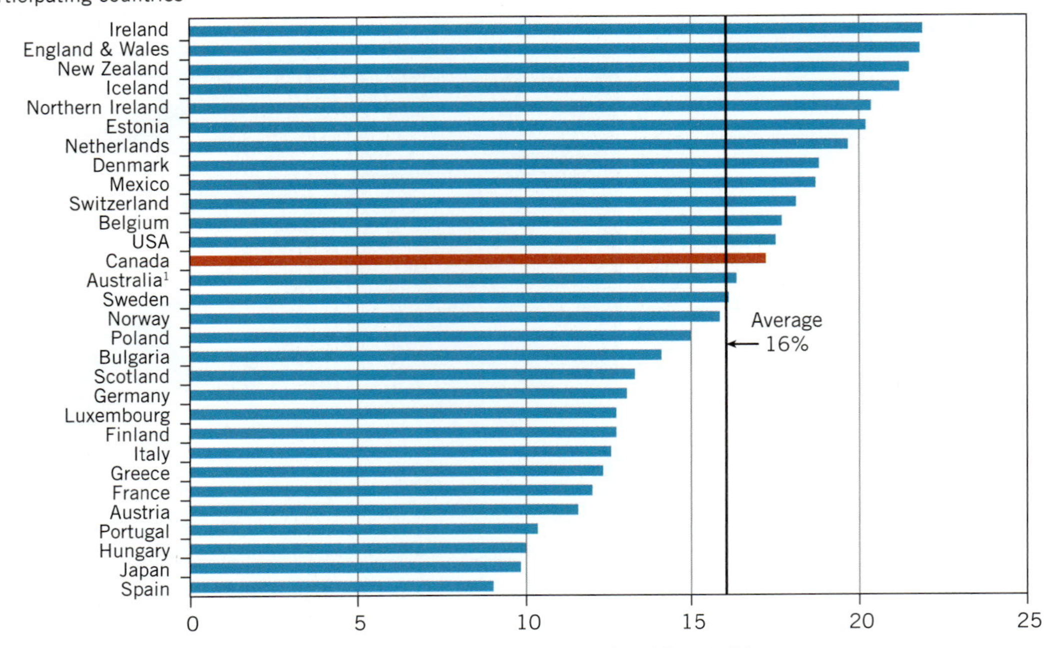


NOTES: Based on responses from victims of at least one out of the 10 types of offences in the year preceding the survey. In general, a difference less than 2.5 percentage points between two countries is not statistically significant.

[1]. Questions on sexual assault incidents were excluded from the survey in Australia. Thus, their national rate is estimated to be 1% lower.

SOURCE: Statistics Canada, An international perspective on criminal victimization, March 1, 2012. Reproduced and distributed on an "as is" basis with the permission of Statistics Canada.

## JUST or BUST?

### HOW SAFE DO WE THINK WE ARE?

Canadians, in general, feel satisfied with their personal safety in Canada, meaning that they do not believe that they are at a high risk of being victimized. The GSS 2009 indicated that 93 percent of Canadians reported feeling satisfied with their personal safety. When responding to specific examples about their safety, 90 percent of Canadians said they felt safe when walking alone in their neighbourhood at night, while 80 percent said that they had no concern about their safety while alone in their homes. When asked about specific situations, Canadians indicated that they felt as safe as they had in 2004. When asked about public transportation, 58 percent of Canadians who used public transportation reported that they were not at all worried when waiting for or using these services after dark. The level of confidence identified in this survey indicates that Canadians generally believe that they are not likely to become a victim of crime.

**FIGURE 10.3** Reasons for Not Reporting Victimization Incidents to Police, 2009

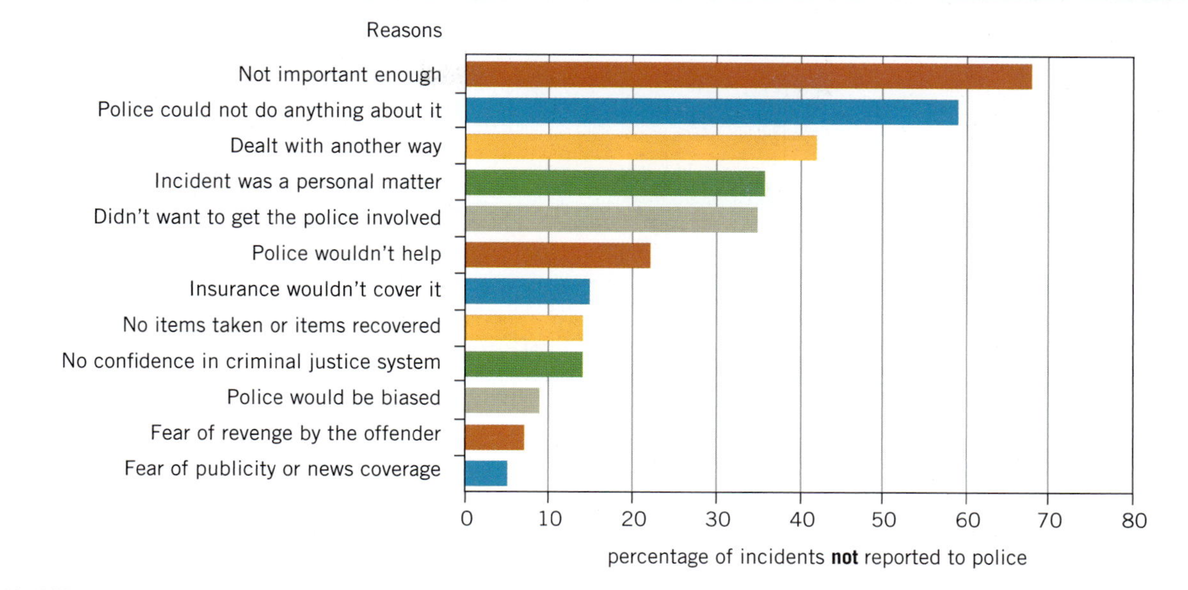


SOURCE: Statistics Canada, Criminal victimization in Canada, 2009 (see chart 4), March 1, 2012. Reproduced and distributed on an "as is" basis with the permission of Statistics Canada.

## LO4 The Impact of Victimization

Being a victim of crime is a traumatic experience that can have a lifelong effect on the victim. The victim may suffer emotional, physical, financial, psychological, and social consequences after a crime. Victimization may extend to secondary parties including the principal victim's family members, friends, associates, as well as the community at large.

It is difficult to measure the impact of victimization; we do know that victims experience a range of emotions from shock and disbelief to anger and fear. According to the 2009 GSS, the most common emotional response is anger. Anger is commonly directed towards God, the criminal justice system, the offender, and the victims themselves. The survey found that all victims had common emotional reactions, regardless of the type of crime (GSS 2009). Victims of property crimes were just as likely to experience emotional reactions as victims of violent crimes. The most common reactions are noted in Figure 10.4.

Victims also report that they experience feelings of confusion, guilt, shame, humiliation, and grief or sorrow (Canadian Resource Centre for Victims of Crime). They experience consistent physical consequences of victimization, even when the crime was not physical. The immediate physical reactions include shaking, hyperventilation, tears, numbness, and dryness of the mouth. In the longer term, some victims report experiencing insomnia, appetite disturbance, lethargy, headaches, nausea, and depression. Victims who are harmed physically may be disabled or may experience physical discomfort indefinitely. Some victims report that their friends avoided or abandoned them after the victimization, usually because their presence was uncomfortable (Devalve, 2005). In general, victims of crime report that the victimization changed their lives permanently. Many victims described changes to once regular habits, their general level of trust in the world, and diminished self-confidence. For some, the victimization resulted in a diagnosis of depression, panic, anxiety, or post-traumatic stress disorder (PTSD). For some the devastation is so severe that they contemplate suicide (Devalve, 2005).

The financial impact of victimization can include the loss of possessions, higher insurance rates, medical expenses, counselling, funeral and burial expenses, loss of employment, and the cost of attending court. One third of the victims of household crime said that the value of damaged or stolen property exceeded $500 (GSS 2009).

**FIGURE 10.4** Emotional Consequences of Self-Reported Victimization Incidents, 2009

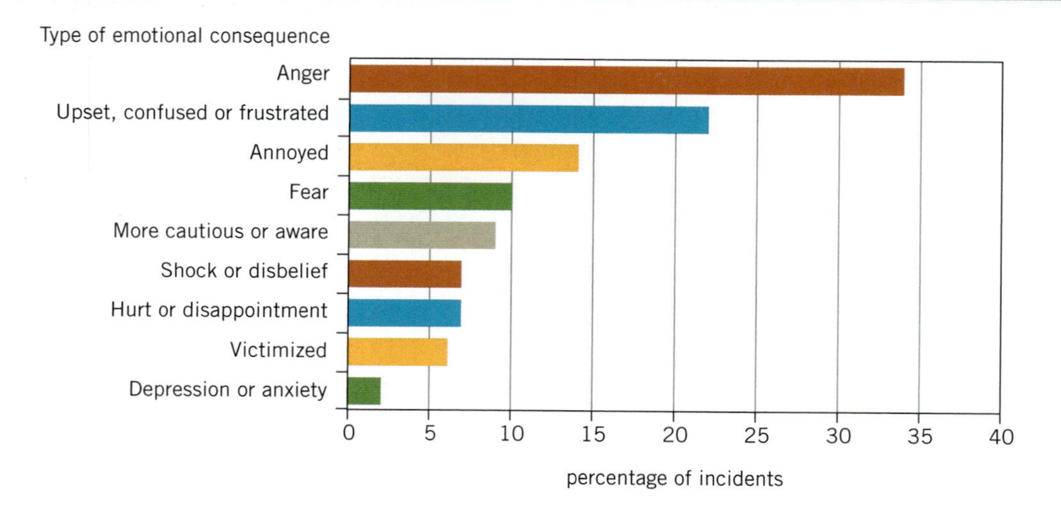


NOTE: Excludes all incidents of spousal sexual and physical assault. Excludes data from the Northwest Territories, Yukon and Nunavut which will be published at a later date.

SOURCE: Statistics Canada, Criminal victimization in Canada, 2009 (see chart 5), March 1, 2012. Reproduced and distributed on an "as is" basis with the permission of Statistics Canada.

Victims must also deal with the aftermath of the crime in the courts. There may or may not be charges laid. If charges are not laid, the victim lives indefinitely with the fact that the offender was not apprehended, and may never be. If a person is arrested, the victim is then required to be a part of the court process. Many victims are required to attend court as a witness, which is a stressful experience.

## LO5 Legislation and Agencies that Support Victims

There are a number of pieces of legislation that support the rights of victims, both on an international and a national level. On an international level, the United Nations *Declaration of Basic Principles of Justice for Victims of Crime and Abuse of Power* provides all member countries with a universal statement about the need to respect victims involved in the criminal justice system. Though the United Nations does not have any authority to formally sanction a country that does not comply with the declaration, it is important that it exists as a model to all countries because it sets an international standard for the treatment of victims.

The international community agreed in the 1985 United Nations victims' declaration on the following rights for victims:

- The right to be treated with respect and recognition;
- The right to be referred to adequate support services;
- The right to receive information about the progress of the case;
- The right to be present and give input to the decision-making;
- The right to counsel;
- The right to protection of physical safety and privacy;
- The right of compensation, from both the offender and the State.

SOURCE: http://www.un.org/events/10thcongress/2088a.htm.

In addition to rights identified by the United Nations, all federal, provincial, and territorial Ministers responsible for criminal justice in Canada endorsed the *Canadian Statement of Basic Principles of Justice for Victims of Crime* in 1988, and then a renewed version in 2003.

The Statement provides a comprehensive overview of the manner in which victims should be treated, particularly during the criminal justice process. However, because it is not law, it does not provide victims with additional rights beyond those outlined in the United Nations' declaration. The Statement is intended to guide the provinces and territories in developing policies, programs, and legislation related to victims. It states:

> In honour of the United Nations' Declaration of Basic Principles of Justice for Victims of Crime, and with concern for the harmful impact of criminal victimization on individuals and on society, and in recognition that all persons have the full protection of rights guaranteed by the *Canadian Charter of Rights and Freedoms* and other provincial Charters governing rights and freedoms; that the rights of victims and offenders need to be balanced; and of the shared jurisdiction of federal, provincial, and territorial governments, the federal, provincial, and territorial Ministers Responsible for Criminal Justice agree that the following principles should guide the treatment of victims, particularly during the criminal justice process.
>
> The following principles are intended to promote fair treatment of victims and should be reflected in federal/provincial/territorial laws, policies and procedures:
>
> 1. Victims of crime should be treated with courtesy, compassion, and respect.
> 2. The privacy of victims should be considered and respected to the greatest extent possible.
> 3. All reasonable measures should be taken to minimize inconvenience to victims.
> 4. The safety and security of victims should be considered at all stages of the criminal justice process and appropriate measures should be taken when necessary to protect victims from intimidation and retaliation.
> 5. should be provided to victims about the criminal justice system and the victim's role and opportunities to participate in criminal justice processes.
> 6. Victims should be given information, in accordance with prevailing law, policies, and procedures, about the status of the investigation; the scheduling, progress and final outcome of the proceedings; and the status of the offender in the correctional system.
> 7. Information should be provided to victims about available victim assistance services, other programs and assistance available to them, and means of obtaining financial reparation.
> 8. The views, concerns, and representations of victims are an important consideration in criminal justice processes and should be considered in accordance with prevailing law, policies, and procedures.
> 9. The needs, concerns and diversity of victims should be considered in the development and delivery of programs and services, and in related education and training.
> 10. Information should be provided to victims about available options to raise their concerns when they believe that these principles have not been followed.

SOURCE: Canadian Statement of Basic Principles of Justice for Victims of Crime, 2003, pp. 10–15. http://www.justice.gc.ca/eng/pi/pcvi-cpcv/pub/03/princ.html. Supreme Court of Canada. Reproduced with the permission of the Minister of Public Works and Government Services Canada, 2012.

The views, concerns, and representations of victims are an important consideration in criminal justice processes and should be considered in accordance with prevailing law, policies, and procedures.

On a national level, there are a number of organizations and agencies in Canada that are devoted to issues related to victims. The Policy Centre for Victim Issues is a part of the Department of Justice Canada and its mandate is to "work toward improving the experience of victims of crime in the criminal justice system by pursuing a range of activities and initiatives." (*Federal Victims Strategy Evaluation, Final Report*. February 2011. Evaluation Division, Strategic Planning and Performance Management. Department of Justice Canada) In addition to ensuring that victims and their families are aware of their role in the criminal justice system, the Centre provides services and financial assistance to support victims including a program that provides financial assistance to enable victims to attend Parole Board of Canada hearings. This funding is important because it is common to have a board hearing convened in a correctional institution in a different province/territory from where the victim lives. This fund provides victims with the financial ability to attend a hearing without incurring financial hardship.

In 2007, a program to provide financial assistance to Canadians who are victimized abroad was introduced (Emergency Financial Assistance for Canadians Victimized Abroad). This program is intended for those who are victims of a violent crime in a foreign country. It is limited to those who have been the victims of sexual assault, aggravated assault, and assault with serious personal violence, including against a child, as well as family members of a homicide victim.

The National Office for Victims was created in 2005, by the Department of Public Safety Canada, to provide information to victims who have concerns and questions about offenders, the federal correctional system, and the Canadian justice system. This office focuses on victims of federally-sentenced inmates; however, it has published a number of documents to inform victims and they offer a toll-free number where victims can ask questions, and be re-directed to programs or services, as required. (Public Safety Canada, http://www.publicsafety.gc.ca/prg/cor/nov/nov-bnv-eng.aspx.)

## FEDERAL OMBUDSMAN FOR VICTIMS OF CRIME IN CANADA

In 2007, the federal government created the Office of the Federal Ombudsman for Victims of Crime. It is an independent resource for victims that was created to ensure that the federal government meets its responsibilities to victims of crime. This office operates at arm's length from the federal departments responsible for victim issues and reports directly to the Minister of Justice. Its mandate relates exclusively to matters of federal responsibility and includes:

- promoting and facilitating victim access to existing federal programs and services by providing them with information and referrals;
- addressing victim complaints about compliance with the provisions of the *Corrections and Conditional Release Act* that apply to victims of offenders under federal supervision, and providing an independent resource for those victims;
- promoting awareness among criminal justice personnel and policy makers of victim needs and concerns and the applicable laws that benefit victims of crime, including promoting the principles set out in the *Canadian Statement of Basic Principles of Justice for Victims of Crime* with respect to matters of federal jurisdiction; and,
- identifying and reviewing emerging and systemic issues that have a negative impact on victims of crime.

## PROVINCIAL AND TERRITORIAL LEGISLATION FOR VICTIMS

Each province and territory is responsible for administering victim services. Each jurisdiction has its own legislation related to victims that identifies their commitment to victim services and financial compensation for victims. There are variations across the country regarding the amount and type of services and compensation.

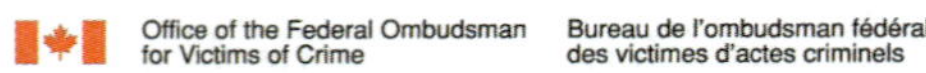


The Office of the Federal Ombudsman for Victims of Crime was created in 2007.

## LO6 VICTIM SERVICES

In recent years we have seen a number of victim services introduced in Canada. According to the Victim Services Survey 2007/2008, which is sponsored by the Policy Centre for Victim Issues of the Department of Justice Canada, approximately 686 different agencies or organizations provided victim assistance to 406,000 victims across Canada (Sauve, 2008). Female victims received assistance three times more often than did men. The same survey showed that police-based victim services are the most common type of victim service available. Many service providers offer specialized services to victims of specific crimes, such as sexual assault centres. Other victim service agencies offer services to victims in specific demographic groups such as children or youth, as well as for the elderly and people with disabilities.

Victim service agencies report that most people who use their services do so because they are looking for general information and emotional support when dealing with the aftermath of their ordeal. The majority of victims who receive the services are victims of violent crime. A Victim Services Survey snapshot was undertaken on May 28, 2008, and on that day 9,808 victims across Canada received formal assistance from a victim service agency and 67.1 percent of them were victims of violent crime (Public Safety Canada, 2010).

The cost of providing services to victims through these service agencies was $178.7 million in 2007/2008 (Sauve, 2009).

Victim services are administered at a provincial/territorial or local level. Victim services are police-based, court-based, and community-based. Other types of victim services include sexual assault centres, which provide assistance specifically to victims of sexual assault. Generally, the goal of victim service agencies is to lessen the trauma and impact that victims and their families' experience. They also strive to offer the victim support throughout their involvement in the criminal justice system.

Police-based victim services are made available to victims at the time of their contact with the police. Police access victim services on behalf of the victim, to provide them with support, information, referral, and court orientation in the immediate aftermath of the crime, and throughout their journey within the criminal justice system. These services are often located in police divisions,

**FIGURE 10.5** Victims Receiving Formal Assistance, by Gender and Crime Type

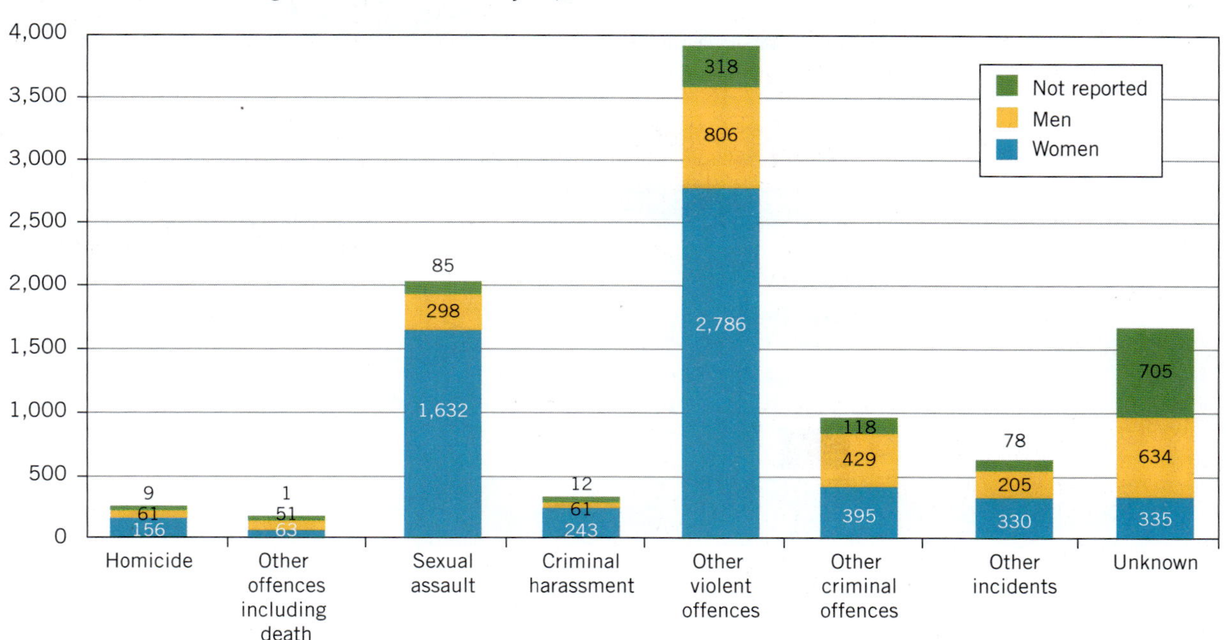


SOURCE: Statistics Canada, Corrections and conditional release statistical overview, March 1, 2012. Reproduced and distributed on an "as is" basis with the permission of Statistics Canada.

Victims of crime are helped by services offered by the public and private sectors.

though they are not always police employees. Police-based victims services rely on both staff and volunteers to respond to calls from the police.

Court-based victim services provide support for those who have become involved in the criminal justice process as either victims or witnesses. They strive to make the court process less intimidating by providing a court orientation to prepare the victim or witness for court attendance. They will accompany the victim, provide updates, and coordinate meetings with the Crown attorney as required. There are court-based victim services that provide support to children who are witnesses or victims. There are provisions that address protecting child witnesses and victims. In some provinces, these are included in the victim bill of rights, and in others they are a part of separate pieces of legislation, such as legislation related to evidence. These provisions again vary amongst the provinces and territories but generally include:

- a person of any age is presumed competent to give evidence in court;
- a child's evidence does not need to be corroborated and is admissible if the child takes an oath, makes a solid affirmation, promises to tell the truth, or if the judge decides the child's testimony is reliable;

**FIGURE 10.6** Victim Services in Canada

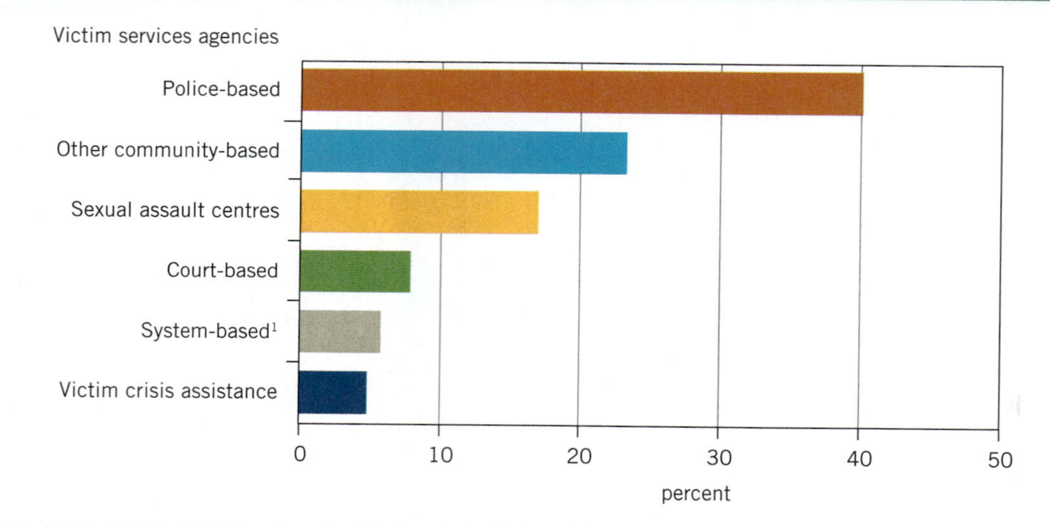


[1]. Services under this model assist victims throughout their contact with the criminal justice system, from the police stage through to the corrections stage. This model can be characterized as one-stop service delivery.

NOTE: Percentages do not add up to 100% due to rounding.

SOURCE: Statistics Canada, Victim Services in Canada, 2007/2008 (see chart 1), March 1, 2012. Reproduced and distributed on an "as is" basis with the permission of Statistics Canada.

- a child's testimony may be accepted on videotape where:
    - the videotape is recorded at a pre-trial examination of the child with parties, lawyers, and the judge present; and
    - the child testifies and agrees with the evidence he or she gave on videotape.
- a child may testify with the assistance of a one-way screen, closed circuit television, or with the accompaniment of a support person; and
- the court has discretion to exclude personal cross-examination of a child by an adverse party; for example, where the adverse party is not represented by a lawyer and wishes to conduct the cross-examination of the child by himself or herself.

These provisions are important for protecting children who may have been a victim of or a witness to a crime, and are meant to safeguard their well-being and protect them from further duress.

Sexual assault centres support those persons who are victims of sexual assault by providing them with counselling and **advocacy**. They also provide education to the general community about the devastation of sexual assault and the myths that exist in our society related to sexual assault.

**advocacy**
the act of providing public support for a particular cause or policy

Child Witness Programs prepare and protect children who are witnesses in court proceedings.

In January 2011, a Toronto police officer made a statement that "women should avoid dressing like sluts in order not to be victimized." This unleashed a series of events, including several "slut walks," intended to raise awareness of the shocking attitude that a woman invites rape through her clothing or actions.

**MYTH VS FACT** **Myths Related to Sexual Assault**

**Myth:** Only females are victims of sexual assault.

**Fact:** According to the Canadian Centre of Justice Statistics (2003), 29 percent of child victims, 12 percent of youth victims, and 8 percent of adult victims of sexual assault reported to 154 police agencies were males.

**Myth:** Women cannot be sexually assaulted by their husbands or boyfriends.

**Fact:** Women have the legal right to say no to any form of sex, even in a marriage or dating relationship. Sexual assault within relationships has been illegal in Canada since 1983, though few women report such incidents to the police.

**Myth:** "She asked for it." Women provoke sexual assaults by their own behaviour or clothing choices.

**Fact:** This myth blames the victim—no one asks to be sexually assaulted. People have the right to be safe from sexual violence. The offender must be held responsible for the crime.

**Myth:** Women lie about being sexually assaulted.

**Fact:** Sexual assault is a vastly under-reported crime. According to the GSS 2009, fewer than 12 percent of sexual assaults are ever reported to the police.

## FINANCIAL COMPENSATION FOR VICTIMS

Each province and territory determines the type of benefits that it offers and the costs for which it will compensate victims. The compensation programs are intended to ease the financial burden that accompanies victimization. The programs are generally available to victims of violent crime as well as the dependents of homicide victims. The types of **compensation** can include:

**compensation**
money given to someone who has suffered loss or injury

- expenses incurred as a result of an injury or death,
- counselling services or expenses,
- prescription drug expenses,
- protective services or expenses (for those who continue to be at risk),
- income support for loss of earnings,
- reimbursement for funeral or transportation costs,
- support of a child who is born out of a sexual assault,
- home medication expenses, and
- crime scene cleaning.

Immediate family members and witnesses are also eligible for certain types of compensation, depending on the circumstances of the offence (Canadian Resource Centre for Victims of Crime). In order to qualify for compensation victims must report the crime to police and then apply for funding based on the time periods specified in each jurisdiction.

In 2007/2008, 45 separate agencies across Canada reported that they awarded $131 million in compensation to victims of crime across Canada (Sauve, 2009). The money was awarded for pain and suffering, loss of support to dependents, medical costs, child maintenance, counselling services, and funeral costs.

**JUST or BUST?**

Should all victims of crime in Canada automatically be granted financial compensation, regardless of the extent of the victimization?

## Victim Satisfaction

LO7

**Victim satisfaction** is measured in several ways. The first measurement of victims' satisfaction relates to their contact with the police. According to the GSS, victims expressed a 64 percent level of satisfaction with the police and a 32 percent level of dissatisfaction. The satisfaction level of victims was higher when the victims were victims of violent crime, compared to the victims of non-violent crime (Statistics Canada, 2005). A Prince Edward Island study on victim satisfaction indicated that when a victim expresses dissatisfaction with the police it is most often because he or she believes the police have minimized the seriousness of the crime or because they failed to keep the victim informed (Bradford, 2005). Over 70 percent of the respondents said that there was a need for more information regarding the progress of their case. This is consistent with research that indicates that when victims are notified of the ongoing developments in their cases, they are more likely to feel that the process has been fair than when they are not notified (Wemmers, 2008). Victims also report that they seek recognition by being heard during the criminal justice process, meaning that they wish to have their views heard (Wemmers and Cyr, 2008).

Historically, victims expressed concerns about their lack of involvement within the criminal justice process. Research indicates that victims generally want to be recognized during the criminal justice trial process (Wemmers and Cyr, 2006) and are often left feeling frustrated when they are not included. This insensitivity to their needs has been referred to as a form of re-victimization. Victims are often faced with a tremendous amount of confusion and uncertainty as they try to understand and navigate a complex criminal justice system. There have been efforts made to respect victims who find themselves involved in the criminal justice system, and to provide them with an improved level of satisfaction; however, it appears that many victims continue to be left out of the process. Victims have also expressed dissatisfaction related to the lack of preparation that they receive for attendance at court and information regarding legal procedures.

"If the criminal justice systems of the world were private companies, they would all go out of business, because half of their main customers—that is, the victims of crime—are dissatisfied with their services"

-JAN VAN DIJK, PRINCIPAL OFFICER OF THE UNITED NATIONS CENTRE FOR INTERNATIONAL CRIME PREVENTION

### Victims Who Fought Back to Improve the World

Gary Rosenfeldt's 16-year-old son Daryn was sexually assaulted and murdered by notorious serial killer Clifford Olsen in 1981. After his family's horrific experience with the criminal justice system, Rosenfeldt began Victims of Violence, an organization that advocates on behalf of victims. The organization lobbied the government and was a strong advocate for introducing significant changes to the system, including using victim impact statements in court, financial assistance programs for victims, and tougher parole legislation.

Priscilla deVilliers' daughter Nina was abducted and murdered in 1991 by Jonathan Yeo, who was out on bail at the time. In 1992, Ms. deVilliers founded CAVEAT—Canadians Against Violence. CAVEAT advocated for reforms to the justice system and educated Canadians on the prevention of violence. In 2001, Ms. deVilliers was appointed Special Advisor to the Ontario Office for Victims of Crime.

Lesley Parrott's 11-year-old daughter Alison was lured from their family home, and then sexually assaulted and murdered in July, 1986. Francis Carl Roy was eventually charged and convicted of the offence in 1999, with the use of DNA evidence. Ms. Parrott was instrumental in developing a national crime prevention campaign called Stay Alert...Stay Safe, which delivered safety messages to over 600,000 children across Canada.

## Chapter Summary

This chapter highlighted the following key areas related to victims in the criminal justice system:

- The role of the victim in the criminal justice system is formalized in two areas—delivering a victim impact statement in the sentencing phase of a trial, and having the right to receive information about a federally incarcerated offender. It is a policy of the Parole Board of Canada to encourage victims to provide victim impact statements during parole board hearings.
- The rate of violent victimization in Canada in 2009 was 118 per 1,000 population, and the rate of household victimization was 237 per 1,000 population.
- One of three victims report incidents of crime to the police.
- The impact of victimization can be traumatic and have a lifelong effect. The impact can be physical, emotional, social, and financial.
- There is international legislation to support the rights of victims as well as national and provincial/territorial legislation. The administration of victim services, including compensation, rests with the provinces and territories and there is some inconsistency across the country. The largest number of victim services is police-based; however, there are also court-based and community-based services.
- Victim satisfaction depends upon the victim's experience. Victims generally want to be recognized and to be kept informed during the trial process.

## Relevant Legislation

*Consolidation of Victims of Crime Act*, R.S.N.W.T. 1988, c. 9 (Supp.)

*Crime Prevention and Victim Services Trust Act*, RSY 2002, c 49

*Victims of Crime Act* R.S.B.C. 1996, c. 478.

*Victims of Crime Act*, RSA 2000, c V-3

*Victims' Bill of Rights* C.C.S.M. c. V55

*Victims' Bill of Rights*, 1995, S.O. 1995, Chapter 6

*An Act Respecting Assistance for Victims of Crime*, RSQ, chapter A-13.2.1

*Victims of Crime Services Act*, 2005 c24; 2009 c35 s1

*Criminal Code*, R.S.C. 1985, c. C-46

*Corrections and Conditional Release Act* S.C. 1992, c. 20

United Nations *Declaration of Basic Principles of Justice for Victims of Crime and Abuse of Power*

## Key Terms

Advocacy

Compensation

General Social Survey

International victimization rate

Victim impact statement

Victim satisfaction

## For Review

1. Who is most likely to be a victim of crime?
2. How are victims represented in the criminal justice system?
3. What is the impact of not reporting crime to the police?
4. What is the rate of victimization in Canada and how does it compare to other countries?
5. What are the services available to victims in Canada?
6. What are the factors that have an impact on the level of victim satisfaction?
7. How are children, who are victims or witnesses, protected in the criminal justice system?

## Thinking Critically

1. Should the status of the victim have any impact on how that victim is viewed by police, the public, or the courts?
2. Do you believe that the rights of the victim clash with the rights of the offender?
3. Should victim services and compensation be consistent across Canada, even though the administration of victim services rests with the provinces and territories?
4. To what extent is the involvement of the victim beneficial to the court process?
5. How could our current legislation be amended in order to provide victims with more support?
6. What measures can be taken to improve the level of victim satisfaction?
7. What measures can be taken to improve the rate of reported crime by victims?

CHAPTER 11

# Emerging Technology in the Criminal Justice System

The Future

NEXT EXIT

## DNA in Action

On July 25, 1986, 11-year-old Alison Parrott was lured from her Toronto home by a male caller who claimed that he was a photographer assigned to take publicity photos for an upcoming track and field meet that Alison was involved with. Excited about the call, Alison headed for Varsity Stadium, a part of the University of Toronto. When she didn't return home that day, her parents alerted the police. Her body was found two days later in a Toronto park—Alison had been raped and strangled. Ten years later, police arrested Francis Carl Roy for Alison's murder, an ex-con who had a lengthy record that included burglary, theft, fraud, assault, and rape. When he murdered Alison he was on parole for having raped two teenage girls, 14 and 19 years of age. It was DNA evidence that conclusively linked Roy to Alison's death. On April 13, 1999, he was convicted of first degree murder and was sentenced to life imprisonment without the possibility of parole for 25 years.

### LEARNING OBJECTIVES

By the end of this chapter, you should be able to:

- **LO1** Describe the impact that emerging technology has had on creating new offences in Canada.
- **LO2** Identify the differences between traditional crime and virtual crime.
- **LO3** Identify specific ways in which law enforcement has benefitted from emerging technology.
- **LO4** Explain the impact of social media on law enforcement.

Alison Parrott is buried at Mount Pleasant Cemetery in Toronto, Ontario.

King's Mill Park: The location where Alison's remains were discovered.

## LO1 Emerging Technology and the Creation of New Crimes

Introducing new forms of technology has resulted in the creation of a host of new crimes that are technology based. The new crime is often referred to as **cybercrime**. As a result, law enforcement agencies have created new units designed to respond to and keep ahead of the new technology. Cybercrime is defined as "a criminal offence involving a computer as the object of the crime, or the tool used to commit a material component of the offence" (Melanie Kowalski, 2002). Offences that can now be committed through the use of a computer (or like tool) include **child pornography**, criminal harassment, fraud, intellectual property violations, and the sale of illegal goods. Other offences related to the use of computer technology include **hacking** or unauthorized use of computer systems, defacing of web sites, and creating and disseminating computer **viruses**. Offences such as cyberbullying and child luring have also emerged and grown, along with the new technology. It is anticipated that as technology continues to develop, so too will new crimes.

Incidents of cyberbullying are seldom reported to the police

### CYBERBULLYING

The 2010 Canadian Internet Use Survey indicated that 8 out of 10 Canadian households had Internet access (The Daily, 2011). British Columbia had the highest rate of household Internet access at 84 percent, followed by Alberta (83 percent) and Ontario (81 percent). The relationship between Internet use and victimization is evident in the 2009 General Social Survey (GSS) on Victimization. The survey indicates that 7 percent of Internet users, aged 18 and older, self-reported that they have been a victim of cyberbullying. **Cyberbullying** is defined as receiving threatening or aggressive emails or instant messages, or being the target of hateful comments. Users of social networking sites and chat sites are three times more likely to be cyberbullied than those who do not use the sites (Perreault, 2011). About 1 in 10 adults that live in a household that includes a child reported a case of cyberbullying against at least one of the children in their household. Of the child victims, girls were more likely to a victim of cyberbullying and the ages of 12–13 are the ages when most cyberbullying incidents took place. Children who are victims of cyberbullying are most likely to be bullied by a classmate. Incidents of cyberbullying are seldom reported to the police or to the Internet provider. The most common response to cyberbullying is to block messages from the sender, meet with school officials, or to limit the victim's access to the Internet.

**cyberbullying**
receiving threatening or aggressive emails or instant messages, or being the target of hateful comments

### LURING A CHILD THROUGH THE INTERNET

Luring a child through the Internet was introduced as a criminal offence in 2002. It is an offence that presents significant challenges to the police and to parents because in some respects, the Internet affords perpetrators of this offence a degree of anonymity. The *Criminal Code* defines Luring a Child in section 172.1:

## FIGURE 11.1 Adult Internet Users Who Self-Reported Cyberbullying, by Relationship to the Bully, 2009

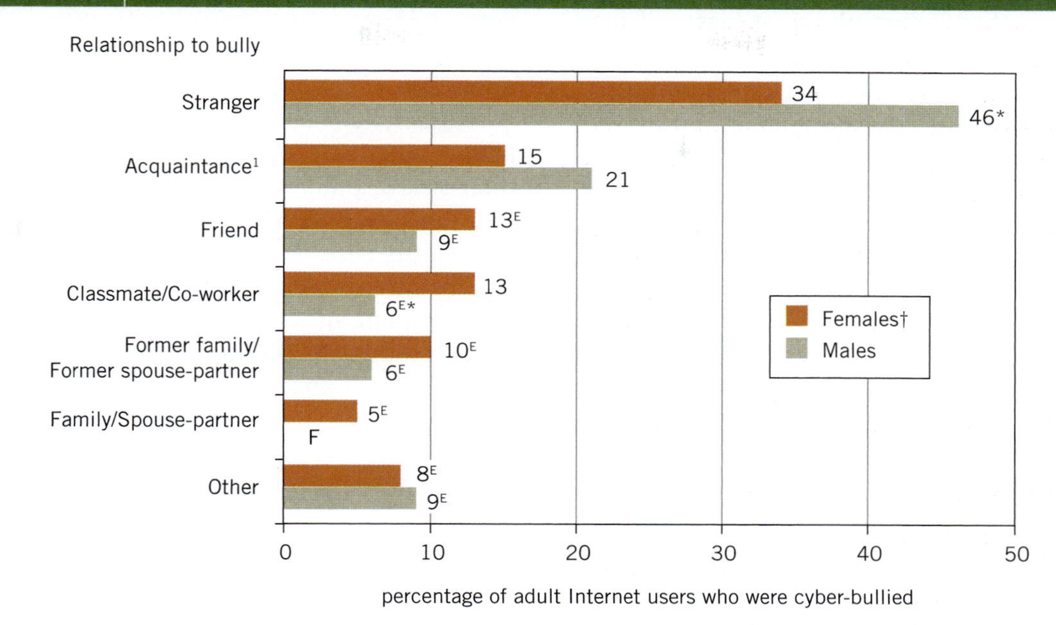


† reference category
E use with caution
F too unreliable to be published
* significantly different from reference category ($p < 0.05$)
[1]. Includes neighbour, acquaintance, Internet friend and known by sight only.
Note: Excludes data for Yukon, the Northwest Territories and Nunavut.

SOURCE: Self-reported Internet victimization in Canada, 2009, http://www.statcan.gc.ca/pub/85-002-x/2011001/article/11530-eng.htm, April 1, 2012. Reproduced and distributed on an "as is" basis with the permission of Statistics Canada.

**172.1** (1) Every person commits an offence who, by means of a computer system within the meaning of subsection 342.1(2), communicates with

(*a*) a person who is, or who the accused believes is, under the age of eighteen years, for the purpose of facilitating the commission of an offence under subsection 153(1), section 155 or 163.1, subsection 212(1) or (4) or section 271, 272 or 273 with respect to that person;

(*b*) a person who is, or who the accused believes is, under the age of 16 years, for the purpose of facilitating the commission of an offence under section 151 or 152, subsection 160(3) or 173(2) or section 280 with respect to that person; or

(*c*) a person who is, or who the accused believes is, under the age of 14 years, for the purpose of facilitating the commission of an offence under section 281 with respect to that person.

(2) Every person who commits an offence under subsection (1) is guilty of

(*a*) an indictable offence and liable to imprisonment for a term of not more than ten years; or

(*b*) an offence punishable on summary conviction and liable to imprisonment for a term not exceeding eighteen months.

(3) Evidence that the person referred to in paragraph (1)(*a*), (*b*) or (*c*) was represented to the accused as being under the age of eighteen years, sixteen years or fourteen years, as the case may be, is, in the absence of evidence to the contrary, proof that the accused believed that the person was under that age.

(4) It is not a defence to a charge under paragraph (1)(*a*), (*b*) or (*c*) that the accused believed that the person referred to in that paragraph was at least eighteen years of age, sixteen years or fourteen years of age, as the case may be, unless the accused took reasonable steps to ascertain the age of the person.

Luring a Child is a hybrid offence and it is one that takes into consideration the perceived age of the child. There is also a clear statement that it is not a defence for the accused to have "believed" the child to be an older age, unless the accused took reasonable steps to ascertain the child's age.

Statistics Canada states that between 2006 and 2007, there were 464 reported incidents of child luring over the Internet in Canada. The accused was identified in about one third of the cases only, leaving 64 percent of the cases unsolved. Of those accused who were identified, about 6 in 10 were males between the ages of 18 and 34. Though the clearance rate is low, of those who were prosecuted during the two year period studied, approximately three quarters of the cases resulted in a finding of guilt and in half of those cases the offender received a custodial sentence averaging 374 days in length (Statistics Canada, 2009). Most people charged with child luring (87 percent) were also charged with other offences, most commonly an invitation to sexual touching or child pornography.

Researchers suggest that there are specific behaviours that youth engage in that may increase their risk of online sexual exploitation. Wittreich, Grewall and Sinclair (2008) caution that behaviours such as sharing personal information, posting photos online, chatting with strangers, and visiting adult sites and chat rooms may increase risk. A study of 5,200 children and youth in grades 4 to 11 across Canada, determined that 3 in 10 used their real names and addresses to sign up for free email or to create a social media profile. Some of the students (16 percent) admitted to intentionally visiting pornographic web sites and 9 percent had visited an adult chat room in the previous year (Media Awareness Network, 2005). Children may accidentally end up on pornographic sites, mainly because many of the sites embed popular, child-friendly terms or names that a child is likely to search.

**FIGURE 11.2** Number of Child Luring Incidents Cleared by Police in 2007

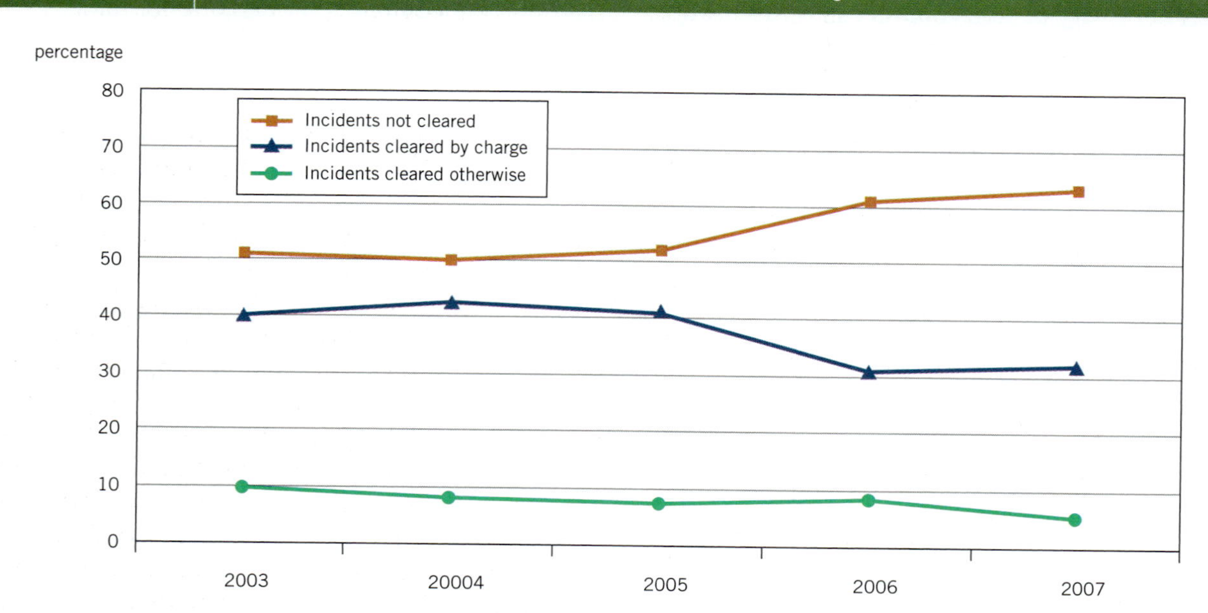


SOURCE:STATISTICS Canada, Child luring through the Internet, April 1, 2012. Reproduced and distributed on an "as is" basis with the permission of Statistics Canada.

## MYTH VS FACT

"The myth of being anonymous on the Internet is dead. We need to stop assuming that our actions online exist in a virtual world where we can remain safe and anonymous. Governments from across the world, in countries like US, China, India and Brazil, have asked for and even subpoenaed information from the search engines to track citizens doing everything from espionage, terror, murder, etc. And guess what? Search engines comply."

VIKRAM, "Ending the Myth of Online Anonymity, Once and For All", January 19, 2010, http://www.evisionworldwide.com/learning/myth-online-anonymity/ (August 2012)

Individuals are often reminded that anonymity on the Internet is indeed a myth. It is possible to trace one's activities on search engines, in chat rooms, and through email messaging. Users are regularly reminded to govern their online actions accordingly.

## CHILD PORNOGRAPHY ON THE INTERNET

In 2002, the *Criminal Code* amended the definition of child pornography to include the use of Internet for the purpose of committing child pornography offences. Law enforcement agencies have created special units and expertise to battle child pornography. In 2010, there were 2,190 police-reported incidents of child pornography (an increase of 36 percent) with a rate of 6 per 100,000 population (The Daily, 2011).

As outlined in the *Criminal Code* (section 163.1), the term "child pornography" refers to any written material or visual representation, whether photographic, film, or video, made by any mechanical or electronic means, that:

- shows or depicts a person who is, or appears to be, under the age of eighteen, engaging in (or depicted as engaging in) explicit sexual activities
- has as its dominant characteristic the depiction, for sexual purposes, of a sexual organ or the anal region of a person under the age of eighteen years
- advocates or counsels sexual activity with a person under the age of eighteen years

The *Criminal Code* makes it an offence to:

- make, print, publish or possess for the purpose of publication any child pornography (section 163.1(2)),
- transmit, make available, distribute, sell, advertise, import, export or possess for the purpose of transmission, making available, distribution, sale, advertising or exportation any child pornography (section 163.1(3)), and
- possess any child pornography (section 163.1(4))

Profiting from the sale and distribution of child pornography is an aggravating factor that may be taken into consideration by the court (*Criminal Code*, s. 163.1(4.3)).

The *Criminal Code* recognizes that there are exceptions to the offence and in section 163.1 declares:

> (6) No person shall be convicted of an offence under this section if the act that is alleged to constitute the offence
> (*a*) has a legitimate purpose related to the administration of justice or to science, medicine, education or art; and
> (*b*) does not pose an undue risk of harm to persons under the age of eighteen years.

## ONLINE FRAUD

Fraud committed online is a new and growing area of crime. The Canadian Anti-Fraud Centre (CAFC) was created in 1993 and is jointly managed by the RCMP, the Competition Bureau Canada, and the Ontario Provincial Police; it is Canada's central fraud depository. It tracks online fraud and educates the public about **Mass Marketing Fraud**, including internationally-based scams. According to the CAFC, they received over 126,000 calls in 2010, an increase over the previous year (Annual Report, 2010). Telephone and facsimile machine communication was reported as the most prevalent method of soliciting Canadians; however, the use of email, the Internet, and text messaging resulted in the highest dollar loss (Annual Report, 2010).

**Mass Marketing Fraud**
a campaign that targets large groups of people via the Internet, phone, or mail

The RCMP reports that some of the common online scams include:

1. The Inheritance Scheme: You receive an email from a stranger seeking your assistance in moving large amounts of money into your bank account and you are promised a percentage for simply providing your bank account details. Your bank account is then taken over and funds are depleted.
2. Lottery Emails: You receive an email advising you that you have won a lottery and you are asked to provide a bank account number to deposit the winnings, or to pay a fee up front (taxes or a security deposit) in order to receive the winnings.
3. Advance Fee Loans: You receive an email advising you that you are guaranteed a loan, with bad credit or no credit. They request an upfront fee that you send and then never hear from the company again.
4. Scareware: Your computer is frozen after receiving a pop-up message warning you that you have been associated with child pornography. The message claims to be from CSIS or the RCMP, and advises you to pay a sum of money to unlock the computer.

### PHISHING

**Phishing** is when an Internet user receives fraudulent emails that represent the sender as a reputable and legitimate organization requesting personal information. It represents a significant security risk because unknowing users send personal information, believing that the request is legitimate. In 2009, 39 percent of all Internet users reported experiencing at least one phishing attempt. Internet users who are aged 35 to 44, who possess a university degree, have a personal income over $100,000, and who live in a metropolitan area are more likely to be subject to phishing attempts (Perreault, 2011). Once personal information is received through a phishing attempt, identity theft and/or fraud usually follows. Many phishing attempts look credible. Figure 11.3 is an example of a phishing attempt detected by Public Safety Canada's Canadian Cyber Incident Response Centre.

**phishing**
fraudulent emails that represent the sender as a reputable and legitimate organization requesting personal information

**FIGURE 11.3** An Example of Phishing

Dear Tax Payer,

You are entitled to your tax refund now. The tax refund is $241.34. You are required to follow the link below to login to our secure Epass site with your Social Insurance number and complete the required information in order for your refund to be processed.

http://www.cra-arc.gc.ca/gol-ged/gov/confirmtaxrefund?REF128328-Jh28877a

Yours sincerely,

Gilles Dompierre, Department of Revenue, Canada

SOURCE: Canada Revenue Agency screenshot, URL: http://www.publicsafety.gc.ca/prg/le/bs/_images/cra-eng.jpg. Canada Revenue Agency of Canada. Reproduced with the permission of the Minister of Public Works and Government Services, 2012.

The most common security issue for Internet users is the infections caused by a virus, spyware, or adware. Two thirds of Internet users report having had problems related to Internet security, including those who run antivirus programs. In order to combat the problem, 91 percent of Internet users possess an antivirus program. Many Internet users also engage in regular habits to prevent problems, such as:

- dealing with well-known organizations only,
- deleting emails from unknown sources, and
- clearing the browser's cache and deleting cookies.

Surprisingly, only 33 percent of users report that they regularly change their passwords.

### IDENTITY THEFT

**Identity theft** involves the theft of an individual's personal information usually with the intention to use that information for a criminal purpose. Identity fraud is using another person's (living or dead) identity information in a fraudulent manner. In 2010, the *Criminal Code* (section 402.1) was amended to make it a crime to posses another person's identity information for criminal purposes. According to the CAFC, Canadians reported $9.5 million dollars in losses as a result of identity theft in 2010 (Annual Report, 2010). The RCMP said that there are many incidents of identity theft and fraud that go unreported. Once your identity is stolen (either through phishing or actual documents), the information can be used to access bank accounts, open new bank accounts, transfer bank balances, apply for loans, credit cards, make purchases, obtain passports, or receive government benefits. The RCMP also reports that the use of stolen identities can facilitate organized criminal and terrorist activities (RCMP, 2011).

**identity theft**
stealing someone's personal information in order to use that information for a criminal purpose

### INTERNET BANKING FRAUD

Banking online has become a common occurrence—in 2009, over two thirds of Canadians reported that they did at least some banking online (GSS, 2009). The self-reported level of bank fraud in 2009 was 4 percent of all Internet users, with British Columbia and Ontario having the highest number of victims, at 5 percent of their Internet users. Of those who made online purchases, 14 percent reported that they encountered problems, though the problems were lessened when the online transactions were made with well-known organizations (Perreault, 2011).

## PROMOTING HATE ON THE INTERNET

The Internet has provided a new platform for the promotion of hate. In 2009, 16 percent of Internet users reported that they were exposed to content online that promoted hate or violence. The groups

## FIGURE 11.4 Victims of Online Bank Fraud

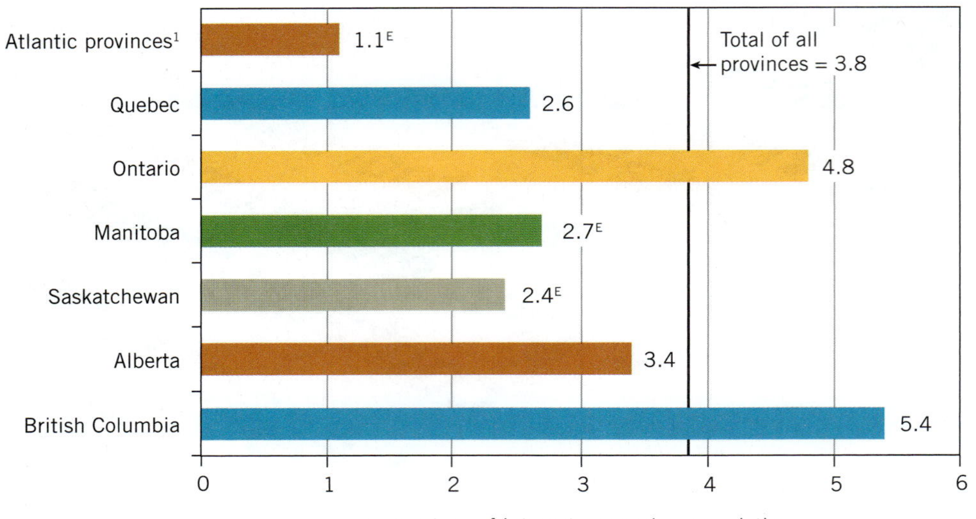


[E] use with caution

1. Due to small numbers, Atlantic provinces were grouped. See Table 1 for data for individual provinces.

NOTE: Percentages are based upon Canadians who used the Internet in the 12 months preceding the survey. Excludes data for Yukon, the Northwest Territories and Nunavut.

SOURCE: Statistics Canada, Self-reported Internet victimization in Canada, 2009, April 1, 2012. Reproduced and distributed on an "as is" basis with the permission of Statistics Canada.

## FIGURE 11.5 Internet Users Who Came Across Hate Content on the Internet, by Target Group of the Hate Content, 2009

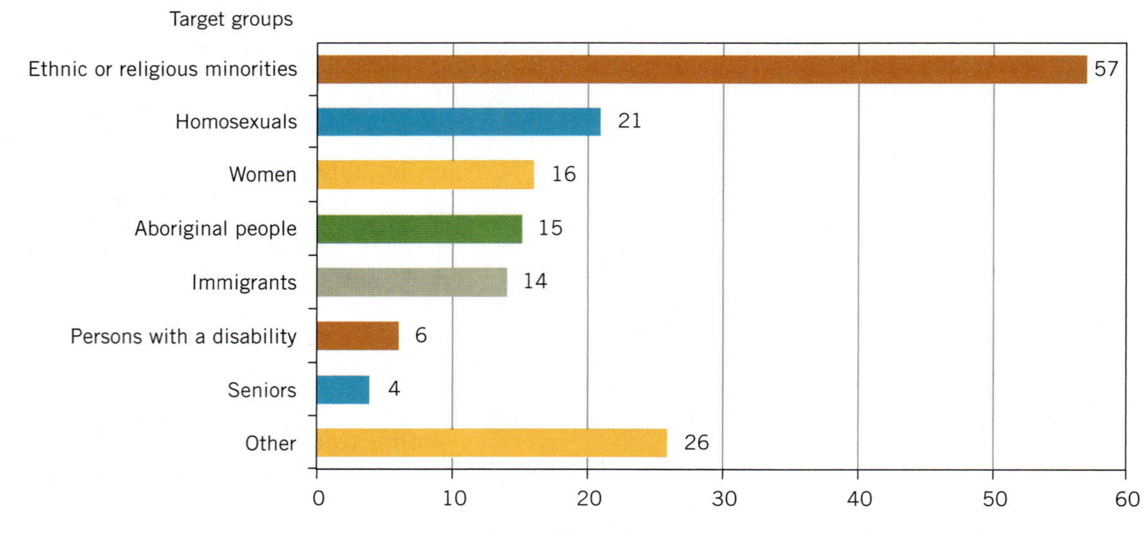


Note: Percentages are based upon Internet users who came across hate content in the 12 months preceding the survey. Categories are not mutually exclusive. Respondents who came across content promoting hate or violence toward a specific group could report more than one target group, therefore totals do not add up to 100 percent. Excludes data for Yukon, the Northwest Territories and Nunavut.

SOURCE: Statistics Canada, Self-reported Internet victimization in Canada, 2009, April 1, 2012. Reproduced and distributed on an "as is" basis with the permission of Statistics Canada.

"Most experts agree that the IT revolution represents the most significant global transformation since the Industrial Revolution beginning in the mid-eighteenth century... Biotechnology will drive medical breakthroughs that will enable the world's wealthiest people to improve their health and increase their longevity dramatically... Terrorists, proliferators, narcotraffickers, and organized criminals will take advantage of the new high-speed information environment and other advances in technology to integrate their illegal activities and compound their threat to stability and security around the world"

-GLOBAL TRENDS, 2015, NATIONAL INTELLIGENCE COUNCIL 2000 (IN SCHAEFER, J.A., 2007)

targeted online parallel those groups that are targeted by hate in general, with ethnic or religious groups being the most common target. The other groups reported by Internet users to be targets of hate content included homosexuals (reported by 21 percent of Internet users who came across hate content), women (16 percent), Aboriginal people (15 percent), and immigrants (14 percent).

## Traditional Crime versus Virtual Crime

Through the introduction of new technology, traditional crimes now have virtual counterparts. The virtual world has created a new landscape where one's physical presence is no longer required in order to commit a crime. Crimes now

**TABLE 11.1 Traditional Crime versus Virtual Crime**

| Traditional Crime | Virtual Crime | Description |
| --- | --- | --- |
| Racketeering | Virtual Extortion | Traditionally, business owners had to pay protection money to organized crime groups to purchase protection services against criminal harm. Today, with evolving technology, criminals make online stores pay protection money against virtual attacks. |
| Bank Robbery | Hacking | Traditionally, criminal gangs robbed money from banks and secured vans. Today, criminals hack into bank computer systems and wire funds electronically to payment systems. |
| Credit Card Theft | Credit Card Theft Online | Traditionally, criminals went through people's garbage to steal their credit card statements and utility bills, and then make fraudulent use of their victims' identity. Today, cybercriminals steal thousands of credit card numbers at once by hacking company databases. |
| Boiler Room Share Scam | Pump-and-dump Share Scam | Traditionally, criminals posing as brokers sold company stocks by phone at artificially inflated prices. Today, these criminals buy company stocks and then issue falsified financial statements on shared sites to inflate stock prices and sell them for profit. |
| Fraudulent Calls | Phishing | Traditionally, criminals called their victims posing as bank security personnel to obtain the victim's personal information. Today, criminals send fraudulent emails, which are deceptive replicas of emails from legitimate financial institutions, to get users to disclose their personal information. |
| Burglars | Computer Viruses | Traditionally, burglars knocked directly at their victim's door to create a diversion while an accomplice went in through the back door and stole valuables. Today, the same process is used online, with malware used to access a computer and infect it with a virus. |

SOURCE: © 2012, Royal Canadian Mounted Police.

cross borders via the Internet, and they target numerous victims at once. The RCMP identified traditional crimes and their virtual counterparts, as listed in Table 11.1.

## LO3 Emerging Technology and Its Impact on Investigation, Enforcement, and Identification

New technology has had an impact on the criminal justice system—on investigation, enforcement, and identification. The new technology has given law enforcement agencies additional tools to support them in investigations. In addition, there have been several attempts at creating new non-lethal devices to support law enforcement officers. Some of the new technological advances are profiled in this chapter.

### DNA

DNA is probably the most well-known technological advance. **DNA** refers to deoxyribonucleic acid, the hereditary material that exists in all humans. Every one of a person's cells contains the same DNA, located in the cell nucleus. DNA is a long, double-stranded molecule that looks like a twisted rope. It is the foundation of a person's genetic makeup. DNA evidence can be collected and preserved for the purpose of identifying suspects. With the exception of identical twins, DNA is unique to each human being. DNA can be obtained from a sample of blood, semen, skin cells, tissue, organs, muscle, brain cells, bone, teeth, hair, saliva, mucus, perspiration, fingernails, urine, feces, and other types of human samples. DNA is extracted from the sample and then used for identification purposes. Canada has a DNA data bank created through the authority of the *DNA Identification Act*, June, 2000. This legislation permits a judge to order persons convicted of certain designated offences to provide blood, mouth, or hair samples for the purpose of extracting their DNA profiles. In April, 2011, it became mandatory for convicted sex offenders to provide a sample of their DNA to the databank. The National DNA Data Bank supports law enforcement by:

- linking crimes where there are no suspects;
- helping to identify suspects;
- eliminating suspects where there is no match between crime scene DNA and a DNA profile in the National DNA Data Bank; and,
- determining whether a serial offender is involved.

The DNA Data Bank has assisted in solving numerous crimes. The 2010/11 Annual Report indicates that there are 279,293 DNA profiles contained in the data bank and that 21,006 investigations were assisted by the data bank since 2000—4,239 in 2010 alone (National DNA Data Bank, 2010/11). These matches involved offences such as murder, sexual assault, attempted murder, break and enter, assault, and others.

### DNA AND WRONGFUL CONVICTIONS

DNA analysis of evidence obtained at crime scenes has played a large role in identifying the fact that there have indeed been several wrongful convictions in recent history. The indisputable science of DNA evidence can make a clear connection between an offender and a crime. DNA first appeared in courtrooms in the 1980s. One of DNA's clear strengths is that it uses a statistical approach based on population genetics theory and empirical testing, whereby matches are evaluated between a suspect and a crime scene based on the probability of random matches across the population (Saks and Koehler, 2005). Wrongful convictions that were overturned in Canada thanks to the introduction of DNA evidence include those of Donald Marshall Jr., David Milgaard, Kyle Unger, and Guy Paul Morin.

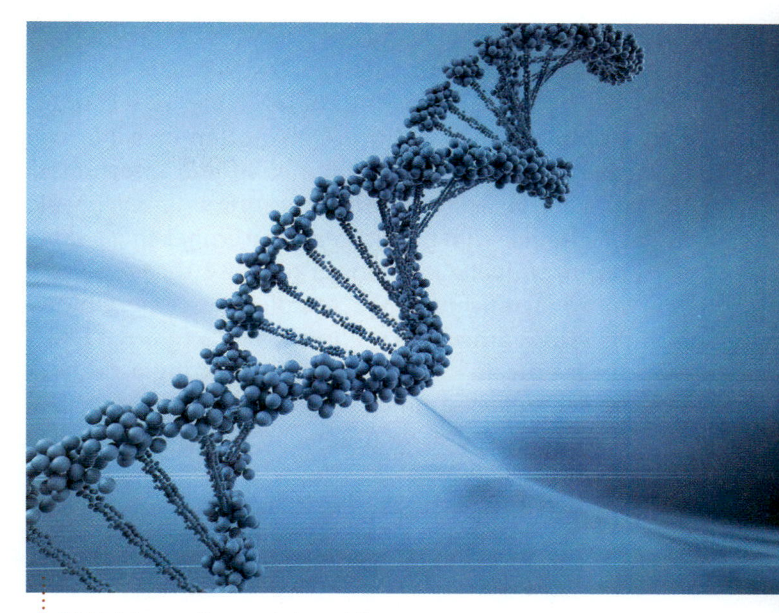

DNA (deoxyribonucleic acid).

## FLASHBACK:
### FORENSIC HISTORY OF DNA: HIGHLIGHTS

**1983** A young woman was found sexually assaulted and murdered in a small town near Leicester, United Kingdom. After an intensive police investigation, the case remained unsolved. Three years later, under similar circumstance and in a nearby town, another young woman was sexually assaulted and murdered.
A suspect was eventually identified in the second case. Police investigators sent samples of forensic evidence from both crime scenes and a sample of the suspect's blood to Dr. Alec Jeffreys, a prominent British scientist conducting research in evolution using DNA. Dr. Jeffreys was able to tell the police two things:

- The DNA evidence collected at both crime scenes came from the same person (thereby linking the crime scenes and identifying a serial offender); and
- The suspect's DNA did not match the DNA evidence from the crime scenes and the first prominent use of forensic DNA evidence led to an exoneration of an individual who confessed to the crime.

Blood samples were later taken from more than 4,500 men in the surrounding communities. A DNA match was found, and one man was convicted of both murders/sexual assaults.

**1989** In early April, the RCMP first used DNA analysis in an investigation of a sexual assault in Ottawa, Ontario. The victim visually identified her assailant but the suspect denied any involvement in the sexual assault. DNA analysis later confirmed the suspect was the perpetrator. In mid-trial, but after the DNA evidence was presented, the suspect suddenly changed his plea to guilty.

**1995** Parliament made history when Bill C-104 was unanimously passed in a single day, which enabled a judge to issue a warrant allowing police to obtain DNA evidence from suspects in a criminal investigation.

**1998** A special DNA-typing task force led by the RCMP, which included scientists from both the RCMP and the Centre of Forensic Sciences, used DNA analysis to help identify human remains from the Swissair Flight 111 disaster.

**2000** Canada's National DNA Data Bank was launched, as well as the proclamation of Bill C-3, enabling a judge to authorize collection of DNA samples from offenders convicted of designated offences.

SOURCE: http://www.rcmp-grc.gc.ca/nddb-bndg/histo-eng.htm.

### TRACE DNA

**Trace DNA**, also referred to as touch DNA, is when only trace amounts of DNA are used in order to make a match. Trace DNA, often invisible, can be collected, and then amplified and interpreted. Trace DNA allows for generating a larger profile of suspects who have committed crimes that simply require touch, as opposed to those that require a more significant DNA sample like semen, blood or saliva. Trace DNA allows one to remove DNA from objects that were touched during a robbery or a break and enter. Trace DNA, introduced in 1997 (Raymond, van Oorschot, Walsh and Roux, 2007), is a new innovation that continues to be studied and researched by scientists.

## BIOMETRICS

**Biometrics** refers to a form of identification whereby unique features are used to recognize or confirm a person's identity. The most common form of biometric identification is fingerprinting. Fingerprinting has advanced from the days of ink rolling, to the use of new automated systems that capture and store fingerprints in a database. Other forms of biometric identification include DNA matching, iris and retinal scanning, voice recognition, handwriting recognition, facial recognition, ear shape, body odour, gait pattern, and vein pattern.

Biometric identification can provide assistance to various sectors in our society. The banking industry, the information technology sector, telecommunications, health and social services, as well as various consumer products, have all taken advantage of the technological advances in biometrics. Law enforcement and correctional services have used biometrics to confirm the identity of persons during court appearances, to gain admission to correctional facilities, as well as while tracking offenders. Biometrics is used in video and audio surveillance in order to identify individuals.

Voice authentication relies on digitizing the speaker's recorded voice and then using it for authentication in future (Onyema, 2011). The iris, also unique to each person, has various patterns and lines that can be captured and used to authenticate identity. The pattern remains stable throughout a person's entire lifetime, enabling long-term authenticity.

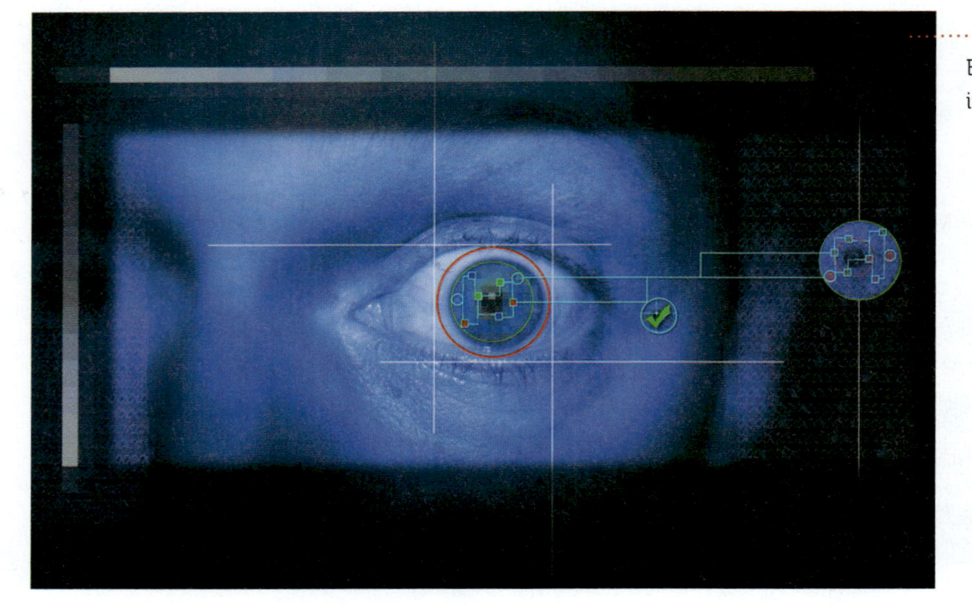

Biometric identification—iris/retinal scanning.

#### THE BIOMETRIC PASSPORT

By spring 2013, all new Canadian passports will be ePassports, which will include an embedded electronic chip. The chip will include personal information about the carrier, as well as a country-specific signature that proves that it was issued by the government of Canada. The chip is secured—it cannot be altered and can only be read within 10 centimetres of the passport reader. The ePassport will include holographic images and a hidden photo of the bearer that can only be viewed under ultraviolet light. The ePassport is intended to increase the accuracy of identifying people at border crossings.

### 3D CRIME SCENE TECHNOLOGY

New technology now allows three dimensional (3D) crime scene reconstruction. Using computer and photographic technology, investigators can create diagrams with 3D surfaces. The purpose of the diagrams is to allow for a more accurate presentation of evidence such as bullet holes, blood spatter, and distance assessment. A more accurate presentation can be helpful to a judge or jury when hearing about evidence. Specific software and an accurate measuring device or scanner are used to capture the data to create a 3D view of the scene.

### FORENSIC DATABASES

Databases designed to assist law enforcement agencies are not new. The automated fingerprint identification system (AFIS) is a database of fingerprints, and the DNA database stores DNA information. Both the sex offender registry and the gun registry are also examples of databases. There are a number of lesser-known forensic databases that were created to help law enforcement investigators by coordinating information in a central location. Some of the current databases include:

#### INTEGRATED BALLISTIC IDENTIFICATION SYSTEM: IBIS

This database was adopted by the American Bureau of Alcohol, Tobacco, Firearms and Explosives (ATF) as the platform for the National Integrated Ballistic Information Network program.

Recreating a crime scene with 3D technology.

It contains bullet and cartridge casings that have been retrieved from crime scenes and test-fires of guns found at a crime scene or on a suspect. The database allows for the comparison of bullet-to-bullet finds.

### PAINT DATA QUERY: PDQ

This database is maintained by the RCMP, and contains the chemical compositions of paint from most domestic and foreign car manufacturers and the majority of vehicles marketed in North America after 1973. The German Forensic Institute and the Japanese National Police Agency added samples to the database in 1998. The paint layers of an automotive paint job are examined and coded into the database. These samples are then compared against any paint sample that is retrieved from a crime scene or a suspect's vehicle.

### NATIONAL AUTOMOTIVE PAINT FILE

The United States Federal Bureau of Investigation maintains a database of over 40,000 automotive paint received from manufacturers.

### GLASS EVIDENCE REFERENCE DATABASE

The United States Department of Defence and the United States Department of State maintain a database of over 700 glass samples from manufacturers, distributors, and vehicle junkyards. The database contains an elemental analysis of glass to determine if there is a match with case samples.

## SHOE AND BOOT PRINTS

There are a number of databases that track shoe prints. These databases assess the impression of the footwear by analyzing pattern, size, damage, and wear. The information can then be used to match suspects in custody or at crime scenes.

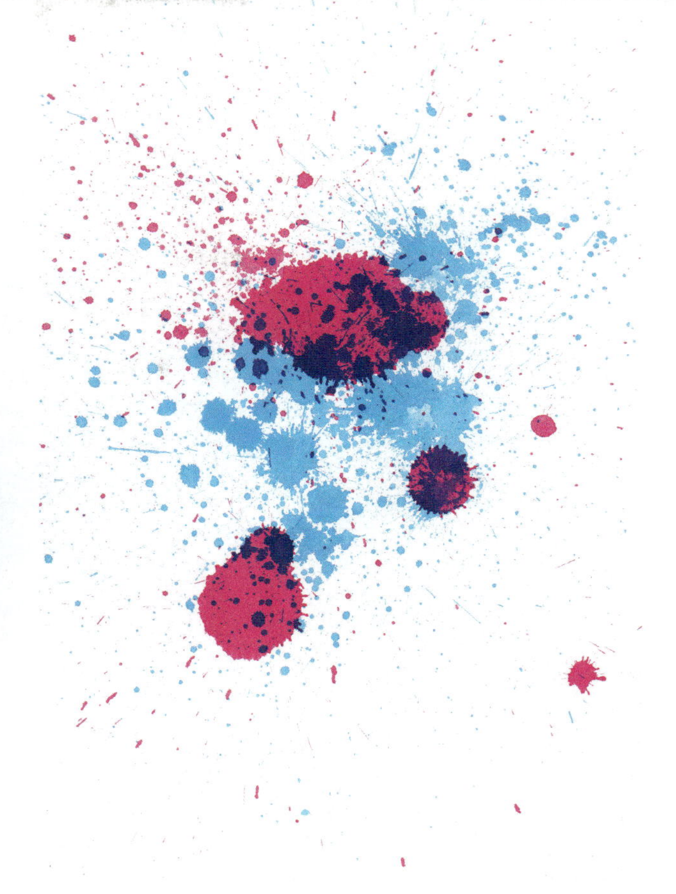

## INTERNATIONAL INK LIBRARY

This database is maintained by the United States Secret Service and the United States Internal Revenue Service. It includes more than 9,500 inks, beginning in 1920. Each year pen and ink manufacturers are asked to submit their new ink formulas, which are chemically tested and added to the database. Samples can be chemically analyzed and compared with library specimens.

## TREADMATE

This database is maintained in the United Kingdom and contains information on over 5,000 vehicle tires and tire tread patterns. The treads are coded for pattern features such as waves, lines, diamonds, zigzags, curves, and blocks.

## FOCUS ON The Incapacitating Flashlight

The United States Department of Homeland Security has introduced a non-lethal alternative to firearms—a flashlight that can be used to disorient subjects by inducing nausea and vomiting. The LED flashlight shoots out pulses of light, which change in colour and duration, and result in a range of responses from vertigo to nausea. The disorientation wears off in moments, allowing for the subject to be apprehended without using greater force. The flashlight is most effective at night and when the subject is directly in front of the officer.

SOURCE: http://www.technologyreview.com/files/11797/Maglite_x220.jpg.

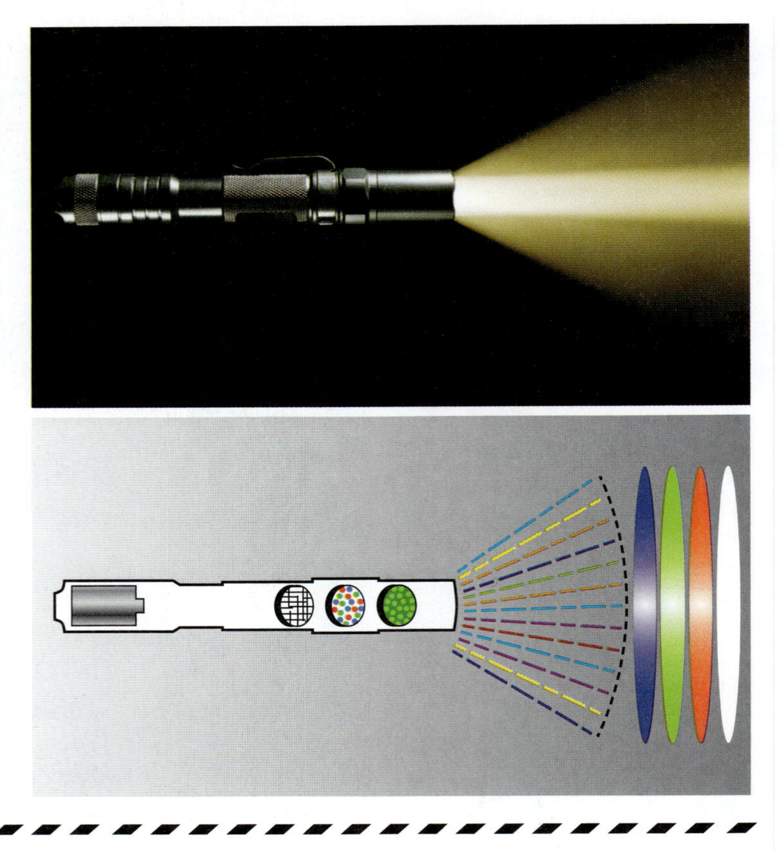

## CELLPHONES

The near-universal use of cellphones has had an impact on law enforcement. Law enforcement agencies are training their officers on that impact by providing them with courses on digital media, enabling them to better investigate cases where mobile devices are used to commit a crime. Tracking cellphone use and collecting and analyzing digital media are examined. Police must prove that digital media evidence is collected and preserved in a way that is consistent with the rules and regulations that currently exist. Police must also be able to gather electronic evidence that exists at crime scenes, including computers, cellphones, and other electronic devices. As the technology continues to advance, so too does the need to update police personnel. Cellphones are used to facilitate certain types of crimes. In her examination of cellphone use and crime, McEwen (2010) observes:

> …there are a number of ways that the features of mobile phones accommodate the social practices of those involved in drug-dealing. Mobile phones are used for social coordination and reorganization in the buying and selling of drugs, and mobile phone use indicates the performative features of a network of actors as opposed to that of single individuals. Finally, the use of coded content in mobile communication assists the buyers and sellers in insulating their activities and collective identities from law enforcement.

Excessive cellphone use has resulted in cellphone bans for drivers, introduced in several jurisdictions throughout North America. All Canadian provinces and territories are bound by similar legislation. Newfoundland and Labrador was the first to ban hand-held use of cellphones in 2002, and the last jurisdiction to pass the

Cellphones, a new form of contraband, are seized from inmates.

legislation was the Northwest Territories in 2012 (CBC, 2011).

Cellphones have created significant security issues for correctional facilities, where they are smuggled into the institutions and used to facilitate unauthorized communications. The unauthorized communication allows for engaging in criminal activity from within the prison (Seglins and MacNaughton, 2010). The cellphones are also used within the inmate economy, where inmates "pay" the inmate owner of the cellphone to make calls. One cellphone seized by prison officials had logged 7,000 calls in a month. Since traditional detection methods have been inefficient, prisons are now looking at the ability to jam or silence unauthorized telephone transmissions within the institutions.

**TABLE 11.2 Number of Cellphones Seized by Corrections Canada, by Region**

| Region | 2007–08 | 2008–09 | 2009–10 | Total |
|---|---|---|---|---|
| Atlantic | 1 | 0 | 1 | 2 |
| Quebec | 0 | 3 | 9 | 12 |
| Ontario | 1 | 13 | 8 | 22 |
| Prairies | 3 | 23 | 43 | 69 |
| Pacific | 2 | 8 | 14 | 24 |
| Total | 7 | 47 | 75 | 129 |

SOURCE: Correctional Service Canada.

## The Impact of Social Media on Law Enforcement LO4

In recent history, we have seen several examples of the impact social media can have on law enforcement. In the aftermath of the Vancouver riot that followed the Vancouver Canucks' loss to the Boston Bruins on June 17, 2011, social media was used to help track down suspects who had engaged in illegal activity. Photos and videos appeared on Tumblr, Flicker, Facebook, and Twitter, many in real time. Within 10 minutes of the end of the game, a Facebook page entitled "Vancouver Riot Pics: Post Your Photos" appeared and people did just that (Vancouver Sun, 2011). The page was "Liked" by 70,000 people within 24 hours, and hundreds of photos appeared of people looting stores, setting fires, and destroying property. While some posted pictures, others reported social media users who were bragging about their riot-related activities. The Vancouver police thanked the public for its assistance and used the volunteered evidence throughout the investigation. Photos and videos were also posted by the Vancouver Police Department, looking for the identity of rioters (Vancouver Riot 2011—Help Identify Suspects, Integrated Riot Investigation Team; https://riot2011.vpd.ca). Social media provided the police with a roadmap of the destruction and enabled them to go on to charge 78 people, as of March 2012 (Vancouver Police, 2012).

Police services have begun to use social media, primarily Facebook and Twitter, to varying degrees across the country. Police services in western Canada are the earliest adopters of the technology, with over 70 percent of them using social media, compared to Ontario at 36 percent and Quebec at 9 percent (Vancouver Sun, 2012). Police are recognizing that social media can become a tool to engage the community, gather intelligence, and investigate crime. Facebook stings have been used to apprehend online criminals engaged in child pornography and other online crimes. The use of social media in law enforcement activities does have its critics—both police and civilians have expressed the need for caution as we move forward into this new platform.

Photos and videos shared through social media had a big impact on the police investigation of the Vancouver Riot of June, 2011.

## Chapter Summary

This chapter introduced the role of emerging technology within the criminal justice system. There has been an emergence of new crimes as a result of the technology, which include:

- cyberbullying,
- child-luring,
- child pornography,
- identity theft, and
- Internet banking fraud.

Emerging technology has also had an impact on investigation, enforcement, and identification within the criminal justice system. Advances in DNA have resulted in convictions and have had a significant impact on wrongful convictions in Canada.

## Relevant Legislation

*Criminal Code*, R.S.C., 1985, c. C-46

*DNA Identification Act*, S.C. 1998, c. 37

## Key Terms

Biometrics
Child pornography
Cyberbullying
Cybercrime
DNA
Hacking
Identity theft
Mass Marketing Fraud
Phishing
Trace DNA
Viruses

## For Review

1. How has technology improved the ability of law enforcement officers to do their jobs?
2. How can children be protected from being victims of computer crime?
3. What has the impact of DNA been in Canada?
4. Identify the most common forms of online fraud.
5. What impact will biometric advances have on law enforcement?

## Thinking Critically

1. What strategies can law enforcement engage in to anticipate the impact of technology?
2. How might average Canadians be affected by extra vigilance that law enforcement applies to the use of technology?
3. What are the advantages and the disadvantages of law enforcement's use of social media?
4. How will technology affect the future of law enforcement?
5. How should the success of the DNA database be measured?

**Practise and learn online with Connect**

# Glossary

**Absolute discharge** accused person is found guilty but is not subject to a penalty of any kind (p. 109); not accompanied by obligation or sanction but remains on young person's record for one year (p. 192)

**Accident** a common law defence where the accused admits to having committed the *actus reus*, but denies that he or she had the intention to commit the crime (p. 41)

**Acquittal** being found or proved not guilty (p. 40)

***Actus reus*** a guilty action or omission (p. 38)

**Administrative law** a form of public law that addresses the actions of governments and government agencies (p. 14)

**Adversarial system** two opposing parties present their case before an impartial arbiter (p. 15)

**Advocacy** the act of providing public support for a particular cause or policy (p. 241)

**Aggravating factors** facts or circumstances that increase the severity of the offence (p. 118)

**Alibi** a common law defence whereby the accused asserts that he/she was in a different place than where the offence took place (p. 41)

**Appeal** examination by a higher court of the decision of a lower court (p. 96)

**Auburn system** a penitentiary model where inmates are together during the day, but separated at night (p. 130)

**Automatism** this rarely used common law defence excuses behaviour that might normally be criminal, if the accused was in an automatic state and did not act voluntarily (p. 43)

***Autrefois acquit*** the Latin phrase meaning "formerly acquitted" and refers to a rule that a person cannot be tried for the same offence more than once (p. 41)

***Autrefois convict*** the Latin phrase meaning "formerly convicted" and refers to a rule that a person cannot be tried for the same offence more than once (p. 41)

**Bail** to free a person arrested or imprisoned after a date and place to appear in court are set and security is taken (p. 86)

**Bail supervision programs** provide supervision to accused persons who lack financial resources to give them access to pre-trial release (bail) with an alternative to pre-trial detention (p. 159)

**Biometrics** a form of identification, such as fingerprinting, whereby unique features are used to recognize or confirm a person's identity (p. 258)

**Breached** violated a condition of community supervision (p. 162)

**Burden of proof** a duty to produce evidence to prove facts necessary to establish a cause of action or a defence (p. 7)

***Canadian Charter of Rights and Freedoms*** the supreme law of Canada, which outlines our fundamental freedoms and basic rights (p. 5)

**Cat-o-nine tails** a multi-tailed whipping device, usually made of leather (p. 131)

**Cautions** a formal warning from the Crown attorney indicating that although there are sufficient grounds to prosecute the offence, the prosecutor will not be proceeding with the charge. This advises the young person to avoid involvement in crime in the future (p. 190)

**Charge to the jury** a judge gives instructions to a jury before it deliberates with regard to the law as it applies to the case before it (p. 95)

**Child pornography** visual representation or written material depicting a person under the age of 18 engaging in explicit sexual activities or which advocates sexual activity with a person under the age of 18 (p. 248)

**Circumstantial evidence** evidence that requires the court to draw inferences and make connections to the fact (p. 93)

**Civil law** overarching term for all areas of private law that regulate private individuals and groups in our society (p. 14)

**Civilian review process** offers complainants an opportunity to share their story with an independent investigator, confident that their complaint will be reviewed in an impartial manner (p. 70)

**Classification** a process to determine an inmate's security level and individual program needs (p. 142)

**Clearance rate** the number of cases that police solve, or otherwise discharge, in a given period (p. 62)

**Clemency** reserved for those individuals who have suffered excessive hardship as a result of a court imposed penalty; decisions are made by the Parole Board of Canada or Royal Prerogative of Mercy (p. 166)

**Closing argument** a statement made by counsel at the closing of a criminal trial (p. 94)

**Common law** a body of law that is continually developing as it is created by court decisions that become judicial precedent (p. 12)

**Common law defences** defences that are created through case law and authorized in the *Criminal Code* (p. 40)

**Community-assisted hearings** circles administered by the Parole Board of Canada, intended to prepare Aboriginal offenders for release (p. 219)

**Community-based residential facilities** provide offenders with a place where they can adjust to life beyond the correctional institution in a supportive, supervised setting (p. 173)

**Community release** includes day parole, full parole, statutory release, as well as those who are under temporary release programs and long-term supervision orders (p. 159)

**Community service** offender must perform volunteer service for agency or community member for a specific number of hours (p. 192)

**Compensation** money given to someone who has suffered loss or injury (p. 242)

**Concurrent sentence** a sentence that is served at the same time as another sentence (p. 113)

**Conditional discharge** discharge accompanied by a probation order with terms and conditions (p. 109); remains on record for three years and is accompanied by specific conditions (p. 192)

**Conditional release** a general phrase encompassing all forms of release from custody with conditions attached (p. 159)

**Conferencing circle** a facilitator brings together victim, offender, family, friends, and other supporters to address outcome of the crime (p. 213)

**Consecutive sentence** a sentence that is served following another sentence (p. 113)

**Consent** a common law defence where the accused contends that permission to commit the offence was received from the victim. This defence only applies to certain types of offences (p. 44)

**Constitutional law** a form of public law referring to laws that identify the powers and limitations of the government and how the powers are exercised (p. 13)

**Contraband** any object that is not permitted within a correctional institution (p. 148)

**Corporal punishment** physical punishment (p. 131)

**Correctional plan** a plan of care designed to support an inmate's reintegration into the community (p. 143)

**Crime** an act or an omission that is prohibited by law (p. 33)

**Crime control model** protects the public through the capture, prosecution, and conviction of offenders (p. 11)

**Crime rate** measures the overall volume of crime in a population (p. 27); a measurement of police-reported crime (p. 54)

**Crime Severity Index (CSI)** complements the crime rate by measuring the severity of the crimes that are reported in Canada (p. 30)

**Criminal law** a form of public law referring to laws that prohibit certain acts (p. 12)

**Cross-examination** re-examination of the witness by the party who did not call him or her; required to test the witness's credibility to ensure that the evidence has legal integrity (p. 94)

**Cyberbullying** receiving threatening or aggressive emails or instant messages, or being the target of hateful comments (p. 248)

**Cybercrime** a crime that is technology-based (p. 248)

**Dangerous offender** offender who poses a high risk of continuing to commit violent and/or sexual offences (p. 113)

**Dark figure of crime** the unknown amount of true crime that is committed (p. 32)

**Day parole** a form of conditional release generally granted for up to a six-month period to prepare inmates for full parole or statutory release; they must return to the penitentiary, community-based residential facility, or provincial/territorial correctional facility each night (p. 161)

***De minimus*** a defence whereby the accused admits to having committed the offence, but asserts that the crime was so minor that a penalty is not warranted (p. 43)

**Deferred custody** young offender is permitted to continue to live in the community, under specific conditions, with the understanding that any breach in the conditions will result in serving the rest of the sentence in custody (p. 194)

**Democratic rights** defined in sections 3, 4, and 5 of the *Canadian Charter of Rights and Freedoms* and include the right to vote (p. 5)

**Deterrence** discouraging the criminal behaviour of persons (or a society) by exposing them to successful conviction (p. 12)

**Direct evidence** evidence that proves a fact and does not require additional explanation or assessment (p. 93)

**Direct examination** the questioning of a witness by the lawyer who called him or her to the stand (p. 94)

**Discharge** the release of an accused without obligation (p. 91)

**Disclosure** the requirement for the Crown attorney and the police to provide the details (and copies) of all of the Crown's evidence against the accused, to the accused prior to the trial (p. 89)

**Discretion** the ability to make decisions on various matters based on his/her opinion within general legal guidelines (p. 61)

**Diversion programs** programs that offer accused persons a community alternative to the traditional criminal justice system (p. 213)

**DNA** hereditary material unique to each human being and which can be obtained from a blood sample, skin sample, or other type of human sample (p. 256)

**Dual procedure offence** (see also *hybrid offence*) an offence that can be either an indictable or summary conviction offence, as determined by the Crown attorney (p. 36)

**Due process** the right to be treated within the principles of fundamental justice (p. 4)

**Due process model** stresses the importance of the presumption of innocence and recognizes a responsibility on the part of the judiciary to identify and respond to any abuse of power (p. 10)

**Duress** there are both common law and statutory versions of this defence whereby the accused asserts that he/she was compelled to commit the crime by threats of immediate death or bodily harm (p. 44)

**Earned remission** an incentive for provincial/territorial inmates to earn "good time" of 15 days for every month served (p. 166)

**Electronic monitoring** enables offenders to live in the community while under electronic surveillance (p. 167)

**Entrapment** occurs when police actions go beyond what is permitted by law (p. 43)

**Equality rights** ensures equal benefit and protection of the law without discrimination based on personal traits such as race, national or ethnic origin, colour, religion, sex, age, or mental or physical disability (p. 7)

**Escorted temporary absence** a temporary release from custody with an escort for administrative, medical, community service, socialization, personal development, or humanitarian reasons (p. 160)

**Evidence** an assertion of fact, opinion, belief, or knowledge (p. 93)

**Expert witness** someone who has specialized knowledge in a given area and is entitled to provide opinion evidence during the proceedings (*Canada Evidence Act*, s. 7) (p. 86)

**Extrajudicial measures** provides young offenders with options that divert them from traditional criminal justice system (p. 190)

**"Faint hope clause"** permitted those convicted of first degree murder to apply for parole after serving 15 years of their sentence, even though they had been sentenced to life imprisonment without parole eligibility for 25 years. This was repealed in February, 2011 (p. 163)

**Field training** training that occurs while on the job (p. 67)

**Fine** a financial payment to the court, and the most common of the sentencing options available (p. 110)

**Fine option programs** available to judges as an alternative to a custodial sentence. (p. 159)

**Full parole** full-time conditional release under supervision normally at one third of the sentence (p. 161)

**Fundamental freedoms** guaranteed in section 2 of the *Canadian Charter of Rights and Freedoms*, and include freedom of conscience and religion, freedom of peaceful assembly, freedom of speech, and freedom of association (p. 5)

**General deterrence** sentencing an offender with a view to deterring the general public from committing the same offence (p. 107)

**General intent** a form of *mens rea* where the accused may not have planned to commit the criminal act (p. 41)

**General Social Survey** a survey that collects data related to victimization, conducted every five years (p. 230)

**Gladue courts** courts that allow the cases of Aboriginal offenders to be heard with a view to being sensitive to their needs (p. 124)

**Hacking** unauthorized use of computer systems intended to defraud or disrupt (p. 248)

**Halfway houses** community-based residential facilities that are available to offenders who are being reintegrated into the community (p. 173)

**Harm reduction** an approach designed to reduce harm of a specific behaviour (p. 147)

**Hate crimes** criminal offences that are motivated by hate towards an identifiable group (p. 39)

**Healing circles** circles that are convened with the intention of specifically addressing or healing an individual or individuals (p. 219)

**Hearsay evidence** what a witness knows based on what was told to him or her by another person (p. 93)

**Honour-based violence** violence that occurs when family members kill or commit a violent act against another family member because they believe that the victim has dishonoured the family name and reputation (p. 42)

**Hung jury** a jury that is unable to reach a unanimous decision (p. 95)

**Hybrid offence** (see also *dual procedure offence*) an offence that can be either an indictable or a summary conviction offence (p. 36)

**Identity theft** stealing someone's personal information in order to use that information for a criminal purpose (p. 253)

**Impartial** without bias (p. 92)

**Incarceration rate** the rate at which offenders are imprisoned (p. 185)

**Indefinite sentence** used for dangerous offenders, who remain under federal supervision indefinitely (p. 114)

**Indictable offence** the most severe type of criminal offence (p. 36)

**Informed consent** you understand what is being asked of you, and you are aware of your right to refuse (p. 73)

**Inmate culture** the values, beliefs, attitudes, and actions of incarcerated individuals (p. 146)

**In-service training** training during the course of one's career (p. 67)

**Intermittent sentence** a sentence that has a break within it that permits the offender to leave the institution for employment or education (p. 113)

**International victimization rate** identifies Canada's rate as being about average in comparison between 30 countries (p. 233)

**Involuntary intoxication** involuntarily consuming drugs and/or alcohol (p. 44)

***Juvenile Delinquents Act*** first piece of legislation to address criminal behaviour of youths in Canada (p. 184)

**Lay an information** documentation against a suspect, indicating why the police believe the person should be arrested (p. 20)

**Leave to appeal** the granting of permission to hear an appeal in the Supreme Court of Canada (p. 82)

**Legal rights** guaranteed in sections 7 to 14 of the *Canadian Charter of Rights and Freedoms*, and include the right to life, liberty, and security of the person (p. 6)

**Levels of restraint** the extent to which a young person's freedom is limited (p. 197)

**Life imprisonment** the maximum sentence in Canadian law (p. 140)

**Lifer** a person sentenced to life imprisonment (p. 113)

**Long-term offender** an offender who poses a "substantial risk" but does not qualify as a dangerous offender; following release from prison this offender receives a long-term supervision order in the community up to a maximum of 10 years (p. 115)

**Long-term supervision order** provides for the supervision of sex offenders at risk of reoffending after a prison sentence expires (p. 171)

**Mass Marketing Fraud** a campaign that targets large groups of people via the Internet, phone, or mail (p. 251)

***Mens rea*** guilty mind and/or criminal intention (p. 38)

**Mistake of fact** a common law defence where an accused makes an honest mistake, in a situation where his or her actions were normally lawful (p. 43)

**Mitigating circumstances** circumstances that may reduce the severity of the sentence (p. 118)

**Mobility rights** guarantees (in section 6 of the *Canadian Charter of Rights and Freedoms*) Canadian citizens the right to live and work anywhere they choose in Canada (p. 6)

**Motions** applications made to the court by either the Crown or the accused (p. 88)

**Necessity** a common law defence whereby the accused asserts that the criminal act should be excused because it was committed in order to avoid a greater injustice (p. 43)

**Not Criminally Responsible on account of a Mental Disorder** accused is determined to be incapable of appreciating the nature/quality of the act or omission, or of knowing it was wrong (p. 45)

**"Notwithstanding" clause** the clause allowing federal and provincial governments the ability to override specific *Charter* rights in certain situations (p. 7)

**Operational stresses** refers to stress that flows from officers' daily operations (p. 67)

**Organizational stresses** refers to stress that comes from the police service itself, specifically the policies and practices of the organization (p. 67)

**Pardon** see *record suspension*

**Peace bond** a written promise to the court to keep the peace (p. 80)

**Pennsylvania system** a penitentiary model designed to keep inmates separate from each other day and night (p. 130)

**Perjury** a criminal offence where a person knowingly makes a false statement while under oath, as in a court of law. Perjury is an indictable offence and the penalty is a term of imprisonment not exceeding 14 years (*Criminal Code*, s. 132) (p. 94)

**Personal service** young offender may be ordered to assist victim with tasks such as cutting grass or painting (p. 193)

**Phishing** fraudulent emails that represent the sender as a reputable and legitimate organization requesting personal information (p. 252)

**Plea** a defendant's response to the question, "are you guilty or not guilty?" (p. 88)

**Police Services Board** consists of both politicians and civilians and is responsible for hiring the police chief, creating budgets, engaging in collective bargaining, and establishing rules and regulations for the police service (p. 69)

**Precedent** is a judicial decision used as a standard in similar, subsequent cases (p. 12)

**Pre-sentence report** a report prepared before sentencing with information concerning the offender's history and background, in order to assist the court (p. 88)

**Principle of proportionality** the principle that considers the gravity of the offence and the extent to which the offender is blameworthy (p. 108)

**Private law** laws that resolve disputes between individuals and private entities (p. 12)

**Probation** a court order that requires the offender to keep the peace, be of good behaviour, and to appear before the court when required to do so for a specific period of time. Additional optional conditions may also apply (p. 109); convicted person is placed under court-ordered community supervision for a specific period of time (p. 159)

**Procedural law** a category of law that defines procedures within the justice system (p. 14); law that provides direction on how to proceed within the criminal justice system (p. 26)

**Professional Standards** a unit that engages in internal investigations and reports its findings to the Chief of Police (p. 69)

**Provincial director** a person, group, or class of persons or a body appointed by the provinces to take responsibility for the administration of the *Youth Criminal Justice Act* (p. 191)

**Public law** laws that are administered on behalf of the state (p. 12)

**Pursuit** a chase (p. 61)

**Real evidence** evidence that is physical itself or is able to identify physical evidence, such as a weapon or a ransom note (p. 93)

**Recklessness** a form of intention where the accused knows the potential consequences of an action but does not take into consideration the potential for harm that the action may inflict on others (p. 41)

**Recidivism** the rate at which an offender reoffends (p. 152); the rate of reoffending (p. 186)

**Recognizance** a document signed by an accused person indicating that he or she promises to appear in court for a trial (p. 87)

**Record suspension (formerly known as a pardon)** someone convicted of a federal offence may apply for a record suspension after an identified waiting period based on the severity of the original offence (p. 165)

**Recruit training** standardized, basic training for new officers (p. 66)

**Reintegration plan** used to plan a young person's release into the community (p. 194)

**Remand** pre-trial custody (p. 204)

**Reparation** making amends for a wrong or an injury done (p. 213)

**Reprimand** mildest sentence available and remains on offender's record for two months (p. 192)

**Retribution** punishment that is considered to be morally right and fully deserved (p. 213)

**Revoke** withdraw privileges (p. 164)

**Security of tenure** a judge is eligible to serve on the bench until the age of retirement in the jurisdiction (p. 83)

**Self-defence** a statutory defence whereby the accused claims that his/her actions were permitted by law (p. 44)

**Self-harm** self-injurious behaviour (p. 140)

**Sentencing circle** a process whereby all persons affected by a criminal offence address the crime and arrive at an appropriate sentence (p. 215)

**Sentencing disparity** occurs when similar persons who are convicted of the same offence receive different sentences (p. 122)

**Sex Offender Registry** a database holding the names and addresses of convicted sex offenders, used by the police as an investigative tool (p. 121)

**Show cause hearing** a hearing where the Crown must state reasons why the accused should be detained in custody (p. 86)

**Special Investigation Unit (SIU)** a civilian unit in Ontario, independent of the police, that investigates circumstances involving police and civilians that have resulted in serious injury (p. 70)

**Specific deterrence** sentencing an offender with a view to deterring that individual from committing another criminal offence (p. 107)

**Specific intent** a form of *mens rea* where the accused is fully aware of his or her intentions and their consequences (p. 41)

**Split-jurisdiction** responsibility for providing a service falls to two different departments (p. 132)

**Stare decisis** refers to precedent; a Latin phrase that means "to stand by what has been decided" (p. 12)

**Statute law** laws that are made through a parliamentary process (p. 12)

**Statute of limitations** a time period after the commission of an offence within which a charge must be laid (p. 37)

**Statutory defences** defences that are codified in the *Criminal Code* (p. 40)

**Statutory release** legal entitlement to release under supervision after completing two thirds of a sentence (p. 166)

**Substantive law** identifies the substance of law in that it clearly states the actions that are against the law (p. 14); law that defines actions that are prohibited (p. 26)

**Sudden provocation** a partial defence of acts, performed in the heat of passion (p. 45)

**Summary conviction offence** the least severe type of offence (p. 36)

**Surety** one who is willing to pledge to be answerable to the court (financially) if the accused does not appear in court (p. 87)

**Suspended sentence** requires the accused to comply with the probation conditions for the length of the probation order (p. 109)

**Trace DNA** when only small amounts of DNA are used to make a match (p. 258)

**Unescorted temporary absence** a temporary release from custody without an escort for administrative, medical, community service, socialization, personal development, or humanitarian reasons (p. 160)

**Uniform Crime Reporting (UCR) Survey** a census of reported crime collected by police services across Canada (p. 26)

**Verdict** the finding of a jury and/or judge (p. 95)

**Victim fine surcharge** a charge imposed on convicted offenders that benefits victim services in the specific jurisdiction (p. 110)

**Victim impact statement** a verbal or written statement delivered by, or on behalf of, the victim at the time of sentencing (p. 228)

**Victim-offender reconciliation programs** programs where victims may share their feelings and describe their loss to the offender (p. 222)

**Victim satisfaction** victim's assessment depends on the victim's experience with the police and legal system (p. 242)

**Viruses** disruptive computer infections (p. 248)

**Voluntary intoxication** voluntarily consuming drugs and/or alcohol (p. 44)

**Warnings** often issued to young offenders before more severe action taken (p. 190)

**Wilful blindness** the accused chooses not to consider the potential criminality of his or her actions because he or she does not want to know the truth (p. 41)

***Young Offenders Act*** replaced *Juvenile Delinquents Act* and reflected policy shift from social welfare approach to an approach requiring young people to take responsibility for their actions (p. 184)

***Youth Criminal Justice Act*** introduced in 2001 and includes legal framework introduced in the *Young Offenders Act* while maintaining focus on social needs as identified in the *Juvenile Delinquents Act* (p. 186)

**Youth justice committees** comprised of citizens empowered to work toward identifying community solutions to dealing with young offenders (p. 195)

# References

## CHAPTER 1:


Bala, N. "Polygamy in Canada: Justifiably Not Tolerated." JURIST—Forum, December, 2011. http://jurist.org/forum/2011/12/nicholas-bala-canada-polygamy.php (accessed August 2012).

Bentham, J. *An Introduction to the Principles of Morals and Legislation*. Buffalo, N.Y.: Prometheus Press, 1988. (Original work published 1789.)

Bingham, T. *The Rule of Law*. London: The Penguin Group, 2010.

Brennan, S. and M. Dauvergne. "Police-reported crime statistics in Canada, 2010," *Juristat*, July 21, 2011.

*Canadian Charter of Rights and Freedoms* (Part I of the Constitution Act, 1982).

Canadian Judicial Council. "The Canadian Justice System and the Media," November 2007. http://www.cjc-ccm.gc.ca/cmslib/general/news_pub_other_cjsm_en.pdf (accessed August 2012).

Case Study: The Montreal Massacre. http://www.gendercide.org/case_montreal.html (accessed August 2012).

CBC News. "Polygamy charges in Bountiful, B.C., thrown out," September 23, 2009, http://www.cbc.ca/news/canada/british-columbia/story/2009/09/23/bc-polygamy-charges-blackmore-oler-bountiful.html (accessed August 2012).

*Criminal Code*, RSC 1985, c C-46.

Department of Justice Canada. *Canada's Court System*. Ottawa: Minister of Justice and Attorney General of Canada, 2005.

Doyle, A. *Arresting Images: Crime and Policing in Front of the Television Camera*. Toronto: University of Toronto Press, 2003.

Forde-Mazrui, K. "Ruling out the Rule of Law." *Vanderbilt Law Review*, 60, no. 5 (2007), p. 1497.

Goff, C. *Criminal Justice in Canada*. 5th ed. Toronto: Nelson Education, 2011.

Kappler, V.E., and G.W. Potter. *The Mythology of Crime and Justice*. Illinois: Waveland Press, 2005.

Karmen, A. *Crime Victims: An Introduction to Victimology*. Belmont, CA: Thomson Wadsworth, 2001.

Office of the Auditor General of Canada. *May 2006 Status Report of the Auditor General of Canada*. 2006.

Packer, H.L. "Two Models of Criminal Process." *University of Pennsylvania Law Review*, (1964) 113, pp. 1–68.

Parliament of Canada. Guide to the Canadian House of Commons. 2005. http://www.parl.gc.ca (accessed August 2012).

R. *v.* Mernagh, 2011 ONSC 2121.

Rathjen, H., and C. Montpetit. *December 6th: From the Montreal Massacre to Gun Control*. Toronto: McClelland and Stewart, 1999.

Reiner, R. "Media Made Criminality: The Representation of Crime in the Mass Media." In *The Oxford Handbook of Criminology*, eds R. Reiner, M. Maguire, R. Morgan. Oxford, UK: Oxford University Press, 2002. pp. 302–337.

Roberts, J., and M. Grossman. *Criminal Justice in Canada: A Reader*. 3rd ed. Toronto: Thomson Nelson, 2008.

Rodriguez *v.* British Columbia, (Attorney General) (1993), 24 C.R. (4th) 281 (S.C.C.).

Sharpe, R.J. and K. Roach, K. *The Charter of Rights and Freedoms*. 3rd ed. Toronto: Irwin Law Inc., 2005.

Smith, M. *The Rodriguez Case: A Review of the Supreme Court of Canada Decision on Assisted Suicide*. BP-349. Ottawa: Parliamentary Information and Research Service, Library of Parliament, 1993.

Statistics Canada. 2009 General Social Survey: Victimization.

Statistics Canada, CANSIM table 254-0002 (Police Officers, by province and territory).

Surette, R. *Media, Crime and Criminal Justice*. 4th ed. California: Wadsworth Publishing, 2011.

Tiederman, M. and D. Valiquet. *Euthanasia and Assisted Suicide in Canada*. Parliament of Canada: Law and Government Division, 2008.

*Youth Criminal Justice Act* (S.C. 2002, c. 1).


## CHAPTER 2:


Alderman, J. 2003. Study in Blue and Grey, Police Interventions with People with Mental Illness: A

Review of Challenges and Responses. Vancouver, Canadian Mental Health Association, British Columbia Division.
*Bill C-10: Safe Streets and Communities Act*. First Session, Forty-first Parliament, 60–61 Elizabeth II, 2011–2012.
Brennan, S. "Canadians' perceptions of personal safety and crime, 2009." *Juristat*, December 1, 2011.
Brennan, S. and M. Dauvergne. "Police-reported crime statistics in Canada, 2010." *Juristat*, July 21, 2011.
CBC News. "Greyhound killer Li granted walks," June 3, 2010. http://www.cbc.ca/news/canada/manitoba/story/2010/06/03/mb-vince-li-priveleges-winnipeg.html (accessed August 2012).
CBC News. "Muslim community grapples with Shafia verdict," January 30, 2012. http://www.cbc.ca/news/canada/story/2012/01/30/shafia-trial-verdict-reaction.html (accessed August 2012).
Dauvergne, M. and J. Turner. "Police-reported crime statistics in Canada, 2009." *Juristat* 30, no. 2 (July 2010).
Department of Justice Canada. "Legislation to Reform Mental Disorder Laws Receives Royal Assent," May 19, 2005. http://www.justice.gc.ca/eng/news-nouv/nr-cp/2005/doc_31516.html (accessed August 2012).
Fedorowycz, O. "Breaking and Entering in Canada—2002." *Juristat* 24, no. 5 (July 2004), p. 1.
Freeze, C. "Canada looks for ways to prevent honour killings in wake of Shafia trial," January 31, 2012, http://www.theglobeandmail.com/news/national/canada-looks-for-ways-to-prevent-honour-killings-in-wake-of-shafia-trial/article2322016/ (accessed August 2012).
Garner, B.A. *Black's Law Dictionary*. Toronto: Thomson Reuters Westlaw, 2009.
Hackett, K. "Criminal harassment." *Juristat* 20, no. 11 (November 2000). Statistics Canada—Catalogue no. 85-002-XIE.
Keeping, J. "Honour killings—premeditated executions—must be stopped in Canada," November 20, 2009, http://www.chumirethicsfoundation.ca/main/page.php?page_id=261 (accessed August 2012).
Kong, R., and K. AuCoin. "Female offenders in Canada, 2008." *Juristat* 28, no. 1 (January 2008).
Loughlin, J., and A. Taylor-Butts. "Child luring through the Internet." *Juristat* 29, no. 1 (March 2009).
MADD Canada. "MADD Canada Challenges Myths about the 'Hard-Core' Drinking Driver." July 6, 2011, http://madd.ca/madd2/en/media/pr/p20110706.htm (accessed August 2012).
Malea, P. *The Fear Factor: Stephen Harper's "Tough on Crime" Agenda*. Ottawa: Canadian Centre for Policy Alternatives, 2010.
O'Grady, W. *Crime in Canadian Context*. Toronto: Oxford University Press, 2011.
Perreault, S. and S. Brennan. "Criminal victimization in Canada, 2009." *Juristat* 30, no. 2 (September 2010).
Pilon, M. *Review of the Mental Disorder Provisions of the Criminal Code*. Ottawa: Parliamentary Research Branch, Law and Government Division, 2011.
Pottie Bunge, V., H. Johnson, and T. Balde. "Exploring Crime Patterns in Canada." *Crime and Justice Research Paper Series*. Ottawa: Minister of Industry, 2005.
R. *v*. Mack, [1988] 2 S.C.R. 903.
R. *v*. Morgentaler, [1988] 1 S.C.R. 30.
R. *v*. Stone, [1999] 2 S.C.R. 290.
Roberts, J.V. *Fear of Crime and Attitudes to Criminal Justice in Canada: A Review of Recent Trends*. Ottawa: Public Works and Government Services Canada, 2001.
Siegel, L., G. Brown, and R. Hoffman. *Criminology: The Core*. Toronto: Thomson Nelson, 2005.
Sinha, M. "An Investigation into the Feasibility of Collecting Data on the Involvement of Adults and Youth with Mental Health Issues in the Criminal Justice System." *Crime and Justice Research Paper Series*. Ottawa: Minister of Industry, 2009.
Stansfield, R. T. *Understanding Criminal Defences and Procedure*. Toronto: Thomson Reuters Carswell, 1992.
Statistics Canada. "Police-Reported Hate Crimes," June 14, 2010. Statistics Canada. http://www.statcan.gc.ca/daily-quotidien/100614/dq100614b-eng.htm (accessed August 2012).
Statistics Canada. *The Daily*, June 14, 2010.
Verdun-Jones, S.N. *Criminal Law in Canada: Cases, Questions and the Code*. 4th ed. Toronto: Nelson College Indigenous, 2006.
Wallace, M., et al. *Measuring Crime in Canada: Introducing the Crime Severity Index and Improvements to the Uniform Crime Reporting Survey*. Ottawa: Minister of Industry, 2009.

## CHAPTER 3:

Butts, E. *Line of Fire: Heroism, Tragedy, and Canada's Police*. Toronto: Dundurn Press, 2009.
Canadian Security Intelligence Service. *Public Report 2009/2010*. Public Works and Government Services Canada, 2010.

Carrington, P.J. and J.L. Schulenber. "Structuring Police Discretion: The Effect on Referrals to Youth Court." *Criminal Justice Policy Review* 19, no. 3 (September 2008), pp. 349–367.

Cooley, D., ed. *Re-imagining Policing in Canada*. Toronto: University of Toronto Press, Scholarly Publishing Division, 2005.

Craven, K. "Foot Patrols: Crime Analysis and Community Engagement to Further the Commitment to Community Policing." *Community Policing Dispatch*, 2, no. 2 (February 2009).

First Nations Chiefs of Police Association and Human Resources Development Canada. *Setting the Context: The Policing of First Nations Communities*. (n.d.) http://www.fncpa.ca (accessed August 2012).

Frontier Centre for Public Policy. "One-Officer Versus Two-Officer Police Cars in Winnipeg." *Frontier Backgrounder*, February 2001.

Haydon, A.L. *The riders of the plains: A record of the Royal North-West Mounted Police of Canada 1873-1910*. Toronto: The Copp Clark Co. Limited, 1910.

Hurd, D. *Robert Peel: A Biography*. London: Weidenfeld & Nicolson, 2007.

Jane Doe *v*. Metropolitan Toronto (Municipality) Commissioners of Police, 1998.

Kari, S. "Chinatown arrest trial kicks off." June 21, 2010, http://news.nationalpost.com/2010/06/21/chinatown-arrest-trial-kicks-off/ (accessed August 2012).

Kohan, A., and D. Mazmanian. "Police work, burn-out, and pro-organizational behavior: A consideration of daily work experiences." *Criminal Justice and Behavior* 30 (2003), pp. 559–583.

Lafreniere, G. *Police Powers and Drug-Related Offences*. Parliamentary Research Branch, Library of Parliament, Government of Canada, 2004.

Landau, T. "When police investigate police: A view from complainants." *Canadian Journal of Criminology and Criminal Justice* 38 no. 3(1996), pp. 291–315.

LeSage, P. *Report on Police Complaints System in Ontario*. Attorney General Office of Ontario, 2005. http://www.attorneygeneral.jus.gov.on.ca/english/about/pubs/LeSage/en-fullreport.pdf.

Li, G. "Private Security and Public Policing." *Juristat*, 2008.

Marin, A. *Oversight Undermined: Investigation into the Ministry of the Attorney General's Implementation of Recommendations Concerning Reform of the Special Investigations Unit*. Ombudsman of Ontario, 2011.

Mason, P. "The Thin Blurred Line: Reality Television and Policing." *British Society of Criminology Conference: Selected Proceedings* 5, 2003.

McKenna, P.F., and C. Murphy. *Police Investigating Police: A Critical Review of the Literature and Annotated Bibliography, for the Commission for Public Complaints Against the RCMP*. 2010

McKenna, P.F. *Canadian Government and Administration: A Policing Perspective*. Toronto: Pearson Education, 2003.

McKenna, P.F. *Police Powers II*. Toronto: Pearson Education, 2003.

Miller, J., and C. Merrick. *Civilian Oversight of Policing: Lessons from the Literature*. New York : Vera Institute of Justice, 2002.

Murphy, C., and P. McKenna. *Rethinking Police Culture, Governance & Management*. Public Safety Canada, 2007.

Ottawa Citizen. *The Williams Case*, http://www.ottawacitizen.com/news/williams-investigation/index.html (accessed August 2012).

Perry, R.A. *Mission Failure: Civilian Review of Policing in New York City 1994–2006*. New York: New York Civil Liberties Union, 2007.

Policing & Security Management Services Inc. *Patrick Shand Inquest Verdict*, http://www.policingsecurity.ca/shand%20inquest%20rec.pdf (accessed August 2012).

Prenzler, T. "Stakeholder perspectives on police complaints and discipline: towards a civilian control model." *Australian and New Zealand Journal of Criminology* 37, no. 1(2004), pp. 85–113.

Public Safety Canada. *First Nations Policing Program*, http://www.publicsafety.gc.ca/prg/le/ap/1index-eng.aspx (accessed August 2012).

R. *v*. Buhay, [2003] 1 S.C.R. 631, 2003 SCC 30.

Royal Canadian Mounted Police, Public National Communication Services Directorate. *The Origins of the Royal Canadian Mounted Police*. Minister, Public Works and Government Services Canada, 2002.

Royal Canadian Mounted Police. *Cadet Training Program*, http://www.rcmp-grc.gc.ca/fs-fd/cadet-eng.htm (accessed August 2012).

Sewell, J. *Police in Canada: The Real Story*. Toronto: Lorimer, 2010.

Soulierre, D. "Policing on prime-time: A comparison of television and real world policing." *American Journal of Criminal Justice* 28 no. 2 (March 2004), pp. 215–233.

*Special Investigation Unit: Annual Report 2010–2011*. Government of Ontario.

Statistics Canada. "Police personnel and expenditures, 2011." December 13, 2011. http://www.statcan.gc.ca/daily-quotidien/111213/dq111213-eng.pdf (accessed August 2012).

Statistics Canada. *Police Resources in Canada 2010*. Canadian Centre for Justice Statistics.

Stribopoulos, J. "In Search of Dialogue: The Supreme Court, Police Powers and the Charter." *Queen's Law Journal* 31, no. 1 (Fall 2005), p. 74.

Swenson, D.X., D. Waseleski, and R. Hartl. "Shift Work and Correctional Officers: Effects and Strategies for Adjustment." *Journal of Correctional Health Care* 14, no. 4 (October 2008), pp. 299–310.

Tanovich, D.M. *The Colour of Justice: Policing Race in Canada*. Toronto: Irwin Law, 2006.

*The General Social Survey: an overview*. Minister of Industry, 2004.

Wortley, S. and J. Tanner. "Data, Denials and Confusion: The Racial Profiling Debate in Toronto." *Canadian Journal of Criminology and Criminal Justice* 45 no. 3 (July 2003), p. 367.

Wortley, S. *Civilian Governance and Policing in a Multicultural Society: A Discussion Paper*. Prepared for the Multiculturalism Directorate Canadian Heritage. 2003.

Young, R. et al. "Informal Resolution of Complaints Against the Police: A Quasi-Experimental Test of Restorative Justice." *Criminal Justice* 5 no. 3, pp. 279–317.

## CHAPTER 4:

"Court Preparation Participant's Guide," Victim Services Division, Nova Scotia Department of Justice. http://www.gov.ns.ca/just/publications/docs/courtprep.pdf (accessed August 2012).

Anderson, B. and D. Anderson. *Manufacturing Guilty: Wrongful Convictions in Canada*. Halifax: Fernwood Publishing, 1998.

Assmann, W. ed. *Representing yourself in a criminal trial: provincial court edition*. Legal Services Society BC, 2009.

Bajer, R., et al. "Wrongful Convictions." *Conference Proceeding, International Society for the Reform of Criminal Law*, Vancouver, Canada, June 2007. http://www.isrcl.org/Papers/2007/YMC.pdf (accessed August 2012).

Canadian Judicial Council. *Ethical Prinicples for Judges*. Ottawa: Canadian Judicial Council, 2004.

Canadian Sentencing Commission. *Sentencing reform: A Canadian approach*. Ottawa: Minister of Supply and Services Canada, 1987.

CBC News. "Accused in Manitoba bus killing fit to stand trial: court," October 6, 2008. http://www.cbc.ca/news/canada/manitoba/story/2008/10/06/beheading-court.html (accessed August 2012).

CBC News. "Canada's wrongful convictions: cases where the courts' got it wrong," October 14, 2010. http://www.cbc.ca/news/canada/story/2009/08/06/f-wrongfully-convicted.html (accessed August 2012).

CBC News. "Dr. Charles Smith: The man behind the public inquiry," August 10, 2010. http://www.cbc.ca/news/canada/story/2009/12/07/f-charles-smith-goudge-inquiry.html (accessed August 2012).

CBC News. "Shafia Case Evidence," December 12, 2011. http://www.cbc.ca/news/canada/montreal/story/2011/12/11/mtl-shafia-evidence.html (accessed August 2012).

CBC News. "Steven Truscott to get $6.5M for wrongful conviction," July 7, 2008. Retrieved from: http://www.cbc.ca/news/canada/story/2008/07/07/truscott-bentley.html (accessed August 2012).

CBC News. "Wrongfully convicted Donald Marshall Jr. dies," August 6, 2009. http://www.cbc.ca/news/canada/story/2009/08/06/donald-marshall-wrongful-conviction-dies342.html (accessed August 2012).

Cohn, M. and D. Dow. *Cameras in the Courtroom, Television and the Pursuit of Justice*. Jefferson, N.C.: McFarland, 1998.

Coughlan, S. *Criminal Procedure*. Toronto: Irwin Law, 2008.

*Criminal Code*, RSC 1985, c C-46.

CTV Edmonton. "Homolka plea bargain still causes controversy." June 19, 2005.

Department of Justice Canada. *Canada's system of justice*. Ottawa: Government of Canada, 2005.

Fleming, T., et al. *The Canadian Criminal Justice System*. 2nd ed. Toronto: Pearson Education, 2008.

Goff, C. *Criminal Justice in Canada*. 5th ed. Toronto: Nelson Education, 2011.

Government of Canada. Drug Treatment Court Funding Program. National Anti-Drug Strategy, http://nationalantidrugstrategy.gc.ca/dtc-ttt.html (accessed August 2012).

Government of Saskatchewan. "Milgaard Family and Province Settle on Compensation Package," May 17, 1999.

Griffiths, C.T. *Canadian Criminal Justice: A Primer*. 4th ed. Toronto: Nelson Education, 2007.

Hon. Goudge, S.T., Commissioner. *Inquiry into Pediatric Forensic Pathology in Ontario*. Toronto: Ontario Ministry of the Attorney General, 2008.

Hon. Kaufman, F. "Report of the Kaufman Commission on Proceedings Involving Guy Paul Morin," 1998. http://www.attorneygeneral.jus.gov.on.ca/english/about/pubs/morin/ (accessed August 2012).

Hon. MacCallum, E.P. "Report of the Commission of Inquiry into the Wrongful Conviction of David Milgaard," 2008. http://www.milgaardinquiry.ca (accessed August 2012).

Justinian I, Law Code, A.D. 535.
Katz, H. *Justice Miscarried: Inside Wrongful Convictions in Canada*. Toronto: Dundurn, 2011.
Law Reform Commission of Canada. "Plea discussions and agreements. Working Paper no. 60." Ottawa: Information Canada, 1975.
Linton, J. "Camera Access to Courtrooms: Canadian, U.S., and Australian Experiences." *Canadian Journal of Communication* 18, no. 1 (1993).
McCormick, P. *Supreme at Last: The Evolution of the Supreme Court of Canada*. Toronto: Lorimer, 2000.
Mitton, C., et al. "Calgary Diversion Program: A Community-based Alternative to Incarceration for Mentally Ill Offenders," *Journal of Mental Health Policy and Economics* 10, no. 3 (2007) pp. 145–151.
Nguyen, L. "Crown, defence agree to change of venue in Tori Stafford case," February 7, 2012. Postmedia News.
R. *v*. Askov [1990] 2 S.C.R. 1199.
R. *v*. Milgaard (1971), 2 C.C.C.(2d) 206 (Sask. C.A.), leave to appeal refused (1971), 4 C.C.C. (2d) 566 (S.C.C.).
R. *v*. Stinchcombe, [1991] 3 S.C.R. 326.
Roll, J.M., et al. "Identifying Predictors of Treatment Outcome in a Drug Court Program." *The American Journal of Drug and Alcohol Abuse* 31 (2005), pp. 641–656.
*Royal Commission on the Donald Marshall, Jr. Prosecution: Commissioner's Report: Findings and Recommendations, Vol 1*. Halifax: Royal Commission, 1989.
Salhany, R.E. *The Practical Guide to Evidence in Criminal Cases*. 7th ed. Toronto: Thomson Reuters Carswell, 2010.
Schneider R.D., H. Bloom, M. Heerema, M. *Mental Health Courts: decriminalizing the mentally ill*. Toronto: Irwin Law, 2007.
Sher, J. *"Until You Are Dead": Steven Truscott's Long Ride into History*. Toronto: Vintage Canada, 2002.
Thomas, J. "Adult criminal court statistics, 2008/2009," *Juristat* 30, no. 2 (July 2010).
Ursel, J., L.M. Tutty, and J. Lemaistre, eds. *What's Law Got to Do With It? The Law, Specialized Courts and Domestic Violence in Canada*. Toronto: Cormorant Books, 2008.
Verdun-Jones, S.N. and A.A. Tijerino. *Victim Participation in the Plea Negotiation Process in Canada: A Review of the Literature and Four Models for Law Reform*. Ottawa: Department of Justice, 2004.

## CHAPTER 5:

Bonta, J., et al. *Presentence Reports in Canada 2005–03*. Public Safety and Emergency Preparedness Canada, 2005.
Campbell Research Associates. *Evaluation of the Aboriginal Legal Services of Toronto Gladue Caseworker Program: Year Three October 2006–September 2007*. 2008.
Canadian Resource Centre for Victims of Crime. *Restitution*. http://www.crcvc.ca/docs/Restitu tion.pdf (accessed August 2012).
Canadian Sentencing Commission. *Sentencing reform: A Canadian approach*. Ottawa: Minister of Supply and Services Canada, 1987.
CBC News. "Cancer faker Kirilow spared jail: Ontario woman gets 15-month conditional sentence for fraud," April 7, 2011. http://www.cbc.ca/news/canada/toronto/story/2011/04/07/kirilow-sentencing.html (accessed August 2012).
*Criminal Code*, RSC 1985, c C-46.
CTV News. "Alleged cancer scammer appears thin, frail in court," August 9, 2010. http://www.ctv.ca/CTVNews/Canada/20100809/fake-cancer-court-100809/#ixzz1qA0oEpnA (accessed August 2012).
Edgar, A. "Sentencing Options in Canada." In *Making Sense of Sentencing*, Roberts, J.V. and D.P. Cole, eds. Toronto: University of Toronto Press, 1999.
Fleury, T. "Sentence statement by Theo Fleury and Todd Holt," http://theofleury14.com/2012/03/20/sentence-statement-by-theo-fleury-and-todd-holt-2/ (accessed August 2012).
Global News. "Timeline: Graham James, decades of abuse," March 20, 2012. http://www.globalnews.ca/timeline+graham+james+decades+of+abu se/6442537452/story.html (accessed August 2012).
Graveland B., and S. Montgomery. "Junior hockey predator Graham James pardoned, April 5, 2010." Canadian Press, http://www.tsn.ca/nhl/story/?id=316693 (accessed August 2012).
LaPrairie, C. "Aboriginal over-representation in the criminal justice system: A tale of nine cities." *Canadian Journal of Criminology and Criminal Justice* 44, no. 2 (April 2002), pp. 181–208.
LaForme, H.S. "The Justice System in Canada: Does it work for Aboriginal people?" *Indigenous Law Journal*, 4, 2005.
Law, M.A., and S.M. Sullivan. *Federal Victim Surcharge in New Brunswick: An Operational Review*. Department of Justice Canada, 2006.
Makin, K. "Judges must weigh cultural factors in native sentencing, court rules," March 23, 2012. http://www.theglobeandmail.com/news/national/

judges-must-weigh-cultural-factors-in-native-sentencing-court-rules/article2379145/ (accessed August 2012).

Motiuk, L.L., and M. Nafekh. "The long-term offender in federal corrections: A profile," *FORUM on Corrections Research* 12, no. 3 (September 2000), pp. 3–5.

Ontario Victims Services Secretariat. *A Report to the Community, Victims, Survivors and Service Providers*. Toronto: Ministry of the Attorney General, 2010.

Public Safety Canada. National Sex Offender Registry.

Public Safety Canada. *The Investigation, Prosecution and Correctional Management of High-RiskOffenders: A National Guide*. Ottawa: Government of Canada, 2009.

Puxley C., and S. Edmonds. "Graham James apologizes to victims, players, hockey community," February 22, 2012. The Canadian Press, http://www.globalnews.ca/graham+james+apologizes+to+victims+players+hockey+world/6442586611/story.html (accessed August 2012).

Puxley, C., and S. Edmonds. "Graham James apologizes to victims, players, hockey community," February 22, 2012. Canadian Press, http://www.globalnews.ca/graham+james+apologizes+to+victims+players+hockey+world/6442586611/story.html (accessed August 2012).

R. *v*. Ferguson, [2008] 1 S.C.R. 96, 2008 SCC 6.

R. *v*. Gladue, [1999] 1 S.C.R. 688.

Roberts, J.V. *Mandatory Sentences of Imprisonment in Common Law Jurisdictions: Some Representative Models*. Government of Canada. http://www.justice.gc.ca/eng/pi/rs/rep-rap/2005/rr05_10/p2.html (accessed August 2012).

Roberts, J. "Sentencing Trends and Sentencing Disparity." In *Making Sense of Sentencing*, Cole, D.P., and J. Roberts, eds. . Toronto: University of Toronto Press, 1999.

Rudin, J. Aboriginal Peoples and the Criminal Justice System, (n.d.) http://www.attorneygeneral.jus.gov.on.ca/inquiries/ipperwash/policy_part/research/pdf/Rudin.pdf (accessed August 2012).

Statistics Canada. *The Daily*, July 17, 2008.

Stenning, P., and J. Roberts. "Empty Promises: Parliament, the Supreme Court, and the Sentencing of Aboriginal Offenders." *Saskatchewan Law Review* 64, 2000, pp. 137–168.

Williams, T. "Sentencing Black Offenders in the Ontario Criminal Justice System." In *Making Sense of Sentencing*, Roberts, J. and D.P. Cole, eds. Toronto: University of Toronto Press, 1999.

## CHAPTER 6:

Arbor, L. *Commission of Inquiry into certain events at the Prison for Women in Kingston*. Ottawa: Queens Printer, 1996.

Babooram, A. "The changing profile of adults in custody 2006/2007," *Juristat* 28, no. 10 (December 2008).

Barrett, M.R., K. Allenby, and K. Taylor. *Twenty Years Later: Revisiting the Task Force on Federally Sentenced Women*. Ottawa: Correctional Service of Canada, 2010.

Boe, R. "Aboriginal inmates: Demographic trends and projections," *FORUM on Corrections Research* 12, no. 1 (January 2000), pp. 7–9.

Boe, R. "Population aging and the federal inmate profile of 2010," *FORUM on Corrections Research* 12 no. 3 (September 2000), pp. 29–34.

Boe, R. *A two-year follow-up of federal offenders who participated in the Adult Basic Education (ABE) Program*. Ottawa: Correctional Service of Canada, 1998.

Bonta, J., C. LaPrairie, and S. Wallace-Capretta. "Risk prediction and re-offending: Aboriginal and non-Aboriginal offenders," *Canadian Journal of Criminology and Criminal Justice* 39, no. 2 (April 1997), pp. 127–144.

Bonta, J., et al. "The prediction of recidivism among federally sentenced offenders: A re-validation of the SIR scale," *Canadian Journal of Criminology and Criminal Justice* 38 (1996), pp. 61–79.

Bonta, J., T. Rugge, and M. Dauvergne. *The reconviction rate of federal offenders 2003-02*. Ottawa: Solicitor General Canada, 2003.

Bottos, S. *Profile of Offenders in Administrative Segregation: A Review of the Literature*. Ottawa: Correctional Service of Canada, Research Branch, 2007.

Brown, R. *Behind Bars: Inside Ontario's Heritage Gaols*. Toronto: Natural Heritage, 2006.

Brown, S. L., and L.L. Motiuk, *The Dynamic Factors Identification and Analysis (DFIA) Component of the Offender Intake Assessment (OIA) Process: A Meta-Analytic, Psychometric and Consultative Review*. Ottawa: Correctional Service of Canada, 2005.

Canadian Human Rights Commission. *Protecting Their Rights: A Systemic Review of Human Rights in Correctional Services for Federally Sentenced Women*. Ottawa: Government of Canada, 2003.

CBC News. "Inmates shouldn't get pensions: poll," April 9, 2010, http://www.cbc.ca/news/canada/story/2010/04/08/ekos-poll-inmates-pensions.html (accessed August 2012).

CBC News. "Prison tattoo parlours get the axe," December 4, 2006, http://www.cbc.ca/news/canada/story/2006/12/04/tattoo-program.html (accessed August 2012).

Clarke, L., et al. "Fathering Behind Bars in English Prisons: Imprisoned Fathers' Identity and Contact with Their Children." *Fathering* 3 no. 3 (2005), pp. 221–241.

Cole, D.P. "The Umpire Strikes Back: Canadian Judicial Experience with Risk-Assessment Instruments." *Canadian Journal of Criminology and Criminal Justice* 49, no. 4 (October 2007), pp. 493–517.

Commissioner's Directive 730. *Inmate Program Assignment and Payments*. Ottawa: Correctional Service of Canada, 1999.

Commissioner's Directive 768. *Institutional Mother-Child Program*. Ottawa: Correctional Service of Canada, 2003.

Cooley, D. *Victimization Behind the Walls: Social Control in Male Federal Prisons*. Ottawa: Research and Statistics Branch, Correctional Service of Canada, 1992.

Correctional Service of Canada. *Task Force on Administrative Segregation*. 2008.

*Corrections Today* 63 (2001).

*Creating Choices: The Report of the Task Force on Federally Sentence Women*. Ottawa: Correctional Service of Canada, 1990.

Delveaux, K., K. Blanchette, and J. Wickett. *Employment Needs, Interests, and Programming for Women Offenders*. Ottawa: Correctional Service of Canada, 2005.

Duguid, S. and R. Pawson, "Education, Change, and Transformation: The Prison Experience." *Evaluation Review* 22, (August 1998), pp. 470–495.

Duguid, S. *British Columbia Prison Education Research Project Final Report, 1998*.

Duguid, S., C. Hawkey, and W. Knights. "Measuring the Impact of Post-Secondary Education in Prison: a Report from British Columbia." *Journal of Offender Rehabilitation* 27, no. 1 (October 2008), pp. 87–106.

Feature Issue: Correctional Education. *FORUM on Corrections Research* 3, no. 1 (1991).

Gabor, T. *Deaths in Custody—Final Report*. The Correctional Investigator Canada, 2007.

Gendreau, P., C. Goggin, and T. Little. *Predicting Adult Offender Recidivism: What Works! (User Report No. 1996-07)*. Ottawa: Department of the Solicitor General of Canada, 1996.

Gerber, J. and E.J. Fritsch. "Adult Academic and Vocational Correctional Programs: A Review of Recent Research." *Journal of Offender Rehabilitation* 22, no. 1 (1995), pp. 119–142.

Gillan, T. "The Correctional Officer: One of Law Enforcements Toughest Positions."

Griffiths, C.T. *Canadian Corrections*. 3rd ed. Toronto: Thomson Nelson, 2010.

*Hands at Work: CORCAN Annual Report 07/08*. Ottawa: Correctional Service of Canada, n.d.

Hanson, R. K., and K.E. Morton-Bourgon. *The Accuracy of Recidivism Risk Assessments for Sexual Offenders: A Meta-analysis. User Report 2007-01*. Ottawa, ON: Public Safety and Emergency Preparedness Canada, 2007.

Harman, J.J., V.E. Smith, and L.C. Egan. "The Impact of Incarceration on Intimate Relationships." *Criminal Justice and Behavior* 34, no. 6 (June 2007), pp. 794–815.

Hassine, V., R. Johnson, and S. Tabriz. *Life Without Parole: Living and Dying in Prison Today*. 5th ed. New York: Oxford University Press, 2010.

Hrabowski III, F.A., and J. Robbi. "The Benefits of Correctional Education." *Journal of Correctional Education* 53, no. 3 (2002), pp. 96–100.

Issue: Prison Violence and Inmate Suicide and Self-Injury. *FORUM on Corrections Research* 4, no. 3 (1992).

John Howard Society of Alberta. *Offender Risk Assessment*. 2000.

Journal of Correctional Education, 53(3), p96-100.

Kerr, T., et al. "Harm reduction in prisons: a 'rights based analysis.'" *Critical Public Health* 14, no. 4 (2004), pp. 345–360.

Kong, R., and K. AuCoin. "Female Offenders in Canada." *Juristat* 28, no. 1 (January 2008), pp. 1–28.

LaPrairie, C. "Aboriginal over-representation in the criminal justice system: A tale of nine cities." *Canadian Journal of Criminology and Criminal Justice* 44, no. 2 (April 2002), pp. 181–208.

Mason, R. "Aboriginal Correctional Programs." *Let's Talk: A New Generation of Correctional Programs* 34, no. 2 (March 2010), p. 10.

Morton, J. "The Elderly in Prison." *Journal of Criminal Law* 69 no. 3 (2005), pp. 189–191.

*Moving Forward With Women's Corrections: The Expert Committee Review of the Correctional Service of Canada's Ten-Year Status Report on Women's Corrections 1996–2006*. Ottawa: Correctional Service of Canada, n.d.

Olotu, M.K., D. Luong, and A. Brews. *Evaluation Report: Lifeline Program*. Ottawa: Correctional Service of Canada, 2009.

Performance Assurance Sector. *Report on the Evaluation of the Okimaw Ohci Healing Lodge*. Ottawa: Correctional Service of Canada, 2002.

Porporino, F.J., and D. Robinson. *Can Educating Adult Offenders Counteract Recidivism?* Ottawa: Correctional Service of Canada, 1992.

Power, J., and D.L. Riley. *A Comparative Review of Suicide and Self-Injury Investigative Reports in a Canadian Federal Correctional Population*. Ottawa: Correctional Service of Canada, 2010.

Public Safety Canada. *Corrections and Conditional Release Statistical Overview Annual Report 2010*. Ottawa: Public Works and Government Services Canada, 2010.

Roberts, J. "Risk Management: The Views of the Public and the Challenge to Corrections." *FORUM on Corrections Research* 5, no. 2 (May 1993).

Sapers, H. *A Preventable Death*. Correctional Investigator of Canada, 2008.

Sapers, H. *Annual Report of the Office of the Correctional Investigator 2009–2010*. The Correctional Investigator Canada, 2010.

Sapers, H. *Annual Report of the Office of the Correctional Investigator 2010–2011*. The Correctional Investigator Canada, 2011.

Statistics Canada. *The Daily*. October 26, 2010.

Stevens, D.J. "Education programming for offenders." *FORUM on Corrections Research* 12, no. 2 (May 2000), pp. 29–31.

Stevens, D.J. and C.S. Ward. "College Education and Recidivism: Educating criminals is meritorious." *Journal of Correctional Education* 48, no. 3 (1997), pp. 106–111.

Tadman, P. *Fallen Angels: Inside Canadas Toughest Womens Prison*. Calgary: Detselig Enterprises Ltd., 2001.

Tapper, J. and P. Fong. "Serial killer Clifford Olson dead, Quebec coroner's officer confirms," *Toronto Star*.

*The Closing of the Prison for Women in Kingston July 6, 2000*. Ottawa: Correctional Service of Canada, 2000.

*The National Strategic Plan for Aboriginal Offenders 2006–2011*. Ottawa: Correctional Service of Canada, 2006.

*The Report of the Correctional Service of Canada Review Panel: A Roadmap to Strengthening Public Safety*. Ottawa: Correctional Service of Canada, 2007.

Winterdyk, J.A. *Corrections in Canada: Social Reactions to Crime*. Toronto: Pearson, 2001.

## CHAPTER 7:

Sapers, H. *Annual Report of the Office of the Correctional Investigator 2010–2011*. The Correctional Investigator Canada, 2011.

Berinbaum, R.N. "Bridging the Gap Between Prison and the Community: An exploration of resettlement and desistance among female offenders in England and Canada." *Internet Journal of Criminology*, 2009.

Bottos, S. *An Overview of Electronic Monitoring in Corrections: The Issues and Implications*. Ottawa: Research Branch, Correctional Service of Canada, 2007.

Brodeur, J.P. "The attrition of parole." *Canadian Journal of Criminology and Criminal Justice* 32 (1990), pp. 503–510.

Correctional Service of Canada (2008). Protecting Society Through Community Corrections.

Correctional Service of Canada (2009). Federal Community Corrections Strategy: Vision to 2020.

Correctional Service of Canada (2011). Departmental Performance Report.

Correctional Service of Canada (2010). Revised National Community Strategy for Women Offenders.

Coyle, J. "Help wasn't just a call away for Gillian Hadley." *Toronto Star*, November 27, 2001.

Desai, A. *Community Connections: The key to community corrections for individuals with mental health disorders*. Ottawa: Public Safety Canada, 2010.

Fry, R. "Community Corrections' Core Mission." *Corrections Today*, American Correctional Association, 2007.

Government of British Columbia. "Toward More Inclusive Neighbourhoods: Property Values Unaffected by Non-Market Housing," 1996, http://www.housing.gov.bc.ca/pub/htmldocs/pub_neighbour/p_value1.htm (accessed August 2012).

Government of Ontario, 2000 Government of Ontario, Bill 102, An act in memory of Christopher Stephenson, to establish and maintain a registry of sex offenders to protect children and communities, (2000), Legislative Assembly of Ontario, Toronto.

Government of Saskatchewan. "Bail Verification and Supervison (Judicial Interim Release)," 2010, http://www.cpsp.gov.sk.ca/Judicial-Interim-Release (accessed August 2012).

Griffiths, C., Y. Dandurand, and D. Murdoch. *The Social Reintegration of Offenders and Crime Prevention*. Ottawa: National Crime Prevention Centre, Public Safety Canada, 2007.

Gunnison, E., and J.B. Helfgott. "Factors That Hinder Offender Reentry Success: A View from Community Corrections Officers." *International Journal of Offender Therapy and Comparative Criminology* 55, no. 2 (April 2011), pp. 287–304.

Johnson, S. "Outcomes of Probation and Conditional Sentence Supervision: An Analysis of Newfoundland and Labrador, Nova Scotia, New Brunswick, Saskatchewan and Alberta,

2004/2004 to 2004/2005." *Juristat* 26, no. 7 (December 2006).

John Howard Society of Alberta. "Electronic (Radio Frequency) and GPS Monitored Community Based Supervision Programs," 2006, http://www.johnhoward.ab.ca/pub/pdf/monitorupdate.pdf (accessed August 2012).

Kong, R., and K. AuCoin. "Female Offenders in Canada." *Juristat* 28, no. 1 (January 2008), pp. 1–28.

Makin, K. "The psychopath, the system, and the fatal flaw," *Globe and Mail* A1, (December 27, 2003), p. A9.

McDonough, J. "Come on now… do Correctional Programs Really Work?" *Let's Talk: A New Generation of Correctional Programs* 34, no. 2 (March 2010), p. 4.

Mackay, R. *Legislative Summary: Bill C-48: An Act to amend the Criminal Code and to make consequential amendments to the National Defence Act (Protecting Canadians by Ending Sentence Discounts for Multiple Murders Act)*. Ottawa: Library of Parliament, 2011.

Murray, J.L., A. Gates and E. Hansen. "Managing addictions in the community." *FORUM on Corrections Research* 15, no. 1 (May 2003), pp. 28–30.

Nafekh, M. and J. Flight. *A review and estimate of time spent in prison by offenders sentenced for murder*. Ottawa: Correctional Service of Canada, Research Branch, 2002.

Performance Monitoring Report 2004–2005. Ottawa: Performance Measuring Division, National Parole Board, 2005.

O'Brien, Rosemary T. (2006). "Community Corrections in Canada: Women Offenders" in *An Overview of Community Corrections in China and Canada*. International Centre for Criminal Law Reform and Criminal Justice Policy Programme, 2006.

Olotu, M.K., M. Beaupre, and P. Verbrugge. *Evaluation Report: Electronic Monitoring Program Pilot*. Correctional Service of Canada, Evaluation Branch, Policy Sector, 2009.

Trevethan, S., and C.J. Rastin. "A profile of offenders serving time in the community." *FORUM on Corrections Research* 15, no. 1 (May 2003), pp. 12–15.

Padgett, K.G., W.D. Bales, and T.G. Blomberg. "Under surveillance: An empirical test of the effectiveness and consequences of electronic monitoring." *Criminology and Public Policy* 5, no. 1 (February 2006), pp. 61–92.

Payne, B.K. and M.T. DeMichele. "Electronic supervision for sex offenders: Implications for work load, supervision goals, versatility and policymaking." *Journal of Criminal Justice* 38, no. 3 (2010), pp. 276–281.

Petrunik, M. and R. Weisman. "Constructing Joseph Fredericks: Competing narratives of a child sex murder." *International Journal of Law and Psychiatry* 28 no. 1 (2005), pp. 75–96.

Roberts, J.V. *Punishing Persistent Offenders: Exploring Community and Offender Perspectives*. New York: Oxford University Press, 2008.

Roberts, J.V. *Public Opinion and Corrections: Recent Findings in Canada*. Ottawa: Correctional Service of Canada, 2005.

Russo, J. "Emerging Technologies for Community Corrections." *Corrections Today* (October 2006).

Taylor, K., and J. Flight. "A profile of federally-sentenced women on conditional release." *FORUM on Corrections Research* 16, no. 1 (2004), pp. 24–27.

Trevethan, S., and C.J. Rastin. "A profile of offenders serving time in the community." *FORUM on Corrections Research* 15, no. 1 (May 2003), pp. 12–15.

Trevethan, S., N. Crutcher, and J.P. Moore. *A Profile of Federal Offenders Designated as Dangerous Offenders or Serving Long-Term Supervision Orders*. Ottawa: Correctional Service of Canada, Research Branch, 2002.

Winterdyk, J.A. *Corrections in Canada: Social Reactions to Crime*. Toronto: Pearson, 2001.

Wodahl, E.J., et al. "Utilizing Behavioural Interventions to Improve Supervision Outcomes in Community-Based Corrections." *Criminal Justice and Behavior* 38 no. 4 (April 2011), pp. 386–405.

Yazar, R. "The Community Maintenance Program: A new strategy for providing treatment follow-up in the community." *FORUM on Corrections Research* 15, no. 1 (May 2003), pp. 25–27.

## CHAPTER 8:

Beattie, S. and A. Cotter. "Homicide in Canada, 2009." *Juristat* 30, no. 3 (2010).

Boe., R.E. 2002. "Future demographic trends may help Canada's Aboriginal youth." *FORUM on Corrections Research* 14, no. 3 (2002).

Calverley, D., A. Cotter, and E. Halla. "Youth custody and community services in Canada, 2008/2009." *Juristat* 30, no. 1 (2010).

Waller, I., and D. Weiler. Crime Prevention through Social Development: An Overview with Sources. Canadian Council on Social Development, 1984.

CBC News. "Medicine Hat girl guilty of first-degree murder," July 9, 2007, http://www.cbc.ca/news/

canada/calgary/story/2007/07/09/med-hat.html (accessed August 2012).
Corrado, R., et al., eds. *Juvenile Justice in Canada: A Theoretical and Analytical Analysis*. Toronto: Butterworths, 1992.
Criminal Intelligence Service Canada. *2010 Report on Organized Crime in Canada*. Government of Canada, http://www.cisc.gc.ca/annual_reports/annual_report_2010/street_gangs_2010_e.html (accessed August 2012).
CTV News. "Teens plead guilty to Kimberly Proctor's murder," October 27, 2010, http://bc.ctvnews.ca/teens-plead-guilty-to-kimberly-proctor-s-murder-1.567698 (accessed August 2012).
Curtis, E., et al. *Kingston Penitentiary: The First Hundred and Fifty Years*. Ottawa: Correctional Service of Canada, 1985.
Dickson, L. "Proctor's killer sent to adult prison...," *Alberni Valley Times*, January 20, 2012.
Gelsthorpe, L. and A. Worrall. "Looking for Trouble: A recent history of girls, young women and youth justice." *Youth Justice* 9 (209) 2009.
Holman, B. and J. Ziedenberg. *The Dangers of Detention: the impact of incarcerating youth in detention and other secure facilities*. Washington D.C.: Justice Policy Institute, 2006.
Hotton Mahony, T. *Women and the Criminal Justice System*. Statistics Canada: Catalogue no. 89-503-X, 2011.
International Cooperation Group. The Evolution of Juvenile Justice in Canada. Department of Justice Canada, 2004.
John Howard Society of Alberta. *The Youth Criminal Justice Act—Handbook*. 2007.
Kellerman, A. L., et al. "Preventing Youth Violence: What Works?" Annual Review of Public Health, 19, 271–293. 1998
Kong, R., and K. AuCoin. "Female Offenders in Canada." *Juristat* 28, no. 1 (January 2008), pp. 1–28.
La Prairie, C. "Aboriginal over-representation in the criminal justice system: A tale of nine cities." *Canadian Journal of Criminology and Criminal Justice* 44, no. 2 (April 2002), pp. 181–208.
Leschied, A., P. Jaffe, and W. Willis. *The Young Offenders Act: A Revolution in Canadian Juvenile Justice*. Toronto: University of Toronto Press, 1991.
Leshied, A., et al. "Childhood Predictors of Adult Criminality: A Meta-Analysis Drawn from the Prospective Longitudinal Literature." *Canadian Journal of Criminology and Criminal Justice* 50 no. 4 (2008), pp. 435–468.
Linden, R. *Comprehensive Approaches to Address Street Gangs in Canada*. Public Safety Canada, 2010.
Marron, K. *Apprenticed in Crime: Young Offenders, the Law and Crime in Canada*. Toronto: Seal Books, 1992.
Maxim, P. and P. Whitehead. *Youth in Conflict with the Law*. 3rd ed. Toronto: Nelson Education, 2009.
Montréal Police. *Provincial Action Plan on StreetGangs*. Québec: Department of Public Safety, 2004.
Office of the Provincial Advocate for Children and Youth for Ontario. *The Roy McMurtry Youth Centre: A summary of Advocacy Activities and Issues, August 2009 to February 2010*.
Pollock, J.M. and S.M. Davis. "The Continuing Myth of the Violent Female Offender." *Criminal Justice Review* 30, no. 1 (2005).
Sawdon, J. Youth Justice in Canada: a resource manual. Toronto: Canadian Training Insitute, 2003.
Sharpe, G. "The Trouble with Girls Today: Professional perspectives on young women's offending." *Youth Justice* 9 (254). 2009
Sher, J. *"Until You Are Dead": Steven Truscott's Long Ride into History*. Toronto: Vintage Canada, 2002.
Spergel, I.A. *Reducing Youth Gang Violence: The Little Village Gang Project in Chicago*. Lanham, Maryland: AltaMira Press, 2007.
Standing Committee on Justice and Legal Affairs. *Renewing Youth Justice*. House of Commons, Canada. 1997
Statistics Canada, The Daily, July 21, 2011.
Statistics Canada. *Juristat* 28, no. 4 (2008).
Statistics Canada. *Juristat* 30, no. 2 (2010).
Statistics Canada. Police-reported crime statistics, 2009.
Statistics Canada. *The Daily*, January 24, 2008.
Statistics Canada. *The Daily*, March 29, 2010.
Statistics Canada. *The Daily*, September 25, 2007.
Stutzman Amstutz, L. and J.H. Mullet. *The Little Book of Restorative Discipline for Schools*. Intercourse, P.A.: Good Books, 2005.
Taylor-Butts, A. and A. Bresson. "Youth Crime in Canada, 2006." *Juristat* 28 no. 3 (May 2008).
Tita, G.E., and G. Ridgeway. "The Impact of Gang Formation on Local Patterns of Crime." *Journal of Research on Crime and Delinquency* 44 (2007), pp. 208–237.
Winterdyk, J.A. *Issues and Perspectives on Young Offenders in Canada*. 3rd ed. Toronto: Thomson Nelson, 2005.

## CHAPTER 9:


Brazemore G. and M. Schiff, *Restorative Community Justice*. Cincinnati: Anderson Publishing, 2001.

Canadian Resource Centre for Victims of Crime. Restorative Justice in Canada: What victims should know. 2011.

CBC News. "Father of girls who froze to death gets 3 years in prison," March 6, 2009, http://www.cbc.ca/news/canada/saskatchewan/story/2009/03/06/sk-pauchay-sentence.html (accessed August 2012).

Centre for Justice and Reconciliation. *What is Restorative Justice?—Restorative Justice Briefing Paper*. Washington: Prison Fellowship International, 2008.

Clark, J.N. "The three R's: retributive justice, restorative justice, and reconciliation." *Contemporary Justice Review* 11, no. 4 (December 2008), pp. 331–350.

Companion, A. Peace and Justice Shall Embrace. Lincoln: Writers Club Press, 2001.

Consedine, J. Restorative Justice—Healing the Effects of Crime. Restorative Justice and Probation Conference, Warsaw, 2 December, 2003.

Cormier, R.B. Restorative Justice: Directions and Principles, Developments in Canada 2002-02. Department of the Solicitor General Canada.

Correctional Service of Canada. *Restorative Opportunities: Fact Sheet for Victims*.

CTV News. "Emotions run high at Pauchay's sentencing circle," February 13, 2009, http://www.ctv.ca/CTVNews/TopStories/20090213/sentencing_circle_090213 (accessed August 2012).

Dhami, M.K., G. Mantle, and D. Fox. "Restorative justice in prisons." *Contemporary Justice Review* 12 no. 4 (2009), pp. 433–448.

Doerner, W.G.,and S.P. Lab. *Victimology*. 6th ed. New York: Anderson, 2012.

Economic and Social Council. Basic principles on the use of restorative justice programmes in criminal matters. United Nations, 2002.

Federal-Provincial-Territorial Working Group on Restorative Justice. *Restorative Justice in Canada: A Consultation Paper*. Department of Justice Canada, 2000.

Garvey, S. "Restorative Justice, Punishment, and Atonement." Utah Law Review (2003) pp. 303–317.

Gaudreault, A. "The Limits of Restorative Justice." *Proceedings of the Symposium of the Ecole nationale de la magistrature*, Paris: Edition Dalloz, 2005.

Godfrey, R. *Under the Bridge: The True Story of the Murder of Reena Virk*. Toronto: Harper Collins Limited, 2005.

Golbach, T.S. "Sentencing Circles, Clashing Worldviews, and the Case of Christopher Pauchay." *Illumine: Journal of the Centre for Studies in Religion and Society* 10, no. 1 (2011).

Griffiths, G.T. "The Victims of Crime and Restorative Justice: the Canadian Experience." *International Review of Victimology* 6 (1999), pp. 265–316.

Guertin, I. "A New Way of Addressing Crime: Restorative Justice," 2010, http://deal.org/blog/a-new-way-of-addressing-crime-restorative-justice (accessed August 2012).

Hurley, M. "Restorative Practices in Institutional Settings and at Release: Victim Wrap Around Programs." *Federal Probation* 73, no. 1 (2009), pp. 16–22.

Johnstone, G. "Critical Perspectives on Restorative Justice." *Handbook of Restorative Justice*, D. Van Ness and G. Johnstone, eds. Portland: Willan, 2006.

Latimer, J., C. Dowden, and D. Muise. *The Effectiveness of Restorative Justice Practices: A Meta-Analysis*. Ottawa: Department of Justice, 2001.

Law Commission of Canada. *Transforming Relationships Through Participative Justice*. Ottawa: Department of Public Works and Government Services, 2003.

Leung, M. "The Origins of Restorative Justice." Restorative Justice Online, 1999, http://www.restorativejustice.org/articlesdb/articles/362 (accessed August 2012).

Lilles, The Honourable H. "Circle Sentencing: Part of the Restorative Justice Continuum." *Third International Conference on Conferencing, Circles and other Restorative Practices*, 2002, Minneapolis, Minnesota, http://www.iirp.org/library/mn02/mn02_lilles.html (accessed August 2012).

Lockhart, A., and L. Zammit. *Restorative Justice: Transforming Society*. Toronto: Inclusion Press, 2005.

Lokanan, M. (2009). "An open model for restorative justice: is there room for punishment?" *Contemporary Justice Review* 12, no. 3 (2009), pp. 289–307.

Macready, T. "Learning social responsibililty in schools: a restorative practice." *Educational Psychology in Practice* 25, no. 3 (2009), pp. 211–220.

Martin, S. "Parents of slain teen talk about restorative justice." *Bowen Island Undercurrent*, April 15, 2011.

McCullough, M.E. *Beyond Revenge*. San Francisco: Jossey-Bass, 2008.
O'Reilley, N. "Community, police turn to restorative justice," November 23, 2010, http://www.thespec.com/news/crime/article/278249--community-police-turn-to-restorative-justice (accessed August 2012).
Plouffe, J., and R. Godfrey. "Murder and Mercy," Reader's Digest, http://www.rdasia.com/murder_and_mercy/ (accessed August 2012).
Public Safety Canada. Restorative justice: Promising beginnings. *Research Summary* 7, no. 5 (2002).
R. *v*. Gladue, [1999] 1 S.C.R. 688, 133 C.C.C. (3d) 385, 23 C.R. (5th) 197.
R. *v*. Moses, [1992] 3 C.N.L.R. 116.
R. *v*. Pauchay [2009] S.J. No. 2 (2009) 4 SKPC 1, [2009] 1 C.N.L.R. 317.
Schachter, R. "Discipline gets the boot: While zero-tolerance polices come into question, urban districts are trying alternatives-and seeing considerable success." District Administration (January, 2010).
Sharpe, S. *Restorative Justice: A Vision for Healing and Change*. Edmonton: Edmonton Victim Offender Mediation Society, 1998.
Sherman, L.W., and H. Strang. *Restorative Justice: The Evidence*. London: The Smith Institute, 2007.
Wheeldon, J. "Finding common ground: restorative justice and its theoretical constructions(s)." *Contemporary Justice Review* 12, no. 1 (2009), pp. 91–100.
Zaslaw, J. "Restorative Resolution." *Education Digest* 76, no. 2 (2010), pp. 10–13.
Zehr, H. *Changing Lenses: A New Focus for Crime and Justice Waterloo*. ON: Herald Press, 1990.
Zehr, H. *The Little Book of Restorative Justice*. Intercourse, PA: Good Books, 2002.

## CHAPTER 10:

Beauchamp. "Sexual Orientation and Victimization 2004." *Canadian Centre for Justice Statistics Profile Series*, Statistics Canada, 2008.
Bradford, B. *Victim Satisfaction Survey 2005: A Prince Edward Island study of victims of crime*. Charlottetown: Equinox Consulting Inc., 2005.
Cameron, S. *On the farm: Robert William Pickton and the tragic story of Vancouver's Missing Women*. Toronto: Random House, 2011.
Statistics Canada. *Juristat* 23, no. 6 (July 2003).
Canadian Resource Centre for Victims of Crime. "The Impact of Victimization," October 2005, http://www.crcvc.ca/docs/victimization.pdf (accessed August 2012).
CBC News. "B.C. gay basher gets 17-month sentence," April 30, 2010, http://www.cbc.ca/news/canada/british-columbia/story/2010/04/30/bc-kandola-sentence.html (accessed August 2012).
Cooper, S. "Victim escaped Pickton, but claims ignored." Postmedia News, January 31, 2011, http://www.canada.com/Victim+escaped+Pickton+claims+ignored/6076683/story.html.
Department of Justice Canada. *Canadian Statement of Basic Principles of Justice for Victims of Crime, 2003*. http://www.justice.gc.ca/eng/pi/pcvi-cpcv/pub/03/princ.html (accessed August 2012).
DeValve, E.Q. "A qualitative exploration of the effects of crime victimization for victims of personal crime [Electronic Version]." *Applied Psychology in Criminal Justice* 1, no. 2 (2005), pp. 71–89.
Evans, J. "Missing Women: Commission of Inquiry British Columbia," http://www.vancouversun.com/pdf/EXHIBIT-34-DC-EVANS-REPORT-AND-APPENDICES-A-AND-B-ONLY.pdf (accessed August 2012).
Hagan, J. *Victims before the Law: The Organizational Domination of Criminal Law*. Toronto: Butterworths, 1983.
Hall, N. "Failures of Pickton investigation similar to Bernardo probe, inquiry told," January 16, 2012, http://www.vancouversun.com/news/Failures+Pickton+investigation+similar+Bernardo+probe+inquiry+told/6003237/story.html#ixzz1nPgNq88R (accessed August 2012).
Jiwani, Y. and M. Young,. "Missing and Murdered Women: Reproducing Marginality in News Discourse." *Canadian Journal of Communication* 31, (2006) pp. 895–917.
Kennedy, L.W., and V.F. Sacco. *Crime Victims in Context*. New York: Oxford University Press, 2007.
Leyton, E. "Death on the pig farm: take one," *Globe and Mail*, June 16, 2007, http://www.missingpeople.net/death_on_the_pig_farm.htm (accessed August 2012).
Makin, K. "Supreme Court rejects Pickton's bid for new trial." *Globe and Mail*, July 30, 2010.
O'Hear, M. "Victims and criminal justice: What's next?" *Federal Sentencing Reporter* 19, (2006), pp. 83–90.
Office of the Federal Ombudsman for Victims of Crime. *Shifting the conversation: A look at refocusing Canada's justice system to better meet the needs of victims of crime*. Government of Canada, 2011.
Public Safety Canada Portfolio Corrections Statistics Committee. *Corrections and Conditional Release Statistical Overview 2010*.

Public Works and Government Services Canada, 2010.
Roberts, J.V. "Victim Impact Statements: Lessons Learned and Future Priorities." *Victims of Crime Research Digest*, 2008, http://canada.justice.gc.ca/eng/pi/rs/rep-rap/rd-rr/rr07_vic4/p1.html (accessed August 2012).
Sauve, J. "Victim Services in Canada." *Juristat* 29, no. 4 (October 2009).
Sauve, J. and K. Hung. "An International Perspective on Criminal Victimization." *Juristat* 28, no. 10 (December 2008).
Sexual Orientation and Victimization, Canadian Centre for Justice Statistics Profile Series, 2004.
Statistics Canada. *Aboriginal Peoples in Canada in 2006: Inuit, Métis, and First Nations, 2006 Census*. Catalogue no. 97-558-xie, 2008.
Statistics Canada. Criminal Justice Indicators, 2005. Catalogue no. 85-227-XIE2002000. Government of Canada, 2005.
Statistics Canada. *General Social Survey*. 2004.
Statistics Canada. *General Social Survey*. 2009.
Umbreit, M. "Victim offender mediation in Canada." *International Social Work* 42 (1999), p. 214.
United Nations Congress on the Prevention of Crime and the Treatment of Offenders (April 2000). Press Release.
Wemmers, J. "Where do they belong? Giving victims a place in the criminal justice process." *National Victims of Crime Conference*, Adelaide, Australia, September 2008.
Wemmers, J., and K. Cyr, "What fairness means to crime victims: A social psychological perspective on victim-offender mediation." *Applied Psychology in Criminal Justice* 2, no. 2 (2006).

## CHAPTER 11:

"DNA National Data Base, RCMP," http://www.nddb-bndg.org/main_e.htm (accessed August 2012).
Bowen, R., and J. Schneider. "Forensic Databases: Paint, Shoe Prints, and Beyond." *National Institute of Justice Journal* 258 (2007).
Canadian Anti-Fraud Centre Criminal Intelligence Analytical Unit. *Mass Marketing Fraud and ID Theft Activities: Annual Statistical Report 2010*.
CBC News. "Facts About Stun Guns and Their Use in Canada," March 18, 2009.
CBC News. "MAP: Cellphone bans in Canada," August 31, 2011, http://www.cbc.ca/news/interactives/map-cellphone-bans-canada/ (accessed August 2012).
Dauvergne, M., and S. Brennan. "Police-reported hate crime in Canada, 2009." *Juristat* (June 7, 2011).
Kowalski, M. *Cyber-Crime: Issues, Data Sources, and Feasibility of Collecting Police-Reported Statistics*. Statistics Canada Catalogue no. 85-558, 2002.
McEwen, R. *Tools of the Trade: Drugs, Law and Mobile Phones in Canada*. New Media Society, 2010.
Steeves, V., and C. Wing. *Young Canadians in a Wired World: Phase II*. Ottawa: Industry Canada, 2005.
Onyema, F.A. "What Is Biometrics? Technologies, Issues, Opportunities And Challenges," May 30, 2011, http://tekedia.com/7908/what-is-biometrics-technologies-issues-opportunities-and-challenges/ (accessed August 2012).
Perreault, S. "Self-Reported Internet Victimization in Canada, 2009." *Juristat* (September 15, 2011).
Public Safety Canada. "National strategy to combat child exploitation on the Internet," January 24, 2005, http://www.publicsafety.gc.ca/media/bk/2005/bg20050124-eng.aspx (accessed August 2012).
Raymond J.J, et al. "Trace DNA analysis: do you know what your neighbour is doing? A multi-jurisdictional survey." *Forensic Science International* 2, no. 1 (2008).
Saks, M.J., and J.J. Koehler. "The Coming Paradigm Shift in Forensic Identification Science." *Science*, 309 (2005).
Schaefer, J.A. *Policing 2020: Exploring the future of Crimes, Communities and Policing*. Futures Working Group, Behavioral Science Unit, FBI Academy, 2007.
Seglins, D., and L. MacNaughton, "Cellphones Pour Into Prisons." CBC News, June 8, 2010.
Sinclair, R.L., and D. Sugar. "Internet Based Child Sexual Exploitation Environmental Scan. Royal Canadian Mounted Police." Ottawa, Ontario, Canada, 2005.
Statistics Canada. "Canadian Internet Use Survey." *The Daily*, May 25, 2011.
Statistics Canada. *The Daily*, July 21, 2011.
Statistics Canada. *The Daily*, March 12, 2009.
Wittreich, A., M. Grewal, and R. Sinclair. *Technology: Shaping Young People's Global World*. The National Child Exploitation Coordination Centre, Ottawa, Canada, 2008.
Wolak, J., et al. "Online 'Predators' and their Victims: Myths, Realities and Implications for Prevention and Treatment." *American Psychologist* 63, no. 2 (2008), pp. 111–128.

# Photo Credits

## CHAPTER 1

Page 2: Wakenphotography/GetStock.com
Page 3: Alain/GetStock.com
Page 6: Michael Hudson/The Canadian Press
Page 9: CHUCK STOODY/The Canadian Press
Page 10: The Canadian Press/Jonathan Hayward
Page 11: Steve Russell/GetStock.com
Page 13: The Canadian Press/Bill Graveland
Page 14: Ryan Remiorz/The Canadian Press
Page 15: Francis Vachon/GetStock.com
Page 17: Wikimedia Commons
Page 18: Richard Levine/GetStock.com

## CHAPTER 2

Page 24: Alphababy/Getstock.com
Page 25 (top): Mike Aporius/The Winnipeg Free Press/The Canadian Press
Page 25 (bottom): JOHN WOODS/The Canadian Press
Page 34 (top): Dennis MacDonald/GetStock.com
Page 34 (bottom): John Lehmann/The Canadian Press
Page 36: Image Source/CORBIS
Page 37: Diane Bondareff/AP/The Canadian Press
Page 39: Reuters/CORBIS
Page 42 (top): Nathan Denette/The Canadian Press
Page 42 (bottom): Peter McCabe/GetStock.com
Page 45: Peter Power/GetStock.com

## CHAPTER 3

Page 50: Alain/GetStock.com
Page 51 (top): Steve Russell/GetStock.ocm
Page 51 (middle): Pupkis/GetStock.com
Page 51 (bottom): Jim Rankin/GetStock.com
Page 52: Goetzman, Library and Archives Canada, accession number 1996-400 NPC, item 418, PA-202188.
Page 54: Georgios/GetStock.com
Page 55: Ron Bull/GetStock.com
Page 56 (top): Mario Beauregard/The Canadian Press
Page 56 (bottom): JoeFox/Getstock.com
Page 57: Francis Vachon/The Canadian Press
Page 58: Jake Wright/The Canadian Press
Page 62: Ashley Cooper/GetStock.com
Page 63: Toronto Star Archives/GetStock.com
Page 64 (top): Marmaduke St. John/GetStock.com
Page 64 (bottom): Bernard Weil/GetStock.com
Page 71: Rich Madonik/GetStock.com
Page 73: Vince Talotta/GetStock.com

## CHAPTER 4

Page 76: Courtesy of Alison Derry
Page 77 (left): Lucas Oleniuk/GetStock.com
Page 77 (right): Toronto Star/GetStock.com
Page 79: Jonathan Hayward/The Canadian Press
Page 81: Wikipedia.org: http://en.wikipedia.org/wiki/File:Toronto_-_ON_-_Old_City_Hall.jpg
Page 82: Fred Chartrand/The Canadian Press
Page 85: Lucas Oleniuk/GetStock.com
Page 89: Dave Chidley/The Canadian Press
Page 91: FRANK GUNN/The Canadian Press
Page 93: Darryl Dyck/The Canadian Press
Page 99 (top): Andrew Wallace/GetStock.com
Page 99 (middle): Darren Calabrese/The Canadian Press
Page 99 (bottom): John Mahler/GetStock.com

## CHAPTER 5

Page 104: Reimar 8/GetStock.com
Page 105: John Woods/The Canadian Press
Page 106: Bernard Weil/GetStock.com

Page 107: Paul Irish/GetStock.com

Page 109: Jacky Chapman/GetStock.com

Page 114: Wikipedia.org: http://en.wikipedia.org/wiki/File:Millhaven-Perimeter.jpg

Page 115: Rozum/GetStock.com

Page 117: Peter Power/The Globe and Mail/The Canadian Press

Page 120: Peter Power/The Globe and Mail/The Canadian Press

Page 123: J.B. Tyrrell, Library and Archives Canada, accession number 1970-088 NPC, item no. p. 2, PA-053620.

## CHAPTER 6

Page 128: Peter Power/The Globe and Mail/The Canadian Press

Page 129: Tom Hanson/The Canadian Press

Page 130: David Bebee/The Waterloo Region Record/The Canadian Press

Page 131: Courtesy of Alison Derry

Page 133 (left): Wikipedia.org: http://en.wikipedia.org/wiki/File:DonJail1860s.jpg

Page 133 (right): Wikipedia.org: http://en.wikipedia.org/wiki/File:New_Don_Jail.jpg

Page 134: Wikipedia.org: http://en.wikipedia.org/wiki/File:Grierson_Centre.jpg

Page 135 (top): Courtesy of the Parole Board of Canada

Page 135 (bottom): © ZUMA Wire Service/Alamy

Page 137: Roy Antal/The Canadian Press

Page 138: Dave McCord/The Canadian Press

Page 139: Bekupe/GetStock.com

Page 140: Wikipedia.org: http://en.wikipedia.org/wiki/File:P4w-kingston-demolition-march-2008.JPG

Page 141: © Alison Derry/McGraw-Hill Ryerson

Page 142: Lucas Oleniuk/GetStock.com

Page 145: © Spencer Grant/Alamy

Page 149: Paul Chiasson/The Canadian Press

Page 151: Patrick Doyle/The Canadian Press

## CHAPTER 7

Page 156: Erdosain/GetStock.com

Page 157: Terdonal/GetStock.com

Page 163: Mikael Karlsson/GetStock.com

Page 165: Softdreams/GetStock.com

Page 167: Jim West/GetStock.com

Page 168: Steve Yeater/The Canadian Press

Page 171: HP Canada/GetStock.com

Page 172: Snaprender/GetStock.com

Page 174: DNY59/iStockphoto.com

Page 175: Basphoto/GetStock.com

Page 176: Georgios/GetStock.com

## CHAPTER 8

Page 182: Maford/GetStock.com

Page 183: BRUCE STOTESBURY, TIMES COLONIST

Page 188: Bishop Barker Co., Patent and Copyright Office, Library and Archives Canada, accession number 1966-094 NPC, item 36549, PA-030472

Page 191: Sharon Graham Sargent/The Canadian Press

Page 192: Richard Green/GetStock.com

Page 194: Courtesy of Government Communications and Public Engagement, Ministry of Children & Family Development, British Columbia

Page 196: David Crausby/GetStock.com

Page 198: Robert Dall/The Canadian Press

Page 199: Rich Madonik/GetStock.com

Page 200: Zhagunov/GetStock.com

Page 201: Photo by Mike Maloney/London Community News

Page 203: Toronto Star/GetStock.com

Page 206 (top): © Alison Derry/McGraw-Hill Ryerson

Page 206 (bottom): CP Photo/The Canadian Press

## CHAPTER 9

Page 210: © ZUMA Wire Service/Alamy

Page 211 (left): Georgeman/GetStock.com

Page 211 (right): Susan Sterner/AP/The Canadian Press

Page 215: Jkerrigan/GetStock.com

Page 216: Winnipeg Free Press—Joe Bryksa/The Canadian Press

Page 217: Troy Fleece/The Canadian Press

Page 218: Arbon8/GetStock.com

Page 219: HP Canada/Alamy
Page 220: Americanspirit/GetStock.com
Page 222: Petesaloutos/GetStock.com
Page 223: Design Pics/Darren Greenwood

## CHAPTER 10

Page 227: Michelloiselle/GetStock.com
Page 228: Rick Madonick/GetStock.com
Page 230: Jonathan Hayward/The Canadian Press
Page 231: Evgenyatamanenko/GetStock.com
Page 233: laverrue was here/Getty Images
Page 240: Toronto Star/GetStock.com
Page 241 (top): Hamdan/GetStock.com
Page 241 (bottom): © Janine Wiedel Photolibrary/Alamy
Page 243: © iQoncept/Shutterstock.com

## CHAPTER 11

Page 246: iStockphoto.com
Page 247 (left): With permission of Patrick Ross
Page 247 (right): Wikipedia.org: http://en.wikipedia.org/wiki/File:Humber_River,_Toronto.jpg
Page 248: Eteimaging/GetStock.com
Page 253: Alexkopje/GetStock.com
Page 256: © Anatema/Shutterstock.com
Page 257: Cornelius20/GetStock.com
Page 258: Lorna/GetStock.com
Page 259: louise murray/Alamy
Page 260 (top): Dohnal/GetStock.com
Page 260 (bottom): Royalty-Free/CORBIS
Page 261 (left): Pupkis/GetStock.com
Page 261 (right): Oriontrail/GetStock.com
Page 261 (bottom): Peanutroaster/GetStock.com
Page 262: Kyolshin/GetStock.com
Page 263: Bakalusha/GetStock.com
Page 264 (top): ZUMA Wire Service/Alamy
Page 264 (bottom): Ferenz/GetStock.com

# Index

## D

## E



## F

## G



## H



## I



## J

## K



## L



## M



## N

## O



## P

## Q



## R

## S

## T



## U



## V